SO-BEU-565

THE
LEWIS CARROLL
HANDBOOK

I. THE REVD. C. L. DODGSON

From Herkomer's (posthumous) portrait in the hall of Christ Church, Oxford, painted in 1899

THE
LEWIS CARROLL
HANDBOOK

Being a New Version of

A HANDBOOK OF THE LITERATURE OF
THE REV. C. L. DODGSON

by

SIDNEY HERBERT WILLIAMS
F.S.A., Barrister-at-Law

and

FALCONER MADAN
M.A., Hon. Fellow of B.N.C.

———

First published in 1931
Now Revised, Augmented and brought up to 1970 by
ROGER LANCELYN GREEN
B.Litt., M.A. (Oxon.)

———

'Ah well, they may write such things in a *Book*,'
Humpty Dumpty said in a calmer tone

1970
BARNES & NOBLE INC.
New York
and
DAWSONS OF PALL MALL
Folkestone & London

R

the
Oxford University Press
New material © Oxford University Press 1962

First published 1931
Revised edition 1962
Revised reprint 1970

Dawsons of Pall Mall
Cannon House
Folkestone, Kent, England

Barnes and Noble Inc.

New York

SBN: 389 01560 1

Printed in Great Britain
by Photolithography
Unwin Brothers Limited
Woking and London

PROLOGUE

LEWIS CARROLL
1862 · 4 JULY · 1962

All in the golden afternoon
A boat goes stealing by,
While Oxford points her shining spires
Against the distant sky.

There is no splash of hastening oars,
No ripple in the stream;
The Godstow rabbits know full well
This dream within a dream.

They lift their heads and prick their ears,
'Tis theirs alone this night
To see the boat and hear the tale—
If one of them is White!

Three little girls who pull the oars,
And two strong arms as well;
But one slight figure in the bows
The deathless tale to tell . . .

That tale has echoed round the world,
The voyagers are no more;
But 'in an evening of July'
They haunt the Godstow shore.

ROGER LANCELYN GREEN

CONTENTS

LIST OF ILLUSTRATIONS

The Publisher wishes to acknowledge the kind permission given by Mr. Philip D. Jaques, on behalf of the Dodgson family, for the publication of the illustrations, particularly those which are new to this edition of the *Handbook*; the friendly assistance of Mr. W. H. Bond, of the Houghton Library, Harvard University, in obtaining the photographs of an illustration by Tenniel in the 1865 and 1866 editions of *Alice's Adventures*, which were reproduced in his article 'The Publication of *Alice's Adventures in Wonderland*' (*Harvard Library Bulletin*, vol. x, 1956); and the courtesy of the S.P.C.K., Mr. Warren Weaver, and the Princeton University Library in allowing publication of a photograph of the two pages of 'Alice' in Swahili (published by the Sheldon Press, London, in 1940 under the auspices of the S.P.C.K.) which was made from the copy in Mr. Weaver's collection.

CHARLES LUTWIDGE DODGSON
(*LEWIS CARROLL*)

Born 27 January 1832, at Daresbury, Cheshire.

Educated at Richmond School, Yorkshire, 1844–5.

At Rugby School, under Tait, in School House, February 1846–50.

Matriculated at Oxford from Christ Church, 23 May 1850.

Came into Residence 24 January 1851.

1st Class in Mathematics, 2nd in Classics (Moderations), 1852.

1st Class in Mathematics (Final Schools), 1854.

B.A. 18 December 1854. A 'Master of the House' 15 October 1855. M.A. 1857.

Senior Student of Christ Church, and resident there, 1855–98.

Mathematical Lecturer there, 1855–81.

Ordained Deacon, 22 December 1861.

Died 14 January 1898, at Guildford, aged 65.

(*Alice's Adventures*, 1865; *Through the Looking-Glass*, 1872; *Notes by an Oxford Chiel*, 1874; *The Hunting of the Snark*, 1876; *Euclid and his Modern Rivals*, 1879; *Sylvie and Bruno*, 1889, 1893.)

PREFACE

THE present volume represents the evolution and development of my former book, *A Bibliography of the Works of Lewis Carroll*, and what was originally begun as a second edition of that book has so grown and extended its scope of research, that it has been decided to issue it under another title, a title more comprehensive than that of a bibliography. I have thought it better to alter entirely the arrangement of the book and its treatment, with a view of making its contents more accessible, and the references easier to follow. The Notes too have been amended where necessary, and very much extended. Statistics and analyses of editions and issues of the more important items are supplied.

That a book of this nature should develop beyond its original intention is perhaps to be expected, since a first edition of any bibliography can only hope to break the ground, as it were. The very publication of such a book draws attention to the author, stimulates interest in his writings, and excites search for unrecorded items, articles in periodicals, &c., which otherwise would never be heard of; indeed many such have turned up and are duly recorded.

In addition to this there has arisen among collectors and lovers of *Alice* a desire to know more than the bare collations of Dodgson's works; for many of the lesser-known items have topical allusions to affairs at Christ Church and Oxford, and when the key to the allusions is provided, an otherwise dull composition becomes interesting and often entertaining.

These items with their morals or hidden allusions are mostly closed books to the present generation, and except for the help of contemporaries of Dodgson would soon become meaningless.

So too, there are not many of Dodgson's contemporaries left who can throw light on the many humorous innuendoes which he loved to write (e.g. in *Facts, Figures, and Fancies*), and it must be remembered that Dodgson only became a celebrity in after years, long after *Alice* was written, so that many of his pamphlets and leaflets were unnoticed, or having fulfilled the purpose for which they were written quickly went the way of all such ephemeral productions.

Even when they are preserved (and it is wonderful how many have been preserved) it is almost impossible for any one not well acquainted with Oxford and its doings to read between the lines, and discover the intention of the author. It would have been impossible for me to have done more than supply the collations with possibly some short notes of the items in this book, but for the kindness and help of my friend and collaborator Mr. Falconer Madan of Oxford, whose personal knowledge of Dodgson, and whose memory, have supplied most of the explanatory notes to the items. To him also are due the majority of the Supplements.

My thanks are also due to Mr. M. L. Parrish of Philadelphia, the proud professor of the largest collection of Dodgson's works in the world, who has been in constant communication with me, supplying me with photostats, and notes of many out-of-the-way pieces, also for his excellent catalogue, which I have found of the greatest service in checking the collations, and points of the various pieces.

It is with pleasure that I acknowledge my indebtedness to Messrs. Sotheby, and to Messrs. Hodgson for allowing me to inspect and examine items passing through their hands, and to Mr. Sidney Mudie of Messrs. Quaritch, who has at all times been ready to place his knowledge at my disposal, and has drawn my attention to more than one Carrollian rarity. Professor Zanetti of the Columbia University, New York, has shown a most kindly interest in the making of this book, and has helped me with photostats, and suggestions, for which I most heartily thank him; and I must here thank another kindly helper in New York, Miss Jean Macalister, also of the Columbia University, whose elaborate list of Dodgson's works has enabled me to extend the list of editions of *Alice* and other books.

Help on a considerable scale has been given by two ladies on the staff of the libraries of Harvard University, Mrs. Florence Milner who has given no little time and attention to supplying details and answering queries, and Mrs. Flora Livingstone, of whom the same may be said: they are both keen Carrollians. Mrs. Florence Becker [Lennon], of New York, who is herself writing an account of Mr. Dodgson, has kindly sent a long list of articles and notices of Dodgson in the Columbia University Library [originally prepared by Miss Ellen Wilkinson of Columbia University].

The authorities of the great Library of Congress at Washington, from Mr. Putman downwards, have taken personal interest in supplying lists of American editions—which we hope may be regarded as a feature of the present volume, and will show the widespread interest taken on that side of the Atlantic in Lewis Carroll. Last, but not least, we owe gratitude to Mrs. Ffooks of Dorchester, one of Lewis Carroll's girl-friends; ever since Dodgson's death she has collected out-of-the-way pieces, editions and papers, as they came out, and perhaps possesses the best collection of twentieth-century Carrolliana (as our references partly testify)—which she has freely allowed us to consult.

Thanks are due also for help to Major C. H. W. Dodgson, of Breinton House, near Hereford, and to Miss F. M. Dodgson; to Colonel W. G. C. Probert; and to the Very Rev. the Dean of Christ Church, Oxford (Dr. H. J. White: see p. 196). Other aid is acknowledged in the course of the book.

But no amount of welcome help can relieve the two authors of the Handbook from responsibility for its numerous shortcomings, and inequalities, of which they are fully conscious.

In conclusion, to all the collectors both here and abroad, who have spontaneously written to me and helped me, I render my thanks. It may please them to know that they have made my task a real pleasure, and whatever merit the book may possess, many lovers of *Alice* may well feel that they have contributed to it.

SIDNEY HERBERT WILLIAMS

32 Warrior Square
St. Leonards-on-Sea
December 1931

SUPPLEMENT TO PREFACE

My first debt of gratitude is to Sidney Herbert Williams and Falconer Madan, both now deceased, whose admirable work is still the foundation and indeed the main edifice of the present *Handbook*.

The majority of entries in the main portion, up to 1931, remain largely in their words. The most important exception is in the case of the First Issue of the First Edition of *Alice's Adventures in Wonderland*: as there is now a perfect copy in the British Museum I have been able to make an entirely new description of it. Other items have been revised or augmented where necessary, and of course all descriptions later than 1931 are my own.

A number of new items have been added throughout, a few of which are my own discoveries, but the majority due to the publication of *The Diaries of Lewis Carroll* in 1953, which I edited at the request of Lewis Carroll's nieces Miss F. Menella Dodgson and her sisters. By their kindness I have been allowed to quote from the *Diaries* the relevant note on the composition and publication of each item mentioned there by Dodgson, thus adding many interesting details unknown to Williams and Madan.

I have also included a number of quotations (never before published) from Dodgson's letters to his publishers Messrs. Macmillan. For these and for all other copyright material I have to thank Miss Menella Dodgson, representing her uncle's trustees.

I should also like to thank Mr. A. J. Beale and Mr. Stanley Godman for descriptions of and references to several rare items; Mr. R. E. Thompson for preparing an admirable Index to this book; Dr. T. B. Heaton and Mr. Geoffrey Bill of Christ Church, and the Deputy Librarian Mr. W. G. Hiscock in connexion with the new material discovered in the Senior Common Room in 1952 by Professor Duncan Black—whose list has led me to the inclusion of several new items. For answering special inquiries I should like to thank Mr. Lovat Dickson of Macmillan & Co.; the Rev. H. Wyndham Lewis, Vicar of Daresbury; Mr. Martin Gardner, editor of *The Annotated Alice*; Mr. John Mackay Shaw of the Florida State University Library; and Mr. Derek Hudson, author of the latest and most complete life of Lewis Carroll.

But these are only specific debts. The work which I have done on this *Handbook* is in the main based on many years of study of Lewis

Carroll and his works which dates indeed from my own first term as an undergraduate at Oxford in 1937 and may be traced by an alarmingly large trail of books and articles duly noted in Part III of the volume now offered. I cannot begin to list all those who have helped me during the past twenty years and more, either personally or by way of books and articles: from those whom I have met only in their books, such as S. D. Collingwood, Langford Reed, A. L. Taylor—and Messrs. Williams and Madan themselves, by way of those such as Mr. Helmut Gernsheim and Mrs. Becker Lennon whose books on Lewis Carroll led to personal meetings, and so via many of Dodgson's former child-friends (many, alas, since dead) including Miss Isa Bowman and her sisters Nellie and Empsie, Miss Price, Professor Clement Rogers and others, to those to whom I owe most, Lewis Carroll's four nieces Menella, Violet, Lucy and Gladys whose friendship during the last twelve years has been amongst my most precious possessions.

ROGER LANCELYN GREEN

Poulton-Lancelyn
Bebington, Wirral
April 1961

NOTE

By an unfortunate oversight the descriptions of items 286 to 300 were retained as given by Williams and Madan, who used lower case and abbreviated slightly for books published after Dodgson's death. The title-pages of these items should not be accepted as accurate transliterations: in most cases they were printed in capital letters.

R. L. G.
1970

METHOD OF DESCRIPTION

(Subject to details being available)

PART I endeavours to give a full description of each piece (short title in italic, with date; full title, usually in quasi-facsimile; imprint; date; size; pagination [and, when desirable, signatures], contents, notes, references). Every unnoted page is blank. π indicates a sheet without a signature.

In Parts II and III there are common-sense simplifications of the scheme, according to the principle of Degressive Bibliography, the more important pieces being given more attention than the lesser; but in some cases desirable information is lacking.

The order is usually chronological. | implies the end of a line in the original title: || implies more than $\frac{1}{2}$ inch of blank interval: ||| more than 1 inch: |||| more than $1\frac{1}{2}$ inches.

The table for sizes, the number of leaves in a sheet being prefixed when not suggested by the linear size, is:

Narrow		Square
folio	12–18 in.	la. 4°
la. 8°	9–12	4°
8°	7–9	sm. 4°
12° or sm. 8°	6–7	squ. 12°

Omissions are indicated by . . . : [ ] imply information not obtained from the book itself.

F. M.

THE original numbers to each item as used by Williams and Madan are retained in heavy type and square brackets to the *right* of each item. The new numbering of major items is given to the *left*, before each title; wherever possible cross-references are given to items by means of these new numbers.

All items that appear in it are referred to *Nonesuch*, with page numbers. As there have been two editions each differently paginated, reference to the First Edition (1939) is given first, followed by reference to the Second Edition (1949) given in round brackets.

The following abbreviations are used for titles appearing frequently:

Nonesuch for *The Complete Works of Lewis Carroll* published by the Nonesuch Press (No. *313*).

Collingwood for *The Life and Letters of Lewis Carroll* by S. Dodgson Collingwood, 1898 (No. I).

L.C.P.B. for *The Lewis Carroll Picture Book*, edited by S. Dodgson Collingwood, 1899 (No. *287*).

Diaries for *The Diaries of Lewis Carroll*, edited and supplemented by Roger Lancelyn Green, 1953 (No. *315*).

R. L. G.

PART I

A list, with notes, of all pieces and editions printed or issued by Dodgson from 1845 to 1898 and editions of his work containing new material or reprints of exceptional interest from 1898 to 1960, in order of date

---

[1845]

1. *Useful and Instructive Poetry*, 1845 [First published 1954]

Lewis Carroll || USEFUL AND | INSTRUCTIVE | POETRY || with an introduction by | DEREK HUDSON |||| LONDON | GEOFFREY BLES

London Geoffrey Bles; [Date on verso of title-page '*First published 1954*']. 8v. pp. [48], no signn. CONTENTS: p. [1] half-title: [2] blank: [3] Title, as above: [4] Imprint: *Printed in Great Britain by | Butler & Tanner Ltd Frome | for Geoffrey Bles Ltd | 52 Doughty Street London W.C. 1.* | and date: 5 'Contents': [6] blank: 7–13 Introduction signed Derek Hudson: [14] blank: 15–45 TEXT: [46–48] blank.

Issued in white parchment with decorations reproduced from the MS. in gold, green and red on front; and printed on spine *LEWIS CARROLL*—[so far in green] *USEFUL AND INSTRUCTIVE POETRY* [this in red] from bottom upwards. White end-papers. Eight pages on shiny paper of illustrations or letterpress from the MS. folded in, but un-numbered.

This is Dodgson's earliest work and was composed in 1845 when he was thirteen. Although nothing in it was published until after his death, it has seemed better to describe it here than at the end of this bibliography.

To the list of Contents following notes have been added of earlier appearances in print of several of the items.

My Fairy. *Collected Verse*, 1932, p. 3. *Nonesuch*, 779 (700).
The Headstrong Man.
Punctuality. *Collected Verse*, 1932, pp. 4–5. *Nonesuch*, 780 (701).
Charity.

C 90   B

Melodies. *Collected Verse*, 1932, p. 6. *Nonesuch*, 781 (702).
A Tale of a Tail.
A quotation from Shakespeare with slight improvements.
Brother and Sister. *Collected Verse*, 1932, pp. 7–8. *Nonesuch*, 782 (702–3).
The Trial of a Traitor.
The Juvenile Jenkins.
Facts. *Collected Verse*, 1932, p. 9. *Nonesuch*, 783 (703).
The Angler's Adventure.
A Fable.
Rules and Regulations. *Collected Verse*, 1932, pp. 10–11. *Nonesuch*, 784–5 (704–5).
Clara.
A Visitor.

Published in U.S.A. by the Macmillan Company.

2. *The Unknown One* (1845)   [1

A story contributed by Dodgson to the Richmond School Magazine, in 1845, bore the title 'The Unknown One'. Mr. Collingwood (*Life*, p. 24) states that it was 'probably of the sensational type in which small boys usually revel'. Dodgson was a schoolboy of twelve when this piece was issued, and it is by far his earliest appearance as a writer. But no copy of the magazine has at present been found, and it is just possible that it was not printed.

F. M.

c. 1850

3. *The Rectory Magazine* (1850)

Strictly speaking this item should not be included in a Bibliography since it has never been published in its entirety—but as the only survivor of the 'Family Magazines' still unprinted, I felt justified in stretching a point to include some description of it here.

The original MS. remained in the Dodgson family until 1932 when, after being shown in the Centenary Exhibition in London, it was sold at Sotheby's and passed into a private collection.

It is described in the Preface to *Mischmasch* as follows: 'THE REC-TORY MAGAZINE. This was first started for general contribution, and at first the contributions poured in in one continuous stream, while the issuing of each number was attended by the most violent excitement through the whole house: most of the family contributed one or more articles to it. About the year 1848 the numbers were bound into a volume, which still exists.'

The date may be a mistake, since the title-page of the magazine reads as follows:

THE | RECTORY MAGAZINE | — | Being | a | Compendium of the best tales | poems, essays, pictures etc. | that | the united talents | of | the Rectory inhabitants | can produce | — | Edited and printed | by | C. L. D. [in monogram] | — | Fifth Edition, carefully | revised, & | improved | — | 1850 | —.

The above description and the following list of contents (only those by C. L. D. himself being mentioned here) are taken from the typescript copy made before the sale of the MS. and kindly lent for the purpose by Miss F. Menella Dodgson.

The MS., in the Exhibition Catalogue (p. 67, item 323) is described as 'in octavo, 98 pages'. However, the page numbers as given in the typescript go up to 106.

In the MS. the contributions by C. L. D. are signed variously 'V. X., B. B., F. L. W., J. V., F. X., Q. G.', and 'Ed.'—but a key is added ascribing all these to him, and giving those employed by other members of the family.

Reasonings on Rubbish. Included in 'The Earliest Work of Lewis Carroll' in the *Strand Magazine*, June 1932.

Sidney Hamilton [in nine chapters].

Thoughts on Thistles. Included in 'Earliest Work', as above.

Horrors. [Poem of 24 lines.] First printed in *The Lewis Carroll Centenary* (Catalogue), 1932; included in *Collected Verse* (1932), p. 12; *Nonesuch*, p. 786 (705–6), &c.

Crundle Castle. [Story in nine chapters.] First printed as Appendix A, pp. 547–53, to *The Diaries of Lewis Carroll*, 1953.

Things in General. Included in 'Earliest Work'.

Tears. [Poem of 12 lines.]

Rust. Included in 'Earliest Work'.

As it Fell upon a Day. [Poem of 18 lines.] Included in 'Earliest Work' and reprinted in *Collected Verse* (1932), p. 14, *Nonesuch*, p. 788 (707), &c.

Terrors. [Poem of 32 lines.] Eight lines first published in Appendix to this *Handbook*, p. 287.

But. Included in 'Earliest Work'.

Woes. [Poem of 54 lines.] The last stanza (6 lines) quoted by the editor in *The Diaries of Lewis Carroll* (1953), p. 22.

Yang-Ki-Ling. [Poem of 24 lines.]

Musings on Milk. First published in *The Lewis Carroll Centenary* (1932), p. 118.

Misunderstandings. [Poem of 26 lines.] First published in *Collected Verse* (1932), p. 13; included in *Nonesuch*, p. 787 (706), &c.

Screams. [Poem of 20 lines.]

Ideas upon Ink. Included in 'Earliest Work'.

Thrillings. [Poem of 20 lines.] First published in editorial notes to *The Diaries of Lewis Carroll* (1953), pp. 21–22.

Twaddle on Telescopes. Included in 'Earliest Work'.

Cogitations on Conclusions. Included in 'Earliest Work'.

The eight pieces (excluding the poem) included in 'Earliest Work', and 'Musings on Milk' printed in the Centenary Catalogue, are short prose essays or 'editorials' of about 250 words each.

Miss Menella Dodgson's typescript, while including a complete list of contents, does not contain every item in the MS. magazine: but it contains all those by Lewis Carroll, except the serial story 'Sidney Hamilton'.

[1850?]

4. *La Guida di Bragia* (*c.* 1850. Published 1931)

'The Ballad Opera "Guida di Bragia" for the Marionette Theatre, a skit on Bradshaw's Railway Guide (an early work, about 1845?), is fully described with quotations in Sotheby's Sale Catalogue for Feb. 14, 1929, lot 875. It occupies thirteen quarto pages and parodies Shakespeare, Dulce Domum, "Auld Lang Syne", &c. The Marionette Theatre itself was sold at Sotheby's on Nov. 14, 1928, lot 664.'

F. M.

This very immature work is probably a little later than Madan suggests, as the parodies contained in it suggest the period of *The Rectory Umbrella* rather than *The Rectory Magazine*.

The 'Prologue' was printed in the Sotheby Catalogue, and is included in *Collected Verse* (1932), p. 107; *Nonesuch*, p. 823 (737).

The whole work was first published in *The Queen*, vol. clxx, No. 4430, pp. 37–40 and p. 66, 18 Nov. 1931, being the Christmas Number of that periodical.

It is not included in *Nonesuch*, and does not seem to have been reprinted elsewhere.

[1850-62]

5. *The Rectory Umbrella* (*c.* 1850–3)
6. *Mischmasch* (1853–62) } Published 1932

THE | RECTORY UMBRELLA | AND | MISCHMASCH | *by* | LEWIS CARROLL | *With a Foreword* | *by* | FLORENCE MILNER | *Harvard College Library* |||| [*Imprint and date as below*]

Cassell & Company, Ltd. London, Toronto, Melbourne & Sydney. Date on verso of title-page '*First Published 1932*'.

Small 4to. P. [i] Half-title; p. [ii] blank; [iii] Title, as above; [iv] imprint and date; v–xii Foreword, signed Florence Milner; xiii Contents; [xiv–xv] blank; [xvi] Frontispiece to *The Rectory Umbrella*; 1–[85] Text of *The Rectory Umbrella*; [86] blank; [87] facsimile half-title of *Mischmasch*; [88] blank; 89–193, Text of *Mischmasch*; [194–6] blank.

Published Oct. 1932. Issued in blue cloth with title on spine and front in gold; decoration on front in green of the maze from p. 165.

The Rectory Umbrella

CONTENTS

Preface. Included in 'Before *Alice*' by S. Dodgson Collingwood, *Strand Magazine*, Dec. 1898.

The Walking-Stick of Destiny. [Story in 8 chapters.]

Ye Fatalle Cheyse. [Poem of 40 lines.] First published in 'Before *Alice*'; included in *The Lewis Carroll Picture Book* (1899), pp. 10-11; *Collected Verse* (1932), pp. 15-16; *Nonesuch*, pp. 789-90 (707-9), &c.

The Vernon Gallery. Quoted in Collingwood's *Life* (1898), p. 33.

Moans from the Miserable.

'The Scanty Meal'. Collingwood's *Life* (1898), p. 33.

Zoological Papers. No. 1: Pixies.

The Storm. [Poem of 35 lines.] Quoted complete in Editorial notes to *The Diaries of Lewis Carroll* (1953), pp. 23-24.

'The Woodland Gait'.

Zoological Papers. No. 2: The Lory. Quoted in 'Before *Alice*' and in Editorial notes to *The Diaries* (p. 24); &c.

'The First Earring'. Quoted in Collingwood's *Life* (1898), p. 35.

Difficulties No. 1. ['Where does the day begin?'] Included in 'Before *Alice*' (1898), *Lewis Carroll Picture Book* (1899), pp. 4-5; Langford Reed's *Further Nonsense* (1926), pp. 97-98, &c.

Zoological Papers No. 3: Fishs. *Lewis Carroll Picture Book* (1899), pp. 7-9.

Lays of Sorrow, No. 1. [Poem of 69 lines.] First published in 'Before *Alice*' (1898); then in *Lewis Carroll Picture Book* (1899), pp. 12-14; *Further Nonsense* (1926), pp. 36-38; *Collected Verse* (1932), pp. 17-19; *Nonesuch*, pp. 791-3 (709-11), &c.

'The Wooden Bridge'.

Representative Men [Three 'Lectures' of a page each.]

Zoological Papers No. 4: The One-Winged Dove.

'High Life and Low Life'.

Lays of Sorrow, No. 2. [Poem of 122 lines.] First published in Collingwood's *Life* (1898), pp. 37-42, and included in 'Before *Alice*' the same year. Reprinted in *Collected Verse* (1932), pp. 20-26; *Nonesuch*, pp. 794-8 (712-16).

'The Duett'.

Difficulties No. 2. ['The Two Clocks'.] First published in 'Before *Alice*' (1898) and included in *Lewis Carroll Picture Book* (1899), p. 6; *Further Nonsense* (1926), pp. 99-100; Editorial notes to *Diaries* (1953), p. 26.

The Poet's Farewell. [Poem of 48 lines.] First published in 'Before *Alice*' (1898). Reprinted in Editorial notes to the *Diaries* (1953), pp. 27-28.

Note. The items between inverted commas are short prose descriptions of drawings parodying pictures in The Vernon Gallery.

Mischmasch

CONTENTS

Preface (dated 13 Aug. 1855). Published in *Lewis Carroll Picture Book* (1899), pp. 15-17.

The Mermaids. [Poem by Louisa Dodgson.]

*The Two Brothers. [Poem of 56 lines, dated 1853.] Published in *L.C.P.B.* (1899), pp. 18–24; *Further Nonsense* (1926), pp. 48–53; *Collected Verse* (1932), pp. 27–32; *Nonesuch*, pp. 799–804 (716–20), &c.

Poetry for the Million. See under the *Comic Times* (1855) (No. *13*).

*The Dear Gazelle. See under the *Comic Times* (1855) (No. *13*).

From Our Own Correspondent. [Comic drawings with descriptions.]

*She's All My Fancy Painted Him. See under the *Comic Times* (1855) (No. *13*).

*Photography Extraordinary. See under the *Comic Times* (1855) (No. *13*).

*Hints for Etiquette. See under the *Comic Times* (1855) (No. *13*).

Notice to the Public.

*Wilhelm von Schmitz. See under the *Whitby Gazette* (1854) (No. *12*).

*The Lady of the Ladle. See under the *Whitby Gazette* (1854) (No. *12*).

*The Palace of Humbug. See under this title (No. *16*).

Stanza of Anglo-Saxon Poetry. [First stanza of 'Jabberwocky' with notes; dated 1855.] First published in this form in 'Before *Alice*' (*Strand Magazine*, Dec. 1898); then in *L.C.P.B.* (1899), pp. 37–38; and in many places subsequently. [See Appendix.]

*The Three Voices. See under the *Train* (No. *14*) and *Phantasmagoria* (No. *68*).

Tommy's Dead. [Poem of 54 lines, parodying Sydney Dobell; written 31 Dec. 1857.] This is the first publication, and it has only been reprinted in Editorial notes to *Diaries* (1953), pp. 134–5 (No. *315*).

*Ode to Damon. See under *College Rhymes* (1861) (No. *22*).

'A Monument—all men agree'. [Verse riddle in 7 lines.] First published in 'Before *Alice*', Dec. 1898; reprinted in the first edition of this *Handbook* (1931), p. 220, with the answer given as 'Tablet'.

*Melancholetta. See under *College Rhymes* (1862) (No. *22*) &c.

*The Willow Tree. Written 1859. See under *Phantasmagoria* (1869) (No. *68*), where it appeared as 'Stanzas for Music'.

*Faces in the Fire. See under this title (1860) (No. *21*).

Review: Photograph Exhibition. See under sub-title (1860) (No. *20*).

Blood. [Poem by Wilfred Dodgson.]

*Lines. [Poem in 42 lines, written Feb. 1860.] Revised as 'A Valentine': see *Phantasmagoria* (1869) (No. *68*).

*Bloggs' Woe. See under *College Rhymes* (1863) and *Phantasmagoria*, where it appears as 'Size and Tears'.

Note. All items above preceded by an asterisk * will be found in *Nonesuch* (and the verse items in *Collected Verse*) though in their revised versions where such were made.

[1 8 5 1 - 6 2]

Miscellaneous and Unpublished Juvenalia

For the sake of completeness the following items may be listed here.

7. *1851.* Autograph MS. of *The Christ Church Commoner*, Chapters I and II, with the following notation at the end in the author's

autograph: '(fragment of an unpublished novel by G. P. R. James)' written on mourning stationery.

Humorous account of an examination at Oxford, in mock heroic style, parodying James.

This unpublished item, then in the collection of Owen D. Young, was shown in the Columbia Exhibition in 1932 and described in the printed Catalogue as Exhibit 391.

8. 1853. 'Autograph MS. of *The Ligniad*, a poem of 100 lines, dated May 23, 1853 (beginning "Of man in stature small"), addressed to George Girdlestone Woodhouse, of Christ Church. It has twice occurred in sales, and twelve lines of it are printed in the sale catalogues (1922 and 1927).'   F. M.

It was exhibited in the Columbia Exhibition (also from O. D. Young's Collection) and described in the Catalogue as Exhibit 392.

9. 1858. The Legend of Scotland

In his *Diary* for 16 Jan. 1858, Dodgson wrote: 'Finished for the Longleys the "Legend" which has been promised them ever since the 12th August last year.'

It was first published in *The Lewis Carroll Picture Book* (1899), pp. 331–9, and was reprinted in *Further Nonsense* (1926), pp. 82–88, and several other places—e.g. *Nonesuch*, pp. 1111–17 (999–1005).

10. 1862. Miss Jones

Written in Oct. 1862—'it is a medley-song, which I composed when last at Croft, with the help of Margaret, Henrietta, etc., the tunes running into each other', wrote Dodgson in his *Diary* on 28 Oct. 1862.

The MS. (in the possession of the Dodgson family) was shown in the Lewis Carroll Centenary Exhibition in London, 1932, and is described on p. 69 of the Catalogue (Item 341).

It was first published in *Collected Verse* (1932), pp. 47–50 where it appears in a reduced facsimile of the words and music as written out by Margaret Dodgson.

The words only are included in *Nonesuch*, pp. 816–18 (730–2).

1854

11. The Oxonian Advertiser (1854)   [2, 3

Writing on 13 Aug. 1855, in the family magazine *Mischmasch* (No. 6), Dodgson, speaking of himself in the editorial plural, said:'In the summer of 1854 we contributed two poems to the *Oxonian Advertiser*, neither at all worth preservation.' M. and W. failed to find a copy of this periodical, but an almost complete file (1853–6) exists in the British Museum, catalogued as *Hall's Oxonian Advertiser*. The paper itself, averaging four sheets per monthly number, bears the heading *The Oxonian Advertiser and Family Newspaper*.

Few of the poems contained in it are signed, and none by Dodgson under any of his known pseudonyms. 'Curiosity or Inquisitiveness' (Feb. 1854) is signed 'I. B. B.', and 'B. B.' was a pseudonym used later the same year by Dodgson—but February is hardly 'the summer of 1854'.

In 'Lewis Carroll's First Publication' (*Times Literary Supplement*, 13 Sept. 1957) I suggested that 'The Farewell: By a Mother to a Child at Sea' and 'Cockney Enigma, on the Letter W' (both in the April number) might be Dodgson's two contributions, and reprinted them on this assumption. A correspondent in the *T.L.S.* (Miss Dorothy Wormald) on 11 Oct. 1957 identified the second as by Henry Mayhew; but 'The Farewell' still seems a probable Dodgson item, and resembles 'The Sailor's Wife' published in the *Train* in 1857.

The poem is of little merit—but later possibilities are of even less worth. 'The Past and the Future' (June); 'There's a tongue in every leaf' (July), and 'The Sailor's Evening Song' (August) are the only runners-up. But without further proof, all is guess-work.

12. *The Whitby Gazette* (1854)   [4, 5

Two pieces are contained in this, both signed 'B. B.', and both identified as by Dodgson by being included in *Mischmasch* (No. 6). They are:

The Lady of the Ladle: 31 Aug. 1854. (Verse.)

Wilhelm Von Schmitz: 7 Sept. 1854. (Prose, in four chapters.)

The first was reprinted in Langford Reed's *Further Nonsense* (1926), pp. 31–35, and subsequently in *Collected Verse* (1932), pp. 33–35; *Mischmasch* (1932), pp. 133–5; *Nonesuch*, pp. 805–6 (721–2), &c.

The second was reprinted in Langford Reed's *Further Nonsense* (1926), pp. 66–78. In *Mischmasch* (1932) only Chapters III and IV are included. The whole story was reprinted in *Nonesuch*, pp. 1097–1110 (986–98).

1855

13. *The Comic Times* (1855)   [6

'*The Comic Times*, a penny rival of *Punch* edited by Edmund Yates, consists of sixteen numbers issued from Saturday Aug: 11, to Saturday Nov: 24, 1855, in London. Collingwood (*Life and Letters of Lewis Carroll* (1898), pp. 62-64) declares that Frank Smedley introduced Dodgson who "became one of the contributors", that several of his poems are in it, that 100,000 copies of the first number were printed, and that Yates congratulated Dodgson on his verses. No copy of the *Comic Times* has yet been found to verify these statements, which were no doubt based on Dodgson's diary or journal.'   F. M.

The *Diaries* give the following contributions to the *Comic Times*, with dates of publication. The first two are copied into *Mischmasch* (No. *6*), the rest cut out and pasted in.

1. *Poetry for the Million* [Prose heading to the following item] Aug. 18, 1855.
   Reprinted in *The Lewis Carroll Picture Book* (1899), p. 25, and in *Mischmasch* (1932), p. 104, and in Langford Reed (No. *298*).
2. 'The Dear Gazelle.' Aug. 18, 1855.
   Reprinted in *Rhyme? and Reason?* (1883) and many subsequent verse collections, e.g. *Nonesuch*, pp. 878-9 (788-9). In all reprints, except L.C.P.B. (No. *287*), *Mischmasch*, and Langford Reed there is a new prose heading. 'The Dear Gazelle' (later called 'Tema Con Variazione' or 'Theme with Variations') is in four stanzas of four lines each: the first line of each stanza is quoted from four concurrent lines in Thomas Moore's *Lalla Rookh* (Moore's *Poetical Works*, 1868, vol. vi, pp. 217-18). The first line is a misquotation, and should read: 'I never nurs'd a dear gazelle.' Mrs. Lennon (*Victoria Through the Looking-glass*, 1945, pp. 267-8) compares Dodgson's verses with Calverley's parody—but misquotes both Calverley and Moore.
3. 'She's all my Fancy painted Him.' Sept. 8, 1855.
   Revised and cut, this forms the Evidence read by the White Rabbit in *Alice's Adventures*. The original version was reprinted in L.C.P.B., *Mischmasch*, &c., *Nonesuch*, pp. 807-8 (723-4).
4. *Hints for Etiquette: or Dining Out made Easy*. Oct. 13, 1855.
   Reprinted in L.C.P.B. (pp. 33-34); *Mischmasch*; Langford Reed, &c., *Nonesuch*, pp. 1235-7 (1113-14).
5. *Photography Extraordinary*. Nov. 3, 1855.
   Reprinted in L.C.P.B. (pp. 28-32); *Mischmasch*, &c.; *Nonesuch*, pp. 1231-5 (1109-13).

[NOTE: M. & W. list the above items in their Nos. [7, 8] as possible contributions to the *Illustrated Times* or the *Whitby Gazette*. They also include, from L.C.P.B., 'The Two Brothers' and 'Stanza of Anglo-Saxon Poetry', neither apparently published before this—they both occur in *Mischmasch* in manuscript. They also include 'The Palace of Humbug', for which see No. *16* below.]

1856

14. *The Train* (1856-7)   [9

THE | TRAIN: || A First-Class Magazine. || [Small picture of a train emerging from a tunnel, with motto below 'Vires acquirit eundo.' || [*a wavy line*]| VOL. I.—FROM JAN. TO JUNE, 1856.||[*a wavy line*]||

London: Groombridge and Sons, Paternoster Row. MDCCCLVI. | [The Authors of articles in 'The Train', reserve to themselves the right of translation.]: 1856: 8°: pp. iv+384. CONTENTS:—p. [i]. Title: p. [ii]. In the centre of the page is London: Printed by Taylor and Greening, 4 and 5, Graystoke Place, Fetter Lane: pp. iii–iv, Index: pp. 1–384, the text, divided equally between the six months, January–June. Vols. ii–v have similar titles and indices, except that the publisher of vol. ii is S. O. Beeton, 18 Bouverie Street, Fleet Street: vol. ii contains pp. iv+384: vol. iii, pp. iv+384; vol. iv, pp. iv+380: vol. v, pp. iv+384, and are divided between the months of the year; the last number is for June 1858.

The *Train* was a monthly magazine started by Edmund Yates and his friends after the failure of his first venture, the *Comic Times*, for which see No. *13*.

To the *Train* Dodgson contributed:

1. 'Solitude'. By Lewis Carroll (vol. i, pp. 154–5, March 1856). Eleven four-line stanzas, beginning 'I love the stillness of the wood', with an illustration. A serious poem on the pleasures of reminiscence. Dodgson's pseudonym of 'Lewis Carroll' here first occurs: for the choice of it out of five submitted to Edmund Yates see Collingwood's *Life*, p. 67. Reprinted in *Phantasmagoria* (1869) and *Three Sunsets* (1898).

2. 'Y^e Carpette Knyghte' (vol. i, p. 191, March 1856). Unsigned. Three six-line stanzas, beginning 'I have a horse, a ryghte goode horse—': a humorous poem. Reprinted in *Phantasmagoria* (1869) and *Rhyme? and Reason?* (1883).

3. 'The Path of Roses'. By Lewis Carroll (vol. i, pp. 286–8, May 1856). A serious poem, chiefly in blank verse, on woman's mission in time of war, showing Tennyson's influence both in subject and style. There is one illustration. Reprinted in *Phantasmagoria* (1869) and *Three Sunsets* (1898).

4. 'Novelty and Romancement. A broken Spell'. By Lewis Carroll (vol. ii, pp. 249–54, October 1856). A prose piece, rather long drawn out, in which 'Leopold Edgar Stubbs' had 'long yearned for poetry, for beauty, for novelty, for romancement' and found the last word on a mechanic's signboard—where it turned out to be 'Roman cement'—a somewhat frigid conceit. Dodgson was feeling his way to better things. There is one illustration. Reprinted, unsigned, in *The Harp of a Thousand Strings* (New York, 1858) from the *Train* with (a reproduction of) the illustration. This is the first reprint of any part of Dodgson's writings, and was, of course, unauthorized. Mr. Parrish kindly communicated to us Mr. R. Edgar's discovery of this early reprint as described in

the New York *Publishers' Weekly* at p. 2738 (1930?). Mr. Edgar states that all the poems in the *Harp* are unsigned, though the *Novelty* was signed 'Lewis Carroll' in the *Train*, and is able to claim for America the first reprint of any part of Dodgson's works, at a date before Dodgson had signed any separate piece with his own name. Reprinted separately by Randolph Edgar at Boston (U.S.A.) in 1925.

5. 'Upon the lonely moor' (vol. ii, pp. 255–6, Oct. 1856). Unsigned. Nine eight-line stanzas, beginning 'I met an aged, aged man': a parody on Wordsworth's 'Resolution and Independence'. Reprinted in the *Cornhill Magazine* (Apr. 1924) and re-written with the title 'An Aged Aged Man' in *Through the Looking-glass* (1872). Both are reprinted in the *Collected Verse of Lewis Carroll* (1929).

6. 'The three Voices'. By Lewis Carroll (vol. ii, pp. 278–84, Nov. 1856). Eighty-four three-line stanzas, beginning 'The First Voice. With hands tight clenched through matted hair'. Reprinted in *Phantasmagoria* (1869), in *Rhyme? and Reason?* (1883) and *Collected Verse*. A description of an overpowering and argumentative woman and a feeble and distracted man, in parody of Tennyson's *Two Voices*, very wittily expressed.

7. 'The Sailor's Wife'. By Lewis Carroll (vol. iii, pp. 231–3, Apr. 1857). Seventeen four-line stanzas, beginning 'See! there are tears upon her face', with one illustration. A serious poem about a dream of shipwreck, reprinted in *Phantasmagoria* (1869).

8. Hiawatha's Photographing. By Lewis Carroll (vol. iv, pp. 332–5, Dec. 1857), with a short introduction in prose. A parody of Longfellow's 'Hiawatha', in blank verse, beginning 'From his shoulder Hiawatha', narrating a failure to satisfy a family photographed separately and as a group. Reprinted in *Phantasmagoria* (1869); and in *Rhyme? and Reason?* (1883) with a few omissions and changes.

It seems to be just possible from internal evidence that Dodgson wrote 'A Fragment from an unpublished drama entitled "Going down for the Long"', but did not care to reprint it (vol. ii, pp. 318–39, Nov. 1856). [But it is not mentioned in the *Diaries*, R.L.G.] And his later parodies of Euclid's Definitions may have been suggested by a reminiscence of 'The Social and Political Euclid' in vol. v, pp. 230, 365.

F. M.

All eight items are included in *Collected Verse* and *Nonesuch*.

1857

Questions on the Pickwick Papers (1857)

A set of thirty questions on Dickens's *Pickwick Papers*, dated 'Christ's College, Christmas 1857'. A reference to this humorous set is made by Mrs. Florence Milner in an article in *St. Nicholas Magazine*, Nov. 1927, as if it were by Dodgson, referring to a copy in the Huntington Library, Pasadena, California. She quotes four of the questions, such as 'Deduce from expressions used on the occasion, Mr. Pickwick's maximum of speed', and 'Give Weller's Theories for the Extraction of Mr. Pickwick from the Fleet'.

But the piece is by Charles Stuart Calverley (*d.* 1884: of Christ's College, Cambridge). It is rare, but printed, with the key, in the 1901 edition of Calverley's works.

15. *Where does the Day Begin?* (1857)

In his *Diary* for 23 Feb. 1857, Dodgson says: 'Wrote a letter to the *Illustrated London News* on the subject of "Where does the day begin?", which I see is now being discussed in that paper. (It is a difficulty which occurred to me some years ago—I wrote on it in The Umbrella.) I signed myself "A Mathematical Tutor, Oxford".' (Cf. the *Rectory Umbrella* (No. *5*), pp. 31–33.)

The letter appeared on 18 Apr. 1857: vol. xxx, p. 372. It is reprinted in *Diaries* (*315*), pp. 104–5.

16. *"The Palace of Humbug"* (1857)

This humorous poem was written late in 1855, and having been refused by the *Comic Times*, the *Train*, and *Punch*, was published in the *Oxford Critic*, No. 1, 29 May 1857. It was copied into *Mischmasch* and is in the printed version (*6*), pp. 136–9, as well as *L.C.P.B.*, &c. *Nonesuch*, pp. 810–12 (725–7). M. and W. include it under Nos. [7, 8]; see above (*13*).

1858

17. *The Fifth Book of Euclid* (1858)

The Fifth Book of Euclid treated algebraically by a College Tutor. (Oxford, 1858).

This has been attributed to Dodgson, but he was never a College Tutor: he was Student and Mathematical Lecturer at Christ Church, and always careful in his use of such terms. Dodgson's own book on the subject was issued in 1868 [see No. *64*], and is wholly different in treatment and details. The present work may have been written by Dr. Thomas Fowler, Tutor of Lincoln College, afterwards President of Corpus.   F. M.

Nevertheless the *Diary* for 31 May 1855 suggests that this *is* by Dodgson. He says: 'During the last month I have again written out, in an improved form, *The Fifth Book of Euclid Proved Algebraically*.' Moreover the letter to the *Illustrated London News* (No. *15*) proves that, even if incorrectly, he *did* refer to himself as a Tutor.

1860

18. *A Photographer's Day Out* (1860)   [10

The | South Shields | Amateur Magazine, | consisting of | Original Articles, | in prose and verse, | By | Amateurs in South Shields and the neighbourhood. | [*a line*] | [Four lines beginning 'The Readers' and ending 'not the cook'.] | [*a line*] | Published in aid of the Building fund of the | South Shields Mechanics' Institute. | [*a line*] |

South Shields: 1860: 8°: size $8\frac{3}{16} \times 5\frac{7}{16}$ in.: pp. vi+42. CONTENTS: p. [i] title as above: [iii] contents: v–vi, 'To our readers': [1]–42, the text. At the bottom of p. 42 under a double line is 'Published in aid of the building fund of the South Shields Mechanics' Institute.'

On pp. 12–16 is an article entitled | 'A Photographer's Day Out. | By Lewis Carroll' |, beginning 'I am shaken and sore' and finishing on p. 16 'I haven't the faintest idea'. Issued in blue paper wrappers, with the title-page reproduced on the front cover within a border. Pp. 2, 3, and 4 are blank.

This is a rare item. A copy was sold at Sotheby's on 12 Nov. 1929: it was without the wrappers and was bound by Riviere in dark-green Levant Morocco, and is perhaps the same as art. 406 in W. H. Robinson's (of Newcastle) *Catalogue of Rare First Editions* (Dec. 1929), priced £50.

M. L. Parrish.

Reprinted in *Nonesuch*, pp. 1089–96 (979–85).

19. *Rules for Court Circular* (1860)   [11

RULES | FOR | COURT CIRCULAR. | (*A New Game of Cards for Two or More Players.*) | [*an ornamental line, followed by the text*] |

[*No place*]: 1860: (Two) 8vo: size $7\frac{3}{16} \times 4\frac{1}{2}$ in.: pp. [4], p. [1] title and sixteen lines of the text: pp. [2–3] the rest of the text: at the end of the text is 'January, 1860'. Anonymous.

The game is peculiar, and it may be doubted whether it attained any vogue. Each player has to 'make a line' by laying down six cards dealt to him, three on each side of a 'lead' card, and obtaining superiority by having a Trio (three of the same value), Sequence (of three or four), Sympathy (three or four Hearts), or Court (three or four Court cards; four are a Court circular) and so on. The process is repeated until the pack is exhausted. Sir Harold Hartley owns a copy with Dodgson's corrections.

For the second edition see 1862 (No. 20).

Williams, i. 1 (p. 3); *Collingwood*, p. 431; *Parrish Catalogue*, p. 99: F. Madan, Sir H. Hartley.

The *Diary* for 25 Jan. 1858 says: 'Completed the rules of the game at cards I have been inventing during the last few days, *Court Circular*.'

20. *Photographic Exhibition* (1860)

This unsigned Review appeared in the *Illustrated Times*, vol. x, p. 57, 28 Jan. 1860. It was cut out and stuck into *Mischmasch*, and is printed in the volume published in 1932 (No. 6) on pp. 178–85. It has not been reprinted elsewhere, but is quoted extensively on pp. 156–9 of the *Diaries* (No. 315).

21. *"Faces in the Fire"* (1860)

This poem was first published in *All the Year Round*, No. 42, 11 Feb. 1860, and collected in *Phantasmagoria* (1869)—see No. 68. *Nonesuch*, pp. 975–6 (875–6). It was copied into *Mischmasch* and appears on pp. 175–7 of the published edition in its original unrevised form.

22. *College Rhymes* (1860–3)   [12

COLLEGE RHYMES: | CONTRIBUTED BY MEMBERS OF | 𝕿𝖍𝖊 𝖀𝖓𝖎-𝖛𝖊𝖗𝖘𝖎𝖙𝖎𝖊𝖘 𝖔𝖋 𝕺𝖝𝖋𝖔𝖗𝖉 𝖆𝖓𝖉 𝕮𝖆𝖒𝖇𝖗𝖎𝖉𝖌𝖊. | 'The blossom of the flying Terms'. —Tennyson. | [*Arms of the University of Oxford*] | Vol. I. |

London: R. Griffin, Bohn and Co. Cambridge: Macmillan and Co. Oxford: W. Mansell: 1861: (eights) 12°: pp. [8]+153+[1]: printed by W. Mansell. Vols. ii–iv have similar titles, with the conjoined Arms of the Universities, and adding 'Vol. II', &c. In vol. iii the London imprint disappears, and the form 'Oxford: T. and G. Shrimpton. Cambridge: Macmillan and Co.' is substituted and continued. From vol. iv onward the printer is H. Alden, printer, Corn Market, Oxford.

A number with its own wrapper was issued every term from the October term of 1859, and a volume of these numbers was published in the summer. In all fourteen volumes were issued in 1860 to 1873, comprising forty-two numbers. Collingwood states in his *Life and Letters* (p. 56) that Dodgson was at one time Editor of *College Rhymes* [1 July 1862 until 25 Mar. 1863]. The Cambridge contributions gradually diminished, and the paper became increasingly Oxonian, and largely drew from Christ Church writers.

The following contributions were from Dodgson:

1. 'A Sea Dirge' (vol. ii, pp. 56–58, Oct. T. 1860). Sixteen four-line stanzas, beginning 'There are certain things—as, a spider, a ghost'. Signed at the end

'Lewis Carroll Ch.Ch.' An amusing apology for hating the sea. It was reprinted in *Phantasmagoria* (1869), *Rhyme? and Reason?*, Collingwood's *Life and Letters*, p. 66, the *Cornhill Magazine*, Apr. 1924, *Further Nonsense*, Dent's *Alice &c.*, *Collected Verse*.

2. 'The Dream of Fame' (vol. iii, pp. 3–7, No. 7, Oct. T. 1861). Eighteen six-line stanzas, beginning 'He saw her once, and in the glance'. Signed at the end 'C.L.D. Ch.Ch.' A serious poem of hopeless love. Reprinted in *Three Sunsets*.

3. 'Ode to Daman from Chloe' (vol. iii, pp. 9–11: as No. 2). Twelve four-line stanzas, beginning 'Oh, do not forget'. Signed 'B. B. [a signature which Dodgson used in 1854 in the *Whitby Gazette*] Ch.Ch.' In Praed's style. Reprinted in the *Cornhill Magazine*, Apr. 1924.

4. 'Those horrid Hurdy-gurdies! A monody, by a victim' (vol. iii, p. 23, as No. 2). Four four-line stanzas, beginning 'My mother bids me'. Signed 'B.B. Ch.Ch.'

5. 'Only a Woman's Hair' (vol. iii, pp. 58–60, No. 8, Lent T. 1862). Ten four-line stanzas, beginning 'Only a woman's hair! Fling it aside!' Signed at the end 'C.L.D. Ch.Ch.' This article has reference to a lock of hair owned by Dean Swift. It is reprinted in *Phantasmagoria* and *Three Sunsets*. Composed 17 Feb. 1862.

6. 'Melancholetta' (vol. iii, pp. 67–71, No. 8, Lent T. 1862). Eighteen six-line stanzas (the last has two extra lines), beginning 'With saddest music'. Signed at the end 'B.B. Ch.Ch.': A humorous poem, reprinted in *Phantasmagoria*, *Rhyme? and Reason?*, *Collected Verse*, but only ten of the stanzas survived the original edition.

7. 'Stolen Waters' (vol. iii, pp. 106–11, No. 9, Summer T. 1862). Twenty-six six-, five-, and four-line stanzas, beginning 'The Light was faint'. Signed 'C.L.D. Ch.Ch.' A serious poem on the penalty of youth sowing wild oats. Reprinted in *Phantasmagoria* and *Three Sunsets*. Composed 9 May 1862.

8. 'Poeta fit non nascitur' (vol. iii, pp. 112–16, as No. 7). Eighteen six-line stanzas, beginning 'How shall I be a poet?' Signed 'K. Oxford.' Mutton pies are described as 'dreams of fleecy flocks | Pent in a wheaten cell': an example of epithets is 'The wild man went his weary way | To a strange and lonely pump'. Reprinted as No. 6.

9. 'Disillusionized' (vol. iii, pp. 129–30, as No. 7). Four eight-line stanzas, beginning 'I painted her a gushing thing'. Unsigned, but dated 15 Mar. 1862. Three stanzas revised are reprinted in Collingwood's *Life and Letters* (1898), p. 66, as by Dodgson; and in *Further Nonsense* (entitled 'My Fancy').

10. 'The Lang Coortin'' (vol. iv, pp. 32–39, No. 10; Oct. T. 1862). Thirty-seven four-line stanzas, beginning 'The ladye she stood'. Signed at the end 'R. W. G.' Reprinted as No. 6.

11. 'Beatrice' (vol. iv, pp. 46–49, as No. 10). Nine seven-line stanzas, beginning 'In her eyes'. Signed at the end 'C. L. D. Ch. Ch., Oxford.' On innocent girlhood. Reprinted in *Phantasmagoria* (1869) and *Three Sunsets* (1898). Composed 4 Dec. 1862.

12. 'The Majesty of Justice. An Oxford idyll' (vol. iv, pp. 97–99, No. 11, Lent T. 1863). Nine eight-line stanzas, beginning 'They passed beneath'. Signed 'R. W. G. Oxford. March 1863'. A gentle satire on the Vice-Chancellor's Court. Reprinted as No. 3.

13. 'Size and Tears' (vol. iv, pp. 113–15, No. 12, Summer T. 1863). Eight six-line stanzas, beginning 'When on the Sandy Shore'. Signed at the end

'R. W. G.' This contribution deals with the disadvantage of Stoutness. Reprinted as No. 6.

It does not seem likely that a Latin verse translation of Foote's 'So she went into the garden to cut a cabbage leaf' (beginning 'Illa igitur caulem vulsura', and signed 'X. Ch. Ch., Oxford') in vol. v, p. 16, No. 13, Oct. 1863, is by Dodgson. After his second class in Moderations in 1852 he gave up Classics, and the ascription of this piece at least needs corroboration.   F. M.

Williams, iii. 5, p. 118 (No. 1 only); *Parrish Catalogue*, p. 118; *Collingwood*, p. 66: British Museum, Bodleian, &c.

To the above should be added:

'Prologue' to vol. iv, 1863, published in No. x, Michaelmas Term 1862. Dodgson notes in his *Diary* for 15 Nov. 1862: 'adapted as Prologue for Volume IV some verses written in 1853, intended as preface for a volume of poems.' The only reprint of this 16-line poem is in *Diaries*, p. 189, except for its appearance in 'Lewis Carroll's Fugitive Pieces' in the *Times Literary Supplement*, 31 July 1953.

All the other contributions are included in *Nonesuch*, as well as various collected editions of verse, &c. But all are in their later forms, often cut or revised.

The original versions of 'Ode to Damon' and 'Melancholetta' may be found in *Mischmasch* (pp. 162–4, and 166–74), No. 6 above.

The complete version of 'Disillusioned' will be found in *Diaries*, pp. 162–3 and in *A Century of Humorous Verse* (Everyman Library No. 813), 1959, pp. 62–63. The complete version of 'A Sea Dirge' will also be found in this volume, but otherwise only in the original edition of *Phantasmagoria*. Its original appearance in *College Rhymes* represents the only occasion on which 'Lewis Carroll' admitted that he was a member of Christ Church.

'A Sea Dirge' is a parody—of metre rather than contents—of Edgar Allan Poe's 'Annabel Lee'.

'Disillusioned' is a more direct parody of the popular song 'Alice Gray' (of which Dodgson had already misused the first line: 'She's all my Fancy painted her'), words by William Mee, set to music by Mrs. P. Millard.

'Those horrid Hurdy-gurdies' resembles the 'Dear Gazelle' parody, since the first line of each stanza is the first line of a popular song: the first by Mrs. John Hunter (Anne Home, 1742–1821) set to music by Haydn; the second from Davenant's *The Rivals* (1668) to a traditional air revised by Matthew Locke; the third is the song 'Ever of thee!' by George Linley (1798–1865), while the fourth is the traditional whine of the organ-grinder.

'The Lang Coortin'' is a parody of the Scottish Ballad style.

R. L. G.

23. *Photographs* (1860)   [13
PHOTOGRAPHS.

No place or date, but in or soon after 1860. (Two) 4°: pp. 3+[1]: pp. 1–3, a list in double columns of the subjects of Dodgson's photographs.

An interesting list of 159 photographs taken by Dodgson early in life, before he was ordained (on 22 Dec. 1861), and long before he moved into the well-known rooms in Tom Quad, where his photographic arrangements can still be traced. The watermark of the paper is dated 1859. Anonymous.

The list is in three parts:

I. Portraits. Size 6×5 in.: 84 persons, some in groups; 87 photographs, chiefly of personal friends at Christ Church and elsewhere.

II. Portraits. Size $7\frac{1}{4} \times 6\frac{1}{4}$ in.: 39 persons or groups, 19 photographs, as Part I.

III. Miscellaneous. Size $7\frac{1}{4} \times 6\frac{1}{4}$ in.: 44 places, sculptures, skeletons (from the Christ Church Anatomical Museum), &c.; 53 photographs. Two of the photographs are dated 1857, two 1858, four 1859, twenty-six 1860.

It is well known that Dodgson from 1868 (when he acquired his rooms in the NW. corner of Tom Quad) took an enormous number of photographs of his friends; and he himself in 1868 called these 'His one amusement' (see Collingwood's *Life and Letters*, pp. 133, -197), and this list shows that he began his hobby as early as 1855, or 1856. He developed his (wet collodion process) plates himself. Collections are not uncommon: Mr. Parrish possesses three scrapbooks containing in all more than 380 photographs; and similar albums occur in booksellers' catalogues. The advantages of private photographs are obvious, though they may fail of being artistic. This list is rare, and printed for private circulation. Anonymous, but certainly by Dodgson. Among the names may be mentioned Liddon, Archbishop Longley, Dean Kitchin, Bishop Wilberforce, and Dodgson himself. Several occur in Collingwood's *Life and Letters* and *The Lewis Carroll Picture Book*, as illustrations. Dodgson almost entirely gave up photography in his later years, say from about 1870, when every one of note had to submit to the claims of publicity.   F. M.

Williams, ii. 3, p. 95; *Parrish Catalogue*, pp. 117–19, &c.; *Collingwood*, p. 431; Sir H. Hartley.

Dodgson's important position in the history of photography has been dealt with fully, and the above pamphlet further described in Helmut Gernsheim's *Lewis Carroll—Photographer* (1949) (No. XIX).

24. *Syllabus of Plane Algebraical Geometry* (1860)   [14

A | SYLLABUS | OF | PLANE ALGEBRAICAL GEOMETRY, | SYSTEMATICALLY ARRANGED, WITH FORMAL DEFI- | NITIONS, POSTULATES, AND AXIOMS. | BY | CHARLES LUTWIDGE DODGSON, M.A. | STUDENT AND MATHEMATICAL LECTURER OF | CHRIST CHURCH,

C 99   C

OXFORD. | PART. I. | CONTAINING | POINTS, RIGHT LINES, RECTILINEAR FIGURES, | PENCILS, AND CIRCLES. |

Oxford: printed by James Wright, Printer to the University. Sold by J. H. and J. Parker, Oxford, and 377 Strand, London: M.DCCC.LX. (fours) 8°: pp. xvi+153+[1]. CONTENTS: p. i, title as above: iii–x, Introduction: xi–xvi, contents: 1–153, the treatise: [2] Errata. Black cloth covers, white paper label on the back. White end papers. The price was 5s.

The writer having observed defects in existing treatises, produces the first part of a work designed to 'occupy with regard to Algebraical Geometry, the same position which is occupied by that of Euclid with regard to Pure Geometry'. The Appendix (pp. 124–53) consists of notes and proofs with diagrams. There is no trace of humour; the cobbler sticks to his last.

25. Notes on the First Two Books of Euclid (1860)   [15

NOTES ‖ ON THE ‖ FIRST TWO BOOKS OF EUCLID. | DESIGNED FOR | CANDIDATES FOR RESPONSIONS.|

Oxford: John Henry and James Parker, and at 377 Strand, London: MDCCCLX: (four) 8° (size $8\frac{7}{8} \times 5\frac{3}{4}$ in.): pp. 8: p. 1, title as above: 2, Notes on the Definitions: 3–4, eleven additional Definitions: 4–5, Scheme to explain some of the Definitions: 6–7, Notes on the Propositions: 8, List of the Abbreviations, &c. At the end is 'Printed by James Wright, printer to the University'.

The Notes are scanty, but clear. Some of the additional Definitions are useful, e.g. of Problem, Theorem, A fortiori. Anonymous, but known to be by Dodgson. A one-leaf prospectus states that the price is 6d. Rare.

Williams, ii. 1 (p. 95); *Parrish Catalogue*, p. 99; *Collingwood*, p. 431.

1861

26. After Three Days (1861)   [16

AFTER THREE DAYS, A POEM.

Published in *Temple Bar*, vol. ii (July 1861), at pp. 566–8.

This serious poem on seeing Holman Hunt's picture of Christ in the Temple, beginning 'I stood within the gate' was reprinted in *Phantasmagoria* (1869) and in the *Three Sunsets*. Composed 16 Feb. 1861. *Nonesuch*, pp. 972–4 (872–4).

27. Formulae of Plane Trigonometry (1861)   [17

THE | FORMULÆ | OF | PLANE TRIGONOMETRY, | PRINTED WITH SYMBOLS (INSTEAD OF WORDS) TO | EXPRESS THE 'GONIOMETRICAL

RATIOS.' || [line] || BY | CHARLES LUTWIDGE DODGSON, M.A. | STUDENT AND MATHEMATICAL LECTURER OF | CHRIST CHURCH, OXFORD.

Oxford: Printed by James Wright, Printer to the University; Sold by J. H. and J. Parker, Oxford, and 377, Strand, London: M.DCCC.LXI: 4°: pp. 19+[1]. CONTENTS: p. 1, title as above: 3–6, preface, dated 'Ch.Ch. June 11. 1861': 7–19, the Formulæ: a stitched pamphlet.

Dodgson invents symbols for the terms of Plane Trigonometry, sine (⌒) cosine (⌒) and the rest, seven in all, and explains them. The formulae are then presented in three parts: (1) Goniometry proper, (2) do. by ratios, (3) Trigonometry. A prospectus on one leaf shows that the price was 1s.

Williams, ii. 4 (p. 96); Parrish Catalogue, p. 65; Collingwood, p. 431: British Museum, Bodleian, Harvard, Huntington, &c.

Perhaps all copies have a slight correction of two items on p. 19, by pasting a small piece of paper over the peccant words.

F. M. (Supplement).

28. Notes on the First Part of Algebra (1861)   [18

Notes on the First Part of Algebra: Oxford: Parker: 1861: Octavo, price sixpence.

Only known from Collingwood's Life and Letters, p. 431.

'Done. Will be out this week I hope', wrote Dodgson to his sister Mary Collingwood on 20 Feb. 1861.

Madan noted in his Supplement 'Sir Harold Hartley owns a copy', but I have been unable to trace one for description here.

29. Endowment of the Greek Professorship (1861)   [19

'Endowment of the Greek Professorship.':

No place, but printed at Oxford: (1861): 4°: pp. [2]. CONTENTS: p. [1] title and 35 lines of text, beginning 'In the Alternative Amendment': at the bottom of the page is 'Nov. 22, 1861'.

An anonymous notice in a long controversy about the emoluments and duties of the Professorship, to which it was proposed to elect Mr. Jowett: see notes on No. 35 (1865). The writer makes fun of the 'Corpus element' in the office, in connexion with All Souls. The piece has been ascribed to Octavius Ogle, but is probably by Dodgson.

Williams, ii. 6 (p. 96); Parrish Catalogue, p. 100: Bodleian, Christ Church.

This broadside is reprinted in its entirety in Diaries (p. 166).

1862

30. Rules for Court Circular (1862) Second Edition   [20

RULES | FOR | Court Circular; | [A NEW GAME OF CARDS FOR TWO PLAYERS.] | [ornamental line.] | [text follows].

No imprint: (1862): (two) 16°: pp. 2+[2]: CONTENTS: p. 1, title and 21 lines of text: 2, the remainder of the text: at the end is 'April, 1862.': pp. [3-4] are blank. Size 5¾ × 3⅞ in.

This second edition re-models and simplifies the game, and is for two players only, but is still too elaborate to be amusing. Anonymous. For the first edition see No. 11 (1860). I have given the collation of this item because, although it is only a second edition of No. 11, it is a much condensed form and shows considerable variation in the text.

Williams, i. 2 (p. 4); Parrish Catalogue, p. 99; Collingwood, p. 431: Bodleian, F. Madan, Harvard.

31. Index to In Memoriam (1862)   [21, 22

AN | INDEX || TO | 'IN MEMORIAM' ||| [line] ||||

London: Edward Moxon & Co., Dover Street: 1862: (eights) 12°: pp. [4]+ 40+8. CONTENTS: p. [1] title as above: [2] London: Bradbury and Evans, printers, Whitefriars: [3] preface: 1-40, the Index: 40, 'Bradbury and Evans printers, Whitefriars.': 1-8, Advertisements of Moxon's books, dated Jan. 1862, and including this book priced 2s. bound, or 1s. 6d. in sheets. The brown cloth binding bears 'Index to In Memoriam' on the front side.

This anonymous index to Tennyson's well-known Elegy on Arthur Hallam refers to each clause of the poem under the most important noun, verb, &c., in it, and contains about 3,000 references in double columns: for example, under River occur '70. 4 the river's wooded reach 102. 2 A r. sliding by the wall'. The 'compilers' are referred to in the Preface, and it is known that while Dodgson suggested and edited, one or more of his sisters chiefly compiled the work. The little publication received Tennyson's personal permission. The Advertisements show that the price was 2s. in cloth limp, or 1s. 6d. in sheets for binding with 'In Memoriam', which was first issued in 1850 and was by now in its eleventh edition. The Index was issued not later than Mar. 1862, and the earliest copies (21) in yellow paper covers have no advertisements.

[Dodgson wrote in his Diary for 9 July 1862: 'To Moxon's, who told me that more than 500 copies of the Index are sold.']

A new edition reached at least as far as a proof of the title-page in 1878 (*Parrish Catalogue*, p. 104), perhaps intended to accompany the 1880 (1879) edition of 'In Memoriam' published by Messrs. Kegan Paul.

Another edition is part of Thomas Davidson's Prolegomena to *In Memoriam* (Boston, U.S.A., 1889).   F. M.

32. Circular to mathematical friends (1862)   [23

A circular dated June 1862, and signed 'Charles L. Dodgson, Student and Mathematical Lecturer of Ch. Ch., Oxford', asking the criticism of friends on 'accompanying tables' designed to exhibit the whole of the subject-matter of Pure Mathematics', and to furnish 'a guide for working examples in the whole subject'.

This is a quarto leaf, printed on one side only, in 33 lines, beginning 'Sir, May I beg the favour'. It leads up to No. 26, 'General list of (Mathematical) Subjects, and cycle for working examples: 1863.' The only copy known is owned by Mr. M. L. Parrish, of Philadelphia, U.S.A.

1863

33. Mathematical Subjects (1863)   [26

General List of (Mathematical) Subjects, and Cycle for Working Examples. Oxford: Printed at the University Press. 1863. 8°: 16 pages. Sir H. Hartley owns a copy with Dodgson's corrections.

Williams, ii. 9 (p. 97); *Collingwood*, p. 432.

Dodgson wrote in his *Diary* for 10 Feb. 1863: 'Today I have sent to the Press the MS. for the Cycle: it has taken me many hours to work.'

34. Enunciations of Euclid (1863)   [25

THE ENUNCIATIONS | OF THE | PROPOSITIONS AND COROLLARIES, | | TOGETHER WITH QUESTIONS | ON THE | DEFINITIONS, POSTULATES, AXIOMS, &c. | IN | EUCLID, BOOKS I. AND II. | [*a line*] |

Oxford, printed by T. Combe, M. A.: E. P. Hall, and A. Latham, M.A. Printers to the University: 1863: (eight) 12mo. pp. 16. CONTENTS: p. 1, title: 3-16, text.

The Bodleian copy (the only one known, besides one at Harvard) contains autograph corrections by Dodgson, who undoubtedly compiled this little anonymous piece, for a new edition, with the addition of Books III-VI, for which see No. 78 (1873). There seems to have been a kind of vulgus of this work from at least as early as 1823, which Dodgson took and modified. There is, for instance, an edition of the common form published in 1862, but it is independent of Dodgson's careful improvements in the present issue.

Williams, ii. 8 (p. 96); *Collingwood*, p. 432: Bodleian, Harvard.

Dodgson does not mention in his *Diary* the publication of this item, but appears to refer to it on 17 Nov. 1862: 'I think an interest-collection might be made of axioms tacitly assumed by Euclid.'

35. *Croquet Castles* (1863)   [24

Croquet Castles. | [*an ornamental line*] | For Five Players | [*an ornamental line*] |||| [*followed by fifteen lines of the text.*]

[*No imprint*]: (1863): (two) 8°: pp. 3+[1]. CONTENTS: p. 1, title: 1–3, eight rules and a Note: before the note is 'Ch. Ch., Oxford, May 4, 1863.' Size $7\frac{7}{16} \times 4\frac{1}{2}$ in., on white wove paper.

An ingenious but over-elaborate variety of the old ordinary game of croquet on grass, with ten balls, ten arches, five flags, &c. An arch and flag form a castle, with one ball as defending sentinel and one ball as a soldier for attack. The second edition is so much altered under a changed name that it is dealt with as an original piece. See No. 37 (1866). Anonymous, but certainly by Dodgson. It never achieved vogue. Perhaps it was never published, for the promised 'figure' before the eight rules is not there. Collingwood states in the *Lewis Carroll Picture Book*, which apparently reprints a *third* edition (see p. 27: 1866), that the details were elaborated in a series of games with the Misses Liddell.

Williams, i. 3 (p. 4); *Parrish Catalogue*, p. 101; *Collingwood*, p. 432: Harvard, F. Madan.

See Dodgson's *Diary* for 4 May 1863: 'Wrote out the rules of a new croquet game, for five players, which I have invented and think of calling *Croquet Castles*.'

Reprinted in *Nonesuch*, pp. 1269–71 (1143–5).

1864

36. *Examination Statute* (1864)   [28

EXAMINATION STATUTE.

[No imprint, but Oxford, 1864]: (one) 4to: pp. [2]. CONTENTS: p. [1], a List in rhyming verse. Size 10 × 7½ in.

'A list of those who might, could, would, or should have voted thereon in Congregation Feb. 2, 4681, arranged alphabetically' in twenty-six lines or thirteen rhyming couplets. An anonymous skit on twenty-one members of the University. The following specimens will illustrate the style and humour:

'A is for [Acland], who'd physic the Masses,
B is for [Brodie], who swears by the gases: . . .

I am the Author, a rhymer erratic—
J is for [Jowett], who lectures in Attic:
K is for [Kitchin], than attic much warmer.
L is for [Liddell], relentless reformer!'
&c., &c.

Each name is disguised by a dot for each letter of the name. The other names are Conington, Donkin, Evans, Freeman, Goldwin Smith, Heurtley, Mansel, Norris, Ogilvie, Parker or Pusey, (Quad), Rolleston, Stanley, Travers Twiss, (University), Vice-Chancellor, and Wall: Xpenditure, Young men, Zeal. A facsimile is in the *Parrish Catalogue* (p. 102), showing all the names. The author is no doubt Dodgson, but it was also attributed at the time to Octavius Ogle. For the occasion see the next piece.

Williams, ii. 10 (p. 97); *Parrish Catalogue*, pp. 101–2; Bodleian, Christ Church, S. H. Williams, &c.

See Dodgson's *Diary* for 1 Feb. 1864: 'Invented and wrote out (with a suggestion or two from Bayne) a squib on the division of tomorrow (about the New Examination Statute) consisting of an alphabetical list of the names of voters and others, with the names left blank.'
Reprinted in *Collected Verse*, &c., *Nonesuch*, p. 920 (826).

37. New Examination Statute (1864)   [29

THE NEW EXAMINATION STATUTE. | [*a line*] | [*Thirty lines of text follow*] |

[Oxford, printed by J. Vincent]: 1864: (one) 4to: pp. 2. CONTENTS: p. 1, title: 1–2, a letter signed 'Charles L. Dodgson, Christ Church, March 2, 1864.': at the foot of p. 2 is 'Vincent, printer.' Size 10 $\frac{6}{16}$ × 8¼ in.

A letter to the Vice-Chancellor, Dr. J. P. Lightfoot, resigning the office of Public Examiner in Mathematics, beginning '. . . I much regret the necessity'. The Statute of 2 Feb. 1864 (see last piece) proposed to allow candidates for a degree to forsake Classics after Moderations, except so far as was needed for a Fourth Class in the

Final School of Literae Humaniores, if they wished to graduate in science. This Dodgson considered degrading both to Classics and to Mathematics.

Williams, ii. 11 (p. 97); *Collingwood*, p. 432; *Parrish Catalogue*, p. 66: Bodleian, Harvard.

The *Diary* for 25 Feb. reads: 'The new Examination Statute, giving a degree for a third class in any school, passed in Convocation by 281 to 243. I fear it is the beginning of very grevious changes in the University: this evening I have been seriously thinking about resigning my Examinership in consequence, and have written a sketch of a letter to the Vice-Chancellor on the subject.'

On 2 Mar. he wrote: 'Left the letter at the Vice-Chancellor's. I am also having it printed at Vincent's to be circulated tomorrow.'

The Letter was also published in the *Morning Post*, 4 Mar. 1864, and much of it is reprinted in *Diaries*, p. 211.

38. Guide to the Mathematical Student (1864)   [27

A GUIDE | TO THE | MATHEMATICAL STUDENT | IN READING, REVIEWING, AND | WORKING EXAMPLES. | BY CHARLES LUTWIDGE DODGSON, M.A. | STUDENT AND MATHEMATICAL LECTURER OF | CHRIST CHURCH, OXFORD. | PART I, | PURE MATHEMATICS. |

Oxford: John Henry and James Parker: MDCCCLXIV: | 8°: pp. [4]+27+ [1], signn. A², B⁸, C⁶. CONTENTS: p. [1] title as above: [2] the circular device of the Clarendon Press with a monogram C. H. L. (the three printers): at the bottom of the page: 'Oxford: by T. Combe, M.A., E. Pickard Hall, and H. Latham, M.A. printers to the University': [3–4] Preface, dated 'Christ Church, Oxford, December, 1864: 1–27, the text of the treatise. A stitched pamphlet. 8vo (size 8⅝ × 5 9/16 in.).

Dodgson here tabulates by subject the whole of Pure Mathematics, in twenty-six divisions and about 500 subdivisions; and prints on pp. 19–27 an ingenious cycle of over 1,600 numbers which supplies a scheme for a sequence of working examples for students. The examples themselves are not here. See No. 23 (1862).

Williams, ii. 12 (p. 97); *Parrish Catalogue*, p. 66; *Collingwood*, p. 432: British Museum, Bodleian, Harvard, &c.

This item does not seem to be mentioned in the *Diary*, unless Dodgson is referring to it on 9 Dec. 1864, when he says: 'A day or two ago I cut up two copies of my *Syllabus* and filed the whole, with some additional MS., to serve as scaffolding for the book, it seems an excellent plan.' There is no further reference to 'the book'.

1865

39. American Telegrams (1865) [34

American Telegrams. | (Summary) | [The text follows.]

No place: 4°: [4] all unnumbered, except the third, which is numbered '2': pp. [1] [4] are blank. The size of the piece is $8\frac{16}{16} \times 7\frac{3}{8}$ in.

An amusing anonymous skit on telegrams relating to the American Civil War transferred (under disguised names) to proposed regulations at Christ Church, Oxford, about the Treasury, the Butler, &c. It is dated 17 Feb. 1865, and begins: 'The interview which'.

Only two copies are known, one at Christ Church, Oxford, and one sold by the College at Sotheby's on 15 Dec. 1926, when it fetched £112. Extremely rare.

Williams, i. 4 (p. 5): Christ Church, Oxford.

Dodgson noted in his Diary for 15 Feb.: 'The idea occurred to me in the evening of writing some mock American news embodying some of our proceedings, and I wrote it at night.' And on 17 Feb.: 'Sent American Telegrams, with some additions, to be printed.'

See Diaries, p. 227 for quotations.

40. New Method of Evaluation (1865) [35

THE NEW METHOD | OF | EVALUATION, | as applied to π. | [a small thin line] | [32 lines of the text follow].

[Oxford]: (1865): (two) folio: pp. 4. CONTENTS: p. 1, title as above, then the introduction, and Method I, as far as 'unknown quantities': 2-4, the rest of Method I, and Methods II-V: on p. 4, at the end, on the right-hand side is | March, 1865. |

This item was reprinted, in brown paper wrappers, in 1874, and is also found as part of 'Notes by an Oxford Chiel' (1874). It is an anonymous skit and a humorous contribution to the long controversy about the payment of Benjamin Jowett, Master of Balliol College, Oxford, as Greek Professor. The statutable salary was £40, as fixed in the sixteenth century: should it be raised to £400, or since Jowett was by many regarded as heretical, should it be left as Henry VIII constituted it? E. B. P. (Pusey), H. P. L. (Liddon), H. G. L. (Liddell, Dean of Christ Church), and similar expressions are treated algebraically, with great neatness and ingenuity. Of the five processes suggested for obtaining a value for π (i.e. payment) which should be commensurable with W. (i.e. Work done), only the fifth 'Evaluation under pressure' produced a final result namely £500,000,000.

For issues of this piece appended to *The Dynamics of a Particle*, see No. **36** below; see also *Notes by an Oxford Chiel* (No. **80**, 1874).

Williams, i. 5 (p. 5), *Parrish Catalogue*, p. 67: Bodleian, Christ Church, Oxford, Huntington, &c.

The relevant *Diary* entries read: *March 3.* 'A day or two ago an idea occurred to me of writing a sham mathematical paper on Jowett's case, taking π to symbolise his payment, and have jotted down a little of it.' *March 8.* 'Sat up and wrote out the paper *On the Evaluation of π.' March 14.* 'Coming out of *The New Method of Evaluation as applied to π*. I had about 80 copies sent round to the Common Rooms.'

Reprinted with next item; in *Notes by an Oxford Chiel* (No. *98*), *L.C.P.B.* See *Nonesuch*, pp. 1123–9 (1011–16).

41. *Dynamics of a Particle* (1865) (First Edition)   [36ᵃ

| THE | DYNAMICS OF A PARTI- | CLE, WITH AN EXCURSUS | ON | THE NEW METHOD OF | EVALUATION, | AS APPLIED TO π. || [*a small thin line*].

Oxford: Printed and published by J. Vincent: 1865: (eight, four, two) 8°: pp. i–iv, 5–28: signn. A⁸, B⁴, C²: size $8\frac{9}{16} \times 5\frac{9}{16}$ in. CONTENTS: p. 1, title: 3–4, Introduction, dated June 1865: p. 5, contents of the three chapters.

A stitched pamphlet, issued in green wrappers, the front page of which is lettered as the title-page, but surrounded by a double fine line border, the outside dimensions of which are $6\frac{15}{16} \times 4$ in. The other pages of the wrapper are blank. All edges cut.

Three editions, or issues, came out in 1865, see above and below: the collation is the same as in the first edition.

The whole pamphlet is conceived in a humorous vein.

The first chapter contains parodies on the Definitions, Postulates, Axioms, &c., of Euclid: some of which have become famous, such as 'Let it be granted that a controversy may be raised about any question, and at any distance from that question', and the 'touching allusion to Polar Co-ordinates which is still heard during the races of our own time, $\rho 5$, $\rho 6$, $\cos \phi$, they're gaining !' Chapter II is the Dynamics of a Particle referring to the contest between Gathorne-Hardy (who won) and Gladstone (now a Liberal), to represent the University of Oxford in Parliament, 13–18 July 1865. Chapter III is a reprint of the Evaluation of π, see No. **35** above. 'A.A.' refers to the short-lived degree of Associate of Arts; R.A. and S.A. to the Royal Academy and the Society of Antiquaries.

—— 2nd Edition (1865), precisely as the 1st Edition, adding on the title 'SECOND EDITION'.   [36ᵇ

—— 3rd Edition (1865), precisely as the 1st Edition, adding on the title 'THIRD EDITION'.   [36c

Issued in green wrappers, on the first page of which the title is reproduced, with the words | HARDY V. GLADSTONE | [a line] | IN RE JOWETT. | [a line] above the title. Both the wrappers and the text have a double line round the title.

The print is identical in all three editions, except that in the 2nd and 3rd the words 'on the same side of it' are rightly inserted on p. iii between angles and together.

For the reprint of Chapters I–II and the Evaluation separately as two parts of The Notes of an Oxford Chiel see No. 80.

(1st ed.) Williams, i. 6 (p. 6); Parrish Catalogue, p. 66; Collingwood, p. 432: Christ Church, Oxford, &c.: (2nd ed.) Williams, i. 6 (p. 6): Bodleian: (3rd ed.) Williams, i. 6, p. 6; Parrish Catalogue, p. 67: Bodleian, &c.

There is no reference in the Diary to the actual writing of this squib, but on 27 May Dodgson notes: 'Last night I invented a diagram (and proof) for the second edition of "π", and sent it to Vincent's to be cut on wood'; and on 8 June: 'Received from Vincent's the first copy of Dynamics of a Parti-cle.'

It was reprinted in Notes by an Oxford Chiel, L.C.P.B., &c. See Nonesuch, pp. 1129–39 (1016–26).

42. Alice's Adventures in Wonderland (1865)   [30

ALICE'S | ADVENTURES IN WONDERLAND. || BY | LEWIS CARROLL. || WITH FORTY-TWO ILLUSTRATIONS | BY | JOHN TENNIEL. ||| London | MACMILLAN AND CO. | 1865. | [The right of translation is reserved.] [sic]

8vo: [xii]+192, signn. [a⁴], b², B–N⁸; size $7\frac{1}{2} \times 5$ in. CONTENTS: p. [i] Half-title, viz. ALICE'S [heavy type] | ADVENTURES IN WONDERLAND. |: [ii] blank: [iii] blank recto of frontispiece: [iv] frontispiece, the trial scene [no legend]: [v] title-page, as above: [vi] blank: [vii–ix] prefatory poem of seven six-line stanzas, beginning 'All in the golden afternoon', preceded by two thin lines or rules: [x] blank: [xi] CONTENTS. [of the 12 chapters]: [xii] blank. [1]–192 the text, with two fine lines over the text of p. 190.

[Note: The British Museum copy, here described, has a tissue guard tipped in over frontispiece—but this may have been added later.]

Issued in red cloth with gold lettering on the spine under three gold lines | ALICE'S | ADVENTURES | IN | WONDERLAND | [an ornament]: and at the bottom over three gold lines | MACMILLAN & CO. | The front cover has three gold lines around the border and three circular lines in the centre enclosing a picture of Alice holding the pig: the back cover is the same except that the subject of the picture is the Cheshire Cat: all edges are plain though (according to S.H.W.) they are sometimes found gilt: but Dodgson wrote to Macmillan on

24 May 1865, after seeing a specimen (blank) volume 'I don't quite like the look of gilt edges at one end. As I want it to be a *table*-book, I fancy it would look better with the edges merely cut smoothe, and no gilding.' S.H.W. adds: 'A copy of this book has been reported in white vellum, though I have been unable to trace it.' Dodgson adds in the letter quoted above: 'My present idea is, to send you 50 copies to be bound first, for me to give away to friends, and the rest of the 2000 you can bind at your leisure and publish at whatever time of the year you think best . . . *One* of the 50 I should like bound in white vellum: the rest in red like the specimen.' However, he wrote on 28 Nov. 1865: 'I have got back the copy, bound in vellum, of the 1st impression of *Alice*. Can the vellum back be transferred to a new copy?'

On the other hand, the catalogue for the sale of Dodgson's library in May 1898 describes both its copies of the 1865 edition as 'vellum'.

The first issue of the first edition of *Alice's Adventures in Wonderland*, of which 2,000 copies were printed at the Clarendon Press in Oxford, are bound by Burn, of 37–38 Kirby Street, London, E.C.

It has been questioned whether the First Edition was ever published, in the strict sense of being on sale to the public and sent to the copyright libraries [the British Museum copy is a late acquisition]: the letter quoted above suggests that only Dodgson's 50 presentation copies left the publisher's offices.

Dodgson notes in his *Diary*: 'First copies sent to Macmillan, June 27 . . . Ordered copy to be sent from London so as to be received by Alice on July 4 . . . Called at Macmillan's to speak about the book' on 7 July; 'Went to Macmillan's, and wrote in twenty or more copies of *Alice* to go as presents to various friends.' It is not stated whether he had received all the original 50 copies, or whether (as seems probable) these were some of them.

On 19 July 1865 he 'heard from Tenniel, who is dissatisfied with the printing of the pictures'. On 20 July: 'Called on Macmillan, and showed him Tenniel's letter about the fairy-tale—he is entirely dissatisfied with the printing of the pictures, and I suppose we shall have to do it all again.'

On 2 Aug. Dodgson finally decided on the reprint of *Alice* . . . [see Facsimile of *Diary* here reproduced—Plate VII].

Dodgson apparently wrote letters to those to whom he had given copies, of which a specimen survives beginning: 'Dear Sir, I write to beg that if you have received the copy I sent you of *Alice's Adventures in Wonderland* you will suspend your judgement on it till I can send you a better copy. We are printing it again as the pictures are so badly done. . . .' See No. (43) [31].

Assuming that only a strict 2,000 copies were printed at the Clarendon Press, Dodgson seems to have regained all but 10 copies, having sent out 46 and retained two himself. The 34 (out of the 36 thus in his possession) he sent to hospitals, where all but one copy perished—assuming that the 15 copies recorded in 1932 as known to be in existence are all that now remain. (See *Catalogue of the Columbia University Exhibition*, 1932, p. 4, for the disposition of the copies at that date.)

A note by Falconer Madan is here of interest: 'The following additional facts about the printing of the First Edition of *Alice* (at a time when Messrs. Macmillan & Co., of London and New York, were Publishers to the University of Oxford), will be of interest, and are allowed to be printed by the courtesy of the Clarendon Press.

'As early as May 13, 1864, Dodgson had a specimen of the work printed, the entry in the Press accounts running, on that day, "Fairy Tale (Dodgson). Specimen 2^s 0^d". The 2,000 copies were completely printed off by the end of June 1865. Of these 48 were given away before they were called in, of which about 15 can still be traced. 1,952 copies of the sheets were sold to Messrs. Appleton of New York, and apparently 1,000 "Titles to Alice (American edition)" were printed. The original edition cost £135 ($12\frac{3}{4}$ sheets at £5 15s. 6d., 52 reams of paper at 20s., rolling press work £5 4s. 0d., carriage 4s. 6d.). The Press lost about £20 on the edition, see Plate XII. As a contrast, a copy was sold in the Kern sale at New York, in January 1929 for £2,000. In the Dodgson sale May 10, 1898, there were two copies, lots 680 and 681.   F. M.'

It may be added that Tenniel must have been hypersensitive about his drawings: the only fault in the British Museum copy appears to be that some (e.g. those on pp. 8, 9, 15, 45, 110, 177, and 188) are more lightly printed than the rest. But he wrote to Dalziel the engraver later in 1865: 'Mr. Dodgson's book came out months ago: but I protested so strongly against the disgraceful printing, that he *cancelled the edition*. Clay is now doing it for Xmas.'

For a comparison of the illustrations, &c., see *Carroll's Alice* by Harry Morgan Ayres, 1936 (No. XVII), and W. H. Bond, 'The Publication of *Alice's Adventures in Wonderland*' in *Harvard Library Bulletin*, x. 306–24 (1956).   R. L. G.

Some notes on the issues of editions during Dodgson's lifetime may here be added.

The authoritative Bibliographical Catalogue of Macmillan & Co.'s publications from 1843 to 1889 (London, 1891) informs us that the first edition was published in 1865, the second in 1866, the third in 1867, the fourth in Feb. 1868, and the fifth from electrotype plates in Oct. 1868. The reprints were in 1869, and at intervals, once or twice a year up to 1889, the total number at that date being twenty-six in all. The price varied from 6s. to 7s. 6d.

[From time to time Dodgson discovered various small misprints and wrote to Macmillan about them. Minor corrections were made in 1871, the most important being on p. 116, line 6 from end, where the 1870 impression (twenty-fifth thousand) still reads 'the pattern on their | back was the same as the rest of their pack': Dodgson wrote on 1 Feb. 1871: 'for "back" read "backs" and for "their" read "the".'

The seventy-ninth thousand, issued for Christmas 1886, contains an important alteration which Dodgson describes in a special Preface that runs: 'As Alice is about to appear on the stage, and as the lines beginning " 'Tis the voice of the Lobster" were found to be too fragmentary for dramatic purposes, four lines have been added to the first stanza, and six to the second, while the Oyster has been developed into a Panther.'

Ignorance of this variant has led to certain modern editions being reprinted from pre-1886 copies, with the shorter version of the poem—e.g. that in the Puffin Story Books (1946).   R. L. G.]

A People's Edition was first issued in 1887, from electrotypes, and reprinted in 1888, 1889, &c., at 2s. 6d. In 1887 Alice and the Looking-Glass were issued together (in one volume) both in 'The People's Edition' at 4s. 6d.

The average number of copies in an edition can be estimated from the fact that the book was in its eighty-third thousand in 1881, showing an average of about 3,500. About 110,000 copies must have been sold in the author's lifetime.

Copies of Alice which did not come up to Dodgson's standard of excellence in printing and were called in or not published, and some copies of ordinary editions, were from time to time 'presented by the Author for the Use of Sick Children'. This note, for instance, with the date 'July 1890' is found in a copy of the fifty-fifth thousand (1877), where it is rubber-stamped on the half-title, and (without the date) blocked in blind on the front cover and on the title-page, which is a cancel leaf. See references to this method of distribution under No. 70*.

The eighty-sixth thousand of the 6s. edition, published in 1897, contains a special preface dated Christmas, 1897, and perhaps only to be found in this issue. It supplies a suggested answer to the Mad Hatter's riddle on p. 97; mentions that the whole book has been reset in new type, with new electrotypes of the illustrations from the original woodcuts (which had never been printed from); and reducing the price of the *Nursery Alice* from 4*s.* to 1*s.*, that being all that the public would give for a 'picture-book'!

This eighty-sixth thousand published in 1897 represents Dodgson's finally revised edition of the book: the small revisions made throughout it have been listed with most meticulous care by Mr. Stanley Godman in 'Lewis Carroll's Final Corrections to "Alice"' published in the *Times Literary Supplement*, 2 May 1958.

43. Circular about returning copies of 'Alice' (1865) [31

Following the suppression of the preceding item, a circular is said to have been issued asking purchasers to return their copies, stating that others would be sent in lieu, with better reproductions of the woodcuts.

This circular to my knowledge has never been described, nor have I heard of it ever having been seen. The only authoritative reference to it that I have been able to find is in Mr. Collingwood's *Life and Letters of Lewis Carroll* (p. 104), where a very definite statement is made concerning the circular. The nearest approach to this circular is a letter of 3 Aug. 1865, probably addressed to Tom Taylor making the same request in writing.

So S. H. W. . . . But Collingwood's statement is by no means definite. He says (loc. cit.) 'All purchasers were accordingly asked to return their copies, and to send their names and addresses; a new edition was prepared and distributed to those who had sent back their old copies, which the author gave away to various homes and hospitals.' Moreover Collingwood does not mention any such Circular in the 'Bibliography' attached to his book (pp. 431-43) which lists every item that he mentions in the text—and several others besides. Moreover, as noted above, there were probably no 'purchasers'.

44. Alice's Adventures in Wonderland (1866) [32
(Second [American] issue of the First Edition)

ALICE'S | ADVENTURES IN WONDERLAND. || BY | LEWIS CARROLL. || *WITH FORTY-TWO ILLUSTRATIONS* | BY | JOHN TENNIEL. ||| [*imprint and date as below.*]

New York D. Appleton and Co., 445 Broadway: 1866: 8°: pp. [12]+192, signn. [a^4], b^2, B–N^8, sign. [a 1–2] being two cancel leaves: size $7\frac{1}{2} \times 5$ in. CONTENTS, precisely as the first issue, being a reissue of the sheets, except that the two first leaves are reprints, dividing the half-title thus, | Alice's | Adventures in Wonderland |, omitting the Macmillan mark on p. [2], varying the imprint and omitting the note about translation. Issued in red cloth. Gold lettering on the back under three gold lines | Alice's | Adventures | in Wonderland | [*an ornament*]. At the bottom is | Appleton | over three gold lines. The front and back covers are decorated as the first issue. Rare in England.

Williams, i. 9 (p. 9: with facsimile at p. 13); *Parrish Catalogue*, p. 3: Harvard, Library of Congress, Huntington, S. H. Williams; *Carroll's Alice* (H. M. Ayres) 1936, &c.

This issue consisted of 1,000 copies, bound in England, with the new tipped-in title-page printed at the Clarendon Press, Oxford. The Ledger notes that Dodgson was charged 13*s*. 6*d*. on 26 May 1866, for '1000 Titles to Alice, American Edition'.

Dodgson authorized the sale to America (after consulting Tenniel) on 10 Apr. 1865 (see *Diaries*).

45. *Alice's Adventures in Wonderland* (1866)
(Third [American] issue of the First Edition)

This issue (description as of previous item) consisted of the remaining 952 copies which were apparently shipped in sheets to New York and bound up there with a new title-page printed in America. This imitates the Clarendon Press title-page; but the variants have been examined and described for Flora V. Livingston's *The Harcourt Amory Collection of Lewis Carroll in the Harvard College Library* (1932) by Melvin Loos, supervisor of printing at the Columbia University Press, and his report may be found on p. 96 of Harry Morgan Ayres's *Carroll's Alice* (1936). The differences, which are of letter-placing and spacing, are minute—but convincing.

46. *Alice's Adventures in Wonderland* (1866)   [33
(Second Edition)

ALICE'S ADVENTURES | IN WONDERLAND. || BY | LEWIS CARROLL. || *WITH FORTY-TWO ILLUSTRATIONS* | *BY JOHN TENNIEL.* ||| [*imprint and date as below, then* '[*The Right of Translation and Reproduction is Reserved*]'.]

London: Macmillan and Co.: 1866: (fours) 8°: pp. [12]+192, signn. [*a⁴*], *b²*, B–Z, AA, BB⁴, size 7½ × 5 in. CONTENTS: p. [1] half-title, | Alice's Adventures | in Wonderland. | : [2] Macmillan's mark: [4] frontispiece (the Trial scene): [5] title, as above: [6] Richard Clay's trade-mark: [7–9] the prefatory poem, preceded by a thin double line: [11] contents of the 12 chapters: 1–192, the text, with thin double line heading p. 190: 192, 'R. Clay, Son, and Taylor, printers, Bread Street Hill.', London. Dark green end-papers. Issued in red cloth. Gold lettering on the back under three gold lines, | Alice's Adventures | in | Wonderland. | [*an ornament*] at the bottom is | Macmillan & Co. | over three gold lines. The front cover has three gold lines around the

ALICE'S

ADVENTURES IN WONDERLAND.

BY

LEWIS CARROLL.

WITH FORTY-TWO ILLUSTRATIONS

BY

JOHN TENNIEL.

London

MACMILLAN AND CO.

1865.

[*The right of translation is reserved.*]

11. Title-page of *Alice's Adventures* (London, 1865)

ALICE'S

ADVENTURES IN WONDERLAND.

BY

LEWIS CARROLL.

WITH FORTY-TWO ILLUSTRATIONS

BY

JOHN TENNIEL.

NEW YORK

D. APPLETON AND CO., 445, BROADWAY.

1866.

III. Title-page of *Alice's Adventures* (New York, 1866)

ALICE'S ADVENTURES

IN WONDERLAND.

BY

LEWIS CARROLL.

WITH FORTY-TWO ILLUSTRATIONS

BY JOHN TENNIEL.

London:

MACMILLAN AND CO.

1866.

IV. Title-page of *Alice's Adventures* (London, 1866)

border and in the centre three circular lines containing a picture of Alice hold-ing the pig. The back cover is the same except that the picture within the three circular lines is that of the Cheshire Cat.

In the *Parrish Catalogue*, Plate II (p. 5) is an interesting facsimile of the back end-paper of the author's own copy of *Alice* (London, 1866), bearing thirty-nine corrections, chiefly slight, but some such as 'p. 161 the head-line should be simply "Quadrille"; p. 134, line 15, *for* "otherwise that" *read* "otherwise than"; p. 86, line 2, *read* "the Duchess said"; p. 37, *for* "wasting our breath" *read* "tedious and dry".' The corrections are in the order in which Dodgson de-tected them, and were not all adopted in the end. The whole book is obviously well and carefully printed. See Plate VII.

The British Museum copy was received on 14 Nov. 1865. See also Part II, section A.

Williams, i. 10 (p. 9, with a facsimile of the title-page on p. 14); *Parrish Cata-logue*, p. 3; British Museum, Bodleian, Christ Church (Oxford), Harvard, Huntington, Library of Congress, &c.

There is some doubt as to when copies of this edition were first sent to Dodgson, and when it was actually published. (The Colum-bia Exhibition Catalogue, 1932, states that there is a copy extant dated '14 Sept. '65'.) The following extracts answer both questions. Dodgson wrote to Macmillan on 30 Aug. 1865 asking for copies to be bound and sent to him 'as soon as it is safe to do so'; he is again asking for copies on 2 Nov., as he sees it is advertised—and he later acknowledged 24 copies received on 11 Nov. But he states in his *Diary*: 'Received first proof sheet from Clay, Aug. 11, 1865', and 'Received first copy of new impression [sic], Nov. 9, 1865'. On 12 Nov. he is asking Macmillan: 'When will the book be really out?'

The earliest review which I can trace is in *The Reader* on 18 Nov. 1865.   R. L. G.

47. *Fly-leaf Advertisement of 'Alice'* (1866)

Dodgson notes in his *Diary* for 29 May 1866: 'Received from Mac-millan two hundred of the fly-leaf advertisements of *Alice*, which he has printed by my suggestion.' No copy seems to have survived, and it is uncertain if this should rank as a Lewis Carroll item.

48. *Alice's Adventures in Wonderland* (1866–7)
(American Pirate Edition)

Dodgson wrote to Macmillan on 5 Jan. 1867: 'In the course of these two days I have received two papers from New York. One, *The*

Nation, containing a long and very complimentary review of *Alice*: the other, *Merryman's Monthly* for December, in which they have actually re-printed half the book, and copied about a dozen of the pictures! ending with "Conclusion next month". However, it is so badly printed, both text and pictures, that I don't think it can supersede the purchase of a single copy of the book.'

The only reference to this in the *Diaries* is on 4 Apr. 1867 when he simply notes 'lent to Mrs. Liddell *Merryman's Monthly*, which reprinted *Alice*'.

The first published reference to this edition of *Alice* seems to be that on p. 140 of Percy Muir's *English Children's Books* (1954) which, using the Macmillan letters as its authority, gives the dates but does not name the periodical. The first full reference, naming *Merryman's Monthly* and giving the dates, is in my Bodley Head Monograph *Lewis Carroll* (1960), p. 42.

No copy of *Merryman's Monthly* for Dec. 1866 and Jan. 1867 has so far been located for description.

It is just possible that the single page in quarto, printed in double columns with one illustration which S. H. Williams reproduced in his *Some Rare Carrolliana* (1924), p. 21 as 'a proof of a page . . . of a projected quarto edition' is in fact a page from *Merryman's Monthly*—but I have been unable to trace the original. It is surely unthinkable that Dodgson ever contemplated a double-column quarto edition—and there is no reference to it in the *Diaries* or the Macmillan letters.   R. L. G.

1866

49. *Symbols and Abbreviations for Euclid* (1866)

Dodgson wrote in his *Diary* for 25 Jan. 1866: 'My mathematical publication this term is a card of symbols and abbreviations for Euclid.'

No copy of this is known, but a similar item is mentioned by Collingwood as published in 1872 (see No. *89*). It is possible that Collingwood was mistaken over his date.

50. *Castle Croquet* (1866)   (Second Edition)   [37ᵃ

CASTLE-CROQUET. | FOR FOUR PLAYERS. | [*a thin line*] | [*a plan of the game*] | [*a thin line*] | Rules. | I. | *Ten lines of Rule I, the last*

three of which are in brackets, preceded by 'N.B.' within the brackets. |
II. | [*four lines of Rule II.*]

[No imprint]: (1866): (two) 8°: pp. 4: size $7\frac{1}{16} \times 4\frac{1}{2}$ in. CONTENTS: p. 1, tit'e:
1-3, plan and six rules of the game: 3-4, 'Advice to the player': 4, 'Aug. 1866.',
and at foot, centred, 'Vincent, printer', i.e. Joseph Vincent, of Oxford. On
white laid paper. Anonymous.

Mr. Collingwood describes this as a reprint with additions, of the
first editions (see No. *35*), but so much has been added and altered,
that I think it should be described as a second edition.

The above item is an anonymous second edition of No. *35* (1863)
but recast, and still too complicated for general use. The long piece
of advice is tedious, but very much needed. A 'figure' or plan of
the castle and arches precedes the six rules. Strictly speaking, we
find the present piece to be an Oxford reprint, repaged and reset, of pp. 221-4 of *Aunt Judy's Christmas Volume* (= vol. iii of *Aunt
Judy's Magazine*, 1867), which is part of No. 16, Aug. 1867, where
this edition first appeared as 'by Lewis Carroll'. Rare.

There appears to have been another form of this item printed on
a cream wove paper 8vo (size $7\frac{9}{16} \times 5\frac{3}{16}$ in.), as I have seen in the
Christ Church Library a four-paged leaflet containing a portion of
the text taken verbatim from pp. 2 and 3 of the above and apparently forming the middle pages of an eight-paged pamphlet. There
is, however, something curious about these four pages, because if
they are part of an eight-paged pamphlet, I do not see how it is
paginated, seeing that the first and last pages are blank, and I can
think of no arrangement by which the pages could follow each
other in proper order. Again, I do not think that it can be meant
to be a vital extract from the whole, because then surely the author
would have commenced at the beginning of a paragraph, and ended
at the end of one. However, I give the collation of the four pages
for what it is worth: p. [1] blank, p. 2 has that portion of the text
of the above item which begins 'being a sentinel' and ends 'consist
in keeping', p. 3 has that portion which begins 'your sentinel' and
ends 'one or more', p. [4] blank. Pp. 2 and 3 are headed 'Castle
Croquet'. What seems most likely is that the four pages just described are proofs of pp. 2 and 3 of the second edition collated above,
without being backed up with the matter on pp. 1 and 4. This would
account for the difference in the paper, and for the fact that the two
outer pages are blank. See below. (S. H. W.)

These are signs that Dodgson intended yet another (third) edition
of this game in 1875, for Mr. Parrish and Mr. Madan own the proof
of two pages of a reprint of this second edition, containing from

'being a sentinel' in Rule VI to 'through one or more' in the advice. But the plan fell through. Mr. Madan's copy is dated in manuscript 13 Mar. 1875. (*Parrish Catalogue*, p. 103.) [37ᵇ

It is odd that the piece called 'Castle Croquet for four players', which is printed in Collingwood's *Lewis Carroll Picture Book* (1899), is neither the 1863 edition which it professes to be, nor the 1866 edition. The title cuts it off from the former, the contents from the latter, and the plan from both. The first rule begins: 'This game requires 8 balls, 8 arches, and 4 flags,' and the castles are arranged

$$\begin{matrix} 1 & & 3 \\ 4 & 3, \text{ not as in the second edition } 2 & 4. \end{matrix}$$ There is also a note how the

$$\begin{matrix} 2 & & 1 \end{matrix}$$

game can be adapted for five players, and the number of rules is only five, while the Advice is omitted. No copy of this (fourth?) edition can at present be traced. [No. **37ᶜ**.] F. M.

See No. *108* below.

51. Elections to Hebdomadal Council (1866) [38

THE ELECTIONS TO THE HEBDO- | MADAL COUNCIL. | [*an ornamental line*] | A LETTER | TO THE | REV. C. W. SAND- FORD, M.A., | HAS BEEN ADDRESSED (ON THIS SUBJECT) | BY | GOLDWIN SMITH, | And may possibly reach a | SECOND EDITION. |

Oxford: Joseph Vincent: 1866: (six) 8°: pp. 11+[1]. CONTENTS: p. 1, title, as above: 3–11 the poem, with notes: on p. 11 is the date Nov. 5, 1866.

On 20 Oct. 1866, in an election to nine places on the Hebdomadal Council the Conservatives won, and this stirred Goldwin Smith to write a letter entitled 'The Elections to the Hebdomadal Council. A letter to the Rev. C. W. Sandford, M.A., Senior Censor of Christ Church, by Goldwin Smith', dated 1 Nov. 1866, and printed at Oxford. Dodgson here anonymously makes fun of the letter, of which he professes to be issuing a second edition, satirizing and parodying it in harmonious verse. When Goldwin Smith's age of intellect shall reign, Dodgson prophesies 'From Fagin's lecture-room a class should come | Versed in all arts of finger and of thumb, | To illustrate in practice (though by stealth) | The transitory character of wealth'. These lines are not in the reprints after 1869.

The less obvious points not mentioned in the printed notes are: p. 3, The first lines are a parody of a recent prize-poem; 'Winter' on the same page was the President of St. John's, one of the new members of Council. 'Wait' on p. 6 was the Rev. S. Wayte, of

Trinity. Pussy on p. 7 is of course Pusey (and a recent debate on the position of Bedells is referred to). On p. 11 Michell, Liddon, Wall, and Mansel are indicated.

The piece was reprinted in 1869 (*Phantasmagoria*, No. 54), and, with alterations, in 1874, both separately and (with a valuable introduction) as part of *Facts, Figures, and Fancies* (the third piece in *Notes of an Oxford Chiel* (No. 80 below). The whole of the *Notes* is reprinted in Collingwood's *Lewis Carroll Picture Book* (1899). Rare.

Williams, i. 27 (p. 37); *Parrish Catalogue*, p. 108: Bodleian, Christ Church, Oxford.

Dodgson began writing this on 3 Nov. 1866, and received his first copies on 8 Nov.—having cut out some lines in proof on the advice of two fellow students, Bayne and Faussett.

The verse portion may be found in *Nonesuch*, pp. 909–16 (815–22) preceded by the short prose heading as in *Phantasmagoria*.

52. *Condensation of Determinants* (1866)   [39

CONDENSATION OF DETERMINANTS, | BEING A | NEW AND BRIEF METHOD | FOR COMPUTING THEIR ARITHMETICAL VALUES. || BY THE | REV. C. L. DODGSON, M.A., | STUDENT OF CHRIST CHURCH, OXFORD. |

[London]: (1866): (four) 8°: pp. [1]+'150' to '155': size $8\frac{9}{16} \times 5\frac{9}{16}$ in. CONTENTS: p. [1], title: '150' to '155', the new Method. On p. 150 is 'From the Proceedings of the Royal Society, No. 84, 1866 [London: Taylor and Francis]' in brackets, above the title. A stitched pamphlet, issued in brown paper wrappers.

Determinants belong to higher mathematics, and are the sums of the products (of a particular kind) of a square block of quantities. Their condensation, or reduction to simpler forms, facilitates the solution of simultaneous linear equations, and other similar problems. See No. 57.

Williams, ii. 13 (p. 97); *Parrish Catalogue*, p. 67; *Collingwood*, p.432: Bodleian, Harvard, Huntington, &c.

According to his *Diary*, Dodgson was 'at work on an elementary pamphlet on Determinants' on 28 Oct. 1865, and 'Finished writing out my paper on *Condensation of Determinants*' on 12 May 1866.

53. *Enigma* (1866)   [40

A single leaf 8vo (size $8\frac{1}{4} \times 5\frac{1}{8}$ in.) on the front page of which is: | [*Printed for private circulation*] | ENIGMA. |

[*Text of fifteen lines*, beginning 'I have' and ending 'my whole'.] In the bottom left-hand corner is | Nov. 1866. | The verso is blank. White wove paper.

38 THE LEWIS CARROLL HANDBOOK

This leaflet was issued separately from the other single leaflet, *Explication of the Enigma* which follows (No. *54*), and which see.

54. *Explication of the Enigma* (1866) [41

A single leaflet: 8vo: (size $8\frac{1}{4} \times 5\frac{1}{8}$) on the front page of which is | EXPLICATION OF THE ENIGMA. | [*Twenty-seven lines of prose text*, beginning 'The whole—is Man' and ending '(Ten Dons)'.] In the bottom left-hand corner is | Nov. 1866 |. The verso is blank.

This leaflet was issued separately from the *Enigma* (see No. *53*). The *Enigma* is the well-known riddle in prose, by Bishop Samuel Wilberforce, beginning: 'I have a large box with two lids.' A poetical version is also known beginning: 'Rare old riddle am I truly, | Oldest of the ancient name', in forty lines. The two items are entirely anonymous, and may be mere reprints by Mr. Dodgson, who was rather fond of reprinting or cyclostyling, for circulation among his friends, problems, puzzles, or extracts which interested him; and it seems probable that these are examples.

The only copies at present known of the two together are in a chronological series of University papers in the Bodleian Library, where they occur between two of Dodgson's pamphlets of 1866 (Nos. *41*, *51* (*Dynamics* and *Elections to Council*, above)) bound in all probability in the next year. The answer to the riddle is Man, who is described as having a box (chest), a couple of good fish (soles of the feet), many weathercocks (veins), the steps of a Hotel (insteps), some Spanish Grandees (ten dons), and so on. There is no proof whatever of Dodgson's authorship of this form of the Explication, but the occurrence of it on a separate leaf favours the suggestion. A copy of the Explication has been seen as a four-page piece, pp. [2–4] being blank, so probably also the *Enigma* in the Bodleian has lost a second leaf. Rare.

(Enigma+Explication) *Williams*, i. 11, 12 (p. 21): Bodleian.

55. *The Pall Mall Gazette* (1866–77)

Dodgson contributed eight letters to the *Pall Mall Gazette*, of which only the sixth and seventh are mentioned by Williams and Madan. They appeared as follows:

1. *The Science of Betting* (signed 'Charles L. Dodgson'): 19 Nov. 1866. Dodgson notes in his *Diary* that he wrote it on 15 Nov., that it was reprinted in *The Times* of 20 Nov., and that he wrote to both papers correcting an arithmetical mistake.

Never reprinted, but quoted by the present writer in 'Lewis Carroll's Fugitive Pieces', *Times Literary Supplement*, 31 July 1953, and on pp. 247–8 of *The Diaries of Lewis Carroll* (1953).

V. LEWIS CARROLL AT THE AGE OF 26
From a photograph by H. P. Robinson, Tunbridge Wells

VI. ALICE LIDDELL AT ABOUT THE AGE OF SIX
From a photograph by Lewis Carroll

2. *The Organisation of Charity* (signed 'Charles L. Dodgson'): 24 Jan. 1867. Never reprinted, but quoted in *The Diaries* (1953), p. 250.

3. *Original Research* (signed 'Rusticus Expectans'): 29 Oct. 1874. This letter 'satirising Dr. Appleton's scheme for the endowment of original research', has never been reprinted, but is quoted in *The Diaries*, pp. 332–3.

4, 5. *Architecture in Oxford* (signed 'Charles L. Dodgson') 3 Nov., 5 Nov. 1874. Dodgson wrote the first of these on 29 Oct. 'with the approval of Barclay Thompson, Shute, Stewart, and (partly) Sampson, on the proposal, which seems imminent, to erect cloisters, and so utilise the grotesque foundations we are now enshrining in stone.' It has never been reprinted, but I quote most of it in *The Diaries*, pp. 333–4.

On 4 Nov. Dodgson noted: 'Received a letter of remonstrance from Bayne: he thinks me disloyal in protesting against the decision of a majority. This I had not done: my "protest" being only against cloisters, which are not yet decided on. I wrote again to the *Pall Mall* explaining this.' None of this second letter has been reprinted.

6. *Vivisection as a Sign of the Times* (signed 'Lewis Carroll'): 12 Feb. 1875. This letter [No. 86 in Williams and Madan] was reprinted in full by Collingwood in the *Life* (1898), pp. 167–71.

7. *Natural Science at Oxford* (signed 'Charles L. Dodgson') 19 May 1877. This letter [No. 99 in W. and M.] was reprinted in full by Collingwood, *Life*, pp. 187–91.

8. *Clerical Fellowships* (signed 'Charles L. Dodgson'): 4 June 1877. Never reprinted, but a few sentences quoted in *The Diaries*, p. 363.

1867

56. *Deserted Parks* (1867)   [43

THE DESERTED PARKS. | 'Solitudinem faciunt: Parcum appellant.'

[Oxford]: 1867: (two) 4°: pp. 4. CONTENTS: p. 1, title as above, and twenty-six lines of text: 1–4, the poem: at the end is 'May. 1867.'

In April 1867 notice was given of a decree to allow the University Parks at Oxford to be used in part for College cricket grounds. On 6 June the decree was rejected, in accordance with the views of this anonymous piece by Dodgson. The author, in 104 lines, contrasts the present enjoyment of the Park by University and City alike, especially the children of the latter, with the proposed tyranny of Sport and Abolition of both young and old, together with the rural amenities. The verses begin 'Museum! loveliest building of the plain', and a long passage is quoted by Collingwood. The poem is a parody on Goldsmith's *Deserted Village*. The 'calm Professor' (half way through) is Jowett, 'passing rich on forty pounds a year' (his exact stipend as Professor of Greek) until persuaded to 'evaluate his pie', see No. *40* above. The Latin motto is (with 'Pacem', not 'Parcum') from the *Agricola* of Tacitus. When the subject came up again in 1879, Dodgson sent round to the Common Rooms copies of this poem, as Collingwood tells us, drawing his information no doubt from Dodgson's diary. The poem is reprinted with the title 'The Proposal to convert the Parks into Cricket-grounds', in *Facts, Figures, and Fancies*, part of *Notes by an Oxford Chiel* (No. **80** below, 1874).

Williams, i, p. 27 (part), p. 38; *Parrish Catalogue*, p. 69; *Collingwood*, pp. 161, 207: Christ Church, Oxford.

Written on 22 May 1867. Only 100 copies were printed, half of which Dodgson distributed among Oxford Common Rooms. Reprinted in *Collected Verse* (1932), pp. 250–3; and *Nonesuch*, pp. 917–23 (823–5)—misprinted 'Park' in Contents and Chronological Table.

Journal of 1867

For Dodgson's Journal of his tour abroad with Canon Liddon, written in this year, and printed for private circulation by Mr. M. L. Parrish of Philadelphia in 1928, see No. *299*.

57. *Elementary Treatise on Determinants* (1867)   [44

AN | ELEMENTARY TREATISE | ON | DETERMINANTS | WITH THEIR APPLICATION TO | *SIMULTANEOUS LINEAR EQUATIONS* | *AND ALGEBRAICAL GEOMETRY.* || BY | CHARLES L. DODGSON, M.A. | STUDENT AND MATHEMATICAL LECTURER OF CHRIST CHURCH, OXFORD. ||||

London: Macmillan and Co.: 1867: 4°: pp. viii+143+[1]. CONTENTS: p. 1, title as above: ii, Macmillan's device, and 'Oxford: T. Combe, M.A., E. B. Gardner, E. P. Hall, and H. Latham, M.A. printers to the University': iii–vi, Preface, at the end is 'Ch. Ch. Oxford, Oct 31, 1867.': vi, Corrigenda: vii–viii, contents: 1–143, the treatise.

For Determinants see No. *52*, above: 'The work itself', says Collingwood, 'is largely original, and its arrangement and style are, perhaps, as attractive as the nature of the subject will allow.' Dodgson allows himself new words, *adjugate* as an adjective, *determinantal* (the first example in the *New Oxford Dictionary* is 1879), &c., and a new symbol—all with due apology. Harvard in the Amory Collection possesses another 1867 issue of this piece with errors corrected (No. **44★**).

Williams, ii. 14 (p. 98); *Parrish Catalogue*, p. 68; *Collingwood*, pp. 110, 432: British Museum, Bodleian, Christ Church, Oxford, Harvard, Huntington, &c.

'The *Determinants* have come and look very well indeed in their brown binding', wrote Dodgson to Macmillan on 10 Dec. 1867.

58. *Aunt Judy's Magazine* (1867-82)

To *Aunt Judy's Magazine*, edited by Mrs. Gatty and later by her daughter Mrs. Ewing, Dodgson made the four following contributions:

1. *Castle Croquet: A Game for Four Players*: Aug. 1867, vol. iii, No. xvi, pp. 221-4. See No. *50* above.
2. *Bruno's Revenge*: Dec. 1867, vol. iv, No. xx, pp. 65-78. See No. *60* below.
3. *Puzzles from Wonderland*: Dec. 1870, vol. ix, No. lvi, pp. 101-2. See No. *75* below.
4. *Dreamland*: July 1882, N.S., vol. i, No. ix, p. 547. See No. *149* below.

In addition to these, three songs, already published in book form, were set to music by Alfred Scott Gatty, as follows:

a. 'Will you walk a little faster?' [from *Alice's Adventures*]: Mar. 1871, vol. ix, No. lix, pp. 310-12.
b. 'Pig and Pepper' ['Speak roughly', from *Alice's Adventures*]: Aug. 1871, vol. ix, No. lxiv, pp. 618-20.
c. 'The Walrus and the Carpenter' [from *Through the Looking-Glass*]: Mar. 1872, vol. x, No. lxxi, pp. 310-12.

Two other items are of Lewis Carroll interest:

Solutions to Puzzles from Wonderland by 'Eadgyth': Jan. 1871, vol. ix, No. lvii, pp. 187-8. See No. *75* below.

The Land of Idleness: Aug. 1881, vol. xix, No. clxxxiv, pp. 604-31. On its first appearance this was signed 'Lewis Carroll', but the name was removed in the Annual Volume. It was really by Fräulein Ida Lackowitz; Dodgson merely sent it to the editor.

59. *Punch* (1867-74)

Dodgson contributed one humorous poem, 'Atalanta in Camden Town' (afterwards collected in *Phantasmagoria*, *68*, &c.) which appeared anonymously on 27 July 1867: vol. liii, p. 38. There are a number of variants (particularly in the last two stanzas) from any subsequent reprint.

Dodgson also contributed the anecdote about Lot's Wife quoted by Collingwood (*Life*, pp. 156-7) which appeared with the heading 'Stories for Sunday Evenings' as the legend under a drawing by George du Maurier on 3 Jan. 1874: vol. lxvi, p. 8.

60. *Bruno's Revenge* (1867)   [42

'Bruno's Revenge' is a short tale printed on pp. 65-78 of *Aunt Judy's May-Day Volume for young people. Edited by Mrs. Alfred Gatty* (London, 1868, 8vo). This volume (vol. iv) contains the numbers for Nov. 1867 to Apr. 1868, and the article appeared in No. 20, i.e. Dec.

1867. There is one illustration by F. Gilbert as a frontispiece to the number. The tale is signed at the end 'Lewis Carroll'.

Bruno's Revenge is the germ of *Sylvie and Bruno* (1889), and is a slight and graceful little idyll, in which one may learn how to see fairies, how to help them when seen, and the best way to convert a vengeful little boy named Bruno into a willing helper in good works, to please his sister Sylvie. There is a fairy song with music, beginning 'Rise, Oh rise! The daylight dies: | The owls are hooting, ting, ting, ting!' 'The creation of Bruno was the only act of homage Lewis Carroll ever paid to boy-nature', according to Collingwood, who quotes Mrs. Gatty's appreciation of the contribution to her magazine.

Williams, p. 69; *Parrish Catalogue*, p. 120; *Collingwood*, p. 109: British Museum, Bodleian, &c.

Dodgson began writing the story on 24 June 1867, shortly before his tour in Russia. He sent it to Mrs. Gatty on 22 Oct. By 12 Dec. he had received the number containing it. 'I don't like Gilbert's illustration', he wrote to Harry Furniss on 7 Mar. 1886, 'they both look grown-up, and something like a blacksmith and a ballet-dancer'.

There were three mistakes in the music on p. 75, and an Errata slip is found in many of the bound volumes. This runs:

> Errata in 'Bruno's Revenge' (Page 75)
> 1st line of music 3rd bar, for FFFA read EFGA.
> 2nd   „   „   make same correction.
> 3rd   „   2nd bar, for CBCB read CACB.

Madan notes in his *Supplement* (1935), p. 5: 'The third correction was made in *Sylvie and Bruno* and *The Story of S. & B.*, but the other two appear to have been unnoticed throughout.'

The story differs in many respects from the chapter in *Sylvie and Bruno* into which it was adapted. In its original form it seems only to have been reprinted three times:

1. *Bruno's Revenge*, by Lewis Carroll. Edited by John Drinkwater. **[595]**
   Collins [1924], pp. 48; (twelve) 8°. Bound in limp red cloth.
   Pp. 3–5 Introduction; pp. 7–38 *Bruno's Revenge*; pp. 39–48 consists of seven poems from *Alice's Adventures*.
2. *Alice's Adventures in Wonderland*, with *Bruno's Revenge*. By Lewis **[327]**
   Carroll. With illustrations by Harry Rountree. Nelson [n.d. published 1925]. Pp. viii+160. *Brunos' Revenge* is printed on pp. 135–52. There was a reprint by Nelson, but with Illustrations by Helen Munro, in 1933. The illustrations in both are to *Alice*.
3. *Modern Fairy Stories*. Chosen and Introduced by Roger Lancelyn Green. *Dent.* (Children's Illustrated Classics.) 1955.

'Bruno's Revenge' occupies pages 43-61, and has one illustration (line) by Ernest H. Shepard on p. 52.

1868

61. *Offer of the Clarendon Trustees* (1868)   [45

THE OFFER OF THE CLARENDON TRUSTEES. | [*a line*] | [*the text follows.*]

Oxford: 1888: (one) 4to: pp. 2. CONTENTS: p. 1, title, as above: 1-2, the letter, and at the foot is 'Vincent, printer.'

A series of humorous suggestions, in the form of a letter to the Rev. C. W. Sandford, Senior Censor of Christ Church, signed 'Charles L. Dodgson', 'Ch. Ch. Feb. 6. 1868', beginning 'My dear Sandford, In a desultory conversation'. It parodies a letter with the same title, 25 Jan. 1868, from Professor R. B. Clifton. The subject is the provision of opportunities at the New Museum for mathematical calculations. Examples of the needs are: 'A room for reducing Fractions to their Lowest Terms . . . with a cellar for keeping the Lowest Terms when found, which might also be available to . . . Undergraduates, for the purpose of "keeping Terms" ', 'A narrow strip of ground . . . for . . . testing practically whether Parallel Lines meet or not'. Reprinted (with a motto and with the address 'Dear Senior Censor', and signature 'Mathematicus') in *Facts, Figures, and Fancies*, part of *Notes of an Oxford Chiel* (1874), and in Collingwood's *Life* (1898), pp. 161-3. Rare.

Williams, i. 27 (part), p. 38; *Parrish Catalogue*, p. 70; *Collingwood*, pp. 161-3, 435: Bodleian, Christ Church, Oxford.

Reprinted in *Nonesuch*, pp. 1121-3 (1009-11).

62. *Telegraph-Cipher* (1868)   [46

A small white card (size $4\frac{1}{2} \times 3\frac{1}{16}$ in.), on the front of which is: | THE TELEGRAPH-CIPHER. | [*a small ornamental line*] | DIRECTIONS FOR USE. | followed by four paragraphs of directions, together making twelve lines, and at the bottom right-hand corner is | [T. O. | The verso has two lines of text, and below three short lines of text enclosed in two brackets, then two lines of text, below which is | Key-Alphabet | above one line containing the entire alphabet, followed by a long thin line right across the card, below which is the entire alphabet with an extra a, following z, and underneath the whole is | Message-Alphabet. |

Mr. Collingwood says this cipher was invented by Mr. Dodgson in 1868, but the card is undated and anonymous. The device employed is to divide the two alphabets along a thin line, and slide them in accordance with a key-word agreed upon and carried only in the memory. Rare.

Williams, i. 14 (p. 23); *Parrish Catalogue,* p. 103; *Collingwood,* p. 433: Harvard, S. H. Williams.

Dodgson wrote in his *Diary* for 22 Apr. 1868: 'Sitting up at night I invented a new cipher, which I think of calling *The Telegraph Cipher.*'

63. Alphabet-Cipher (1868) [47

A white card: 8vo (size $7\frac{1}{8} \times 4\frac{15}{16}$ in.). On the front is: | THE | ALPHABET-CIPHER. | [*a small ornamental line*]. Then a square table of letters with a note at the bottom. On the verso is the | *Explanation.* | in twenty-nine lines. The card is undated and anonymous.

The table is a square alphabet, the top line across being a–z, the next b–z, a, the third c–z, a, b; and so on. Two friends agree on a key-word, write it letter for letter over the letters of the message to be sent, and dispatch the letters *suggested* by the two lines and the table. The date of composition is unknown, but may be about the same as the preceding item. Dodgson was undoubtedly the author of both these anonymous ciphers. Rare.

Williams, i. 15 (p. 23); *Parrish Catalogue,* p. 103: Bodleian, Harvard.

Included, from the Parrish copy, in *Nonesuch,* pp. 1283–4 (1156–7), where it is dated 1868 (probably on account of above entry, and entry 79 in *Centenary* (1932), p. 22). It does not seem to be mentioned in the *Diary*—unless the extract quoted under previous item, *62,* suggests that he had recently invented it—and here was a *new* cipher.

64. Fifth Book of Euclid (1868) [49

THE | FIFTH BOOK OF EUCLID | TREATED ALGEBRAICALLY, | SO FAR AS IT RELATES TO | *COMMENSURABLE MAGNITUDES.,* || WITH NOTES. || BY | CHARLES L. DODGSON, M.A. | STUDENT AND MATHEMATICAL LECTURER OF CHRIST CHURCH, OXFORD. ||||

Oxford and London: James Parker and Co.: 1868: 8°: pp. [4]+37+[1]: signn. A⁴ (pp. [1–4], 33–end), B⁸ (pp. 1–8, 25–32), C⁸ (pp. 9–24): size $8\frac{3}{4} \times 5\frac{3}{8}$ in. CONTENTS: p. [1] title: [3] preface: 1–37, the text. Issued in brown paper wrappers, the first page of which reproduces the title-page.

A matter of Ratios, but the theory of Incommensurable Magnitudes is, as far as possible, excluded. Dodgson's object was to produce a clear exposition, with notes and 'hints on proving propositions' (p. 14), of the Euclid (Book V) required for the pass schools at Oxford. The algebraical definitions, axioms, and conventions, compared with Euclid's, are of interest. The edition of 1874 (No. 84) is so different that it will be dealt with independently. Neither has any connexion with works with similar titles issued at Dublin (1842), Oxford in 1858 ('by a college Tutor'), or Oxford in 1862 (by G. S. Ward).

Williams, ii. 15 (p. 98); *Parrish Catalogue*, p. 69; *Collingwood*, pp. 132, 433: British Museum, Bodleian, Harvard, S. H. Williams, &c.

As early as 16 Jan. 1868 Dodgson wrote in his *Diary*: 'I have written almost all of a pamphlet on *Euclid V* by Algebra, with notes', but there is no mention of completion or publication dates.

65. *Algebraical Formulæ* [50

Algebraical Formulæ for Responsions. Oxford: Printed at the University Press . . . 1868: 8°: 4 pages. Sir H. Hartley owns a copy, and also a copy of 'Formulæ in Algebra': 8°: 8 pages [50★].

Collingwood, p. 433.

Dodgson notes (*Diary*, 21 May 1868): 'Took to the University Press the MS. for *Formulæ in Algebra for Responsions*.' It seems probable that [50★] is a proof copy.

66. *Woodstock Election* (1868) [48

'Woodstock Election. To the Editor of the "Oxford University Herald".'

A letter beginning 'Sir—With your well-known impartiality', signed A Liberal of the Liberals', 24 Nov. 1868, on p. 10, column 1, of the *Oxford University Herald* of 28 Nov. 1868.

The contest was between the Hon. G. C. Brodrick (Liberal) and Henry Barnett (Conservative) on Monday, 23 Nov. 1868. Dodgson displays all his humour in the comments on the respectful attention stated by the *Oxford Chronicle* to have been paid to Brodrick, who did not get in, and the uproarious opposition to Barnett, who was successful. The former is described as saying, 'Conservative cravens, where are ye? Brodrick, the son of Brodrick, dares you to the fray. Have ye voices, only to vote with? . . . What is demonstration to a dig in the ribs? Is there any reasoning like rotten eggs?'. The letter appears in one of the Rev. T. Vere Bayne's Scrapbooks of Carrolliana in Christ Church Library, and is no doubt by Dodgson.

Williams, iii. 6 (p. 118): British Museum, Bodleian, &c.

That this is quite certainly by Dodgson is proved by the entry in his *Diary* for 24 Nov. 1868: 'An account of the Woodstock Election has appeared in the *Oxford Chronicle*—written by a Liberal, but so charmingly candid as to the brutal behaviour of the Liberal electors, that I thought it a fair subject for a letter to the *University Herald*.'

The complete letter is reprinted for the first time on pp. 275–6 of my edition of *The Diaries of Lewis Carroll* (1953).

67. *Anagrams* [640

Dodgson was fond of working out anagrams of considerable length. Mrs. Ffooks has a paper of about 1885 covered with them. Examples are:

> William Ewart Gladstone
> A wild man will go at trees.
> Wild agitator! Means well.
> Wilt tear down all images?

> Edward Vaughan Kenealy
> Ah! We dread an ugly knave.

> Florence Nightingale
> Flit on, cheering angel.

Although not published at the time, some at least of these Anagrams were written for publication on 25 Nov. 1868, when Dodgson records that he wrote a letter to the *Standard* on *The Times's* report of Gladstone's defeat, and 'also sent them an anagram which I thought out lying awake the other night [the third quoted above]'. Neither letter nor anagram was published. Dodgson continues that he heard of another on the same name: 'I, wise Mr. G, want to lead all', which he answers 'Disraeli: "I lead, Sir!" '

1869

68. *Phantasmagoria* (1869) [54

PHANTASMAGORIA || *AND OTHER POEMS* ||| BY | LEWIS CAR-
ROLL. ||||

London Macmillan and Co.: 1869: (eights) 12°: pp. viii+202+(2): signn. [A]⁴, B–O⁸: size 6 $\frac{11}{16}$ × 4 $\frac{9}{16}$ in. CONTENTS: p. i, half-title | Phantasmagoria |: ii. Macmillan's circular device in the centre: iii, title as above, and at foot '[*All rights reserved*]': iv, in the centre is 'Oxford: by T. Combe, M.A., E. B. Gardner, E. P. Hall, and H. Latham, M.A., Printers to the University': v, introductory note in brackets, about the origin of the poems: vii–viii, contents of the two parts: 1, in the centre is | Part I. |, 3–202, the text: at the bottom of p. 202 is | The End. | Brown end-papers.

Issued in blue cloth. Gold lettering on the back under four dotted gold lines | Phan- | tas- | ma- | go- | ri- | a |, and at the bottom, over four dotted gold lines is | Macmillan | . The front cover has two gold lines around the border, and a large representation of the Crab nebula in the constellation Taurus in gold, in the centre. The back cover is similar except that the central design is Donati's comet ('two distinguished members of the Celestial Phantasmagoria.'), surrounded with stars of gold. All edges gilt.

This entertaining medley was issued in Jan. 1869 and consists of two parts, the first containing thirteen amusing poems, the second (p. 143) an equal number of serious ones. Dodgson's intention was to have secured illustrations by George du Maurier, but the plan fell through. Later, in 1883, Mr. Frost supplied a very satisfactory series of them.

The title-poem is in seven cantos, and is well adapted to remove all fear of ghosts from nervous people, by representing that it is no pleasure at all to the ghosts to howl on battlements on wet nights, or to clank chains. ('*Scarmoges*' is an old form of 'skirmishes'.) The word Phantasmagoria was invented in 1802, and seems to mean a Gathering of Ghosts.

The poems are as follows, an asterisk showing those which are printed for the first time:

Part I

*Phantasmagoria.

*A Valentine. Written Feb. 1860, to William H. Ranken, who was then a master at Radley. It was copied into *Mischmasch*, which version, the original, differs somewhat from the above.

A Sea Dirge. First published in *College Rhymes*, Nov. 1860. [Set to music by Leonard James Rogers, and issued on a single sheet, n.d. [? Feb. 1869].

Ye Carpette Knyghte. Written before 11 Jan. 1855. Published in the *Train*, Mar. 1856.

Hiawatha's Photographing. Finished 13 Nov. 1857. Published in the *Train*, Dec. 1857.

The Lang Coortin'. Finished 15 Nov. 1862. Published in *College Rhymes*, Nov. 1862.

Melancholetta. Begun 5 Apr. 1857; full version copied into *Mischmasch, c.* 1858–9. Published in *College Rhymes*, Mar. 1862.

The Three Voices. Copied into *Mischmasch,* July 1856. Revised and published in the *Train*, Nov. 1856.

*A Double Acrostic. Written (while listening to the music of the Christ Church Ball) on 25 June 1867.

Size and Tears. Copied into *Mischmasch* as 'Bloggs' Woe', Nov. 1862. Published in *College Rhymes*, June 1863.

Poeta Fit, non Nascitur. Published in *College Rhymes*, June 1862.

Atalanta in Camden Town. Published in *Punch*, 27 July 1867.

The Elections to the Hebdomadal Council. Written 3 Nov. 1866, and printed privately as a pamphlet 8 Nov. See 51.

Part II

The Valley of the Shadow of Death. In *Three Sunsets* Dodgson dates this 'April 1868', but there is no mention in the *Diaries*.

Beatrice. (Probably the child-friend Beatrice Ellison.) Finished 4 Dec. 1862. Published in *College Rhymes*, Nov. [*sic*] 1862.

*Lines. Acrostic of the names 'Lorina, Alice, Edith' [Liddell]. Written in a copy of Catherine Sinclair's *Holiday House* and dated 'Christmas 1861'. [Facsimile in Sotheby's Auction Catalogue for 3 Apr. 1928, Lot 355.]

The Path of Roses. Finished 10 Apr. 1856. Published in the *Train*, May 1856.

The Sailor's Wife. Finished 23 Feb. 1857. Published in the *Train*, Apr. 1857.

Stolen Waters. Finished 9 May 1862. Published in *College Rhymes*, June 1862.

*Stanzas for Music. Dated 1859 in *Three Sunsets*, where it appears as 'The Willow Tree', the original title under which it was copied into *Mischmasch* in or before that year.

Solitude. Dated 16 Mar. 1853 in *Three Sunsets*. Published in the *Train*, Mar. 1856, being the first occasion when the pseudonym 'Lewis Carroll' was used.

Only a Woman's Hair. Dated 17 Feb. 1862 in *Three Sunsets*. Published in *College Rhymes*, Mar. 1862.

Three Sunsets. Dated 'Nov. 1861' in the volume to which it gave its name in 1898. Published in *College Rhymes*, Nov. 1861 with the title 'The Dream of Fame'.

*Christmas Greetings. Printed separately in 1884 (*162*) and included in *Alice's Adventures Underground* (1886) where it is dated 'Christmas 1867' which seems to be the date at which it was written, though there is no reference to it in the *Diaries*.

After Three Days. Dated 16 Feb. 1861 in *Three Sunsets*, though he first saw Holman Hunt's picture 'The Finding of Christ in the Temple', with which it deals, in Apr. 1860. [Letter to Mary Dodgson, quoted in *Diaries*, p. 164.] It was published in *Temple Bar*, July 1861 (vol. ii, pp. 566–8).

Faces in the Fire. Copied into *Mischmasch* and dated Jan. 1860 (date also given in *Three Sunsets*), it was first published in *All the Year Round*, No. 42, on 11 Feb. 1860. In these versions it has a different first stanza, beginning 'I watch the drowsy night expire', and an extra stanza following stanza five. The complete original version is reprinted on pp. 148–50 of *Diaries*.

All the above poems are included in *Collected Verse* (1932) and *Nonesuch*, but all in the revised versions to be found in *Rhyme? and Reason?* (1883) and *Three Sunsets* (1898).

The 'Miniature Edition' of *Phantasmagoria*, published in 1919, makes no mention of the fact that all the serious poems (Part II of the original edition) are omitted, or that five later pieces have been added. It is, in fact, only a reprint of so much of the 1869 edition as was printed in 1883 in *Rhyme? and Reason?*, with a few additions.

As late as 12 Dec. 1868, Dodgson was planning to issue *Phantasmagoria* in two forms: 'I think I shall have *200* private with the squib ["Elections"], and 400 *without*', he wrote to Macmillan on 10 Dec. Two days later he was still insisting: 'I don't think it will do to include the Oxford poem in all the copies', and was planning a 'fly-leaf' to explain the difference between the two issues—5s. 6d. with, and 5s. without the 'squib'.

But on 15 Dec. (see *Diary*) he notes: 'called at the Press to say that I have given up the idea of bringing out the poems in two different forms. The Oxford poem is to be in all the 600 copies.'

There seems to be no record of any copy bound up without the Oxford poem.

69. *Phantasmagoria* (1869) (First Edition, Second Issue)   [55

Phantasmagoria and other poems by Lewis Carroll, author of 'Alice's Adventures in Wonderland' (London, Macmillan & Co., 1869) 'All rights reserved', 8vo (size $6\frac{11}{16} \times 4\frac{9}{16}$ in.). This item is exactly as the first issue, except for the title, which is a cancel leaf. The addition of 'Author of Alice in Wonderland' was no doubt an afterthought.   F. M.

Dodgson records in his *Diary* for 7 Jan. 1869: 'Called on Macmillan and sent off twenty-eight copies of *Phantasmagoria*, which is now ready: 300 or 400 have been already ordered by the trade, and I agreed to Macmillan's proposal to print 1,000 more, (making 1,600 altogether).'

It is doubtful whether the second issue described above consists of this additional 1,000 copies, as Dodgson was writing to Macmillan on 24 Jan. 1869: 'Pray advertise *Phantasma.* in any way you like: my only objection was to having *Alice* mentioned on the title-page.'

But he had already agreed to having a slip inserted loosely advertising *Alice*, and this is sometimes found in copies of the first edition (any issue) tipped in on the front end paper. It measures 3·8 by 4·5 in., and is printed lengthwise on white paper as follows:

|| *By the same Author.* | ALICE'S ADVENTURES | IN | WONDER-LAND, | WITH FORTY-TWO ILLUSTRATIONS BY TENNIEL. | Crown 8vo., Cloth, Gilt Edges, 6s. | MACMILLAN & CO., LONDON. ||

If Madan is correct in describing the title-page as a cancel leaf, his copy must represent yet another issue: but I have found no copy of which it is true in the strict sense he implies. In normal copies the variant title-page is the normal p. [iii] of leaf [iii–iv] returning as leaf [v–vi].

70. *Phantasmagoria* (1869) (First Edition, Third Issue)

This item is exactly as the second issue as far as p. 202; but p. [203], instead of being blank, has the words TURN OVER printed in the bottom right-hand corner, and p. [204], also originally blank, has now Macmillan's advertisement of 'Other works by Lewis Carroll'. This was pointed out by Mr. N. Nathanson of Johannesburg on p. 184 of *The Book Collector*, vol. 8, No. 2, Summer 1959. See also the following number, p. 309, Autumn 1959 for further notes by John M. Shaw of New York, and the present writer.

71. *Alice's Abenteuer* (1869) (First German Edition, first issue) [52

ALICE'S ABENTEUER | im Wunderland | von | Lewis Carroll. | Uebersetzt von Antonie Zimmermann. | [*an ornamental line*] | Mit zweiundvierzig Illustrationen | von | John Tenniel. || [*an ornamental line*] |

London: Macmillan und Comp.: 1869: 8°: pp. [12]+178+[2]: signn. [π]⁶, 1–11⁸, 12²: size 7¼×5 in. CONTENTS: p. [1] half-title | Alice's Abenteuer im Wunderland. | [4] frontispiece: [5] title, as above: [7–9] the prefatory poem, beginning 'O schöner, goldner Nachmittag': followed by a small ornamental line: [10] A note in brackets in the centre of the page, of appreciation and explanation, showing that to preserve the sense, a literal translation has not always been followed, German nursery rhymes having been substituted for the English ones: [11] Inhalt (Contents): 1–178, the text: p. 178 has an ornamental line immediately below the text, and then | Druck von Breitkopf und Härtel in Leipzig. | at the bottom of the page. Dark blue end-papers.

Issued in red cloth. Gold lettering on the back under three gold lines | Alice's | Abenteuer | im | Wunderland. | [*A small ornamental device.*] At the bottom is | Macmillan | over three gold lines. On the front cover are three gold lines around the border, and three circular lines in the centre containing a picture of Alice holding the pig. The back cover is the same except that the figure within the circle is that of the Cheshire Cat. All edges gilt.

The reproductions of the woodcuts in this German edition are excellent, and bear comparison with those in any other issue of *Alice in Wonderland*. In the list of contents the pagination of the English edition has been carelessly reprinted, so that for every chapter except the first it is incorrect!

Williams, i. 17 (p. 25); *Parrish Catalogue*, p. 6; *Collingwood*, pp. 139, 433: British Museum, Bodleian, Harvard, &c.

72. Alice's Abenteuer (1869) (First Edition, second issue) [53

Alice's Abenteuer | im Wunderland | von | Lewis Carroll. | Aus dem Englischen von Antonie Zimmermann. | [*A small ornamental line*] | Mit zweiundvierzig Illustrationen | von | John Tenniel. | Autorisirte Ausgabe. | [*A long ornamental line*]

Leipzig Johann Frederich Hartknoch.: 8vo: size $7\frac{1}{4} \times 5$ in.: pp. [xii]+[1]–178. The collation is the same as the first issue, except for the difference in the title, and the absence of the last blank leaf.

On examination it will be seen that both books were printed from the same setting of type, with the exception of pp. [3]–[10]. These four leaves forming a folding were, I think, reset while the book was in sheets, so as to avoid using a cancel for the new title as above. This is in accordance with the conclusions I have arrived at with regard to these two issues. It is impossible to say with certainty which is the first issue, but I think it most likely that the book with the Macmillan imprint is the first. I imagine that the translator rendered the title-page just as it stood in the English edition, merely adding his name as translator. The printer set up from this translation, and it was not until a number of copies had been struck off that the Macmillan imprint was noticed. It was found easier no doubt to reprint the four leaves than substitute a cancel after the books were bound. This no doubt was done, and the sheets sent to London to be bound. Had the books been bound before the mistake was discovered, the new title would have been a cancel. These conclusions seem to be borne out by the note in Macmillan's *Bibliographical Catalogue*, to the effect that there was no Macmillan imprint in the German edition. That the translator worked carelessly is evident from the fact that he has followed the pagination in the 'Contents' given in the English edition, forgetting that the 'lay-out' would of necessity be different from that in English, and would therefore require fresh pagination, and so has given a wrong pagination for every chapter, except the first. He has also perpetuated the error found in the second English (1866) edition in the pagination in the list of contents. Mrs. Ffooks has an edition of 1885.   S. H. W.

Parrish Catalogue, p. 7: S. H. Williams, Mrs. Ffooks, &c.

Dodgson notes in his *Diary* that 'the German *Alice* came out in Feb. [1869]'. Although he corrected proofs—or at least saw them (he did not know German)—he makes no reference to the misprinted pagination in the Contents!

73. *Aventures d'Alice* (1869) (First French Edition)   [51

AVENTURES D'ALICE | *AU PAYS DES MERVEILLES.* ||| PAR |
LEWIS CARROLL. || TRADUIT DE L'ANGLAIS PAR HENRI BUÉ. |
OUVRAGE ILLUSTRÉ DE 42 VIGNETTES PAR JOHN TENNIEL. |

Londres: Macmillan and Co.: 1869: (fours) 8°: pp. [12]+196, signn. [a]⁴,
b^2, B–Z, AA–BB⁴, CC²: size 7 3/16 × 4 12/16 in.: at foot is [*Le Droit de Traduction et de
Reproduction est reservé.*] | CONTENTS: p. [1] half-title, | Aventures d'Alice | au |
pays de Merveilles. | [2] Macmillan's device in the centre: [4] frontispiece: [5]
title, as above: [6] five lines of acknowledgement and thanks from Lewis
Carroll to the translator, in brackets, in the centre of the page, with | Londres.
—Imprimerie de R. Clay, Fils, et Taylor, Bread Street Hill. | at the foot of the
page: p. [7–10] the introductory poem, beginning 'Notre barque glisse sur
l'onde', preceded by two thin lines: [11] Table of contents: 1–196, the text,
below the text on the last page is | Fin. | and at the bottom is | Londres,—
Imprimerie de R. Clay, Fils, et Taylor, Bread Street Hill. |
Issued in blue cloth. Gold lettering on the back under three gold lines is |
Aventures | d'Alice | au pays des | Merveilles | and at the bottom in most copies
| Macmillan | over three gold lines. The front cover in most copies has three
gold lines around the border. There are three circular lines in the centre of the
cover containing a picture of Alice holding the pig. The back cover is the
same except that the central figure is the Cheshire Cat. All edges gilt.

The difficulties of translators of *Alice* can be imagined. Sometimes
they declined to face the difficulty, as in Chapter VII ('Were they
in the well . . . Of course . . . well in.'), or, when a popular song
was parodied, they parodied a popular song of their own country:
or they twisted or turned as best they could. One great initial advantage was Tenniel's engravings, but only the Italian and Spanish
translators were careful enough to alter 'drink me' in an engraving
in Chapter VII to 'bevi' and 'in this style' in Chapter VII to 'prezzo
fisso', or something similar. In 1870 a French edition with Tenniel's
illustrations was published by Messrs. Hachette in Paris. An abridged
edition was issued in 1912.

Williams, i. 16 (p. 24); *Parrish Catalogue,* p. 7; *Collingwood,* pp. 138–40, 433:
British Museum, Bodleian, Harvard, &c.

Dodgson noted on 3 Aug. 1869 that the French *Alice* 'is just out'.

74. *The Guildford Gazette Extraordinary* (1869)   [57

THE GUILDFORD GAZETTE || EXTRAORDINARY || 'If I
chance to talk a little wild, forgive me.'—*Shakespeare.* || [*double rule*] ||
No. 9999. Dec. 29, 1869 [*both in heavy black*] || [*double rule*] || [*Here
double columns begin, the first commences*] OPENING OF THE NEW
THEATRE. || [*rule*] | (*From our Special Correspondent, Mr.* LEWIS CAR-
ROLL.) | [*rule*] || [*Text begins*].

Pamphlet c. 6″ × 12″. Front cover, in paper as the rest, is p. [1] and bears the title in ruled panel *THE GUILDFORD GAZETTE ||| EXTRAORDINARY*. Pp. 16. P. [2] as title-page given above, and text of 'article' by Dodgson, which is concluded on p. 3. The programme follows, with text of songs and sketches by W. W. Follett Synge, with short connecting links by Dodgson. P. [16] blank, as back cover.

The relevant *Diary* entry, under 28 Dec. 1869, reads: 'Theatrical performance at Mr. Synge's [W. W. Follett Synge, 1826–91, diplomatist and author]—very enjoyable. *The* treat of the evening, to me, was the 'Dirge over Dundee', sung by Alice Shute . . . There was a good scene from *King Lear*, for Mr. Synge; *Kenilworth*, versified, in which Miss S. acted capitally as Queen Elizabeth; *Old Poz*, in which Eva Shute acted the child very sweetly and simply; a few charades in dumb show, in which I took part as an M.D.; ending with [J. M. Morton's] *Poor Pillicoddy*, very fairly acted by Wilfred [Dodgson], Mr. Synge and Miss S. Mr. and Mrs. A. Trollope were present. I am trying to commemorate the evening in print, *The Guildford Gazette Extraordinary*'.

In 1931 'the only known copy' was in the Parrish Collection. The following year Miss Synge and the Dodgson family were found to have copies. All are now in America. In 1952 Professor Duncan Black discovered a copy at Christ Church (see *N. & Q.* 198, 2 Feb. 1953), and Dodgson's 'Introduction' was reprinted for the first time in Derek Hudson's *Lewis Carroll* (1954), pp. 327–30.

1870

75. *Puzzles from Wonderland* (1870) [56

Puzzles from Wonderland. By the Author of 'Alice's Adventures in Wonderland'.

Part of *Aunt Judy's Magazine*, edited by Mrs. Gatty, Dec. 1870 (= *Aunt Judy's Christmas Volume*, 1871), 8vo, pp. 101–2. The Solutions are also in verse, at pp. 187–8, contributed by 'Eadgyth' (i.e. Edith) to the Jan. 1871 number. The Puzzles in verse begin 'Dreaming of apples', 'A stick I found', 'John gave his brother', 'What is most like', 'Three sisters at breakfast', 'Said the moon', 'When the King' (a prose prologue) and 'Seven blind'. The Puzzles are clever, but full of quibbles (such as often = of ten: 'a man blind of both eyes' is *also* 'a man blind of one eye', and so counts twice in a list of blind men in the puzzle).

Dodgson was writing these in July 1870, and records on 30 Nov. having received a copy of *Aunt Judy's Magazine* containing them, 'they were originally written for the Cecil children'. He met Lord Salisbury in June of that year when he came to Oxford to be installed as Chancellor, and photographed and made friends with the children. He stayed several times at Hatfield, and told several stories which afterwards found a place in *Sylvie and Bruno*.

'Eadgyth' has not been identified, but seems not to have been Dodgson himself, since many other contributions—certainly not his—appeared in *Aunt Judy's Magazine* between 1869 and 1878. These include ingenious hidden word-puzzles, but also a life of Sir John Franklin and a long essay on Bewick. It is possible that they are by Horatia K. F. Gatty (later Mrs. Eden) who assisted and later succeeded her mother as Editor.

The Puzzles (and the Answers, except for No. I) do not seem to have been reprinted until *Collected Verse* (1932), pp. 75-79. They may be found in *Nonesuch*, pp. 819-22 (733-6). But all these reprints differ in at least eight respects from the original in *Aunt Judy* (as well as omitting the couplet by 'Eadgyth' answering No. I) —e.g. Puzzle VII originally says 'Five that see with both eyes', which is changed to 'Four' in the reprints—but the answer still retains 'Five'.

W. and M. (p. 334) say that this item is printed in Collingwood's *Life* (p. 140) and in *The Lewis Carroll Picture Book*—but it appears in neither.

76. *Algebraical Formulæ and Rules* (1870)   [58

Oxford: Printed at the University Press. 1870: 8°: 4 pages. Sir H. Hartley owns a copy.

77. *Arithmetical Formulæ and Rules* (1870)   [59

Oxford: Printed at the University Press. 1870.

This item is only known at present from Collingwood's *Life*, p. 433.

78. *Songs from Alice in Wonderland* (1870)   [60

THE SONGS | *FROM* | ALICE'S ADVENTURES IN WONDERLAND | WRITTEN BY | [*a double circle (diameter* $1\frac{5}{8}$ *in.) enclosing a picture of Alice holding the pig*] | LEWIS CARROLL | The Music Composed | BY | WILLIAM BOYD | *Ent. Sta. Hall* | [*an ornamental line*] | *One Shilling Nett* |

London Weeks & Co. 16 Hanover St. W.: [1870]: 8vo: (size $10 \times 6\frac{13}{16}$ in.): pp. [2]+10+wrappers. CONTENTS: [*There is no title-page, the front of the wrapper serving as such and being laid out as above*]: p. [1] dedication | To | Meggie and Ellen | in memory of | Christmas 1869. | these songs are affectionately dedicated |: [2] preface of nine lines beginning 'These Songs' and ending 'of a hat.'

with, below, on the left hand | London 1870 |: 1, Song with music 'Will you walk a little faster', three staves with below the bottom stave | 'The words of these songs are printed through the express permission of the Author of "Alice's Adventures in Wonderland"' |: 2, Quartette, with music 'Il Coro', two stanzas: 3, two verses of the preceding song, and below a song with music 'Twinkle, twinkle, little bat', three staves: 4, Song with music 'Speak crossly', three staves, and below is one verse: 5, song with music, 'You're old Father William', three staves: first verse: 6, second verse of 'You're old Father William', three staves: 7, the six remaining verses of 'You're old Father William': 8, a song with music, 'How doth the little crocodile', four staves: 9, a song with music, "Tis the voice of a lobster', three staves with one verse below: 10, a song with music 'The Queen of Hearts', three staves. The whole is lithographed. 'W. 118'. Issued in a white wrapper, stitched. The front page of the wrapper has the title as above: [2] blank: 3, an advertisement of nine songs published by Weeks and Co., enclosed in a double line border with ornamental corners: [4] blank.

Dodgson wrote additional lines to one of the poems expressly for this book of songs. On turning to the Preface we find that '. . . The author of the words has been good enough to add to one of the poems, so that if on no other ground this publication will be valuable inasmuch as it has furnished the charming absurdity about the Duck and the Dodo, the Lizard and Cat a-swimming in milk round the brim of a hat'. Mr. Beecroft gave some help. There appear to be several variations of the first edition of this item, the difference being in the colour of the wrapper and the arrangement of the advertisements. I have found it impossible to decide which is the first, and Messrs. Weeks have not been able to help me. I conclude, however, that the one collated above is the first, as it was this form of it which was entered at the Stationers' Hall, and it is also this form which was sent to the Bodleian Library under the conditions of the Copyright Act.   S. H. W.

Mr. Parrish has at least four issues: (1) with advt. of seven New Songs on the outside of the back wrapper, (2) with the advt. of Songs on the inside, and of 'VII Songs from a Lilliput Levee', on the outside of the back wrapper, (3) interchanging the advtt. in No. 2, (4) with 'and Simpkin, Marshall & Co.' below the imprint and advtt. of New Songs on inside of the back cover. The Bodleian copy above described has only the advt. of New Songs inside the back cover.   F. M.

Reprinted in 1913, 1921, and 1926. Mr. Parrish has also an undated 6d. edition.

Williams, i. 19 (p. 26); Parrish Catalogue, p. 120: British Museum, Bodleian, Harvard, &c.

79. *Afventyr Isagolandet* (1870)   [64

Alice's Äfventyr Isagolandet . . . Äfoersattning fräu engelsan af Emily Nonnen. Stockholm: 1870: 8°: pp. [6]+184.

Alice's Adventures in Swedish. The only copy at present recorded is in the possession of Mr. M. L. Parrish of Philadelphia.

1871

80. *Suggestions for Committee appointed to consider Senior Studentships* (1871)

PRIVATE [in square brackets and heavy type] || *Suggestions for Committee to consider the expediency of re-* | *constituting Senior Studentships at Christ Church. March, 1871.* || [Folio sheet dividing the suggestions under IX heads: in all 58 lines. Signed] || C. L. D.

Printed on one side of the sheet only.

This item was unknown until Duncan Black discovered Vere Bayne's copy in the Senior Common Room at Christ Church in 1952—just as I was transcribing the following passage in Dodgson's *Diaries* for 4 May 1871: 'I took to the University Press the proof, finally corrected, of my *Suggestions for the Committee appointed to consider Senior Studentships.*'

81. *Prologue to Play* (1871)   [628

At Clevedon House, Park Town, Oxford, the residence of Dr. Edwin Hatch, Vice-principal of St. Mary Hall (*d.* 1889), amateur acting occasionally took place, and on two occasions, since Miss Beatrice Hatch and her sister were among Dodgson's child-friends, he wrote a Prologue for the play. On 1 and 2 Nov. 1871, two pieces were acted, *The Loan of a Lover* and *Whitebait from Greenwich*, and the prologue spoken has been preserved all these years by the wonderful memory of Mr. F. B. de Sausmarez, of Cheltenham.   F. M.

Madan prints this Prologue for the first time on pp. 199–201 of the original edition of this *Handbook*. It was included by F. B. de Sausmarez in his article 'Early Theatricals at Oxford' in *The Nineteenth Century*, Feb. 1932, and may be found in *Collected Verse* (1932), pp. 108–10 and *Nonesuch*, pp. 823–5 (737–9). *Nonesuch* makes the ridiculous assertion that the two plays were written by Dodgson: the first was by J. R. Planché and the second by J. M. Morton.

Though not printed until 1931, it is included here since it was recited in public, and so 'published' in the legal sense, in 1871.

82. *To all Child-readers of Alice* (1871)   [65

TO ALL CHILD-READERS | OF | '𝔄𝔩𝔦𝔠𝔢'𝔰 𝔄𝔡𝔳𝔢𝔫𝔱𝔲𝔯𝔢𝔰 𝔦𝔫 𝔚𝔬𝔫𝔡𝔢𝔯𝔩𝔞𝔫𝔡.' | [Surrounded by a double line border, the inner dimensions of which are $3\frac{1}{2} \times 2\frac{1}{2}$ in.]

[Oxford]: 1871: (two) 24°: pp. 3+[1]: size $4\frac{3}{16} \times 2\frac{3}{4}$ in.: CONTENTS: p. 1, title as above: 2, the text, beginning 'Dear children', and ending 'Friend', followed by the date | Christmas, 1871. | in the bottom left-hand corner, and | 'Lewis Carroll' | in the bottom right-hand corner: White wove paper. Copies of this item are met with in varying sizes of the paper.

A letter of good wishes for Christmas and the New Year, beginning 'Dear children, At Christmas time a few grave words are not quite out of place I hope, even at the end of a book of nonsense'. There is no reference to the New *Alice* (*Through the Looking-Glass*) and the little piece was probably enclosed in copies of the 1872 edition of *Alice*, and also (as the *Athenaeum* of 16 Dec. 1871 shows) in copies of the *Looking-Glass*.

Williams, i. 20 (p. 28); *Parrish Catalogue*, p. 8; *Collingwood*, p. 433: Bodleian, Harvard, Huntington, &c.

This was presumably printed in Dec. 1871, since on 22 Nov. Dodgson noted in his *Diary*: 'Heard from Menella Smedley, approving of the little Christmas address I had sent her in MS.'

It seems only to have been reprinted on p. 246 of *A Selection from the Letters of Lewis Carroll to his Child-Friends* (1933).

83. *A Circular Letter about a Frontispiece* (1871)   [66

An undated leaflet, cream laid (size $7\frac{1}{8} \times 5\frac{1}{12}$ in.), printed on one side only: pp. [2], p. [1] headed on the right-hand side | Ch. Ch., Oxford. | A space is left for the date and name of the correspondent. The body of the letter consists of twenty-two lines, beginning 'I am sending you' and ending 'course is best'.

This item is a circular letter which Mr. Dodgson had printed to send to friends interested in *Alice in Wonderland*, to ascertain their views as to whether the frontispiece for *Alice through the Looking-Glass*, then about to be published, was of such a nature as to frighten his young readers. Until this letter appeared at Sotheby's on 16 June 1926 I had never heard of it, nor have I after many inquiries been able to find anyone else who knew of it. A proof of the frontispiece in question should accompany the letter. The complete letter is as follows:

'I am sending you, with this, a print of the proposed frontispiece for "Through the Looking-glass". It has been suggested to me that it is too terrible a monster, and likely to alarm nervous and imaginative children; and that at any rate we had better begin the book with a pleasanter subject.

'So I am submitting the question to a number of friends, for which purpose I have had copies of the frontispiece printed off.

'We have three courses open to us:

'(1) To retain it [i.e. the hideous Jabberwocky] as the frontispiece.

'(2) To transfer it to its proper place in the book, (where the ballad occurs which it is intended to illustrate) and substitute a new frontispiece.

'(3) To omit it altogether.

The last-named course would be a great sacrifice of the time and trouble which the picture has cost, and it would be a pity to adopt it unless it is really necessary.

'I should be grateful to have your opinion, (tested by exhibiting the picture to any children you think fit,) as to which of these courses is the best.'

The letter in this case was dated Feb. 15. 71, and addressed to Mrs. Barry, and Dodgson has followed on the text by a written personal letter in his usual violet ink, referring to 'the new volume of Alice' which he proposed to present to one of Mrs. Barry's daughters, also saying that he had called on John (presumably Mrs. Barry's son) but had not succeeded in seeing him. Dodgson goes on to say that there did not appear to be any etiquette to prevent Dons and undergraduates associating 'but we are rather shy of each other, and I fancy the undergraduates as a rule don't care for our society.   Very Truly yours

C. L. Dodgson.'

Eventually the plate selected for the frontispiece was the White Knight, and the picture, which is the subject of the above letter, is to be found on p. 23.   S. H. W.

1 8 7 2

84. Through the Looking-Glass (1872)   [67

THROUGH THE LOOKING-GLASS, ‖ AND WHAT ALICE FOUND THERE. ‖ BY | LEWIS CARROLL, | AUTHOR OF 'ALICE'S ADVENTURES IN WONDERLAND.' ‖ *WITH FIFTY ILLUSTRATIONS* | BY *JOHN TENNIEL.* ‖|

London: Macmillan and Co.: 1872: at foot, '[*The Right of Translation and Reproduction is reserved.*]': 8°: pp. [12]+224+[4]: signn. [A]⁶, B–P⁸, Q²: size 7⅜×4¹⁵⁄₁₆ in. CONTENTS: p. [1] half-title: | Through the Looking-Glass, | and what Alice found there. | : [2] | 'Dramatis Personae. | (As arranged before commencement of [a chess] game)' | [*a double line*] | Beneath are four columns of characters in the game, each column having eight characters: [3] a chess problem with the men in position on a chess-board; below is the solution in eleven moves: [4] frontispiece (The White Knight): [5] title, as above: [7–9] a prefatory poem beginning 'Child of the pure unclouded brow', preceded by two fine lines: [10] Macmillan's device: [11] contents of the 12 chapters: 1–222, the text: 223–4, seven three-line verses, beginning 'A boat beneath a sunny sky', preceded by two thin lines: 224, | The End. | P. [1] has signature | Q [Turn over. | at the bottom of the page: [2] Advertisements of the works of Lewis Carroll: [3] Richard Clay's device, central. In addition to the unnumbered pages at the beginning of each chapter, p. 98 in the middle of Chap. V is accidentally unnumbered throughout the whole of the first edition, and p. 95 in some copies. See Plate IX.

Dark green end-papers. Issued in red cloth. Gold lettering on the back under three gold lines | Through | the | Looking-Glass. | [ornament] | and at the bottom is | Macmillan | over three gold lines. The front cover has three gold lines around the border, and three circular gold lines in the centre enclosing a picture of the Red Queen. The back cover is the same, except that the central figure is that of the White Queen. All edges gilt. Some copies are bound in white. A magnificently bound copy is described and illustrated in Maggs's Catalogue No. 443 (1923), art. 447: the front cover bears a chess-board and pawn, with inlaid work in six colours.

Evolution of the Book. According to Collingwood's *Life* (p. 138) 'a few days after the publication of "Phantasmagoria" [Jan. 1869] Lewis Carroll sent the first chapter of his new story [*Through the Looking-Glass*] to the press'. Again there was some difficulty about the title; originally he had thought of *Behind the Looking-Glass and what Alice found there.* This was changed to *Looking-Glass House and what Alice found there.* This title was so far settled that it was sent to the press and proofs exist in the Huntington Library in Los Angeles of some half-dozen sheets which clearly indicate that Dodgson had intended publishing the book under that title in 1870. It is curious that no other record or mention of this early form of title exists. Mr. Collingwood apparently did not know of it, and Messrs. Macmillan, to whom I submitted photostats of the proofs, have no knowledge of it. In their courteous letter to me they say: '. . . We have little doubt, although we cannot prove it, that these were early proofs of the book which was afterwards published under the title of *Through the Looking-Glass and what Alice found there.* . . Unfortunately we have no copies of this proof, nor have the printers, Messrs. Clay & Sons Ltd., any record.'

Some interesting papers about the early form of the book are in the Amory Collection in the Harvard College Library (Columbia, U.S.A.). One is a sheet of paper bearing eight variations of the title-page in Dodgson's hand, dated 1870: another the earliest form of the preliminary leaves, with corrections. That library has also a collection of Press Cuttings formed by Dodgson about many of his books and much else of interest.

It will be seen on reference to the facsimiles which I have had made (Plates VIII, IX) that the layout of this title is much the same as that of the first edition, though rather larger. In addition to the differences in the wording of the title, it will be seen that the book as originally conceived was to have only forty-two illustrations as compared with the fifty afterwards included in the first edition. The page of contents has only eleven chapters instead of twelve, and the following differences are noticeable in the wording of the chapter headings. In the first edition Chapter V has become 'Wool and Water', Chapter VIII 'It's my own invention', and Chapter X 'Waking', before it was divided into Chapter X 'Shaking' and Chapter XI 'Waking'. The layout of the verses following the page of contents is the same as in the first edition, but there are five alterations in the text in Dodgson's hand. In verse 4, line 4, 'Melancholy' is substituted for 'Wilful weary'; verse 5, line 1, 'frost the blinding' for 'whirling wind and' and line 2, in the same verse, 'The storm wind's moody' for 'that lash themselves'. The word *fairy*, where it appears in the poem, was originally spelt 'faery'. All the corrections were carried out in the first edition and subsequent editions. In the last verse of the poem in the proof the word 'pleasures' (though not corrected) was afterwards changed to 'pleasance', a very happy thought as 'Pleasance' is the second Christian name of Miss Alice Liddell.

It is interesting to note, by the way, that at the end of the book there is a very beautiful poem beginning 'A boat beneath a sunny sky', and continued in triolets, making in all twenty-one lines. If the first letter of each line be taken in order they will be found to spell the name 'Alice Pleasance Liddell', the original of Alice. This form of the title and preliminary pages was discarded for the book as we now know it, the title becoming (through a suggestion of Canon Liddon) *Through the Looking-Glass*.

Dodgson had proved so exact, and exacting, as a critic of the way his requirements were carried out, that Tenniel, when approached about the illustrations for *Through the Looking-Glass*, declared he was too busy; and it must have been in 1866 that Dodgson almost despaired of getting him to take the drawings in hand. Sir Noel Paton was then applied to, but he was ill, and declared that Tenniel was *the* man. On 22 Jan. 1867, Dodgson wrote by Tenniel's advice to Richard Doyle, the artist so long connected with *Punch*. Nothing came of this, and Tenniel was approached again, with the result that, in the end, he once more shouldered the task, and an interesting letter from him, dated June 1870 (reproduced in facsimile in Collingwood's *Life*, p. 141), illustrates his difficulties. While on the one hand Dodgson was urging 'Don't give Alice so much crinoline', or

'The White Knight must not have whiskers', Tenniel induced Dodgson to omit the 'wasp' chapter on the ground that it was uninteresting, and that he was quite unable to make a picture for it: 'A wasp in a wig is altogether beyond the appliances of Art'. The effect of these criticisms and counter-criticisms may be gathered from what Tenniel wrote subsequently, that 'with *Through the Looking-Glass* the faculty of making drawings for book illustration departed from me . . . I have done nothing in that direction since . . .'.

Publication. The book was issued in Dec. 1871, but no copies have 1871 on the title-page, and Dodgson's own first copy, received on 6 Dec. 1871 (Dodgson Sale, lot 690), bore 1872, as did Alice Liddell's own (presentation) copy also.

Other editions. An American edition was published in 1872 at Boston (Lee and Sheppard) and New York (Lee, Sheppard, and Dillingham) with a rearrangement of the preliminary leaves and no advertisements at the end. It appears to be a reissue of the original sheets printed in London, for it bears Macmillan's device, and has the misprint 'Wade' for 'Wabe' (*Parrish Catalogue*, p. 9). In London the thirteenth thousand is still 1872, and there were reprints from electrotypes in Apr. and July 1872, 1873, 1876, 1878, and often thereafter. The People's edition was first issued in 1887; and the sixty-first thousand is dated 1897.

As stated, the book, like its famous predecessor, was published during the year preceding that on the title, i.e. in 1871, while the title is dated 1872. The reproduction of the blocks appears to have given satisfaction to Lewis Carroll; at any rate the edition was issued without comment from the author, and other editions quickly followed. It was not until the sixtieth thousand was reached that the fate of the 1865 *Alice* book overtook *Through the Looking-Glass.* Here again Tenniel's drawings were badly reproduced, and efforts were made to suppress the edition. In Dec. 1893 Lewis Carroll issued a leaflet asking that possessors of copies of this edition would return them to Messrs. Macmillan and they would receive new copies in exchange [see No. *249*].

There is a printer's error in the first edition of *Through the Looking-Glass.* On page 21, at the bottom of the page, is the first verse of 'Jabberwocky', in the second line of which the last word is spelt wrongly, with a 'd' instead of a 'b'. In the verse printed backwards on the same page the word is spelt correctly. This error was corrected in subsequent editions; but the first American edition has the same error. I have also noticed that page 98, which is not the beginning of a chapter, is unnumbered, also page 95 in some copies. S. H.W.

The Chess Setting. As *Alice's Adventures* are, in a sense, in a card setting, so *Through the Looking-Glass* is in a chess setting, but the latter is much more conspicuous, for a chess diagram is displayed at the beginning, posed as a problem ('White to play, and win in eleven moves'). The twenty-one moves are duly set out, and the pages of the book at which each move occurs is given. In the earlier editions the names of each of the pieces are also given, such as 'White—Pieces—Tweedledee, Unicorn, Sheep', &c. With all this parade it was proper that.the game should proceed in chess style, and in later editions a special preface claims that the problem 'is correctly worked out, so far as the *moves* are concerned', and excuses some irregularities, but declares that there is a normal check-mate (whereas there is no attempt at one).

But in spite of this explanation the chess framework is full of absurdities and impossibilities, and it is unfortunate that Dodgson did not display his usual dexterity by bringing the game, as a game, up to chess standard. He is known to have been a chess-player, see Collingwood's *Life* (p. 92) and the Dodgson sale in 1898 (lot 196). He might have searched for a printed problem to suit his story, or have made one. But he allows the White side to make nine consecutive moves (!): he allows Alice (a White pawn) reaching the eighth square, and Alice becoming a Queen, to be two separate moves: he allows the White King to be checked without either side taking any notice of the fact: he allows two Queens to castle (!): he allows the White Queen to fly from the Red Knight, when she could take it. Hardly a move has a sane purpose, from the point of view of chess.   F. M.

Re the Chess Setting, it should be noted that Dodgson added a Preface dated 'Christmas 1896' to the revised edition of 1897 explaining that 'the chess problem . . . is correctly worked out, so far as the *moves* are concerned'. In this and subsequent reprints the board shows the White King on Q.B.'s 3rd: he is absent in earlier editions, e.g. fortieth thousand (1877)—as is also Red King who appears later on his 5th. But see item No. *127* below.

In the 1931 *Handbook* Madan adds two pages (46–48) on 'Jabberwocky'. For new essay on this subject, and on the other verses in the *Alice* books see Appendix, pp. 278–87 of present volume.

Looking-Glass dates. Dodgson made no table of dates in his *Diary* as he did for *Wonderland,* but the following notes drawn from *Diaries* and the letters to Macmillan may be of interest:

24 Aug. 1866. Letter to Macmillan. 'It will probably be some time before I again indulge in paper and print. I have, however, a floating idea of writing

a sort of sequel to *Alice*, and if it ever comes to anything, I intend to consult you at the very outset, so as to have the thing properly managed from the beginning.'

24 Jan. 1868. Letter to Macmillan. 'Have you any means, or can you find any, of printing a page or two, in the next volume of *Alice*, in *reverse*?'

On 2 June 1868 he writes to Macmillan that neither Tenniel nor Noel Paton can illustrate *Alice II*, and asks about 'Babs' (W. S. Gilbert). He also tried Dicky Doyle, and possibly Proctor, before persuading Tenniel to undertake the task.

On 8 Apr. 1868 (*Diary*) he is asking George MacDonald for an introduction to Noel Paton 'about the pictures for *Looking-glass House*'. But on 18 June 'I wrote to *Tenniel*, finally accepting his kind offer to do the pictures (at such spare times as he can find) for the second volume of *Alice*. He thinks it *possible* (but not likely) that we might get it out by Christmas 1869.'

Dodgson was interrupted immediately after this entry by the sudden death of his father; but in August he was staying at Onslow Square, and it is probable that this was the occasion when he met Alice Raikes as described in *The Times*, 22 Jan. 1932.

The next entry is for 12 Jan. 1869: 'Finished and sent off to Macmillan the first chapter of *Behind the Looking-Glass, and What Alice Saw There*.' He met Tenniel late in March, but he had not begun any of the illustrations.

Meanwhile he was discussing by letter with Macmillan how to print 'two pages' of the new *Alice* in reverse, deciding by the end of Jan. 1869 to 'limit it to one or two stanzas (with perhaps a picture over them to fill the page) and print the rest of the ballad in the usual way'.

On 15 Apr. 1870 he was writing to Macmillan about trial title-pages (apparently with the final title, since he complains about the letter 'F' in the title—but the 'AND' was between the two lines of title, and not at the beginning of the second line as in Plates VIII and IX). Some of the type is set up, since he refers to a picture to come on p. 11 of Alice getting through the looking-glass.

On 25 June 1870 (*Diary*) he had 'the first seven pictures for *Through the Looking-glass*' to show to Lord Salisbury's children; but Tenniel was still supplying pictures for more than half of 1871: 'I have only received 27 pictures as yet' (25 Apr.); and on 29 Apr. agreeing that the book must be postponed for Christmas instead of coming out at Michaelmas.

As far as the writing was concerned, however, Dodgson noted on 4 Jan. 1871 'Finished the M.S. of *Through the Looking-glass*. It was begun before 69.' He left a space for the month, which probably should be Jan. (see above).

On 1 Nov. '*Alice Through the Looking-glass* is now printing off rapidly'. On 30 Nov. 'Heard from Macmillan that they already have orders for 7500 *Looking-glasses* (they printed 9000), and are at once going to print 6000 more!' On 6 Dec. 'Received the first complete copy of the *Looking-glass*', and on 8 Dec. 'Received from Macmillan three *Looking-glasses* in morocco, and a hundred in cloth.' He inscribed and sent off a hundred that day, including one in morocco for Alice Liddell: he had intended to bind hers with a piece of looking-glass in the centre of the front cover (letter to Macmillan 15 Apr. 1870), but apparently this proved impracticable.

According to a letter of 17 Dec. 1871 to Macmillan 'the pressing between sheets of blank paper in order to dry for binding is the real cause of all the "inequality" which has so vexed Mr. Tenniel in the copies already done', and he urged him to have the sheets of the additional 6,000 dried naturally, i.e. by stacking, even if there was a delay which resulted in loss of income: 'I have already had a bitter lesson in this matter with *Alice's Adventures . . .*'—though this does not refer to the 1865 edition, but to a later 3,000 which were printed too hurriedly—'a blow to the artistic reputation of the book which I doubt if it will *ever* quite recover . . . .

Through the Looking-glass was not suppressed until the 1893 issue: but this suggests that even the first edition had a narrow escape from coming under Tenniel's ban!

But there was no doubt in the minds of the public about the success of the book, and Dodgson noted in his *Diary* on 27 Jan. 1872, after the book had been out barely seven weeks: 'My birthday was signalized by hearing from Mr. Craik [of Macmillan's] that they have now sold 15,000 *Looking-glasses*, and have orders for 500 more!'

85. *Avventure d'Alice, in Italian* (1872) First Edition, First Issue) [68

LE AVVENTURE D'ALICE | NEL PAESE DELLE MERA-VIGLIE || PER | LEWIS CARROLL. | TRADOTTE DALL' INGLESE DA | T. PIETROCÒLA-ROSSETTI. || CON 42 *VIGNETTE DI GIOVANNI TENNIEL.* |||

Londra: Macmillan and Co.: 1872: 8°: pp. [12]+189+[3], signn. [A]⁴, B², B–N⁸, O⁴: size 7 3/16 × 4 13/16 : CONTENTS: p. [1] half-title, | Le Avventure d'Alice | nel paese delle Meraviglie. | : [2] Macmillan's device, central: [4] frontispiece: [5] title, as above, and at foot, '(*Proprietà letteraria dell' autore.)*': [6] imprint, | Londra: R. Clay, figli, E. Taylor, Stampatori, | Bread Street Hill. | : [7–9] the prefatory poem, beginning 'In su' vespri giocondi', preceded by two thin lines: [11] 'Indice', a list of contents [1–189] the text: [1] imprint, | Londra: R. Clay, figli, E. Taylor, Stampatori, | Bread Street Hill. | : p. 186 has two

VII. A page of Dodgson's diary (vol. 9, p. 60) about the 2nd edition of *Alice's Adventures* (London, 1866)

LOOKING-GLASS HOUSE,

AND WHAT ALICE SAW THERE.

BY

LEWIS CARROLL.

AUTHOR OF "ALICE'S ADVENTURES IN WONDERLAND"

WITH FORTY-TWO ILLUSTRATIONS BY JOHN TENNIEL.

London:

MACMILLAN AND CO.

1870.

[The Right of Translation and Reproduction is reserved.]

VIII. Title-page of *Looking-Glass House*, 1870

THROUGH THE LOOKING-GLASS,

AND WHAT ALICE FOUND THERE.

BY

LEWIS CARROLL,

AUTHOR OF "ALICE'S ADVENTURES IN WONDERLAND."

WITH FIFTY ILLUSTRATIONS

BY JOHN TENNIEL.

London:

MACMILLAN AND CO.

1872.

[*The Right of Translation and Reproduction is reserved.*]

IX. Title-page of *Through the Looking-Glass,* 1872

x. Tenniel's Illustrations for *Alice's Adventures* (details, in Dodgson's hand, 1865) thin lines over the text: p. 189 has | Fine. | just below the centre of the page. Dark grey end-papers.

Issued in bright red cloth: gold lettering: on the back under three gold lines: | Le | Avventure | d'Alice | nel paese | delle | Meraviglie. | [*A device*] | and at the bottom of the back is | Macmillan | over three gold lines. The front cover has three gold lines around the border, and three circular gold lines in the centre of the cover, containing Alice holding the pig. The back cover is the same except that the central figure is the Cheshire Cat. All edges gilt.

The reproduction of the cuts in the Italian *Alice* is far from good; either the electrotypes were showing signs of wear, or they were carelessly used. The Italian and Spanish *Alices* are unique among the translations of the book, in that they are the only ones in which the 'Drink me.' on the label in the cut on p. 10 has been translated. As the block or electrotype is obviously the one used for the other printings, I imagine that the label in the present case must have been cut out and another substituted with the Italian 'Bevi' inserted. This laudable attention to detail was extended to the ticket on the Mad Hatter's hat on pp. 101, 166, where 'Prezzo fisso L12.' is substituted for 'In this style 10/6.' Dodgson received his copy of this London edition on 20 Mar. 1872; another Italian edition translated by E. C. Caglio was published in 1924 at Bergamo, with Rackham's illustrations.

I have given the above collation as the first issue of the first edition, but there is no doubt that one copy at least was issued bearing the date 1871. As I have not been able to obtain any information whatever about it, I have come to the conclusion that the date 1871 was a printer's error, instantly detected and corrected, and that the copy is probably unique. [68*

I much regret that I am unable to give any details of this book. It is the only copy with this date (1871) that I have ever heard of, and Messrs. Macmillan are unable to throw any light on it. In their *Bibliographical Catalogue* it is recorded that the first edition in Italian was published in 1872. I cannot help thinking that perhaps it may contain other variations than that of the date. When I saw the copy in question through the courtesy of Messrs. Sotheran, circumstances prevented me from collating it at the time, and when the next opportunity arose the book had been sold.

Hence all I can say about the copy of the Italian *Alice* bearing the date of 1871 is that it exists, and that I have seen and handled it.

There is another form of the first issue of the first edition of the Italian *Alice*, to which attention should be drawn. It differs from the other in that it is invariably found in mint condition, the covers lack the gold lines around the border, and only the top edges are gilt. The binding is a smooth red cloth. The contents are undoubtedly the first issue. The explanation I think is that the demand for the Italian *Alice* was not great, and that a number of sheets were left on Messrs. Macmillan's hands (indeed all the bound copies were not disposed of, for they were still to be had from Messrs. Macmillan at the original price as late as 1930) and it is these sheets recently bound which make up the above form of the first issue of the first edition of the Italian *Alice*. I think it can be of no interest to the collector.   S. H. W.

A copy dated 1871—perhaps the one mentioned above—was noted in Parrish's 1933 *Supplement* to his *Catalogue* as having been added to his library.

86. (First Edition, Second Issue)   [69

LE AVVENTURE D'ALICE ‖ NEL PAESE DELLE MERA-VIGLIE. ‖ PER │ LEWIS CARROLL. │ TRADOTTE DALL' INGLESE DA │ *t. pietrocòla-rossetti.* │ CON 42 *VIGNETTE DI GIOVANNI TENNIEL.*│││

Torino: Ermanno Loescher: 1872: [at foot] (Proprieta letteraria dell' autore.)│ Dark grey end-papers, all edges gilt.

This book is in every respect identical with the first issue, except that p. [5] is on a cancel leaf, with the title as above, and p. [6] is blank: but the Clay imprint removed from p. [6] is still on the page following the text, as in the first issue. All the copies that I have seen have been bound by 'Burn & Co.' (on a label) in a rough orange cloth. See Note to the preceding item (No. **68**).

Williams, i. 24* (p. 34); *Parrish Catalogue*, p. 9: Harvard, S. H. Williams, F. Madan, &c.

87. Circular to Hospitals (1872)   [70

Circular to Hospitals offering copies of the two 'Alice' books. London: Macmillan. 1872.

Only known at present from the above entry in Collingwood's *Life*, p. 434. A similar notice is described in No. **198** (1890), cf. No. **92** (1876). Some copies of these books have 'For the Use of Sick Children' *printed* on the title [**70***].

88. New Belfry (1872)   [71ª

THE NEW BELFRY │ OF │ CHRIST CHURCH, OXFORD. ‖ A MONOGRAPH │ BY │ D.C.L. │ 'A THING OF BEAUTY IS A JOY FOR EVER.' │ [*a square*] │ East view of the new Belfry, Ch. Ch., as seen from the Meadow │

Oxford: James Parker and Co.: 1872: | (four and eight) 12°: pp. 23+[1]: signn. [A]⁴, B⁸, see below: size 6 11/16 × 4 5/8 in. CONTENTS: p. 1, half-title: 3, title as above, within a thin line: 5, contents: 7–23, the text with | Finis. | below the text on p. 23: 24, imprint in the centre of the page, | Oxford: | By T. Combe, M.A., E. B. Gardner, and E. Pickard Hall, | Printers to the University. |

Issued in brick-red wrappers, the front page of which is lettered as the title-page, except that in addition, it has below the thin line border | Price Sixpence.|

There were five issues of this pamphlet: (1) as above, (2) as above, adding J. H. Stacy in the imprint [71^b], (3) adding Second thousand, 1872, on the front page of the wrapper [71^c], (4) as (3) but with 1873 [71^d], (5) according to Collingwood an issue with 2+31 pages (error for 23+1?) [71^e]. No. 4 was afterwards included in the volume entitled *Notes by an Oxford Chiel*, published by Parker of Oxford in 1874 (see No. 80).

This pamphlet is a humorous skit on the bald wooden cube erected to contain the bells extruded from the Cathedral (when the Tower was opened inside up to the base of the spire), and placed over the beautiful staircase leading to the hall, in the south-east corner of Tom Quad. The word Belfry is declared to be from the French 'bel, beautiful, becoming, meet' and the German 'frei, free, unfettered, secure, safe' = meat-safe. Among the personal references are (p. 8) Faussett, Liddon, Bayne: (p. 9) The architect of the House and the alterations of the Cathedral was Sir George Gilbert Scott: Jeeby = G. B., Governing Body. Syllogisms are introduced and much fun is derived from the simplicity of a cube. The criticism is mordant, but good-humoured. A more suitable structure was provided within a short time.

Mr. Parrish owns a long list of the persons to whom Dodgson sent a copy, the earliest date of sending being 5 June 1872. The pamphlet can hardly be called anonymous, D.C.L. being a thin disguise of C. L. D(odgson). Sheet A 4 is made up of pp. 1–4, 21–24.

On 31 May 1872: 'took to the University Press the MS. for a "monograph" on the Belfry, written in the last two days'.

This, the most amusing of the 'Oxford squibs', was reprinted in *The Lewis Carroll Picture Book* (1899). It may be found in *Nonesuch*, pp. 1139–50 (1026–36).

89. Symbols &c. To be used in Euclid (1872)   [72

'Symbols &c. to be used in Euclid, Books I. and II. Oxford: Printed at the University Press . . . 1872.'

Only known from the above entry in Collingwood's *Life and Letters of Lewis Carroll*, p. 434.

90. *Propositions in Euclid* (1872) [73

'Number of Propositions in Euclid. Oxford: Printed at the University Press . . . 1872.'

Only known from the above entry in Collingwood's *Life and Letters of Lewis Carroll*, p. 434.

91. [*Unnamed Pamphlet, printed at Cambridge* (1872)]

This item may never have been printed, but the reference to it is given here so that ardent Carrollians and other book-hunters may set to work searching for it.

Writing to Macmillan on 28 Nov. 1872, in a letter headed *Private*, Dodgson says: 'I want you to execute a little commission for me, in the printing department, *and to keep a secret.* The enclosed MS. is a burlesque on the proceedings of a very advanced school of reformers who met in London the other day, to consider the subject of the "redistribution" of our revenues at Oxford and Cambridge, for the benefit of scientific men, who are not to teach, but only to "investigate". To me (and to others) this seems to savour a little too strongly of a very unscientific affection for the "loaves and fishes"—So that there is a grain of serious meaning in the burlesque: still I hope I have made the whole thing extravagant enough to show it is not to be literally interpreted, and so to save it from being personally offensive to anyone.

'If I get it printed here, people will guess the authorship, and I want to remain "incog." So what I want you to do is, to get it printed at Cambridge, (no doubt they have many such squibs on the subjects of the day, just as we have here), and have it on sale at your establishment there. . . . I think it will fill about 4 pages of a quarto-sheet. Please have it done in a nice readable type, on good paper, and let me have 50 copies.'

Dodgson also asked to have copies sent to all Combination Rooms at Cambridge, and, after copies were on sale at Oxford, to Senior Common Rooms too—'only please take care to have "Cambridge" printed on it, so that it may be known to come from there.'

There is no reference to it in the *Diaries*—but there is a gap from 24 Oct. to 26 Dec. 1872 when no diary was kept.   R. L. G.

1873

92. Enunciations of Euclid (1873) [78

THE ENUNCIATIONS | OF | EUCLID I–VI | TOGETHER WITH | QUESTIONS | ON THE | DEFINITIONS, POSTULATES, | AXIOMS, &c. || [a line] ||

Oxford: By E. B. Gardner, E. Pickard Hall, and J. H. Stacy, Printers to the University: 1873: (eights) 12°: pp. 46+[2]: signn. B–D⁸. CONTENTS: p. 1, title: 3, preface: 5–46, the work.

An enlargement of No. 25 (1863) above. Still anonymous, but certainly by Dodgson. It deals with six, not four, books of Euclid.

On 26 Dec. 1872, when covering two months during which no Diary had been written, Dodgson noted: 'I have printed (for publication next term) *The Enunciations of Euclid I–VI.*'

93. Prologue

Prologue (to a play privately acted in Dr. Hatch's house, written for Miss Beatrice Hatch on 14 Feb. 1873) beginning 'Wiffie! I am sure'.

The *Diary* for 14 Feb. 1873 reads: 'To Mrs. Hatch to see rehearsal of *Checkmate* [by Andrew Halliday]. A Mr. Bainbrigg acted very well, as also De Sausmarez, Tylee, and Arthur Hatch as page. After returning, I wrote a prologue for Wilfred and Beatrice [Hatch] to speak.'

First published (in type and facsimile of MS.) in *Strand Magazine*, Apr. 1898, in Beatrice Hatch's article 'Lewis Carroll'. It was reprinted (in facsimile) in Isa Bowman's *The Story of Lewis Carroll* (1899), p. 122, and in Sotheran's Catalogue 796 (July 1925), No. 366. It may be found in the original edition of this *Handbook* (1931) on pp. 206–7; in De Sausmarez's article 'Early Theatricals at Oxford', *Nineteenth Century*, Feb. 1932; and is included in *Collected Verse* (1932), pp. 111–12, and *Nonesuch*, p. 826 (739).

94. Vision of the Three T's (1873) [74

THE VISION | OF | THE THREE T'S. | A THRENODY | BY | THE AUTHOR OF | 'THE NEW BELFRY'. | 'Call you this, baching of your friends?' | [*A view of the Tunnel*] | *West view of the new Tunnel.* |

Oxford: James Parker and Co.: 1873.: (eights) 12°: pp. 37+[3], signn. [B] C⁸, D⁴: size 6 11/16 × 4 5/8 in. CONTENTS: p. 1, half-title | The Vision | of | the three T's | : 3, title as above, within a thin line border: 5, contents: 7–37, the text in three chapters, beginning 'Chapter I. A conference' and ending 'hook it'.:

[1] Imprint in the centre, | Oxford: | by E. B. Gardner, E. Pickard Hall, and J. H. Stacy, | Printers to the University, | Issued in brick-red paper covers. p. [1] which reproduces the title, having at the bottom outside the border | 'Price Ninepence.' |

—— The second edition.   [75

This was issued as part of *Notes by an Oxford Chiel* (1874) (see No. 80), and also separately: and only differs from the first edition by the words Second Edition added with a short line above and below, both on title-page and wrapper. It still bore the date 1873. Collingwood states that there were *three* editions in this year 1873.

The Three T's are the Tea chest, i.e. Belfry, the Trench at the south-east corner of Tom Quad as part of the south side of the quadrangle, and the Tunnel, the double-arched entrance to the Cathedral at the west end of the last-named. What with an Angler, a Hunter, a Professor, 'One distraught' (Jeeby, as in the *New Belfry*), and a tutor, much humorous criticism is made of these three features of the Quadrangle. Two ballads are also introduced with effect, *The Wandering Burgess*, 'a dumpish ditty' beginning 'Our Willie had been sae lang awa' (p. 15), and *A Bachanalian Ode* beginning 'Here's to the Freshman of bashful eighteen!' (p. 36). A passage on p. 10 about kingfishers and goldfish gave some offence at the Deanery, but the language is studiously moderate. The exuberant fancy which plays round three very limited subjects is striking. The piece may be called a parody of Walton's *Compleat Angler*.   F. M.

Dodgson notes on 19 Mar. 1873: 'The new West entrance to the Cathedral was revealed today and almost rivals the Belfry in ugliness! At night began a manuscript on the subject, which I think of calling *The Vision of the Three T's*.' Next day was that on which the 'adventure' in the skit was supposed to have happened—during the performance of Bach's 'Passion-Music' in the Cathedral 'to about 1200 people. I did not go. I think it a pity churches should be so used'.

On 24 Mar.: 'Drew on wood the small view of the new entrance to the Cathedral, for title-page of pamphlet.' Dodgson does not illustrate his own skit—for the drawing shows railway lines, and Piscator says (p. 21): 'But, Sir, I see no rails,' while the Lunatic answers: 'Patience, good Sir! For railing we look to the Public. The College doth but furnish sleepers.'

In my copy, which Andrew Lang gave to his future wife Leonora Blanche Alleyne in June 1873, he has written in pencil beside the last sentence quoted above: 'Some poplars along the river belonging to Ch. Ch. have just been cut down for sleepers.'

95. Objections (1873) [76

Objections, submitted to the Governing Body of Christ Church, Oxford, against certain proposed alterations in the Great Quadrangle.

[Oxford: Printed at the University Press]: 1873: (two) 4°: pp. 3+[1]. CONTENTS: p. 1, title, as above, followed by 32 lines of text: at head of the page is '[Printed for Private Circulation.]': 1–3, Objections, signed 'Charles L. Dodgson. Ch. Ch. May 16, 1873.': [1] 'Appendix', a passage from Ruskin's 'Stones of Venice', vol. i, p. 171, and a note.

Dodgson objected to (1) a lowering of the terrace in order to uncover the lower part of the shafts of the original (proposed) Cloisters; (2) the narrowing of the terrace; (3) a grass slope in the place of the terrace wall. (1) was carried out, and (2), but Dodgson won on his third contention: there is a low wall and no slope. There is of course nowhere any allusion to D.C.L.'s other criticisms of the Quadrangle (Nos. **71** and **74** above). The Ruskin quotation is made to support the objection to (2). The entrance to a Cathedral should be broad and by one large door, not a relatively small double archway. Dodgson must have enjoyed the passage quoted from Ruskin, where it is suggested that the paltry doors of many English Cathedrals 'look as if they were made, not for open egress, but for the surreptitious drainage of a stagnant congregation'. Rare, as most of the minor Oxford pieces are.

Dodgson returned to the attack in his letter 'Architecture in Oxford' published in the *Pall Mall Gazette*, 3 Nov. 1874, which helped to prevent the building of cloisters in the Great Quadrangle.

96. Discussion (1873) [77

A DISCUSSION | OF | THE VARIOUS | METHODS OF PROCEDURE | IN CONDUCTING | ELECTIONS. || [*ornament*] ||

Oxford: by E. B. Gardner, E. Pickard Hall, and J. H. Stacy, Printers to the University: 1873: (eights) 12°: pp. 15+[1]. CONTENTS: p. 1, title: 3, preface, signed 'C.L.D.' 'Ch. Ch., Dec. 18, 1873': 5, contents: 7–15, [1] the pamphlet in four chapters.

Beginning with this pamphlet, Dodgson occupied himself for a long time in elaborating an approximately perfect way of ascertaining the wishes of electors, where the candidates and issues are more than one. See Nos. *113, 167–9*, &c.

With inexorable logic he shows that election by simple or absolute majority, or by gradual elimination, or by a vote of 'no election', or by a simple system of marks, is, or rather may be, a failure. He proposes a modified system of marks, but confesses in the Preface that the piece was written and printed in great haste, probably in view of an impending College election.

In fact Dodgson found that he had accidentally omitted all mention of the Method of Nomination, and printed a leaf headed '§ 6, The Method of Nomination', and followed by 15 lines of text and a diagram, the verso being blank: the text begins 'In this method'. One copy of this leaf survives in the Bodleian Library, attached in error to the 1874 'Suggestions as to taking Votes'.

The only copy of the Discussion at present known was the author's own, marked with a few corrections, now in the possession of Mr. Parrish, so that it is difficult to be certain that it was ever in circulation. Rare.

Williams, ii. 23 (p. 99); *Parrish Catalogue*, p. 72; *Collingwood*, p. 434.

Still no further copy seems to have been found. The complete pamphlet (with ' The Method of Nomination' and Dodgson's MS. emendations) was reprinted by Duncan Black in his *The Theory of Committees and Elections* (1958), pp. 214–22.

Dodgson notes in his *Diary* for 13 Dec. 1873: 'Began writing a paper (which occurred to me last night) on "Methods of Election", in view of our election of a Lee's Reader in Physics and a Senior Student next Wednesday.' And on Thursday, 18th: 'Election of Baynes and Paget: we partly used my method.'

1874

97. *The Blank Cheque* (1874)   [79

THE BLANK CHEQUE, | A FABLE. | BY | THE AUTHOR OF | 'THE NEW BELFRY' | AND | 'THE VISION OF THE THREE T'S'. || [*a thin line*] | 'VELL, PERHAPS,' SAID SAM, 'YOU BOUGHT HOUSES, VICH IS DELICATE | ENGLISH FOR GOIN' MAD; OR TOOK TO BUILDIN', VICH IS A MEDICAL TERM | FOR BEIN' INCURABLE.' | [*a thin line*] ||

Oxford: James Parker and Co.: 1874: (eight) 12°: pp. 14+[2]: no signatures: size 6 11/16 × 4 5/8 in. CONTENTS: p. 1, half-title, a cancel leaf | The Blank Cheque, | a Fable. |: 3, title as above, within a thin line border: 5–14 the text: [1] 'Moral', eleven lines of text, then | Finis. |, a cancel leaf: [2] 'Oxford: E. Pickard Hall, and J. H. Stacy, Printers to the University.'

Issued in brick-red wrappers, the front of which is lettered as the title-page, with the addition below the thin line border of | Price Fourpence |. The other three pages of the wrapper are blank.

A comment on a proposal to authorize the building of the new Examination Schools before any plan or estimate had been prepared. This clever fable is full of topical allusions. Mrs. Nivers is about to take a holiday, and leaves her maid to select a new school for Angela, with power to select a plan, and if the housekeeper allows the estimates, to carry out the plan. This allegory refers to a decree proposed in Convocation at Oxford on 28 Nov. 1873, that the building of the new Examination Schools on the Angel Inn site in the High Street should be entrusted to a Delegacy of nine who should select a plan, submit estimates to the Curators of the Chest, and with their approval carry it out! This was drawing a Blank Cheque with a vengeance. By a decree passed on 20 Apr. 1874 much of the danger was averted.

Nivers is the University, John is perhaps John Mowbray, Burgess for the University. De Ciel is C. L. D(odgson). Mr. Prior Burgess may be Gathorne-Hardy, the senior Burgess. Harry Parry is Liddon, Pussy is Pusey, Weight is Dr. Samuel Wayte, President of Trinity, Chase is Dr. D. P. Chase, the Principal of St. Mary Hall, Freddy is Dr. Bulley, President of Magdalen, Benjy is Jowett, Arthur is Stanley. There is an allusion to the collapse of the roof of the new Museum. The Moral explains the purport of the fable—which might not have been clear to every voter. It is clear that Dodgson at first did not propose to include this rather crude piece in his 'Notes by an Oxford Chiel' (which see, No. 80), and its wrappers do not betray any connexion between the two; but at last he tacked it on to the other five. In most copies the Moral, like the half-title, is pasted on a stub, as though the original leaves were blank, and the insertion of the Moral an after-thought. This piece was reissued, not reprinted, as part of the 'Notes'. A proof of the title-page with corrections by Dodgson is facsimiled in B. H. Blackwell's Catalogue No. 250 (1929), p. 10. The quotation on the title-page is of course from Dickens's *Pickwick Papers*. F. M.

There is no record in the *Diaries* of when Dodgson actually wrote this, but he noted on 29 Jan. 1874: 'In the afternoon wrote a fair copy of the MS. of *The Blank Cheque* and sent it to the press.' And on 6 Feb. 'Received copies of *The Blank Cheque*.'

It was reprinted in *The Lewis Carroll Picture Book*, and may be found in *Nonesuch*, pp. 1170–6 (1054–9).

98. *Notes by an Oxford Chiel* (1874) [80

𝕹otes | by | an 𝕺xford 𝕮hiel. ||| [*lines*] | "𝕬 𝕮hiel's amang ye takin' notes, | 𝕬nd, faith, he'll prent it." [*line*] |||

Oxford: James Parker and Co.: '1865–1874' [i.e. 1874]: (eights) 12°: pp. [154], see the separate pieces. CONTENTS: p. [1] title, within a line border: [2] 'Oxford: by E. Pickard Hall and J. H. Stacy, Printers to the University.': [3] contents: the fourth page is blank: then follow the six separate pieces as below.

(The following description of the six pieces is as in Williams's *Bibliography* (1924) and preferred as more informative than the descriptions on the plan of the Handbook.) (F. M.)

I (*Evaluation*)

P. 1, half-title: 2, blank: 3, title | The New Method | of | Evaluation | as applied to π. | [*thin small line*] | 'Little Jack Horner | sat in a corner, | eating a Christmas pie'. | [*thin small line*] | First printed in 1865. | Oxford: James Parker and Co. | 1874. | [*all within a thin line border*]: 4, imprint in centre | Oxford: | By E. Pickard Hall and J. H. Stacy, Printers to the University. |: 5, contents: 6, blank: 7–16, the text.

II (*Dynamics*)

P. i, half-title: ii, blank: iii, title | The Dynamics | of a | Parti-cle.| [*thin small line*] | ''Tis strange the mind, that very fiery particle, | should let itself be snuff'd out by an article' | [*thin small line*] | First printed in 1865. | Oxford: | James Parker and Co. | 1874. | [*all within a thin line border*]: iv, imprint in centre | Oxford: | By E. Pickard Hall and J. H. Stacy, | Printers to the University. | : v–vi, introduction, dated June 1865: 7, contents: 8, blank: 9–24, the text.

III. (*Facts, &c.*)

P. 1, half-title: 2, blank: 3, title | Facts, Figures, and | Fancies, | relating to | The Elections to the Hebdomadal Council, | The Offer of the Clarendon Trustees, | and | the Proposal to convert the Parks | into Cricket-grounds. | [*small line*] 'Thrice the brinded cat hath mewed.' | [*thin line*] | First printed in 1866–1868. | Oxford: | James Parker and Co. | 1874. | [*all within a thin line border*]: 4, *imprint in centre* | Oxford: | E. Pickard Hall and J. H. Stacy, | Printers to the University | : 5–8, introductory: 9–19, 'The Elections to the Hebdomadal Council': 20, blank: 21–4, 'The Offer of the Clarendon Trustees.': 25–9, 'The Deserted Parks.': 30, blank.

IV. (*New Belfry*)

P. 1, half-title: 2, blank: 3, title | The New Belfry | of | Christ Church, Oxford. | A Monograph | by | D. C. L. | 'A thing of beauty is a joy for ever' | [*diagram of a square, size 1⅛ in. square*] | 'East view of the New Belfry, Ch. Ch., as seen from the Meadow.' | [*thin line*] | second thousand. | [*thin line*] | Oxford: | James Parker and Co. | 1873. | [*all within a thin line border*]: 4, blank: 5, contents: 6, blank: 7–23, the text: 24, *imprint in centre*, Oxford: | By T. Combe, M.A., E. B. Gardner, E. Pickard Hall, and J. H. Stacy, | Printers to the University. |

V. (*Three T's*)

P. 1, half-title: 2, blank: 3, title | The Vision | of | the Three T's. | a Threnody | by | the Author of | 'The New Belfry.' | 'Call you this, Baching of your friends?' | [*small view of a double tunnel*] | [*thin line*] | Second Edition | [*thin line*] | Oxford: | James Parker and Co. | 1873. | 4, blank: 5, contents: 6, blank: 7–37, the text: 38, *imprint in centre* | Oxford: | by E. B. Gardner, E. Pickard Hall, and J. H. Stacy, | Printers to the University. |

VI. (*Blank Cheque*)

P. 1, half-title: ', blank: 3, title | The Blank Cheque, | A Fable. | By | the Author of | 'The New Belfry' | and | 'The Vision of the Three T's.' | [*short thin line*] | 'Vell, perhaps,' said Sam, 'you bought houses, vich is delicate | English for goin' mad; or took to buildin', vich is a medical term | for bein' incurable.' | *short thin line*] | Oxford: James Parker and Co. | 1874 [*all within a thin line border*]: 4, blank: 5–14, the text: 15, Moral, *and at foot* 'Finis': 16, *imprint in centre* | Oxford: | E. Pickard Hall, and J. H. Stacy, | Printers to the University.|

Issued in green cloth. Back blank except for gilt line at the top and bottom. Front cover has | Notes | by | an Oxford Chiel. | in the centre, and four separate lines forming a border, joined at the corners by four dots, all in gilt. Back cover is blank except for a similar border. All edges cut and gilt. Endpapers yellow.

This volume is composed of six pamphlets (see Nos. *40–41, 51, 61, 56, 88, 94, 97*), five having been before published separately. No fresh matter was added to the text in any case. The four extra pages consist, as shown, of a common title for the pamphlets, and a table of contents. As will be observed from the collation above, the six pamphlets in this bound volume are not the original editions, except in the case of *The Blank Cheque*, and *Facts, Figures and Fancies*, which latter was put together and first issued as part of these *Notes*.

The *Evaluation, Dynamics*, and *Facts* are reprints (or prints) specially made for the *Notes of an Oxford Chiel*. The *New Belfry, Three T's*, and the *Blank Cheque* are reissues, though called in the *New Belfry* '2nd thousand' and in the *Three T's* '2nd. edition'. It appears that none of the six pieces when issued in collected form as the *Notes*, bear any wrappers of brick-red paper, but when it was decided to issue them separately, then in the case of the three reprints appropriate wrappers were printed indicating that they were part of the *Notes*, and in the case of the reissues their original wrappers were left as they were, except that all six bore a price. The first two pieces and the last have no signatures, but all have half-titles. The wrappers of the reprints bear on p. 1 'Notes by an Oxford Chiel', and the motto, and below them the title, imprint, and surrounding line of the title-page proper, and at the foot a price (*Evaluation* Price fourpence, *Dynamics* . . . Six pence, *Facts* . . . Eightpence). Pp. 2 and 3 are blank; p. 4 bears the general title of the *Notes*, and a list of the six pieces, both the *New Belfry* and the *Three T's* being in their 'second thousand', *not* edition. The wrappers of the three last pieces have on p. 1 a mere repetition of the original title and the prices (Ninepence, Ninepence, Fourpence) and pp. 2–4 are blank.

The unique *Notes* owned by Mr. Parrish (No. **80***) which contains the first five pieces was probably an early proof copy, made and bound up before the sixth piece had been admitted, and before any general title and list of Contents had been set up; also the title-page of the *New Belfry* bore the date 1872, *not* 1873. Mr. Parrish possesses also a copy of the six pieces bound up without any general title, presumably a late proof copy.

The whole of the *Notes*, with new introduction to each piece by Lewis Sergeant, are reprinted at pp. 40–124 of Collingwood's *Lewis Carroll Picture Book* (1899).

It may be here noted that the *Academy* of 7 Jan. 1899 contains a long anonymous article on pp. 19–22 with the title 'Lewis Carroll's Suppressed Booklets'. The writer, acting on the assumption that the six booklets which make up the *Notes* were suppressed, gives a full account of each with quotations and explanations, and states that 'for some reason . . . Mr. Dodgson was led to withdraw every copy which the publishers had in their possession'. The Editors of the present volume can only say that each part of the *Notes* was freely published at the price of a few pence and that of more than one part, more than a thousand copies were sold. As they were local in interest and full of half-concealed allusions to Oxford persons and matters, it is probable that smaller quantities were printed than would otherwise have been reasonable, but that there was any justification for the heading of the article in the *Academy* they cannot at present believe. Every one at Oxford knew who wrote these pieces, for the anonymity is of the thinnest kind, and their separate publication extended over ten years.   F. M.

The only *Diary* notes about this volume occur on 10 Mar. and 22 June 1874: 'Settled on a general title . . . viz. *Notes by an Oxford Chiel*', and 'In the last few days I have brought out . . . *Notes by an Oxford Chiel*'.

99. *Facts, Figures, and Fancies* (1874)   [81

Facts, Figures, and Fancies is strictly a part of *Notes by an Oxford Chiel*, and only issued separately after the *Notes* were published. It has been described therefore in the foregoing article.

This item, *Evaluation of π* and *Dynamics of a Particle* were specially reprinted to be included in *Notes by an Oxford Chiel*—but it is not certain from the reference in Dodgson's *Diary* (22 June 1874) when the separate pamphlets in this reprint became available.

100. Suggestions as to taking Votes (1874)   [82

SUGGESTIONS | AS TO THE BEST METHOD OF | TAKING VOTES, | WHERE MORE THAN | TWO ISSUES ARE TO BE VOTED ON. ||| [*a small ornament*] ||

Oxford: by E. Pickard Hall and J. H. Stacy, Printers to the University: 1874: (four) 12°: pp. 7+[1]. CONTENTS: p. 1, title: 2, a preface signed 'C. L. D.' and dated 'Ch. Ch., June 13, 1874.': 5-7, the proposed plan.

The plan proposed to the Governing Body of Christ Church is that every voter should have all the issues to be voted on (including 'that nothing be done') before him, and should indicate his preference, with certain further directions and modifications. Dodgson refers to his former paper (No. *96* above, 1873), but has 'since seen reason to modify some of the views therein expressed'. The aim is that the real opinion of the majority of voters should be clearly ascertained. Perhaps every copy contains a deletion in Dodgson's violet ink of the unnecessary word 'placed' in the last line of p. 5. The Suggestions are in five sections; the extra slip (§ 6) described by Williams in his *Bibliography* (1924) belongs to No. *96* above. See No. *113*.

Reprinted in Duncan Black's *The Theory of Committees and Elections* (1958), pp. 222-4.

101. Examples in Arithmetic (1874)   [83

EXAMPLES | IN | ARITHMETIC | COLLECTED BY | CHARLES L. DODGSON, M.A. | STUDENT AND MATHEMATICAL LECTURER OF CH. CH. OXFORD || [*a line*] || [at the top of the page is '[Unpublished]'.

(Oxford): 1874: (sixteen) 12°: pp. i-iv, 5-31+[1]. CONTENTS: p. i, title: ii, 'Oxford. By E. Pickard Hall and J. H. Stacy, Printers to the University': iii-iv, 'Contents' a list of seventeen subjects: 5-31, the Examples, or sums.

A plain and unadorned set of examples, without solutions; but of the seventeen subjects in the complete plan, five are wholly and eight are partly omitted, without explanation! Also the use of asterisks in Part II is not explained, and certain fractions are called 'continuous' in the list of Contents and 'continued' in the text. These mistakes are very unusual in so careful a writer as Dodgson, and show that the printing was hurried through. Mr. Parrish has a copy with all the answers entered in the author's own hand, and in his catalogue gives a facsimile of pp. 26-27 from his copy.

Preliminary Algebra and Euclid Bk. V (1874)

'Preliminary Algebra, and Euclid Book V. Oxford: Printed at the University Press. 1874.'

So in Collingwood, p. 435, but no copy is known, and the title is probably a loose description of No. *102*, below (Euclid, Book V). This latter was published by Parker, but printed at the University Press.

102. Euclid, Book V (1874)   [84

EUCLID, BOOK V. | PROVED ALGEBRAICALLY | SO FAR AS IT RELATES TO | *COMMENSURABLE MAGNITUDES* | TO WHICH IS PREFIXED | A SUMMARY | OF ALL THE NECESSARY ALGEBRAICAL OPERATIONS, | ARRANGED IN ORDER OF DIFFICULTY. || BY | CHARLES L. DODGSON, M.A., | SENIOR STUDENT AND MATHEMATICAL LECTURER | OF CH. CH. OXFORD. |

Oxford: James Parker and Co.: 1874: 8°: pp. viii+62+[2]: signn. A⁴, B–E⁸. CONTENTS: p. i, half-title: iii, title: iv, 'Oxford: E. Pickard Hall and J. H. Stacy, Printers to the University', v–vi, preface: vii, contents: 1–62, the work, in six parts or chapters. Bound in green cloth, with title in gold on the front cover.

This treatise bears hardly any relation to the earlier pamphlet with a similar title issued in 1868 (No. **49**). In the present case, Part I is occupied with 'Preliminary Algebra' then follow the Propositions of Book V, then the Enunciations, Definitions, and Axioms, with an Appendix on Euclid's definition of Proportion, but the treatment as well as the order is here different. No reference to the former piece is made in the Preface.

Dodgson was writing this on 25 Mar. 1874, but was working on *Euclid I, II* by 3 July.

103. Lize's Avonturen in het Wonderland (1874)
(Early but Abridged Dutch Edition)   [115

Lize's Avonturen in't Wonderland.

[No title-page, but heading to p. 1 of text as given in the collation below.]¹ (Niemegen): [1881?]: 4°: pp. 20+4 plates: size 10¾×9½ in.: signn. 1, 2⁴, 3¹+ four coloured plates. CONTENTS: p. [1] blank: p. [2] frontispiece: pp. 1–20 the text: p. 1 is headed | Lize's Avonturen in't Wonderland | [a thin line] | followed by twenty lines of text beginning 'De kleine Lize': p. 20 ends 'geluisterd naar': and below is | Lize's Avonturen in't Wonderland. | [a thin line] |. There are three pages of very indifferent coloured lithographs (by Enrick and Binger) in addition to the frontispiece, all being enlarged reproductions of Tenniel's drawings. The frontispiece has two pictures, one above the other, the upper one (size 4½×7³⁄₁₀ in.) being the Fish Footman delivering the invitation to play croquet (p. 77 in the original edition), and the lower one (also size $4\frac{1}{2} \times 7\frac{3}{10}$ in.) the interior of the kitchen with the Duchess and the baby (p. 81 in the original edition). Plate No. 1 facing p. 8 of the text is made up of three reproductions from the original edition, one (size $4\frac{1}{2} \times 7\frac{3}{10}$ in.) occupying the upper half of the plate, being The Mad Tea-party (p. 97 in the original edition) while the lower half is divided equally between Putting the Dormouse into the teapot (p. 110 in the original edition) on the left, and the three gardeners (p. 113 in the original edition) on the right, the size of each of the lower reproductions being $4\frac{1}{2} \times 3\frac{11}{16}$ in. Plate No. 2 (size $8\frac{4}{5} \times 7\frac{2}{5}$ in.), facing p. 11, shows the trial scene (p. 186 in the original edition), but the artist has introduced the Queen into the picture, presumably to make it rectangular, the upper right-hand portion in the original being occupied by text. Plate No. 3 (size $8\frac{4}{5} \times 2\frac{2}{5}$ in.), facing p. 14, represents the Queen saying 'Off with his head' (p. 117 in the original edition).

Issued in a grey paper case. The front of the case has a coloured lithograph with | Lize's | Avonturen | in het | Wonderland | naar het Engelsch | in red on a large black circle: In the top left-hand corner is a picture of a gardener, in the top right-hand corner is the Mad Hatter: in the bottom left-hand corner is Alice and a crown, and in the bottom right-hand corner is the March Hare and some playing-cards. Below in a ribbon-like rectangle is | Blomhert & Timmerman | Nijmegen |: The whole is enclosed within a double rustic border, and below this border in the right-hand corner is | Lith Enrick & Binger | . Pp. 2 and 3 of the case are white in colour and blank: p. 4 of the case | Bij Blomhert & Timmerman te Niemegen verscheen | and below an advertisement of his books. The edges are plain and cut level with the case. (The Bodleian copy, from which the above collation was made, appears to have been shaved to fit the case into which it has been bound.)

I do not regard this book as of much importance, while curious in its way; it has small value or interest to a collector of the first editions of Lewis Carroll, for it is obviously abridged, and therefore lacks continuity, or else has had matter introduced to make continuity. It has therefore none of the merits attaching to the French, Italian, and German editions issued by Macmillan, who by the way inform me that if the date 1881 is correct the rights of translation had lapsed at that time.

The chief claims of this Dutch edition to notice rest on the fact that Mr. Collingwood mentions it in the list of books at the end of his *Life and Letters of Lewis Carroll*, and also that a copy has a place in the Bodleian Library among the works of Lewis Carroll.

S. H. W.

As far as Chapter 8 the tale is given with some fullness, but with omission of the songs, but Chapters 9 to 12 are almost entirely omitted. The title and plates are lithographed by Messrs. Enrick and Binger. The text begins 'De Kleine Lize zat op een heel warmen Zomerdag met haar zuster op een bank in den tuin' (*sic*), which shows how paraphrastic the abridgement sometimes is. Neither the author's nor the translator's name is given. The book is rare in England.   F. M.

104. There was also a Danish version, published in 1875, according to Madan (*Supplement*, 1935, p. 11), but he does not describe it, and no copy is available for description here.

1875

105. Vivisection (1875)   [86

Vivisection as a sign of the Times.

A letter in the *Pall Mall Gazette*, 12 Feb. 1875 (headed as above), signed 'Lewis Carroll', beginning 'Sir,—The letter which appeared,' and dated 10 Feb., shows that Dodgson regarded vivisection as tending to the apotheosis of Self, and a significant accompaniment of State-enforced secular education, but he is able to quote not only Herbert Spencer, but also Mr. Squeers. The whole letter, occupying 62 lines in the *Gazette*, is reprinted by Collingwood in the *Life* (pp. 167–71).

This letter has already been included under contributions to the *Pall Mall Gazette* (No. 55) above, but it is repeated here on account of the following entry in Dodgson's *Diary* for 4 Mar. 1875: 'Heard from Mrs. Mosley, secretary of the Northern Branch of the Society for the Prevention of Cruelty to Animals, asking leave to reprint my letter to the *Pall Mall* on a fly-leaf to circulate.'

Dodgson gave his permission—but no copy of the fly-leaf has so far been traced.

106. Fallacies about Vivisection (1875)   [87

SOME POPULAR FALLACIES | ABOUT | VIVISECTION. |||
by | LEWIS CARROLL. |||| Printed for private circulation only | Oxford, June, 1875. |

Oxford: 1875: (ten) 8°: (size $7\frac{2}{3} \times 4\frac{2}{3}$ in.): pp. [1]+16+[1]. The first five words are in thick type: the last eight are underlined. CONTENTS: p. [1], title, as above: 2–16, the text: the rest is blank. All edges are plain and cut.

So far as concerns the separate publication of *Some Popular Fallacies about Vivisection*, I have been unable to trace any history to supplement the above collation. It is not mentioned in Collingwood's chronological list, but in the text of his *Life and Letters* (p. 165) he mentions that Dodgson wrote an article with the above title in 1875, which, after being refused by the *Pall Mall Gazette*, was accepted by the Editor of the *Fortnightly Review*. An examination of the files of the *Review* for that year reveals the article in the issue for 1 June. It commences on p. 847, headed | Some Popular Fallacies about Vivisection. | and ends on p. 854 with below on the right hand | Lewis Carroll | The pamphlet collated above is an exact reprint of the article in the *Fortnightly Review*, and is probably one of a few copies struck off at Dodgson's instigation for circulation among his friends. When the above note appeared in my *Bibliography* (1924), doubt was expressed in some quarters as to whether this pamphlet was a genuine issue of the article in the *Fortnightly Review*, June 1875. I have had no doubt myself, but since the question was raised it is gratifying to be able to state definitely that it was issued by Dodgson, and under his direction. At a sale at Hodgson's on 26 Mar. 1931 a copy was sold corresponding in all respects with the one above, and with it was Dodgson's own proof copy, with directions in violet ink in his hand; this definitely settles the authenticity of the above item.

The proof copy was without the wrapper, and across the title at the top of p. [1] (really p. 2 according to the pagination) is written Press | 150 copies to be printed | title-page | no corrections | The paper is identical with the ordinary issued copy accompanying it, and with the copy collated above in my possession.

This is a rare pamphlet, since only 150 were printed in 1875, and I think few can have survived. The title had been reproduced on p. 42 of the *Bibliography*.

It may be noted that the paging is most unusual, the odd numbers occurring on the verso of the leaves, so that p. 1 is at the back of the title-page, which would otherwise have been considered the front wrapper.   S. H. W.

The pamphlet is a serious attempt to discredit vivisection, which fails to be fully effective from the juxtaposition of pitiless logic with warm and generous sentiment. He counters no fewer than thirteen positions or theses which he regards as fallacious, but regards the infliction of pain on animals as in some cases justifiable, under proper legislation. He argues on p. 7 that the evil charged against vivisection consists chiefly in the effect produced on the operator.

                                                        F. M.

No light is thrown on the pamphlet by Dodgson's *Diary*, but Collingwood's statement about the periodical publication is substantiated on 19 May 1875: 'Heard from Mr. John Morley, editor of the *Fortnightly Review*, that he accepts my article on "Some

Popular Fallacies about Vivisection". It had been sent to him through Miss F. P. Cobbe, having been first offered to the *Pall Mall*, but declined on the ground of the fallacies being unheard of, though eight out of the thirteen came from a *Pall Mall* article!'

For the validity and importance of Dodgson's statement in the campaign against vivisection, see C. S. Lewis's pamphlet *Vivisection* [1948], p. 10.

Dodgson's essay is reprinted in *Nonesuch*, pp. 1189–1201 (1071–82), with letter of 18 July 1924 from Madan to M. L. Parrish pointing out the misquotation of Terence.

107. Euclid, Books I, II (1875) [88

EUCLID ‖ BOOKS I, II | EDITED BY | CHARLES L. DODGSON, M.A. | SENIOR STUDENT AND MATHEMATICAL LECTURER | OF CH. CH., OXFORD ‖ [*a line*] ‖ [At the top of the page is | *NOT YET PUBLISHED* | [*a line*] ‖

Oxford: 1875: (eights) 12°: pp. [8]+102+[2]: signn. A⁴, B–G⁸, H⁴. CONTENTS: p. [1] half-title: [4] a diagram: [5] title, as above: [6] 'Oxford. By E. Pickard Hall and J. H. Stacy, Printers to the University': [7] Preface: 1–76, 77–102, the text: but pp. 14, 34, 38, 54 are blank. Bound in reddish-brown cloth, with a printed label on the side.

Dodgson's idea of the least rectification of the original form of Euclid, Books I and II, which would render them satisfactory for modern use. The changes include the addition of some axioms, postulates, and 'conventions', and some alterations of language and form. Book I is divided into seven chapters, and a diagram before the title exhibits the logical sequence of the theorems of the first book. The published edition, which contains many alterations, especially in the Introduction, did not come out till 1882 (No. *156*): meanwhile Dodgson circulated this impression among friends, and produced *Euclid and his Modern Rivals* in 1879. Rare.

In his *Diary* for 25 Mar. 1874 Dodgson noted: 'Electros of Euclid I, II arrived', and he was planning to work on the book during the Long Vacation of that year. But there is no mention of this edition printed for private circulation.

108. For a contemplated new edition of *Castle Croquet* in 1875, see No. *50* (1866).

The page of proof described by Madan turns out to be a page set up by Macmillan for *Alice's Puzzle Book* in Mar. 1875. Dodgson got no farther than this page—'I enclose the *Castle Croquet* rules to try the experiment on. Would you get a page of it set up in whatever style you think will look best?' he wrote on 9 Mar. 1875. On 19 Mar. he is suggesting titles for the book, for which Tenniel had agreed to supply a frontispiece: but there is no further reference to it.

1876

109. Song for 'Puss in Boots' (1876)

No copy of this item is recorded anywhere, and it is only known from the entry in Dodgson's *Diary* for 13 Jan. 1876 when he was staying with the Barclays at Brighton: 'The children went to help in acting *Puss in Boots* at Mrs. Head's, for which I wrote them a song, and got fifty copies printed to distribute among the audience.'

110-112. Professorship of Comparative Philology   [95-97

PROFESSORSHIP OF COMPARATIVE PHILOLOGY.

Three quarto leaves (size about $10\frac{1}{4} \times 7\frac{3}{4}$ in.) bear the above title, dated respectively 4, 12, and 14 Feb. 1876, and signed 'Charles L. Dodgson' 'Ch. Ch.', with the date.

110. No. 1. The title is followed by a copy of the proposed decree of 15 Feb., and the letter beginning 'There are one or two points'. [95].

111. No. 2. The title is followed by a line, and the letter begins, 'There seems to be good reason'. [96].

112. No. 3. The title is followed by a motto ('Be just before you are generous') and a line. The letter begins 'Since the issue'. Printed on both sides, the other two being printed on one side only. None have any imprint. [97].

The University proposed to relieve Professor Max Müller of the duties of his chair, and to appoint a deputy Professor with half the Professor's salary. Dodgson in these papers objects chiefly to the inadequate remuneration of the deputy, and avoids all personal considerations. The decree was, however, carried by 94 to 35.

Williams, ii. 29 (p. 100); *Parrish Catalogue*, p. 80; *Collingwood*, p. 436 (as if one paper): Bodleian, F. Madan (with additional proof of No. 1, bearing no day of the month, sent round to friends for suggestions). The above own all three: Harvard has the first and second papers, S. H. Williams the third only.

According to his *Diary*, Dodgson wrote No. 1 on 3 Feb. and it 'came out' on 5 Feb., wrote No. 2 on 12 Feb., and sent No. 3 'to all Common Rooms, and had copies distributed at the door of the Convocation-house' on 15 Feb., the day when the question came before Convocation.

113. Method of taking Votes (1876)   [93

A METHOD | OF | TAKING VOTES | ON MORE THAN | TWO ISSUES | '[As I hope to investigate this subject further . . . return it to me any time before   ]' | [A line] | [At the head of the title-page is '[*Not yet published*]'

[Oxford:] March, 1876: (ten) 8vo: pp. 20. CONTENTS: p. 1, title, note and date: 3-20, the Method, in six sections with ten tables.

This is an improved anonymous form of No. **82** (1874), still more elaborate, and still less practicable. The note on the title is printed in full in Williams's *Bibliography* (1924), and by Collingwood.

The blank space is in at least one copy filled in with 'June 1876', in writing, and in another with 'April 1878'. The Author's name does not occur anywhere. On p. 20 '§ 5' is an error for '§ 6'.

114. The Bodleian has a cyclostyled leaf dated 'Dec. 7, 1877', in which Dodgson asks for suggestions: it begins 'Would you kindly consider', and is signed 'C. L. Dodgson'. [94].

On 23 Feb. 1876 Dodgson wrote in his *Diary*: 'Spent the after-noon in writing out a new *Method for Taking Votes* which I sent to the Press to be set up in slip.'

Duncan Black reprints this, and 'The Cyclostyled Sheet' in his *The Theory of Committees and Elections* (1958), pp. 224-34.

115. Hunting of the Snark (1876)   [89

THE HUNTING | OF THE SNARK | an 𝔄gony | in 𝔈ight 𝔉its || BY | LEWIS CARROLL | AUTHOR OF 'ALICE'S ADVENTURES IN WONDER-LAND', and 'THROUGH THE | LOOKING-GLASS', | *WITH NINE ILLUSTRA-TIONS* | BY | HENRY HOLIDAY || [*at foot:—*] [The Right of Translation and Reproduction is Reserved.]

London: Macmillan and Co.: 1876: (fours) 8°: size 7⅛ × 4¹³⁄₁₆ in.: pp. xi + [3] + 83 + [3], signn, [*a*], *b*, B-L⁴, M². CONTENTS: p. i, half-title | The Hunting of the Snark |: iv, frontispiece: v, title, as above: vi, imprint in the centre, London: R. Clay, Sons and Taylor, Printers, Bread Street Hill. |: vii, three lines of dedication 'to a dear Child' over four four-line stanzas, see below: ix-xi, preface: [xiii] list of contents, in Eight Fits or Chapters: each Fit or Chapter has a half-title and a following blank page: 1-83, the poem: [1] imprint, exactly as on p. vi, above: [2] blank except for | [Turn over. | at the bottom right-hand corner: [3] Macmillan's advertisements of Lewis Carroll's works, with press opinions.

Generally issued in buff-coloured cloth, dark-grey end-papers. Black letter-ing along the back, | The. Hunting. of. the. Snark | The front cover has six black lines around the border, broken by ten circles at equal intervals, the space within these lines is devoted entirely to a picture of the Bellman on the yard-arm of a ship, a large sail on the mast bears the words | The | Hunting | of the | Snark | all printed in black. The back cover has the same border, but the picture in the centre is that of a large buoy in a rough sea bearing the words | Was | a | Boojum |. All edges gilt. There are many variations. Some copies were bound in vellum, probably for presentation. Mr. Parrish of Philadelphia, U.S.A. has one bound in green and gold, and occasionally copies are found in crimson and gold. According to Lewis Carroll himself copies were issued variously in light blue, dark blue, light green, dark green, scarlet and white, all having the ship and bell buoy in gold. (See note to *Alice in Wonderland*, 1865 (No. 30) and *Six Letters* (1924), p. 4.)

F. M.

It is doubtful whether any variant coloured bindings were for sale, other than buff or red: the other colours seem to have been bound specially for Dodgson, who wrote to Macmillan on 21 Mar. 1876 ordering : 'IOO in red and gold, 20 in dark blue and gold, 20 in white vellum and gold', he also sent 'four miscellaneous covers to be used for binding 4 copies for me', and noted that 'dark green' was also available.

Publication. The exact date is uncertain: Dodgson asked Macmillan (letter to Craik, 17 Jan. 1876) to advertise *Snark* 'to be published on the 1st. of April—Surely that is the fittest day for it to appear'. He went to London on|Wednesday, 29 Mar. to write in '80 presentation copies' which were just ready. The copy sold at the sale of his books in 1898 bears his signature and the date '30 March 1876'. Macmillan's record 29th as publication day.

Evolution of the Book. Full details will be found in the *Diaries*, and of interest is a reference in 'Alice on the Stage' (see *Lewis Carroll Picture Book*) and in an article by Henry Holiday published in *The Academy* on 29 Jan. 1898. Briefly, the first line (which is the last of the poem—'For the Snark *was* a Boojum, you see!') came into Dodgson's head as he was out walking at Guildford on 18 July 1875, and the rest of the stanza four days later. He 'completed' the poem in 88 stanzas on 6 Nov. 1875, and intended to publish it that Christmas, with a frontispiece only. Earlier still it was meant simply to be one of the poems in *Sylvie and Bruno*. Dodgson continued to add to the poem until 19 Jan. 1876, by which time it consisted of the present 141 stanzas—the last stanza, written that day, being that beginning 'In the matter of Treason'.

On 12 Feb. 1876 Dodgson noted: 'At night wrote a new Preface for *The Snark*.' R. L. G.

The Book. The poem describes with infinite humour the impossible voyage of an improbable crew to find an inconceivable creature. It has been called the 'Odyssey of the Nonsensical', 'a masterpiece with more nonsense to the foot than could be found in an acre of lesser stuff'. It has been noticed that all the crew are B's (Bellman, Baker, Butcher, Beaver, Barrister, Bonnet-maker, Boots, Broker, and Billiard-marker) and even the Snark was a Boojum, after all. The poem is marked off from the two *Alice* books by not being written primarily for children.

Has the book a meaning? Or none at all? The fullest consideration of the question is in 'A commentary on the Snark, by Snarkophilus Snobbs', pp. 87–101 of a special Christmas number of *Mind* (1901), really an elaborate and ingenious skit by Dr. F. Schiller of Oxford, in which he proves the Hunting to be the pursuit of the Absolute. Others think it to be the pursuit of Fame, or Fortune, or Popularity, or the North Pole, or a burlesque of the Tichborne case, or an allegory, or the search after Happiness! Mr. Devereux Court in 1911 considered it a satire on a board of directors. The author consistently denied that the poem had any meaning whatever (see Collingwood's *Life*, p. 173), but allowed that 'words mean more than we mean to express when we use them'. He regarded 'Snark' as compounded of 'Snail and Shark' (*Strand Magazine*, Apr. 1898).

The dedicatory poem (in very small type) consists of four four-line stanzas, beginning 'Girt with a boyish garb for boyish task', addressed to Gertrude Chataway, one of Dodgson's girl friends, as is revealed by the curious double acrostic in the verses. They are repeated with slight changes in *Rhyme? and Reason?* (1883), showing that that book also was dedicated to her; and again in the 1919 edition of *Phantasmagoria*, with the same implication. They were written 24–25 Oct. 1875.

The illustrations are noteworthy as a triumph of art over almost intractable material. It is odd that Holiday should pretend (*loco citato*) that in deference to Dodgson's wishes he abstained from figuring the Boojum—for it is obviously portrayed in the last plate, for those who have eyes. In the illustration of the Hunting on p. 41 the two female figures are Hope and Care referred to in the text on p. 40. The engraver throughout was Joseph Swain.

[Holiday did, in fact, supply a picture of the Snark, but Dodgson refused to include it, writing 'that it was a beautiful beast but that he had made the Snark strictly unimaginable and desired him to remain so'.

The picture was shown in the Centenary Exhibition in London in 1932 (item 473) and published for the first time in *The Illustrated London News*, 9 July 1932.]

In the Preface Dodgson explains some words of the Jabberwock, as that *fruminous* is fuming and furious, that the 'i' in *slithy* is pronounced as eye (which by the way differentiates the word from the dialectal *slithy* meaning slippery), and so on. The word 'uffish' occurs on p. 37.

The pagination is peculiar, in beginning on the last leaf of a sheet. The advertisements show that in Mar. 1876 *Alice* was in its forty-ninth thousand and the *Looking-Glass* in its thirty-eighth thousand.

In the first edition there is a misprint in the last stanza but one of the First Fit, where 'Baker' should read 'Banker'. [Not all copies.]

Other Editions, &c. The circulation reached 18,000 in 1882. In 1876 an American edition, reproduced (and much reduced) by photolithography (an early American example of the process) came out at Boston (James R. Osgood & Company), of which the Parrish Catalogue gives a collation. The *Hunting* was reprinted seventeen times between 1876 and 1908. A 'miniature' edition came out in Oct. 1910 and was reprinted five times before 1921.

In 1929 at the Hours Press at Chapelle Réauville, Eure, Miss Mary Cunard produced a French translation (*La Chasse au Snark*) by 'Aragon', who has not attempted to reproduce metre or rhythm.

F. M.

Chatto and Windus included *The Hunting of the Snark* in their Zodiac Books in 1941, with illustrations by Mervyn Peake. It has been included in several anthologies, such as *The Book of Nonsense* (1956) in Dent's Children's Illustrated Classics.

116. *Easter Greeting* (1876)   [90

|||| AN EASTER GREETING | TO | EVERY CHILD WHO LOVES | "𝔄lice." |||| [This title is in the centre of p. [1], surrounded by a double thin line border, the dimensions of which within the inner line are $4\frac{3}{10} \times 2\frac{1}{2}$ in.]

[Oxford]: 1876: (two) 16°: pp. [4]: size $5\frac{1}{8} \times 3\frac{1}{2}$ in. CONTENTS: p. [1] the title, as above: [2] the text in italic, beginning 'Dear Child' and ending 'kneeling', within a double line border: [3] the text continued in italic, beginning 'figures' and ending 'that is past!' signed below | Your affectionate Friend, | Lewis Carroll. | In the bottom left-hand corner is the date 'Easter, 1876,': p. [4] is blank. The whole of the first edition was printed in Oxford by Parker on E. Towgood's cream-laid large post fine paper, and was issued without wrappers.

In the note to this item in my edition of the *Bibliography* (1924), I stated that I thought it the rarest of the Carroll items excepting the *Alice* books. I now find it necessary to correct this statement. At the time, although I had seen many copies of the *Easter Greeting* only two were the first edition, all the others being subsequent editions. Search, stimulated perhaps by the attention drawn to it by the Bibliography, has produced others, so that though by no means common, it is no longer a great rarity. It appears to have been privately printed by Lewis Carroll for distribution among his many young friends. After repeated requests he allowed it to be printed for the public in 1880 by Macmillan without imprint, who made arrangements with Messrs. Harrison of London to sell the leaflet at one penny each. Macmillan reprinted it in 1881, again in 1883, and again in 1887.

This leaflet lends itself easily to forgery, specimens of which I have seen from time to time, more or less clumsy imitations, but the original may be distinguished, apart from the above collation, by the paper, which should bear the watermark of 'Towgood Fine'; also by the character of the paper, appearance of age, &c., and, further, on examination with a glass, certain defects due to wear, and condition of the type used, are apparent in the original which of course on comparison are not found in the forgery. Particular attention should also be paid to the dimensions within the border, given above, as I have seen fakes which could be distinguished by these measurements being wrong.

A reproduction of p. [1] of the presentation copy in my possession is given on p. 46 of the Bibliography (1924). The inscription is written in violet ink, which Lewis Carroll constantly used.

S. H. W.

On 5 Feb. 1876 Dodgson noted in his *Diary*: 'In the afternoon I wrote a large piece of MS. for *An Easter Letter* which I am again thinking of printing to insert in copies of my Easter book. I am afraid the religious allusions will be thought "out of season" by many, but I do not like to lose the opportunity of saying a few serious words to (perhaps) 20,000 children.' And on 22 Mar.: '2.30 a.m. I have been sitting up, finishing the MS. of a little "Easter Letter" to put into copies of *The Snark*.'

Copies of (presumably) the first issue were on sale, judging from Dodgson's letter to Craik on 18 May 1876: 'Please be prepared to sell *Easter Greetings* separately, if asked for; I have been asked if I will allow them to be sold, and of course I have no objection. You will know best what to charge: only remember that I want neither to gain nor lose by it. . . . Please send me another 200.'

R. L. G.

The first issue, as has been stated above, was printed at Oxford by Parker on paper bearing the watermark 'E. Towgood Fine.' Two presentation copies are known with the date 29 April, 1877 (*Williams*, p. 46, Quaritch Catalogue

418 [1928], article 530). There were at least ten (Nos. 1-10) issues and editions, and some of the tests which distinguish them are:

1. Pp. [2-3] Six spacings between paragraphs (as 3, 8, 9. Nos. 2, 5 want them).
2. Pp. [2-3] The eleven dashes in the text are one piece of type each (Nos. 1, 2, 10: not in two pieces as 3, 7, 9).
3. P. [2] 'Dear Child' (Nos. 1, 2, 3, 5, 10: not 'My Dear child' as 7, 9).
4. P. [3] 'gray-headed' (Nos. 1, 2, 10: not 'grey-headed' as 3, 7, 9).
5. P. [3] 'Righteousness shall arise' (Nos. 1, 2, 3, 5, 10: not as rightly 'Righteousness' shall 'arise').

The present *Easter Greeting*, of the title of which a facsimile is given in Williams's Bibliography, appears to be the first issue of a piece frequently reprinted, with or without authority. The writer has spent many hours on the ten issues known to him, putting them through tests, and has formed a tentative pedigree of dates and mutual connexion. An account of each follows taking this first issue as a standard for comparison.

1. This has been sufficiently described above.
2. (*c*. 1877) Title as No. 1, and letter dated Easter 1876, but the second line of p. 1 is '-To-', not 'To'. A peculiar issue, probably not printed at Oxford, nor authorized. The page and type are a little larger than No. 1, and the pages contain 4, 36, 37 lines. The real date may be 1877 or 1878. It makes the bad error of '*my turn*' for 'my *turn*' on p. 3, l. 12, destroying the right emphasis.
   Parrish Catalogue, p. 12, No. 1, with facsimile on p. 13: F. Madan (in a lambskin cover lettered in gold 'An Easter Greeting—Lewis Carroll').
3. (1880) Title as No. 1 and letter dated Easter, 1880. The first published edition, printed in London in 1880 for Messrs. Macmillan. Dodgson probably found that his genuine issue had been reprinted without authority, but why he reprinted in London, and not Oxford, is not known. With No. 2 it omits the comma after 'sadness' in p. 3, l. 28. (*Williams*, i. 32, p. 47; *Parrish Catalogue*, p. 12, No. 4; *Collingwood*, p. 436: F. Madan.)
4. (1881) In this year Macmillan published an issue, but no copy is identified. No. 5 may be an exemplar of this issue (*Macmillan's Catalogue*, 1901, p. 374).
5. (1882?) Mr. Parrish owns a copy presented on 17 Nov. 1882, by the author. Very similar to No. 1, and dated Easter, 1876, but this has closed-up paragraphs on pp. 2-3. It is printed on paper with the Towgood mark, and so may be supposed to be Oxford printing. (*Parrish Catalogue*, p. 12, No. 2, with facsimile of title on p. 14.)
6. (1885) In this year Macmillan published a reprint of No. 4 (*Macmillan's Catalogue* as above), but no copy has been identified.
7. (*c*. 1885?) A new edition, similar in appearance to No. 1, but undated, and with two important corrections. As it is printed on Towgood paper it seems to be an Oxford impression by Parker. For 'Dear Child' (p. 2, l. 1) there is 'My Dear Child' as in the final form adopted, and Dodgson has also corrected the quotation on p. 3, l. 20:—
   Malachi, iv. 2. Shall the Sun of Righteousness arise . . .
   Nos. 1, 2, 3, 10. The Sun of Righteousness shall arise . . .
   Nos. 7, 9. 'The Sun of Righteousness' shall 'arise . . . (rightly). Incidentally he has suppressed the comma after 'Friend' in p. 2, l. 18, and adopted 'grey-headed' in place of 'gray-headed' in p. 3, l. 17, thereby indicating

that he used No. 3 to reprint from. In all these particulars it agrees with No. 9, below.

8. (1887) In this year Macmillan again published an issue (*Macmillan's Catalogue* as above), but no copy is identified.

This ends the series of separate issues, so far as is at present known.

The next two numbers represent reprints imbedded in later books.

9. (1889 and 1890) In the *Nursery Alice*, an edition of *Alice* written by Dodgson himself in simple words and abridged form, he reprints the *Easter Greeting* in its final form, see No. 7 above. This and No. 1 may be regarded as the standard last and first forms.

10. (1894?) Sheet N of a Dodgson volume not yet identified, bears the *Easter Greeting* on pp. 177–9, followed by *Christmas Greetings*, and advertisements of Lewis Carroll's works up to 1893. It appears to be printed from No. 1.

The pedigree may be nearly as follows:

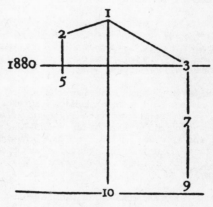

(*place of* 4, 6, 8 *not known*)

117. *Letter to Hospitals* (1876) [92

'Letter and Questions to Hospitals. Oxford: Printed at the University Press. 1876.'

So in Collingwood's *Life and Letters of Lewis Carroll*, p. 436. No copy is at present known. The letter probably offered copies of the two *Alice* books, and inquired whether Vivisection was approved by its council.

Williams, ii. 31 (p. 101); *Collingwood,* p. 436.

This is verified by an entry in Dodgson's *Diary* for 6 July 1876: 'Took to the University Press the MS. of a new circular to send round to hospitals etc. offering *Alice* and *Looking-Glass* for the use of sick children.'

Dodgson had written to Mr. Craik of Macmillan's on 18 May asking him to give an estimate for printing 500 copies each of the *Alice* books 'on cheap (but not thin) paper—no gilt edges nor gilt ornaments outside—but a strong cover which would not easily come to pieces, and if possible a gay one: I might even say *gaudy*. What can you suggest, which would please the eyes of little children and yet would be cheap?'

Dodgson was again sending round circulars to hospitals in June 1877 'to get the information which I could not get satisfactorily last time': there is no indication whether this was a new circular or further copies of the old one.

The 'hospital' editions of *Alice* and *Looking-Glass* (300 of each) seem to have been ready at the end of Dec. 1877, with the inscription 'Presented for the use of Sick Children' printed on the title-pages, but Macmillan's can find no record of the date of issue, &c.

118. *Fame's Penny-Trumpet* (1876) [91

| [NOT PUBLISHED.] || FAME'S PENNY-TRUMPET. | [*a thin line*] | Affectionately dedicated to all 'original re-searchers' who pant for 'endowment.' | [*a thin line*] | [*then follow four four-line stanzas*].

No imprint: (1876): (two) 4°: pp. 3+[1]: size 9¼×7¼ in. CONTENTS: p. 1, title: 1-3, 13 stanzas, beginning 'Blow, blow your trumpets': signed on p. 3 | An Unendowed Researcher. | with the date 'July, 1876'.

Fame's Penny-Trumpet is a severe criticism in verse of researchers who work for money rewards—'vivisectors, log-rollers, flatterers and other mountebanks'. They are bid to 'make' their 'penny-trumpets squeak', while Wisdom is quite out of their reach. This invective is in Tennysonian style, and does not spare to call its objects 'vermin'. It is reprinted in *Rhyme? and Reason?* (1883) with an illustration, and in the second edition of *Phantasmagoria* (1919). Only two copies are known, both in America.

Williams, i. 30 (p. 43); *Parrish Catalogue*, p. 103; *Collingwood*, p. 436: Harvard.

The relevant *Diary* entry, under 24 July 1876, runs: 'Found in Common Room the fifty copies of *Fame's Penny Trumpet* which Bayne has had printed for me (the *Pall Mall*, *Punch*, and *The World* had all declined to publish it).'

Reprinted in various collections and *Nonesuch*, pp. 898-900 (807-8).

1877

119. Responsions (1877)   [98

RESPONSIONS, HILARY TERM, 1877.

A quarto leaf (size about $9\frac{5}{8} \times 7\frac{5}{8}$ in.) printed on one side only, with no imprint, signed 'C. L. Dodgson', 'Ch. Ch., April 18. 1877.'

A letter to the Vice-Chancellor, signed as above, suggesting from statistics of 1875 to 1877 that the standard in one section of the examination in Responsions was 'far too high' and the consequent slaughter of candidates anomalous.

See Nos. 128-9 (1882).

Williams, ii. 32 (p. 101); Parrish Catalogue, p. 81 (a proof without day of month): Collingwood, p. 436: Bodleian.

Diary, 16 Apr. 1877: 'Composed a letter to the Vice-Chancellor on the anomalies of Responsions last term—45 per cent passing in one section, and 69 in the other. Sent it April 18.'

Taking Votes (1877)

For a cyclostyled letter relating to Dodgson's Method, see No. 114 above.

Natural Science at Oxford (1877)   [99

For this letter to the Pall Mall Gazette, reprinted by Collingwood in his Life, pp. 187–91, see No. 55 above.

120. Memoria Technica (1877)

Dodgson noted on 31 May 1877: 'Spent a good part of the day, and of the night, on revising my Memoria Technica', and next day 'The new Memoria Technica works beautifully. I made rhymes for the foundations of all the Colleges (except Univ.). At night I made lines giving "π" to 71 decimal places.' On 20 June: 'Spent the evening in trying an "electric pen" sent from Parkers, with moderate success', and on 27 June 'Did "electric" account of my system of Memoria Technica.'

An exactly similar cyclostyled piece, dated 'June 1888' is described under that date (No. 207) and was reprinted by Collingwood, Life, pp. 268–9. There is no mention of this second Memoria Technica in the Diaries (and no copy of the 1877 version has ever been reported). Possibly Dodgson made only one—and misdated it! But 1877–8 was certainly his 'cyclostyle' period.

121. *The Eastbourne Chronicle* (1877)

Dodgson contributed three letters on the theme 'Is it well to have children vaccinated?' The first was in answer to a letter with this title signed William Hume-Rothery of Merton Lodge, Tivoli, Cheltenham—an ardent 'Anti-Vaccinationist'—who then answered each of Dodgson's letters, becoming more and more discourteous in the process. Dodgson wrote strictly as a mathematician—signing himself 'Charles L. Dodgson' and adding 'Mathematical Lecturer of Christ Church, Oxford' to the first—pointing out a major fallacy in the statistics cited by those of the A.V. persuasion and the conclusions to be drawn from them. His letters appeared as follows:

1. *Eastbourne Chronicle*, No. 1145. Saturday, 18 Aug. 1877 (52 lines).
2.   „   „   No. 1148. Saturday, 8 Sept. 1877 (54 lines).
3.   „   „   No. 1150. Saturday, 20 Sept. 1877 (49 lines).

122. *Circulating Series of Disputable Propositions* (1877)

Known only from the entry in *Diaries* for 29 Nov. 1877: 'Took to Press my "circulating series" of "disputable" propositions.'

1878

123. *Charade* (1878) (Cyclostyle Edition)   [100

A CHARADE | [*two lines*] | [*then follows the text*].

[Oxford]: (1878): (two) 8°: size 8¾ × 5⅝ in.: pp. [4]: cyclostyled. CONTENTS: p. [1] title, a notice signed 'Lewis Carroll', with the date 'Ap. 8. 1878': and the first stanza of the Charade: [2–3] the rest of the Charade, with two illustrations.

A singular and rare piece. The Charade consists of six stanzas (30 lines), beginning 'My first is singular at best: | More plural is my second'. | Preceding it is a notice by Dodgson dated as above, offering £5 for a similar independent charade. There are two clever sketches (on pp. 2 and 3) of a human and a real goose, suggesting, perhaps, that the only answer is anserine. But there *is* an answer, showing that the charade is genuine and exceedingly ingenious.

Dodgson here introduces the cyclostyle writing for the first time (except for the small leaf, No. *114* above, 1877): it forms a kind of stencilling by successive punctures by a minute wheel in place of a nib. Ten or a dozen copies can be taken with ink passing through the punctures, but when the pen is moved too slowly the inside of an 'o' is apt to drop out.

Facsimile reproductions of the Charade will be found in Isa

Bowman's *Story of Lewis Carroll* (1899); also in the *Parrish Catalogue*, pp. 19-21 and the *Strand Magazine* (Apr. 1898, p. 416); and reprints of the text in *Rhyme? and Reason?* (1883), pp. 208-10, and *Phantasmagoria* (1911), pp. 160-2.   F. M.

Williams, i. 33 (p. 48): *Parrish Catalogue*, pp. 16, 19-21; *Collingwood*, p. 436: Harvard (the original manuscript is in the Amory Collection), F. Madan.

124. *Word-Links* (1878) (Cyclostyle Edition)   [101

| WORD-LINKS. | [*a double rule*] | A Game for two Players, or | a round Game. | [*a double rule.*] | [*text follows*]

[Oxford]: (1878): a leaflet on a light-yellow wove paper written with a cyclostyle: (two) 8°: size 8¾ × 5⅝ in.: pp. [4]. CONTENTS: p. [1] title: [1-4] the text, ending 'Ap. 11, 1878', 'Lewis Carroll': between lines 24 and 25 of p. 1 is an oval diagram of words: The | Rules for 2 players.| begin on p. 2: The | Rules for a round game. | begin on p. 3: on p. 4 is an example of a scoring paper, and at end a double line.

The earliest form of the game ultimately called Doublets, which gained considerable vogue, and is still popular. A general account of the game will be found in No. *130*. The present paper, which begins 'The principal feature', is rather diffuse and needs clearer exposition, consisting of a description, rules, and method of scoring. Dodgson numbered each copy of the present piece in ink: No. 4 has been seen, and 6, and 10.

Williams, i. 34 (p. 48); *Parrish Catalogue*, p. 17; *Collingwood*, p. 436: Madan.

125. *Word-Links* (1878) (First Printed Edition)   [102

WORD-LINKS | [*a thin line*] | *A Game for two Players, or a Round Game.* | [*thin line*] | [then twenty-two lines of the text, beginning 'A series of words of the same length'].

[Oxford: 1878]: (two) 12°: size 6¹⁵⁄₁₆ × 4½ in.: pp. 4. CONTENTS: p. 1, the title and text as above: 2-3 | The Rules for two Players | with diagram: 4, | The Rules for a Round Game. | , and examples of Doublets for practice. On white wove paper.

No date or place of publication appears, but Mr. Collingwood in his list of books dates it 1878, and the cyclostyle version (see No. *124*) bears the date 11 Apr. 1878. It is otherwise undated and anonymous.

An improved and simpler form of No. *124* with some suggested Doublets. In these early forms the words 'doublet', 'links' and 'chain' are used, but also 'jewels' and 'necklaces', which latter are not found subsequently.

Williams, i. 35 (p. 49); *Parrish Catalogue*, p. 17; *Collingwood*, p. 436: Bodleian, Harvard.

The first reference to 'Word-Links' is on 12 Mar. 1878, when Dodgson records that he taught the game to Professor Gandell's family.

126. Fun (1878)

On 9, 16, 23, 30 Oct. 1878 there appeared in *Fun*, vol. xxviii, a parody of *Alice* in the series 'Specimens of Celebrated Authors' called *Alice in Numberland*. On p. 174 (30 Oct. 1878) the 'Fish Riddle' from *Through the Looking-Glass* was quoted entire, and on p. 175 the answer was given in the same metre as the riddle, running to four stanzas of four lines each.

Dodgson wrote to Macmillan in Nov. 1878 (undated letter) quoting the first four lines: 'The verses you sent me in [Nov.] '72 began like this . . . The reason I asked the question is that, when you sent me them, I sent you back an *amended* version, as they were rather halting in metre; and I see (in a parody of *Alice* which has appeared in *Fun*) these very verses—not the original ones, but the amended version. So I conjecture that you showed my amended version to the writer (whoever it was), and that he has adopted the new readings. Was it so?'

There is, unfortunately, no further reference to the poem—nor any mention of the author. The last stanza in *Fun* runs:

> 'Get an oyster-knife strong,
> Insert it 'twixt cover and dish in the middle;
> Then you shall before long
> Un-dish-cover the OYSTERS—dishcover the riddle!'

127. Erratum Slip in 'Through the Looking-Glass' (1878)

On 30 Aug. 1878 Dodgson wrote to Macmillan: 'I have made an annoying discovery in the forty-second thousand of *Through the Looking-Glass*. Both the Kings are omitted from the chess diagram. They are in their proper places in a copy I referred to of the tenth thousand: but in *which* thousand the misprint first appeared I have not the means to discover.

'The first thing to be done (and please have it done without delay) is to print a slip of paper, and insert it in all copies still in hand. I enclose MS. of slip.'

No copy of this 'slip' has so far been found.

1879

128. *Euclid and his Modern Rivals* (1879) [103

EUCLID | AND HIS | MODERN RIVALS | BY | CHARLES L. DODGSON, M.A. | *Senior Student and Mathematical Lecturer* | *of Christ Church, Oxford* || [a quotation from Shakespeare's *Midsummer Night's Dream*, Act. V, Sc. 1, lines 114–17 '. . . That you should here repent you . . .']||

London, Macmillan and Co.: 1879: 8°: pp. xxxi+[1]+299+[1]: signn. [a], b, B–T8, U6. CONTENTS: p. i, the half-title: ii, Macmillan's device: iv, diagram of Theorems in Euclid I: v, the title; at the foot is | [All rights reserved] |: vi, 'Oxford: by E. Pickard Hall, M.A., and J. H. Stacy, Printers to the University': vii, 'Dedicated to the memory of Euclid': ix–xi, prologue: xiii–xxix, 'Argument of Drama': xxx–xxxi, the list of Appendixes: 1–199, the work in four acts: 201–99, the six Appendixes. Bound in red cloth, lettered in gold on the back.

One of the outstanding examples of serious argument cast in an amusing style, designed to prove that for elementary geometry a revised Euclid is better than any proposed modern substitute. The form is dramatic: Minos and Rhadamanthus, with occasional help from Euclid himself and 'Niemand', sit in judgement on twelve (or in some sense nearly twenty) Euclid-wreckers and their manuals, and much fun results, with comic but conclusive discomfitures of all kinds. Herr Niemand is a convenient gentleman who is 'ready to defend any thesis, true or untrue' (p. 17). The chief appendix is on methods of treating Parallels. This is the most elaborate mathematical work produced by Dodgson, and at the same time a piece of literature. A presentation copy dated 27 Mar. 1879 has been seen, and a rough draft in manuscript was lot 706 in the Dodgson sale. For a supplement and second edition see Nos. 145, 146 (1885).

129. At Harvard there is an offprint of Appendix IV (36 pages, 12° repaged): about methods of treating parallels. [104.] F. M.

Williams, ii. 33 (p. 101); *Parrish Catalogue*, p. 81; *Collingwood*, pp. 201–7 (with extracts), 437: British Museum, Bodleian, Ch. Ch., Oxford, Harvard, Huntington, &c. Sir H. Hartley has the Appendix.

130. *Doublets* (1879) [105

DOUBLETS || *A WORD-PUZZLE* || BY | LEWIS CARROLL || 'Double, double, | Toil and trouble.' ||

London: Macmillan and Co: 1879: size 5 15/16 × 3 7/8 in.: pp. 39+[1]: signn. A–B8, C4, (eights) 12°. CONTENTS: p. [1] title as above, enclosed within a border of four black lines, the ends of the lines overlapping. The words | Price Two Shillings | are below the black line at the bottom of the page: 2, in the centre in black-letter type | Inscribed | to | Julia and Ethel |: 3–5, preface, signed | Lewis Carroll |: 6, | Rules | : 7, Method of scoring, etc.: 8–9, | Doublets already set |: 10–11, Preface to Glossary: 12, | Abbreviations |: 13–37, Glossary of legitimate words in small type: 38–39 | Solutions of Doublets | March 29–June 21.

Issued in red cloth with white end-papers. The back is blank. The front cover has three blind lines forming a border, and | Doublets | a Word Puzzle | by | Lewis Carroll | in gold on the upper half of the cover, and Macmillan's monogram surrounded by a wreath, in blind tooling at the bottom. The back cover is blank except for three blind lines as border. All edges are cut and plain.

Apparently the first published edition, in which the latest problems are on 21 June 1879. The Preface reprints the note of the Editor of *Vanity Fair*, 29 Mar. 1879, and Lewis Carroll's undated letter about the origin of the game and proposed rules.

The game of Doublets was invented by Dodgson at Christmas 1877, for two young ladies who had 'nothing to do': and was at first called 'Word-Links', see Nos. 124–5, but the word 'doublets' was in use from the first. It consists in connecting two doublets (words with the same number of letters, usually 3, 4, or 5) by links in which each word differs from the preceding one by one single letter only, as HEAD, heal, teal, tell, tall, TAIL. The chain in which there are fewest links gains the highest marks.

The idea of a glossary was due to doubts about admissible words, and about 1,400 words of from three to six letters are given, those which cannot be changed into others being omitted, while only two abbreviations ('e'en' and 'e'er') are admitted. The preface to the glossary presents an amusing passage (from *Vanity Fair*, 17 May 1879) incorporating many impossible words which had been used by solvers, ostensibly written by 'Choker' (i.e. Dodgson himself). See puzzle for 26 July.

The Julia and Ethel of the dedication are probably Julia and Ethel Margaret Arnold, sisters of Mrs. Humphry Ward. No doubt these were the two for whom Dodgson invented the game. For the second edition see 1880 (No. 111); for the third edition see 1880 (No. 112).

The game became popular in private circles, and in Feb. or Mar. 1879 Dodgson wrote about it to the editor of *Vanity Fair*, who was becoming tired of the weekly Acrostics and Hard cases, and took up the new game, beginning with three trials on 29 Mar., 5 Apr., and 12 Apr., and starting a competition on 19 Apr. The following three short papers preceded the first issue of Doublets.   F. M.

131. New Puzzle (29 Mar. 1879)   [106
A NEW PUZZLE.

An offprint from *Vanity Fair*, 29 Mar. 1879, comprising the Editor's note, and also Dodgson's (undated) letter in full, headed 'Doublets—a verbal puzzle': 93 lines in all, printed on one side of a long slip, the text begins, 'The Readers of *Vanity Fair*', and Dodgson's letter 'Dear Vanity,—Just a year ago last Christmas . . .'. These are printed in the preceding first edition of doublets (No. 105). At the foot are the first three doublets (Drive PIG into STY, &c.).

132. Doublets (19 Apr. 1879)   [107
DOUBLETS.

A notice describing the game, with six rules and with notes, signed 'Lewis Carroll'. In all there are 79 lines, the text beginning 'This Puzzle consists', all within a black line, crossing at the corners and headed '[*From 'Vanity Fair'*, *April* 19, 1879.]' At the foot are the conditions of the competition. Printed on one side only of a single long slip.

Parrish Catalogue, p. 18.

133. Doublets already set (1879)   [108
DOUBLETS ALREADY SET.

A single leaf, 8° (size $7\frac{7}{8} \times 5\frac{1}{4}$ in.), on the front page of which, after the title, are six dates with three doublets each as follows: 29 Mar.: 5 Apr.: 12 Apr.: 19 Apr.: 26 Apr.: 3 May: and after two notes, 'May 3, 1879' [in the bottom left-hand corner] | [All within a black line border, the ends of which overlap each other by $\frac{1}{4}$ in., the area within the border being $6\frac{3}{8} \times 3\frac{7}{12}$.] The verso is blank. On white wove paper.

There are twenty-four lines in all, the text beginning 'Mar. 29.—Drive PIG into STY.' Anonymous.

Of these three preceding pieces, Mr. Madan possesses the first and second, Mr. Parrish (*Cat.*, p. 18) the second and third, and the Bodleian the third. They are rare.

134. Doublets (1879) (Abridged Edition)   [109
DOUBLETS | *A WORD-PUZZLE* | BY | LEWIS CARROLL. | [*thin ornamental line*: followed by twenty-three lines of the text beginning 'The rules of the Puzzle' and ending 'society'.]

[Oxford? October?] (1879): (four) 12°: size $6\frac{3}{4} \times 4\frac{7}{16}$ in.: pp. 8. CONTENTS: p. 1, title and text, as above: 2, Rules; Rule 1, four lines; Rule 2, six lines, and Rule 3, six lines: 3–6, Doublets already set in 'Vanity Fair', 29 March–4 October: 7–8, Solution of Doublets, 29 March–31 May: at top of right-hand corner of pp. 4, 5, 6, 8 is '1879'. A stitched pamphlet on brown wove paper.

It would appear that a call was made for a simpler abridged form of No. 105, without a glossary and for popular use: hence this shorter issue, costing a few pence, and hardly to be called a second edition. There can be little doubt that this piece followed the first edition, and not vice versa, for the doublets proposed extend to 4 Oct., and are arranged in competitions. The solutions end at 31 May, as the sheet of eight pages could hold no more. There is no mention of a method of scoring. The letterpress is extracts from No. 130.

135. Game (1879)   [110

A GAME FOR TWO PLAYERS.

An octavo leaf, printed on one side only: containing a title as above, followed by 24 lines of text, the last of which is the date 'Jan. 16, 1879.'

An anonymous early form of Lanrick, before even the name was settled, with two paragraphs of general description, beginning 'the Game is played on a chess-board', followed by six rules (1, 4, 3, 5, 3, 1 lines respectively). The only copy known, in Mr. M. L. Parrish's possession, has a title supplied in Dodgson's violet ink 'LANRICK. | The muster-place be Lanrick mead.' |, and further corrections which change Rule 1 from 'The men are set alternately, on any border-squares.' to 'The Players set their men, in turn, on any border-squares they like'. See No. 139.

For the development of the game see No. 142.

The game was already called Lanrick by 24 Jan. 1879 when Dodgson records playing it with Julia and Ethel Arnold. On 11 Feb. he recorded in the Diaries: 'Received ten proofs of Lanrick, in nearly its final state, I hope.' But there is no further reference to this edition. A variant with 10 instead of 6 rules and dated 1 Mar. 1879 (4 pp., 8°, pp. 2–3 printed) is noted by Madan (Supplement, p. 8).

136. The Educational Times (1879)

Dodgson made ten contributions to the Educational Times (which were often reprinted in Mathematical Questions and Solutions from 'The Educational Times'). See Notes and Queries, 24 Aug. 1940 for article and list by R. C. Archibald of Brown University, Providence, U.S.A.

1. 'Practical Hints on Teaching. Long Multiplication worked with a single line of Figures', *Educational Times*, vol. xxxii, pp. 307–8; 1 Nov. 1879. [Letter to the Editor signed 'Charles L. Dodgson, Senior Student and Mathematical Lecturer of Ch. Ch. Oxford'.]

2. 'Notes on Question 7695', by C. L. Dodgson, M.A., *Educational Times*, vol. xxxviii, page 183: 1 May 1885. [Reprinted in expanded form in *MQS*, vol. xliv, pp. 86–87: (1885).]

3. 'Question 9588'. *ET*, vol. xli, p. 247: 1 June 1888. Solutions by J. C. Simmons and Prof. Tanner, p. 278: 1 July 1888; *MQS*, vol. l, pp. 34–35 (1889).

4. 'Something or Nothing'. *ET*, vol. xli, p. 245: 1 June 1888. *MQS*, vol. xlix, pp. 101–2 (1888).

5. 'Question 9636'. *ET*, vol. xli, p. 280: 1 July 1888. [See *MQS*, vol. lix, pp. 94–95 for partial solution and comments on it by Dodgson.]

6. 'Question 9995', *ET*, vol. xlii, p. 83: 1 Feb. 1889. Solutions on p. 221 and in *MQS*, vol. li, p. 98 (1889).

7. 'Question 11530'. *ET*, vol. xlv, p. 234: 1 May 1892. (Solutions by H. J. Woodall, vol. xlvi, pp. 155–6; 1 May 1893.) *MQS*, vol. lix, pp. 71–73 (1893).

8. 'Question 12650'. *ET*, vol. xlviii, p. 87: 1 Feb. 1895. (Various solutions, pp. 234–5.) *MQS*, vol. lxiii, pp. 92–93 (1895).

9. 'Question 13614'. *ET*, vol. l, p. 391: 1 Sept. 1897. (Apparently no reply to this question was published.)

10. 'Question 14122'. *ET*, vol. lii, p. 93: 1 Feb. 1899 ('By the late Lewis Carroll'.) (Solutions p. 386 and vol. liii, p. 258.) *MQS*, vol. lxxiii, pp. 125–6 (1900).

1880

137. Doublets (Second Edition 1880) [111

DOUBLETS | *A WORD-PUZZLE* || BY | LEWIS CARROLL || 'Double, double, |Toil and trouble.' || SECOND EDITION ||

London, Macmillan and Co.: 1880: (eights) 8°: pp. 73+[1]: signn. A–E8, F4, G1. CONTENTS: p. 1, the half-title: 2, a Macmillan device: 3, the title, within black border lines crossing at the corners, and with 'Price Two Shillings' at the foot: 4, 'Oxford: By E. P. Hall, M.A., and J. H. Stacy, printers to the University': 5, Dedication as in No. 105: 7–20, preface signed 'Lewis Carroll', rules, scoring and 'Doublets already set in 'Vanity Fair': 21–28, Solutions: 29–73, a Glossary with Preface, &c. Bound in brick red cloth, with blind tooling, lettered in gold on the front cover.

A reprint of No. *130* (1879), but larger in size and in larger type. The only differences are that the list of past doublets and solutions extend from 29 Mar. to 20 Dec. 1879, that the solutions immediately follow the Doublets, and that on pp. 29 and 31 'Society' is printed 'society'. The author received his copy on 20 Feb. 1880. This edition is reprinted in Collingwood's *Lewis Carroll's Picture Book* (1899), p. 275, and (1913), p. 199, with a facsimile of the title-page, and an extra note to the preface to the glossary, but the Doublets and Solutions cease after 26 July.

Mrs. Ffooks, F. Madan, Harvard.

138. Doublets (Third Edition, 1880) [112

——Doublets, with title exactly as the second edition, with 'THIRD EDITION', 1880, and with the Doublets and Glossary enlarged to 85 pages. Mr. Parrish possesses a copy bearing 'The party at the Chestnuts [Guildford] from the Author, June 1880'. (*Parrish Cat.*, p. 22.) In Apr. (?) 1880 Dodgson had proposed in a letter to *Vanity Fair* a 'New Method of Scoring', affecting rules 1 and 2 in the marks forfeited for each link beyond the least possible number, and these changes are adopted in this third edition, with other slight changes. The binding is as before.

The Doublets already set are continued to 10 Apr. 1880, and the solutions to 3 Apr. Pp. 23-26, 39-45 are purposely blank for manuscript additions: the pages are 85+[3].

Parrish Catalogue, p. 24: F. Madan.

139. The Monthly Packet (1880) [113

Dodgson contributed the whole of *A Tangled Tale* to this monthly magazine edited by Charlotte Yonge (see No. *182*). The earlier parts were called 'Romantic Problems: A Tangled Tale': the whole is listed under the book itself.

Dodgson's other contributions to the *Monthly Packet* are as follows:

1. 'Problem: Cats and Rats.' Feb. 1880.
2. 'Lanrick: A Game for Two Players.' Dec. 1880.
3. 'Mischmasch: A Game for Two Players.' June 1881.
4. 'Lanrick' [Final form, as in *Lewis Carroll Picture Book*]. Aug. 1881.
5. Letter: 'Girls' Own Shakespeare'. June 1882. See No. *153*.
6. 'Mischmasch' [Final form, as in *Nonesuch*, pp. 1272-3 (1146-7)]. Nov. 1882.

140. Letter from Mabel (1880) [114

[A letter from Mabel to Emily, anonymous, not dated: cyclostyled (as Nos. **94, 100**) on one side of an octavo sheet, beginning 'Edinborough, Feb. 14, My dear Emily, Last Saterday', and ending 'Your loveing Mabel']

[Oxford: 1880]: (one) 8°: pp. [2].

A fabricated letter to illustrate common illiterate errors of spelling and expression. It is certainly by Dodgson, and is dated by Collingwood 1880. Beatrice Hatch (*Strand Magazine*, Apr. 1898, p. 419) states that Mabel and Emily were two of her own dolls. They were named after her American cousins the Misses Kerr, as she had received them from her aunt, their mother.

Mr. Parrish's copy of this piece is the only one known.

Williams, ii. 35 (p. 101); *Parrish Catalogue*, p. 104, with facsimile on p. 107; *Collingwood*, p. 437.

1881

141. *Jabberwocky* (1881)   [116

| JABBERWOCKY | [seven stanzas, and notes, follow on the same page]

[Oxford at the University Press: 1881]: (two) 8°: size $8\frac{7}{8} \times 5\frac{5}{8}$ in.: pp. [4]. CONTENTS: [2] The Jabberwocky in English, 28 lines with three footnotes: [3] 'Mors Iabrochii', a Latin version in fourteen elegiac stanzas, signed 'A. A. V.' with four footnotes.

For the Jabberwocky see No. *84*: this is a fine translation into Latin, made in Mar. 1872 by Augustus Arthur Vansittart, Fellow of Trinity College, Cambridge (*d.* 1882). It begins 'Cæsper erat: tunc lubriciles ultravia circum | Urgebant gyros gimbiculosque tophi', and is reproduced, with the English, in facsimile in the *Parrish Catalogue*, pp. 26–27, and reprinted in Collingwood's *Life* (pp. 144–6). A less good Latin version by Hassard Dodgson, a Master in the Court of Common Pleas, is printed in the *Lewis Carroll Picture Book* (1899), pp. 364–5. The date of the present piece is supplied by Collingwood.

142. *Lanrick* (1881)   [117

'Lanrick' a game for two Players. Oxford: Printed at the University Press . . . 1881.

Four pages, 12mo: 1, Title (with 'Third Edition'); 2–3 the eight rules, dated Oct. 1881; 4 is blank.

Though not issued separately, the version in the *Monthly Packet* of Aug. 1881 bears the words 'Second Edition'.

The earliest notices of the game are No. *135* (1879) above, and in the *Monthly Packet* for Dec. 1880, pp. 613–14 (where Dodgson states that he had been engaged for two years in elaborating the game and supplies the rules); Feb. 1881, p. 207 (help is acknowledged); Mar. 1881, pp. 303–4 (ditto, adding some notes); June

1881, p. 611 (ditto); and Nov. 1881, p. 512 (where the 'third edition' of the rules is printed, eight in number). Rare.

143. Notice about Index (1881)   [118

'Notice re Concordance to "In Memoriam" Oxford: Printed at the University Press . . . 1881.'

Only known from the above entry in Collingwood's Life, p. 437. For the Index to 'In Memoriam' see No. 31 (1862).

This probably resembled the advertisement which appears in copies of Alice's Adventures of this date, e.g. the seventy-second thousand (1883), which gives half of page [194] to it.

144. Purity of Election (1881)   [119
PURITY OF ELECTION (1881)

[An Article on the General Election, in the St. James's Gazette of 4 May 1881.]

From Dodgson's Diary quoted by Collingwood (Life and Letters, p. 212) we learn that Frederick Greenwood asked him to contribute the article. 'Lewis Carroll' advocates not only secret voting, recently introduced, but also sealing the votes till the whole election is over, to avoid that curious effect of a definite tendency in the early results, in influencing in the same direction the later voting. Voters like to be on the winning side. The letter is dated 30 April. Sir H. Hartley has an offprint. Included here as a separate item on account of the offprint—but no copy of it can be found for description, although Dodgson noted (Diaries) on 19 May 1881: 'Received from Mr. Greenwood fifty copies of my letter on Purity of Election and sent off a number of copies—to Gladstone, Lord Salisbury, etc.'

145. The St. James's Gazette (1881–90)

While Frederick Greenwood remained its editor, Dodgson used the St. James's Gazette as his usual means of communicating with the public, his last letter appearing shortly after Sidney Low had succeeded Greenwood. His contributions are as follows:

1. 'The Purity of Election' (signed Lewis Carroll). 4 May 1881.
2. 'Traitors in the Camp' (signed Lewis Carroll). 30 Dec. 1881.
3. 'Education for the Stage' (signed Lewis Carroll). 27 Feb. 1882.
4. Second letter with the same title. 6 Mar. 1882.
5. [On Gladstone and the Cloture]. (As by Lewis Carroll). 23 Mar. 1882.
6. 'Lawn Tennis Tournaments' (signed Charles L. Dodgson). 12 Aug. 1882.

7. 'Fallacies of Lawn Tennis Tournaments' (signed Charles L. Dodgson). 1 Aug. 1883.
8. Second letter on same—4 Aug. 1883.
9. Third letter on same—21 Aug. 1883.
10. 'Proportionate Representation' (signed Charles L. Dodgson). 15 May 1884.
11. Second letter on same—19 May 1884.
12. Third letter on same—27 May 1884.
13. Fourth letter on same—5 June 1884.
14. 'Parliamentary Elections' [Article: reprinted by Collingwood, pp. 233–6]. 5 July 1884.
15. [On 'The Showerbath']. (As by Lewis Carroll). 7 Aug. 1884.
16. 'Redistribution' [Article] (signed Charles L. Dodgson). 11 Oct. 1884.
17. 'Vivisection Vivisected' (signed Lewis Carroll). 19 Mar. 1885.
18. 'Who Shall Offend One of Those Little Ones?' [Article] (signed Lewis Carroll). 22 July 1885.
19. 'Hydrophobia Curable' (signed Lewis Carroll). 21 Oct. 1885.
20. 'Election Gains and Losses' (signed Charles L. Dodgson). 4 Dec. 1885.
21. 'Children in Theatres' (signed Lewis Carroll) [quoted in part by Collingwood, pp. 180–1, and more fully by Green (see below) and by him in Diaries, pp. 452–3]. 19 July 1887.
22. 'Tristan d'Acunha' (signed Charles L. Dodgson). 10 Apr. 1888.
23. 'Telephone Messages' (signed Lewis Carroll) [quoted in full by Green (see below)]. 17 Jan. 1889.
24. 'Mrs. Fawcett and the Stage Children' (signed Lewis Carroll). 20 July 1889.
25. 'Sylvie and Bruno' (signed Lewis Carroll) [quoted in full by Green (see below) and in his The Story of Lewis Carroll (1949), pp. 153–4)]. 10 Jan. 1890.
26. 'On Fasting' (Lewis Carroll). 10 Apr. 1890.
27. 'The Oxford Scandal' (signed Charles L. Dodgson). 6 Dec. 1890.

For these contributions see article 'Lewis Carroll and the St. James's Gazette' by Roger Lancelyn Green in Notes and Queries for 7 Apr. 1945. [Note that a misprint occurs in the quotation of Dodgson's letter (No. 23 above) where the proposed word for a telephone message should read 'tel-tale'.] For the letters on 'Proportionate Representation' see, besides Collingwood, pp. 232–6, Duncan Black's The Theory of Committees and Elections (1958), pp. 189–238.

Following the appearance of No. 27 'The Oxford Scandal' (a profane masquerade at Queen's College) a letter appeared signed 'An Essex Vicar' which identified Dodgson with Lewis Carroll and accused him of irreverence for parodying ''tis the voice of the sluggard'. Dodgson wrote to Sidney Low begging him not to print 'any statement as to my connection with the "nom de plume" of Lewis Carroll . . . it being my earnest wish to remain, personally, in the obscurity of a private individual'. See D. Chapman-Huston: The Lost Historian: Sidney Low (1936), pp. 74–76.

146. *Letter about Christ Church* (1881)   [120

A letter in the *Observer* on 5 June 1881, on recent disturbances in
Christ Church, signed 'Charles L. Dodgson'.

The *Observer* of 29 May 1881 had printed a leading article on a
great disturbance, chiefly by out-college men, in Christ Church on
25 May. Collingwood (*Life*, pp. 212–16) describes the occurrence
and reprints the entire letter, in which Dodgson defends the general
character of the College, and the action of the Dean, both at this
time and in the summer term of 1870.

147. *The Garland of Rachel* (1881)   [121

THE | GARLAND OF RACHEL | BY | DIVERS KINDLY HANDS |||

'Printed at the private press of H. Daniel. Oxford': 1881: (twos) 8°: pp.
67+1.

The *Garland* consists of eighteen poems by Dr. Daniel and his
friends to commemorate his daughter Rachel's first birthday, 27
Sept. 1881. Among the contributors are Austin Dobson, Andrew
Lang, J. A. Symonds, Robert Bridges, Edmund Gosse, and Mrs.
Margaret Woods. The seventh in order is a set of seven four-line
stanzas beginning '[W]hat hand may wreathe thy natal crown',
signed 'Lewis Carroll' (pp. 29–31), followed by a Latin metrical
version of the same by Sir Richard Harington, beginning '[Q]ua
tibi natalis'. But Lewis Carroll's poem was not wrung from him
without a precedent letter dated 23 Nov. 1880, in which he professes himself incapable of acceding to Dr. Daniel's invitation to
contribute, at the same time giving a specimen of what, left to himself, he could write on the subject, beginning 'Oh pudgy podgy
pup'. The *Garland* was issued (36 copies only), on or soon after
18 Oct. 1881.   F. M.

Both poems were reprinted in the first edition of this *Handbook*
(pp. 208–10), in *Collected Verse* (1932), pp. 329–31 and in *Nonesuch*,
pp. 934–6 (838–9).

148. *On Catching Cold* (1881)   [122

On catching cold.

[Oxford: Printed at the University Press. 1881.]: (two) 12°: pp. [4]. CON-
TENTS: p. [1] title: [1–4] the extracts.

Dodgson occasionally reprinted short pieces to distribute among
his friends. The present paper (in one case at least) came straight
from the Dodgson papers secured by Messrs. Parker of Oxford

after his death, and Collingwood also vouches for the fact, and for the date.

The three extracts here anonymously reprinted are:

I. 'The most common cause . . . they had caught cold' from Dr. Thomas Inman's *Restoration of Health* (1870), p. 75.

II. 'On this point we have . . . the air passages', from the same writer's *Preservation of Health* (second edition, 1870), p. 161.

III. 'Sudden change . . . upward of 70°', from Dr. James Copland's *Dictionary of Practical Medicine* (1832?), *sub voce* Catarrh.

The passages tend to show that colds are caught by passing suddenly from a cold atmosphere to a hot room, like chilblains.

The Land of Idleness (1881)

Aunt Judy's Magazine, No. 184 (1 Aug. 1881) contains a story entitled 'The Land of Idleness, by Lewis Carroll'. As a fact the writer was Fräulein Ida Lackowitz, and the tale was only forwarded to the editor by Dodgson. This is stated by Messrs. Macmillan in the advertisements at the end of 'Sylvie and Bruno Concluded' (No. 216, 1893), and perhaps elsewhere.

1882

149. Dreamland (1882)   [123

| Dreamland. | Words by LEWIS CARROLL. | Music by C. E. HUTCHINSON. |

[Oxford. printed at the University Press: 1882]: (two) 8°: size 8 11/16 × 6 5/16 in.: pp. [4]. CONTENTS: p. [2] introduction giving the history of the music, in the words of Mr. Hutchinson, headed by | Dreamland. | and eight lines of text (by Lewis Carroll), beginning 'Of Poetry' and ending 'of the melody', with a thin line underneath: then seventeen lines of text by Hutchinson beginning 'I found myself' and ending 'could not recall', all within a thin line border: size 7×4 11/16 in.: p. [3] heading as title above, followed by three staves of music with the words of the first verse beginning 'When midnight mists', then the four remaining verses in two equal columns, divided by a thin vertical line, all within a thin line border (size 7×4⅔ in.). No date appears, or imprint. On wove paper light brown in colour.

The music of this remarkable and rare piece was composed by Mr. C. E. Hutchinson in a casual dream, which he fortunately was able to recall, and write down on waking. The words are by Lewis Carroll and closely follow the dream, except for 'a slight transposition . . . to meet the rhythmical necessities of the melody'. The piece presents an unusual example, not of dream verses but of dream music. Charles Edward Hutchinson of Brasenose College, Oxford, dreamed that a procession of heroes of old passed before him on a stage, each turning to look at him. He woke with a melody for a four-line stanza ringing in his ears, and only these words 'I see the shadows falling, And slowly pass away'. Dodgson supplied five stanzas to suit the music. Thus the words were written for the music, and not 'vice versa'. Collingwood gives a reprint of the second paragraph of p. 2, and a reduced facsimile of p. 3 (pp. 221-3). F. M.

What Collingwood in fact gives on p. 222 is a facsimile of the music and poem as they appeared in *Aunt Judy's Magazine*, vol. xx, p. 547, July 1882.

150. *Letter to the Dramatic Profession* (1882) [127

A letter to friends and to members of the Dramatic Profession, enclosing and recommending a Prospectus of a scheme of Play-acting, apparently by instituting a school of Dramatic Art.

[Oxford: Printed at the University Press.]: (1882): (two) 8°: size $7\frac{1}{16} \times 4\frac{5}{8}$ in.: pp. [4]. CONTENTS: pp. [1-3] the letter, signed 'Charles L. Dodgson'.

Headed on p. [1] 'Ch. Ch. Oxford 1882' and with space left for the address and subscription. The letter has no reference to Dodgson's proposed expurgated edition of Shakespeare, and the enclosed Prospectus has not been seen. The letter begins 'There is but little I can add'. Collingwood supplies the references to a 'School of Dramatic Art', no doubt from private sources, and he reprints part of the letter at p. 181.

Williams, i. 43(2), (p. 55: correct the entry), ii. 38 (p. 102); *Parrish Catalogue*, p. 82; *Collingwood*, pp. 181, 437: F. Madan.

Dodgson wrote in his *Diary* on 28 Jan. 1882: 'Heard from Mr. Dubourg about the prospectus of the "Dramatic School of Art" which he sent me the other day, and which I had offered to circulate among friends, accepting my offer to do so.'

And on 1 Feb. 1882: 'Sent to the University Press my letter written to circulate along with the prospectus.'

151. *Letter on Oxford Responsions* (1882) [128

A letter in the *Guardian* of 8 Feb. 1882, on 'Oxford Responsions', signed 'Charles L. Dodgson', 'Christ Church, Oxford, Feb. 2, 1882.'

Dodgson disposes of an allegation in the *Guardian* of 1 Feb. 1882, that there was a serious increase in the number of men plucked at Oxford in Euclid, Books i and ii, owing to inadequate preparation and neglect. Not without humour he points out that the failures had in many cases been counted twice, in the calculations. The editor tries to blunt Dodgson's scalpel, in an appended note. See next number.

152. *Responsions Lists* (1882) [129

AN ANALYSIS OF THE RESPONSIONS LISTS | FROM MICHAEL-MAS 1873 to MICHAELMAS 1881. |

[Oxford Printed at the University Press]: (1882): (two) 4°: pp. [4]. CONTENTS: p. [1] the title: [2–3] preface and Calculations, signed 'Charles L. Dodgson', 'Ch. Ch., Feb. 9, 1882.'

Dodgson again (see Nos. *151* and *119*) refutes the allegation about a phenomenal number of failures in Responsions in Michaelmas Term 1881. The elaborate calculations show that the average number who passed in 1873–81 was 64 per cent. and in Michaelmas Term 1881 it was 63. But the variations were considerable (54 to 82). There is no reference to the *Guardian* (No. *151*).

Dodgson noted in his *Diary* on 4 Feb. 1882 that 'this week has gone partly on *Analysis of Responsions* . . .'.

153–4. *Two Circulars about Shakespeare* (1882) [125–6

Two Circulars about a proposed expurgated Edition of Shakespeare.

I

An octavo leaflet (size $8\frac{1}{5} \times 5\frac{1}{2}$ in.) printed on one side only, and signed 'Lewis Carroll', containing a 'request to my lady readers' to supply lists of about fifteen plays, most suitable for children, to be expurgated, and issued in a cheap and handy volume. It begins 'The Editor kindly allows me'.

This is an offprint (not reprint) of a note in the *Monthly Packet*, third series, iii, p. 602 (June 1882), and is undated, and printed in London, no doubt in June 1882. Dodgson's scheme of a 'Girls' Own Shakespeare' began (with the *Tempest*) on 29 Mar. 1885 (Collingwood, *Life*, p. 240), but proceeded no farther. [**125**].

Williams, i. 42 (p. 54); *Parrish Catalogue*, p. 24: *Collingwood*, p. 437?: Bodleian, Harvard.

II

A letter to ladies to the same purport as No. 1, headed 'Ch. Ch., Oxford. 1882', but unsigned.

[Oxford: printed at the University Press]: (1882): (two) 8°: size $7\frac{1}{16} \times 4\frac{3}{8}$ in.: pp. [4]. CONTENTS: pp. [1–4] the letter, with postscript.

No. 1 is here entirely rewritten for sending to Dodgson's lady friends, with space left for address, and for subscription and name. The postscript is a personal recommendation of a lady willing to teach children at their own London homes. The letter is in italics and begins 'May I ask for your kind co-operation', and is unsigned. This form is rare. [**126**].

Williams, i. 43 (2), (p. 55); *Parrish Catalogue*, p. 25; *Collingwood*, p. 437: Harvard.

155. *Mischmasch* (1882)   [**124**

| MISCHMASCH. | [*a thin line.*]

[Oxford: Printed at the University Press]: (1882): (two) 12°: size $6\frac{7}{8} \times 4\frac{1}{2}$ in.: pp. 4. CONTENTS: p. [1] the title as above: [2] | Mischmasch. | a word-game for two players or | two sets of players. | 'Pars pro toto.' |, followed by eighteen lines of text beginning 'The essence of this game' and ending 'the word': 3, text of twenty-seven lines, beginning 'thought of' and ending 'Player': 4, text of seven lines, beginning '6. A "resigned" ' and finishing 'is drawn', followed by the date | November, 1882. | in the bottom left-hand corner. On brown wove paper.

Mischmasch is 'a word-game for two players or two sets of players'. Each side proposes a 'nucleus' of two or more letters (say *emo*) and the other side provides a word containing the nucleus (say *lemons*); there are seven rules, including a system of marks for results. The title is taken from the fanciful name of one of the magazines which Dodgson wrote and edited (but never printed) for his brothers' and sisters' amusement in the fifties, before going up to Oxford. See Collingwood's *Life*, p. 62, and his *Lewis Carroll Picture Book* (1899), pp. 15-28, where it is explained that Mischmasch is a German word equivalent to hodge-podge, medley. The game seems never to have 'caught on'.

The present issue is a revised anonymous reprint of an article with the same heading in the *Monthly Packet*, Nov. 1882, pp. 491-2, where the present rules 5 and 6 change places, and a note asking for advice and criticism follows at the end. It is also there signed 'Lewis Carroll'; but these are the only differences. In the *Monthly Packet*, June 1881, at p. 620 the first form of this 'New Game' is found, also with seven rules: see also Sept. 1881, p. 284. Anonymous.

Reprinted in *Nonesuch*, pp. 1272-3 (1146-7).

156. *Euclid, Books I and II* (1882)   [**130**

EUCLID || BOOKS I AND II || EDITED BY | CHARLES L. DODG-SON, M.A. | STUDENT AND LATE MATHEMATICAL LECTURER | OF CH. CH., OXFORD ||||

London Macmillan and Co.: 1882: (eights) 12°: pp. xi+[1]+108, signn. a⁴, b², B–G⁸, H⁶. CONTENTS: p. i, the half-title: ii, A diagram: iii, the title: at the foot is '[All rights reserved]': iv, 'Oxford: by E. Pickard Hall, M.A., and J. H. Stacy, Printers to the University.': v–xi, Introduction, in two parts: 1–74, Book I: 75–100, Book II: 101–8, three appendixes. Bound in flexible brown cloth, with title-label on the front cover, priced 2 shillings.

The first published edition by Dodgson of Euclid's Elements Books I and II, the first private issue having been printed in 1875, see No. 88. The present edition has an Introduction and Appendixes, and is revised throughout by changes and abridgements, but without alteration of Euclid's methods of proof or logical sequence. There is no specific reference to 'Dodgson's Euclid and his Modern Rivals' (see No. 103), and this little work is intended for beginners only, containing about five-sevenths only of the words contained in the ordinary editions. The subsequent editions, which follow the same lines, are: the second edition (printed at Oxford), 1883, with words instead of such symbols as $=$, $\therefore$ (Bodleian): third edition: fourth edition: fifth edition, 1886: sixth edition, London, 1888: seventh edition: eighth edition, 1889.

No date is given in the *Diaries* for the publication of this, though Dodgson was applying to the Oxford University Press on 2 July 1881 to do so. But an interesting note occurs on 1 Nov. 1882: 'Began today preparing the second edition (I am withdrawing the first from sale) of *Euclid I, II*, by erasing "$+$", "$=$", "$>$", and "$<$" signs, which seem likely to make the book less useful, as all algebraical signs are supposed to be forbidden in Cambridge examinations.'

1883

157. Lawn Tennis Tournaments (1883)　　　　　　　[133

LAWN TENNIS | TOURNAMENTS || THE TRUE METHOD OF ASSIGNING PRIZES | WITH A PROOF OF THE FALLACY | OF THE PRESENT METHOD | BY | CHARLES L. DODGSON, M.A. | STUDENT AND LATE MATHEMATICAL LECTURER OF | CH. CH. OXFORD || Palmam qui meruit ferat ||

Price Sixpence London Macmillan and Co.: 1883: (six) 8°: size $7\frac{1}{2} \times 4\frac{7}{8}$ in.: pp. [2]+9+[1]. CONTENTS: p. [1] the title as above: [2] contents in 6 sections: 3–9, the text: [1] An advertisement of Euclid (No. 130) in the centre, and | Baxter, printer, Oxford | at the bottom: pp. 6 and 7 of the text are unnumbered. A sewn pamphlet, issued without wrappers.

Dodgson easily shows that a tournament in which all competitors beaten in the first round retire, and similarly in the succeeding rounds, does result in the best man winning the first prize, but that the chance of the second best getting the second prize is only 16–31ths, and that it is 12 to 1 that the four best will *not* come out finally in their proper order. But as usual with Dodgson's ideals of scoring or voting, the scheme proposed is too ingenious and elaborate for general use, though terribly near perfection. The results would be many fewer competitors, a shorter tournament, and less gate-money!   F. M.

This followed the letter in the *St. James's Gazette* of 1 Aug. 1883, and was published about the end of the month. It was already printed or being printed on 6 Aug. when Dodgson sent a description to Macmillan, offering to send copies 'at once'. It is reprinted in *Nonesuch*, pp. 1201–11 (1082–91).

F. and W. give a separate entry [132] for the letter, which I omit as it is included in No. *145.*

158. *Circular about Appointments* (1883)   [256

A circular to friends about appointments, &c.

Mr. Collingwood (*Life and Letters*, p. 271) states that so many applications were made to Dodgson for aid in obtaining situations 'that at one time he had a circular letter printed, with a list of people requiring various appointments or assistants, which he sent round to his friends'. No copy of this circular is known, nor any indication of its date.

So Madan on p. 157 of the *Handbook*. But he added an Addenda (p. [xx]) as follows:

I have picked up a copy of the missing 'Circular about Appointments', No. 256 (p. 157). It is a four-page octavo letter, headed 'Ch. Ch. Oxford', and beginning Dear   , 'Having a strong prejudice against "begging-letters", and ending on p. 4 'Yours   , Charles L. Dodgson', followed by two postscripts. It is an attempt to set an Oxford Graduate (whose name and College are given) and his wife and eight children on their feet again after threatened bankruptcy and mentions another case for help. The copy seen is filled in (in violet ink) with 'Dec. 21/83', Dear 'Mrs. Egerton Todd', and Yours 'sincerely'.

On 24 Dec. 1883 Dodgson notes (*Diaries*) that during the last few days his work has included 'sending to my friends about 180 copies of a letter (printed) about the Dymeses'.

159. *Rules for reckoning Postage* (1883)   [134

'Rules for Reckoning Postage.' Oxford: Baxter . . . 1883.

So in Collingwood's *Life* (1898), p. 438, but no copy has at present been found.

160. *Rhyme? and Reason?* (1883) (First Edition)   [131

RHYME? | AND REASON? || BY | LEWIS CARROLL || *WITH*
SIXTY-FIVE ILLUSTRATIONS | BY | ARTHUR B. FROST | *AND NINE* | BY |
HENRY HOLIDAY || 𝔍 𝔥𝔞𝔟𝔢 𝔥𝔞𝔡 𝔫𝔬𝔯 𝔯𝔥𝔶𝔪𝔢 𝔫𝔬𝔯 𝔯𝔢𝔞𝔰𝔬𝔫. |

Price seven shillings London Macmillan and Co.: 1883: (fours) 8°: size
$7\frac{1}{2} \times 4\frac{13}{16}$ in.: pp. xii+214+[2]. CONTENTS: p. i, the half-title: | Rhyme? | and
Reason? |: ii, Macmillan's monogram in the centre: iv, the frontispiece: v,
the title as above, and at foot '[All Rights Reserved]': vi, The imprint in the
centre London: R. Clay, Sons, and Taylor Bread Street Hill, E.C.: vii, the
dedication | 'Inscribed to a dear child . . .' finishing with 'sea', followed by
two thin lines, then four stanzas, and two thin lines: ix, a statement of five
lines as to the origin of the poems in the book here printed for the first time:
xi–xii, 'Contents': 1–214, the text: [1] blank except for | [Turn over. | in the
bottom right-hand corner: [2] Macmillan's advertisements of the works of
Lewis Carroll. At the bottom under a long thin line is 'London: R. Clay, Sons,
and Taylor, Printers.' Issued in olive green cloth. Lettered in gold on the
back under three gold lines: | Rhyme? | and | Reason? | [*A small device*] | and
at the bottom of the back is | Macmillan & Co | over three gold lines. The
front cover has three gold lines around the border, and three circular gold
lines in the centre containing the head of the ghost (p. 57). The back cover
is the same as the front except that the circular lines in the centre contain a
picture of the Bellman (p. 135). All edges yellow.

The text is made up of poems of Lewis Carroll, chiefly reprinted
from *Phantasmagoria* (No. *68*: 1869), but including the whole of
the *Hunting of the Snark* (1876). The whole of Part II of *Phantasmagoria* (the serious poems) is omitted, as well as one poem of which
the interest had passed ('The Elections to the Hebdomadal Council').
In fact the only poems never published before are 'Echoes' (after
Tennyson, beginning 'Lady Clara Vere de Vere'), 'A game of fives'
(beginning 'Five little girls'). The last three of the four riddles (beginning 'Empress of Art', 'The Air is bright', and 'My first is singular')
and 'Fame's Penny Trumpet', and of these the fourth riddle and
'Fame's Penny Trumpet' had been *privately* printed before, see Nos.
123, *118* (1878 and 1876). Also the 'Téma Con Variazióni', beginning
'I never loved a dear Gazelle | Nor anything' | is from the *Comic
Times* of 1855. The volume is therefore a *réchauffé* of printed matter,
except for quite a few pieces. Even the little double acrostic poem
on p. vii, dedicating the book to Gertrude Chataway (beginning
'Girt with a boyish garb') is the same as the dedication of the *Snark*,
except that the second line should end 'loves as well', and in the
fourth line 'he' has been rightly altered to 'one'. Dodgson must
have enjoyed the difficulty in pronouncing the new title in conversation. There is an echo of the title in Vernon Blake's 'Nor

Rhone nor Reason', 1930. The number of separate pieces or parts (excluding the *Snark*) is sixteen.

What is new is the numerous and fine designs by A. B. Frost, 65 in number (24 full-page) which add interest to many of the reprints, especially to 'Hiawatha's Photographing' and the 'Three Voices': with the (reproduced) Holiday pictures they make a fully illustrated volume. Collingwood points out that the (apparently) prose preface to the *Hiawatha* is really itself in the same metre as the poem. The last page in the book bears statements that Dodgson's books will be sold with less abatements in price than were usual, and that 'An Easter Greeting' could be purchased separately for 1d.

The volume was issued on 6 Dec. 1883, and a new edition in 1887, the fourth thousand, bearing that date. The second edition contains the 'Preface to Fourth Thousand' written in Nov. 1887, just in time for insertion. The eighth thousand issued in 1901 (1) omits the motto on the title, (2) has an extra leaf after the Contents reprinting the preface of the fourth edition, which gives a list of the first appearances of the separate items, and informs us that the 'Téma' first appears in the *Comic Times* in 1855, and the 'Atalanta' in *Punch*, in 1867: (3) this edition has no advertisements at the end.

Lot 243 in the Dodgson sale (1898) was 'Thirty-two original pen and ink sketches and drawings for *Rhyme? and Reason?* by Frost'.

The Contents of the book are as follows, + indicating that the piece is from the 1869 *Phantasmagoria*, ★ that the piece is here first printed.

+Phantasmagoria   +Poeta fit
★Echoes   Snark
+Sea Dirge   +Size and Tears
+Carpette Knyghte   +Atalanta
+Hiawatha's Photographing   +The Lang Courtin'
+Melancholetta   Four Riddles (1. +There was an
+Valentine   ancient City; 2. ★ Empress of
+The Three Voices   Art; 3. ★The air is bright; 4. My
   Téma   first is singular)
★ Game of Fives   Fame's Penny Trumpet   F. M.

Dodgson noted (*Diaries*) on 18 Oct. 1883: 'Sent off last sheet of *Rhyme? and Reason?* marked "Press". (Ordered first picture on 7 Feb. 1878 more than five and a half years ago).' And on 6 Dec. 1883: 'Arrival of twelve copies of *Rhyme? and Reason?*' Apparently too small a first edition was printed, for he wrote to Craik of Macmillan's on 9 Dec. apologizing, and directing him to print 2,000 more.

He also notes that Messrs. Dalziel had written to him complaining about the title being similar to one which Routledge published for them. This would be *Rhyme and Reason* by H. W. Dulcken published about 1870. (There was also a book called *Rhymes and Reason* by Clara Hall, published by Edward Lacey about 1844.) 'It is a pity', wrote Dodgson, 'but I fear it's too late to alter the name. We must hope that the two question-marks in *my* title will keep the two books distinct.'

While noting the variations in contents between *Rhyme? and Reason?* and *Phantasmagoria*, Madan makes no mention of the textual variants which are numerous. Besides revision, a great many lines are omitted—notably in 'Hiawatha's Photographing' where passages of as many as eighteen lines have been removed. There were also new lines and stanzas added, largely for the sake of matching text to position of illustration. Dodgson notes (*Diaries*) on 19 May 1883: 'I have now arranged in pages the whole of the volume of poems, (which I think of calling *Rhyme? and Reason?*), having had to write in, as padding, three stanzas at page 4, beginning "Houses are classed" and five at page 106 beginning "He saw" . . .'

There is scope here for research, which no one seems yet to have undertaken. The poem 'The Three Voices', for example, made its first appearance (in MS.) in *Misch-Masch*, and was published in the *Train*, in *Phantasmagoria*, and in *Rhyme? and Reason?*: there are variants in all four versions.   R. L. G.

161. *Christ Church Common Room Notices, etc.* (1883–92)

Madan lists three of these under 1889 [Nos. 190–1, &c.] and mentions several others. Several more have been discovered by Duncan Black, who wrote about them in *Notes and Queries*, Feb. 1953, though without listing them.

It does not seem worth giving full bibliographical descriptions to each of these ephemera, but I have been enabled by the kindness of Dr. Heaton, Librarian of Christ Church, to make the following list. The items are now bound into volumes (not always chronologically): I include only printed items certainly composed by Dodgson—there are numerous notes, letters, lists, accounts, &c., in his handwriting.

A. *Agenda and Notices for Meetings of Common Room*
These are often of several folio pages with long notes, all but the first three with the printed signature C. L. DODGSON, Curator, and were issued for Meetings on the following dates:

   1. 28 Feb. 1884.
   2. 12 June 1884.

3. 19 Feb. 1885.
4. 11 Mar. 1886.
5. 28 May 1886.
6. 29 May 1886 [special meeting, with a small slip enclosed for next meeting].
7. 18 June 1886.
8. 24 Feb. 1887 [for this and all subsequent meetings there is a separate notice giving the date and saying that Agenda will be issued later].
9. 16 Feb. 1888.
10. 7 Mar. 1889.
11. 9 May 1889.
12. 17 May 1889 [special meeting].
13. 20 Feb. 1890.
14. 12 Feb. 1891.
15. 4 Mar. 1892.

B. *Miscellaneous Slips and Folders*

1. Single page. To the Members of Common Room. | 'I have procured samples of the following 16 Liqueurs. . . .' 12 Nov. 1883.

2. Folder: 3 sides printed. Re *Dessert Claret* and *Spirits and Liqueurs*. 23 Nov. 1883.

3. Folder: 4 sides printed. Ch. Ch. Common Room. | Correspondence during April and May, 1884, between the present Curator and six of his predecessors, on the question of 'conditions of membership'. [Imprint of BAXTER, PRINTER, OXFORD.] 1884.

4. Folder: 3 sides printed. Christ Church Common Room. | Begins: MEMBERS of the House, who have taken their | M.A. degree, are eligible as Members of Common | Room . . . July 1884.

5. Folder: 1 side (of 4) printed. Re TEA. Two copies: one dated Nov. [blank] 1887, the other 9 Nov. 1887.

6. Single page. Christ Church Common Room. | [rule] | WINE-CARD | [rule] || 'In vino veritas' | The Curator regrets to find that the Wine-Card | just issued, is incorrect. . . . 14 Nov. 1887.

7. Folder: 1 page (of 4) printed. Christ Church Common Room. | [rule] | CHAMPAGNE | [rule] | [Seven lines of text re a toasting party 'at 1.30, on [blank]'. Nov. [blank], 1887.

8. Single page. For Members of Common Room only [to left of centre] | [Heavy rule] || Periodicals [this in heavy black decorated type] | TAKEN IN DURING 1890 || [short rule] || 21 Jan. 1891.

9. As above, but for 1891 and dated 13 Feb. 1892.

10. Card, printed on both sides. CH. CH. COMMON ROOM | Prices of Wines and Spirits. [And on verso] Prices of Liqueurs. March 1892. [Not signed.]

1884

162. Christmas Greetings (1884) (First Separate Edition)   [135

|| CHRISTMAS GREETINGS. | [FROM A FAIRY TO A CHILD.] | [five four-line stanzas follow, in pearl type, signed at end 'Lewis Carroll'].

[London, Macmillan: 1884]: (one) 16°, printed on one side only, within a double line, the area of which is $4\frac{6}{16} \times 2\frac{9}{16}$ in.: size $5\frac{1}{8} \times 3\frac{1}{2}$ in.

This little poem, which begins 'Lady dear, if Fairies may', was written by Lewis Carroll in 1867, but was not reprinted until 1869, when it appeared in *Phantasmagoria* (see No. *68*) with slight variations and one error (the comma in stanza 1 after 'may', here also supplied but redundant). The type is one size larger than in 1869 (then diamond, now pearl), but still minute. The London printing and date (Macmillan and 1884) are supplied by Collingwood. There was only one edition. Like the *Easter Greeting* (see No. *116*) it has been forged or pirated, several specimens of which I have seen, all differing in some respects from the original, one being dated a year before the poem was written. The Bodleian and Madan copies are identical, and can be distinguished from the other issues by the first 'g' in 'forgetting' being injured at the foot. It is reprinted in the *Nursery Alice* (No. **185**, 1889).   S. H. W.

Williams, i. 48 (p. 60); *Parrish Catalogue*, p. 28; *Collingwood*, p. 438: Bodleian, Harvard (6 copies), F. Madan.

163. Twelve months in a Curatorship (1884)   [136

TWELVE MONTHS IN | A CURATORSHIP ||| BY | ONE WHO HAS TRIED IT |||| [At the head is 'Printed for private circulation', in italic capitals underlined.]

(Oxford, printed by E. Baxter) 1884: (eights) 12°: pp. 53+[3]. CONTENTS: p. 1, title: 3, contents: 5, preface: 7–51, the piece in nine sections: 52, 53 [1–2] appendixes A, B: [3] 'Baxter, Printer. Oxford.' A stitched pamphlet, without covers.

A humorous account of the first year of Dodgson's Curatorship of Common Room at Christ Church, Oxford. It is anonymous, but no doubt the author signed each copy sent round to resident members of Common Room. Dodgson describes the piece as 'largely autobiographical, slightly apologetic, cautiously retrospective, and boldly prophetic . . . at once financial, carbonaceous, æsthetic, chalybeate, literary and alcoholic.' The Curator had, under theoretical supervision, to deal with the accounts, wines and mineral waters, coals, servants' wages, books and newspapers of the Common room, to which the Senior Students and their guests retired after dinner in Hall, and which was open all day for literary use or tea. From it wine, groceries, and the like could be sent out to the rooms of the Senior Students. The cellar had about 25,000 bottles of wine. The piece centres in controversies between the Curator and the Wine Committee, between the end of 1882, when he was elected, and early in 1884. The appendixes give details of rules broken in the letter, and Accounts of the Common Room for 1883. It is clear that Dodgson's management was treated with some asperity by certain members of Common Room, but he did not lose his temper. This piece was issued in Jan. 1884. Senior Students (equivalent to Fellows in other Colleges) are in the twentieth century called Students, and Junior Students, Scholars. See also under No. 190.

Williams, ii. 42 (p. 103); *Parrish Catalogue*, pp. 85-86; *Collingwood*, pp. 84-85, 438: F. Madan; Christ Church.

164. *Supplement to Twelve Months in a Curatorship* (1884)
[137

SUPPLEMENT | TO | 'TWELVE MONTHS IN | A CURATOR-SHIP' | [At the head is 'Printed for private circulation' in Italic capitals, underlined.]

(Oxford, printed by E. Baxter): Feb. 1884: (four) 8°: pp. 57-63+[1]. CONTENTS: p. 57, the title: 59-63, the Supplement: at the foot of p. 63 is | 'Baxter, Printer, Oxford.' |

An early and rare form of No. 139, in which after 'I have referred to' on p. 61, four paragraphs occur beginning 'The hard work—So I elect—I beg—In this letter', extending the text into p. 63.

There is no postscript. In this supplement Dodgson explains his own view on the position, and apologizes for any laxity there may have been in his management. Only Mr. Parrish's copy is known.

Parrish Catalogue, p. 86.

165. *Postscript to Twelve months in a Curatorship* (1884)
[138

POSTSCRIPT | [*a line*] | The text follows.

[Oxford, printed by E. Baxter, 1884.]: (one) 8°: pp. 2: CONTENTS: p. 1, the title, and fifteen lines of text: 2, the remainder of the text.

Dodgson here proposes six 'Rules for the Wine-committee', designed to avoid all future difficulties, with a short preface beginning 'In deference to the wishes of many dear friends'. Given the new rules, he is willing to continue in office. Presumably they were accepted, for he continued in office. See No. 136. It seems probable that this fly-sheet was issued between the two issues of the supplement, for in the fly-sheet rule 4 is rather awkwardly broken into two paragraphs, the second beginning 'In all other': in the supplement, second issue, the two sentences are one paragraph, as being one rule. Anonymous and undated. Rare.

Williams, ii. 44 (p. 103); *Parrish Catalogue*, p. 86; *Collingwood*, p. 438: Harvard, F. Madan.

166. Supplement to Twelve months in a Curatorship (1884)
(Second Issue) [**139**

SUPPLEMENT | [&c. exactly as No. 137.]

(Oxford, as before): Feb. 1884: (&c. exactly as No. 137, but CONTENTS: p. 57, the title: 59-62, the supplement: 62-63, the postscript: at the foot of p. 63 is 'Baxter, Printer, Oxford').

The second and ordinary form of the Supplement, without the four peccant paragraphs in No. 137, but with the Postscript incorporated. Anonymous, see No. 136. This and the *Twelve Months* are found stitched together, as well as separate.

Williams, ii. 43 (p. 103); *Parrish Catalogue*, p. 86; *Collingwood*, p. 438: Harvard (2 copies), F. Madan.

167. Parliamentary Elections (1884) [**140**

PARLIAMENTARY ELECTIONS | [*a line*] | [*Reprinted from the* ST. JAMES'S GAZETTE.] | [*a line*]: [*The text follows in two columns of* 72 *and* 71 *lines*: dated Ch. Ch., Oxford, July 4. 1884. Signed 'C. L. Dodgson']

[London?] (1884): (one) folio: printed on one side only.

A long letter in which Dodgson develops five principles for Parliamentary elections (electoral districts to be approximately equal; minorities to be represented; surplus votes to be transferred; ballot papers to be plain; and counting of votes to be simple), and his proposed rules to carry them out. This is in fact a scheme for Proportional Representation, see No. 152. A reference in Collingwood's *Life*, p. 233, to a previous letter on Purity of Elections, refers to No. *114* (1881).

Williams, ii. 45 (p. 104); *Collingwood*, pp. 232-4: Bodleian, Harvard.

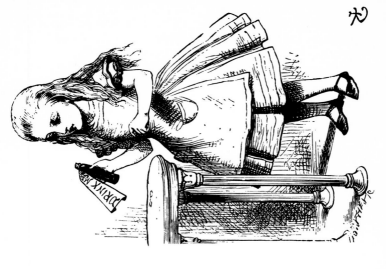

XI. ALICE AND THE BOTTLE

(a) (left) Illustration from the 1865 edition of Alice's Adventures
(b) (right) Illustration from the 1866 edition

XII. The Clarendon Press Ledger: a page showing expenses and receipts connected with *Alice's Adventures*, 1865 (*much reduced*)

168. Principles of Parliamentary Representation (1884) First
Private Edition)   [141

THE PRINCIPLES OF | PARLIAMENTARY | REPRESENTA-
TION ||| BY | CHARLES L. DODGSON, M.A. | STUDENT AND
LATE MATHEMATICAL LECTURER | OF CH. CH., OXFORD |||

| London | Harrison and Sons | 59 Pall Mall | 1884. | 8°: size $7\frac{3}{4} \times 5\frac{1}{4}$ in.:
pp. [8]+47+[1], signn. [A]⁴ B–D⁸. CONTENTS: p. [1] the half-title | the
Principles of | Parliamentary | Representation |: at the top is 'With the author's
compliments' underlined: [3] the title, as above: [5] the preface of six para-
graphs, with | Ch. Ch., Oxford, | Nov. 5. 1884. | at the bottom left-hand
corner, and | C. L. D. | at the right-hand corner: [7] the contents: pp. 1–45,
the text: 46 and 47, Index: on p. 47 is | Baxter, Printer, Oxford. | Without
wrappers, stitched.

A contribution to the controversy which occupied some months
in the newspapers of 1884 about Parliamentary Representation. The
four chapters deal with Desiderata, Electoral Districts and Elections,
and (the last) a summary of practical details. Principles, statistics,
tables, and algebra are all brought in to support Proportional
Representation.

This first issue was one of 150 copies for private distribution, as
is known from a proof copy owned by Mr. Parrish, dated 23 Oct.
with the author's corrections and notes, altering the date to 5 Nov.,
and authorizing the next (priced) issue. It is described, at a time
when it was owned by Messrs. Blackwell, booksellers, of Oxford,
as follows:

I am indebted to Mr. B. H. Blackwell of Oxford for bringing
to my notice Mr. Dodgson's own copy of this pamphlet, as above
described, which is a very interesting item, because it shows from
the notes and corrections on it in Dodgson's hand that 150 copies
of it were issued as complimentary copies. Mr. Dodgson's auto-
graphic instructions are as follows: 'Press all but last sheet—another
proof of index wanted. Correction at P.p. 7. 13. 8. VIII. 150 copies'
['of this sheet' written here but crossed out.] 'to be printed—then
remove words, "with the Author's compliments", and replace "price
one shilling" (above "London") on title-page—to be ready in case
more copies are needed for sale.'   S. H. W.

Parrish Catalogue, pp. 83–84.

169. Principles of Parliamentary Representation (1884) (First
Published Edition)   [142

THE PRINCIPLES OF | PARLIAMENTARY | REPRESENTA-
TION | [&c., precisely as No. 141, omitting 'with the Author's

compliments', and placing | PRICE ONE SHILLING | above the imprint.

The first published edition, with the above and some other slight alterations. Mr. Collingwood's statement that this edition was reprinted in 1885 takes no notice of the important modifications introduced, see No. 141.

Williams, i. 47 (p. 59): Parrish Catalogue, p. 83; Collingwood, pp. 234–6: British Museum, Bodleian, Harvard, Huntington, &c.

170. Profits of Authorship (1884)   [143

THE PROFITS OF AUTHORSHIP |||| BY | LEWIS CARROLL |||| PRICE SIXPENCE || LONDON | MACMILLAN AND CO. | 1884

8vo. Madan was unable to find a copy of this pamphlet, and none has been found since. But I discovered the title-page, as given above, among the Dodgson family papers (or possibly a proof of it) which Miss F. Menella Dodgson has allowed me to transcribe.

Collingwood mentions the pamphlet and quotes a long paragraph from it (pp. 226–8).

There are many letters on the subject from Dodgson to Macmillan between 8 Aug. 1883 and 31 Aug. 1883, but no mention of the pamphlet (but no letters are available between the latter date and 14 Oct. 1884, except one of 9 Dec. 1883 dealing exclusively with Rhyme? and Reason?). Dodgson originally intended his article to appear in the St. James's Gazette (on 21 Aug. 1883 he wrote in Diaries: 'During yesterday and today I have written nearly all of a letter I mean to send to the St. James's on "Authors and Booksellers" . . .'). No such letter can be traced, and he was still asking Macmillan for details to use in it on 31 Aug. 1883.

Even Messrs. Macmillan have no copy of The Profits of Authorship, as Charles Morgan points out on pp. 113–14 of his The House of Macmillan (1943)—where, perhaps, he hints that it was never in fact published, in spite of Collingwood's explicit reference to it as 'a little pamphlet'.

1885

171. Parliamentary Representation (1885). Second edition.

[151

The title and general arrangement are made as in the first edition, No. 142 (1884). The chief differences are as follows: on the half-title is 'with the author's compliments'; on the title 'Second Edition' is added, and 1884 changed to 1885. The Preface is shorter, and dated 1 Jan. 1885. The number of the pages is the same, but the contents are considerably altered. The first edition was too technical for general use or comprehension, so the second relegates the technical parts to an Appendix (pp. 35-45) and to some extent rewrites the pamphlet, while some pages are identical in type with the first edition, though not in paging.

The only recorded copy is owned by Mr. Parrish, but there is no known reason why it should be rare. The following supplement and Postscript suit either edition of the Principles, and are dated later.

172. *Parliamentary Representation*—Supplement (1885)   [152

THE PRINCIPLES OF | PARLIAMENTARY | REPRESENTA-TION ||| [*a short thick line*] | Supplement | [*a short thick line*] ||||

Oxford: printed by E. Baxter: (four) 12°: size $8\frac{1}{8} \times 5\frac{3}{8}$ in.: pp. 7+[1]. CONTENTS: p. 1, the title as above: 3-7, the text: at the foot of p. 7 is | Ch. Ch., Oxford, | Feb., 1885. | in the left-hand corner, and | C. L. Dodgson. | in the right-hand corner.

Dodgson points out 'a serious mistake which the Society (for Proportional Representation) is making "about surplus votes"', and with infinite exactitude corrects it. Collingwood mentions two editions of this supplement, but no second edition (No. 153) has been found.

Diaries, 16 Jan. 1885 give: 'After two days of experiments, I have at last constructed a clear crucial case of failure for the Proportional Representation Society method, which I think of circulating as a supplement to my pamphlet.' And on 2 Feb. 1885: 'Ordered of Baxter 1,000 copies of the supplement to *Parliamentary Representation*, to be posted to all M.P.s and members of the "Prop. Rep. Soc".'

173. *Parliamentary Representation*—Postscript to Supplement (1885)   [154

THE PRINCIPLES OF PARLIAMENTARY | REPRESENTA-TION. | [*short thick line*] | Postscript to Supplement. | [*short thick line*] | The text follows.

(Oxford, printed by E. Baxter: 1885): (two) 12°: size $8\frac{1}{8} \times 5\frac{3}{8}$ in.: pp. 4. CONTENTS: p. 1, title as above, and the beginning of the text: 1-4, the text: below the text on p. 4 is the following | Ch. Ch., Oxford, | Feb. 1885. | C. L. Dodgson. | [*a thin line*] | Erratum in Supplement. | [*a short thick line*] | 'Page 7, line 10 from the end, for 1-4th read 3-4ths. At the foot of the page is | Baxter, Printer, Oxford. | There is no wrapper.

A short but cogent answer to objectors to Dodgson's method (in the Supplement) in the matter of surplus votes. The Society's method is shown to result in a vicious circle.

Diaries, 11 Feb. 1885: 'Sent to Baxter the MS. of a Postscript to the Supplement to meet an objection of Mr. Courtney's.'

174. Supplement to Euclid (1885)   [145

SUPPLEMENT | TO | 'EUCLID AND HIS MODERN RIVALS'|| CONTAINING | A NOTICE OF HENRICI'S GEOMETRY | TOGETHER WITH | SELECTIONS FROM THE REVIEWS |||

London Macmillan and Co.: 1885: 8°: pp. 301–56: signn. [U]⁴, X–Z⁸. CONTENTS: p. 301, the title: 302, 'Oxford printed by Horace Hart, Printer to the University': 303, the preface, signed 'C. L. Dodgson', 'Ch. Ch., Oxford, April, 1885': 305–30, 'Act. ii. Scene VI. Treatment of Parallels by revolving lines. Henrici.': 331–56, 'Appendix VII. Reviews of "Euclid and his Modern Rivals", with the Author's remarks thereon.' Issued in grey paper covers, the front cover reproducing the title, adding 'Price One Shilling' at the foot.

Olaus Henrici's *Elementary Geometry* (London, 1879) supplies a fourteenth victim to the thirteen in No. 103 (1879); and Dodgson intersperses remarks of his own in quoting eight reviews of the original work.

'The *Supplement to Euclid and his Modern Rivals* is off my hands', wrote Dodgson on 25 Apr. 1885, and mentions it (*Diaries*) as 'Published April '85'.

175. Euclid and his modern Rivals (1885) (Second edition)   [146

EUCLID AND HIS MODERN RIVALS.

This is similar in title to No. 103 (the first edition, 1879) but bears 'Second edition' on the title-page. Other differences are that it has xxxi+[1]+275+[1] pages; that it has a short extra Preface prefixed to the original Preface, signed 'C. L. D., Ch. Ch. 1885.'; that it has two additional appendixes, and a rearrangement of the diagram in the frontispiece, and that much of the matter of the Supplement (No. 145) is incorporated. This latter piece (dated Apr. 1885) must have been issued before, or with, the second edition, which, though seldom found, is not likely to be actually 'rare'. Parts are rearranged or altered. A presentation copy to the Author's brother Edwin is dated 1 Jan. 1886. An erratum slip should precede p. 1, and a prospectus is known.

Harvard, M. L. Parrish, F. Madan.

On 10 July 1885 Dodgson noted (*Diaries*): 'I am seeing through the press the second edition of *Euclid and his Modern Rivals.*'

176-7. *Letter, and Prospectus* (1885)   [155, 156

[A Letter and Prospectus]

No place: (1885): (two) 8°: size $7 \times 4\frac{3}{8}$ in.: pp. [4]: on thick laid paper with watermark 'Silver Burn': CONTENTS: p. [1] at the top on the right-hand side is | 7 Lushington Road, | Eastbourne, | Aug. [21], 1885 |. Blanks left for names. Then on the left-hand side | Dear [Dolly] | Then follows the text of the letter | 'I have undertaken, on behalf of a friend, | to circulate the enclosed prospectus, in the hope | of finding a purchaser, or a tenant, for the house. | Would you kindly show it to any friends of yours | whom you think it might suit? | Below on the right-hand is | Believe me, | [Yours affectionately] | [C. L. Dodgson] | pp. [2, 3, 4] are blank.

Unfortunately the prospectus (no doubt another Lewis Carroll item, No. 156) is missing. The blanks in the copy of the above item from which this collation was taken, were filled in by Mr. Dodgson in the usual violet ink. I have shown them in square brackets. Another copy was offered in Magg's Catal. No. 427 (1922), Item No. 2211 (for 21s.) addressed to Dr. Daniel of Oxford. The Prospectus was again missing.

S. H. Williams.

178. *Proposed Procuratorial Cycle* (1885)   [147

THE PROPOSED PROCURATORIAL CYCLE, | [to be submitted to Congregation on Oct. 27, 1885.] | [*a line*, then 27 lines of text.]

[Oxford] (Printed by E. Baxter): (1885): (two) 4°: pp. [4]. CONTENTS: p. [1] the title: [1-2] the paper, signed 'Charles L. Dodgson' 'Ch. Ch. October 24, 1885.': for the second leaf, see the next piece.

Dodgson shows, with relentless logic, that the Cycle of Colleges from which the Proctors of the University were to be elected each year (by simple rotation of Colleges) was constructed on a crude and unfair system. He submits a thirty-year cycle based on the number of persons eligible in each college for the post of Proctor. He issued the paper (which begins 'If, as will be') with a view to a rejection of the proposed cycle rather than to secure (at this stage) the adoption of his own. To make the construction of his own cycle clear, he issued on the second leaf of this four-page paper, to be torn off and *not* sent round to all and sundry, a Postscript for Mathematicians only, see next entry.

The Statute, however, passed Congregation practically un-amended, by 51 to 32.

Williams, ii. 47 (p. 104); *Parrish Catalogue*, p. 87; *Collingwood*, p. 439: Bodleian, Christ Church, Harvard, &c.

179. *Postscript* (1885)   [148

POSTSCRIPT, | [addressed to Mathematicians only.] | [*a line*]

(Oxford, printed by E. Baxter): (1885): one leaf 4°: pp. [2]. CONTENTS: p. [1] the title: [1–2] the paper, signed 'Charles L. Dodgson', 'Ch. Ch. October 24, 1885.'

See No. **147**: the first words are 'It will, I think'; this leaf was to be torn off from the ordinary copies of the preceding entry.

22 Oct. 1885: 'Worked at a fly-leaf, to send round, about the absurd new Proctorial Cycle.'

23 Oct. 1885: 'Wrote a Postscript to the Paper (to Mathematicians only) explaining process of calculation.'

180. *The Proctorial Cycle* (1885)   [149

THE PROCTORIAL CYCLE TO BE VOTED ON IN | CON-GREGATION ON TUESDAY, NOV. 10. 1885. |

[Oxford]: (1885): (two) 4°: pp. [4]. CONTENTS: p. [1] the title: [1–3] the piece, signed 'Charles L. Dodgson', 'Ch. Ch. November 6, 1885.'

Dr. Edward Moore, Principal of St. Edmund Hall, had criticized Dodgson's proposals in a quarto paper, undated, but before the voting on 27 Oct. 1885, and Dodgson here answers the arguments at some length: the first words are 'For two reasons'. In the Congregation of 10 Nov. the cycle approved on 27 Oct. was thrown out by 52 to 47, and to complete the Gilbertian situation, the whole of the proposals to amend the existing statute were rejected by 10 to 3! So Dodgson may be said to have won his plea.

Williams, ii. (p. 104); *Parrish Catalogue*, p. 87; *Collingwood*, p. 439 (with the misleading title 'Further Remarks'): Bodleian, F. Madan.

5 Nov. 1885: 'Wrote a second paper on the Proctorial Cycle.'

181. *Suggestions as to Election of Proctors* (1885)   [150

SUGGESTIONS AS TO THE ELECTION OF PROCTORS.

[Oxford]: (1885): (two) 4°: pp. [4]. CONTENTS: p. [1] the title: [1–4] the piece, dated at the end 'Nov. 21, 1885.'

A longer and more elaborate system for electing proctors with justice to the claims of each College, with a proposed statute establishing a Cycle. The first words are 'In any system', but Dodgson forgot to append his name, so that the piece is anonymous. This rather unpractical elaboration completed the weariness of Congregation, which acted as stated above. The only unwearied person was Dodgson himself, who in April 1886 returned to the attack, see No. 159.

Parrish Catalogue, p. 88; *Collingwood*, p. 439.

20 Nov. 1885: 'Sent MS. for my suggestions for a Proctorial Cycle to Baxter'—the Printer.

182. *Tangled Tale* (1885)   [144

A TANGLED TALE ‖ BY | LEWIS CARROLL ‖ *WITH SIX ILLUS-TRATIONS* | BY | ARTHUR B. FROST ‖ Hoc meum tale quale est accipe.|‖

London Macmillan and Co.: 1885: 8°: size 7 3/16 × 4 13/16 in.: pp. [12]+152+[2]: signn. [A]⁶, B–K⁸, L⁴, [M]¹. CONTENTS: p. [1] the half-title | A Tangled Tale |: [2] Macmillan's circular device, with monogram in the centre: [4] the frontispiece: [5] the title as above, and at foot | [*All Rights Reserved*] |: [6] imprint in the centre | Richard Clay & Sons, | Bread Street Hill, London, E.C. | And Bungay, Suffolk. |: [7] two four-line verses headed by | To my Pupil. | All in black letter type: [9] the preface with date October 1885, and signed 'L. C.': [11] contents: 1–76, the ten Knots: 77–152, Appendix of Answers to the Knots, with the imprint at the foot of p. 152. | London: Richard Clay and Sons, Printers.|: [1] Blank except for | [Turn over | at the bottom right-hand corner: [2] Macmillan's advertisements of the works of Lewis Carroll, and notes of the *Easter Greeting* and new trade terms. Dark grey end-papers.

Issued in red cloth. Gold lettering on the back under three gold lines, |A | Tangled | Tale | [*A device*] |, and at the bottom of the back is | Macmillan & Co. | over three gold lines. The front cover has three lines around the border, and three circular lines in the centre containing the head of the Dragon. The back cover is the same except that the circular gold lines contain the heads of the knights. All edges cut and gilt.   S. H. W.

The Preface explains that each of the ten knots in the Tangled Tale embodies at least one mathematical problem or puzzle. They originally appeared in the *Monthly Packet* (a magazine chiefly read by ladies, and edited by Charlotte Mary Yonge from 1851 to 1898), with the Answers, between April 1880 and March 1885. Some are serious, some almost quibbles, but all amusing. The author says of them (p. 152): 'My puppets were neither distinctly *in* my life (like those I now address) nor yet (like Alice and the Mock Turtle) distinctly *out* of it'. The present reprint is only very slightly altered from the first form.

Some copies bear 'second thousand' on the title-page without other change. The book was issued on 22 Dec. 1885, at the latest: and reprinted in 1886 (third and fourth thousand).

THE KNOTS

	Title	Monthly Packet
I (i)	Excelsior**	1880, Apr. (xxix), pp. 369–70 (the two knights' walk).
	Answers	(xxix) 618–21, xxx. 283, 610, 612 (27 competed).
II (v)	Eligible apartments (two problems)*	1881, Apr. (3rd series, i) 394–7 (doors in a square, and genealogy, see Collingwood's Life and Letters, pp. 244–7).
	Answers	(i) 608–11, ii. 509 (10 and 25 competitors).
III (ii)	Mad Mathesis	1880, July (xxx) 76–78 (about trains passing each other).
	Answers	(i) 281–3, 612 (46).
IV (iii)	The Dead Reckoning*	1880, Oct. (xxx) 388–90 (about weight of sacks).
	Answers	(xxx) 610–13 (97).
V (iv)	Oughts and Crosses	1881, Jan. (i) 67–69.
	Answers	(i) 302–3, 397, 412, 610 (22).
VI (vi)	Her Radiancy (2 problems*)	1881, July (ii) 93–96 (Bank of England, and quantities of scarves).
	Answers	(ii) 282–4, 509–11 (2 and 29)
VII (vii)	Petty Cash*	1882, April (iii) pp. 378–80 (Expenses of lunch)
	Answers	(iii) 596–602 (45).
VIII (ix)	De omnibus rebus (two problems)	1883, Aug. (vi) 179–80 (placing pigs, and omnibuses).
	Answers	(vi) 490–1 (2 and 4).
IX (viii)	A serpent with corners (three problems)*	1883, Jan. (v) 77–79 (buckets, immersed solids, garden walk).
	Answers	(v) 292, 384–7 (5, 3 and 12).
X (x)	Chelsea buns (three problems)	1884, Nov. (viii) 474–8 (maimed soldiers, where does the day begin?, ages of three men).
	Answers	(ix) 95, 295–7, 497 (1st), 495–7 (3rd) (19–20). The second problem was 'left to another time' (ix, p. 297), 'postponed' (ix, p. 495), 'postponed sine die' (p. 145 of the published volume).

In some of the answers Dodgson playfully used such expressions as 'malefactors' and 'wrong-doers', e.g. in *M.P.* ii. 283, for which he was seriously taken to task (ii. 511, iii. 102)! In general his tricks and quibbles were accepted quietly. 'Mad Mathesis' (the spirit of Mathematics) occurs in more than one Knot, and so does 'Her Radiancy'.

Frost's six illustrations, marked with an asterisk in the above list of knots, are fully adequate, and all but one are full pages. The engraver was Joseph Swain. Lot 245 in the Dodgson sale (1898) was 'original unused drawings in pen and ink for "The Tangled Tale", by Frost'. The pupil to whom the book is dedicated in eight lines, beginning 'Beloved Pupil! Tamed by thee' was Mary Edith Rix (Collingwood's *Life*, p. 250). Each of the ten knots was reprinted separately in octavo (No. 144*) from the type of their first issue in the *Monthly Packet*, and at least the first seven were paged from 1 to 34. The first bears a first draft of the Preface to the present reprint in book form. There were also similar reprints of the first two Answers (No. 144**), paged from 1 to 12. All these (without Knots viii–x) are owned by Mr. Parrish, and no other sets are known to have survived.   F. M.

Williams, i. 49 (p. 60); *Parrish Catalogue*, p. 28 (a copy, and proofs of the first 8 preliminary pages); *Collingwood*, pp. 238, 244–7, 439: British Museum, Bodleian, Harvard, Huntington, &c.

The *Diaries* note on 3 July 1885: 'Wrote to Macmillan and Swain [the engravers] about *A Tangled Tale*, which I hope to get out as a Christmas book this year.'

On 10 July 1885: 'As Mr. Frost declines to re-draw the pictures for *A Tangled Tale*, I am going to use six of them.'

On 3 and 5 Nov. he was still writing to Macmillan about the cover and price of the book, but he noted in his own copy (*Sale Catalogue*) that he received it on 22 Dec. 1885.

On 27 Mar. 1886 he wrote to Macmillan: 'Many thanks also for a long series of notices, condemnatory of *Tangled Tale*. I feel rather tempted to send a few of them to Miss Yonge (at whose request it was written) and say "and this blighted reputation I owe to your baneful influence!" Spite of this chorus of blame, it is selling pretty well, don't you think?'

A Tangled Tale was included in *Nonesuch*, pp. 981–1078 (881–969). It was previously reprinted in the Everyman *Alice, &c.*, 1929.

There was a translation into French, projected in 1958, and made by Dr. Jean-Claude Cuzin. It will be published under the title *Un Fil Embrouillé* by the Collège de Pataphysique as one of its quarterly 'Dossiers Acénonètes'. But as yet no date has been given. The 'Beloved Pupil' to whom the book is dedicated was Edith Rix (whose name may be found by taking the *second* letter of each line in the poem)—born 1866 and died about 1918. Dodgson taught her mathematics (she became a Computer at Greenwich Observatory) and refers to her frequently in the *Diaries*.

A Tangled Tale was reprinted (with the Frost illustrations) in Volume II of *Mathematical Recreations of Lewis Carroll*, 1958, by Dover Publications, Inc., New York. See No. *318* below.

1886

183. Three Years in a Curatorship (1886)   [160

THREE YEARS IN A | CURATORSHIP ||| BY | ONE WHOM IT HAS TRIED ||||

Oxford, printed by E. Baxter: 1886: (sixteen) 8°: pp. 31+[1]. CONTENTS: p. 1, the title; at the head is 'Printed for private circulation': 3, the preface, signed 'C. L. Dodgson, Curator', 'Ch. Ch. March, 1886': 5, contents, in five sections: 7–31, the Report. Issued without covers.

On Christ Church Common Room affairs—ventilation, lighting, furnishing ('Airs, Glares and Chairs'), expenditure and receipts, wine for 'biburients', and the like. There is an interesting table of the 'Present Stock of Wine' (over 20,000 bottles), and their prices. Fifty copies were printed. Selections in *Nonesuch*, pp. 1182–5 (1064-7).

Williams, ii. 50 (p. 105); *Parrish Catalogue*, p. 89; *Collingwood*, p. 439: Christ Church, Oxford, F. Madan.

184. Remarks on Finance Committee (1886)   [161

Remarks on the Report of the Finance Committee. Oxford: Printed by E. Baxter. Pp. 8, cr. 8vo . . . 1886.

So in Collingwood's *Life* (1898), p. 439, but no copy has at present been found. The position in Collingwood's book seems to indicate that it came in date between the foregoing and the following pieces.

In *Diaries*, 8 Mar. 1886, comes the entry: 'Stood at desk from 9 to 6, writing paper on *Report of Finance Committee*' (which is a covert attack on Faussett).

Even the new finds in Christ Church Common Room do not seem to include a copy of this pamphlet.

185. Remarks on Mr. Sampson's Proposal (1886)   [162

REMARKS | on Mr. Sampson's proposal (to be brought | before Common Room on May 28, 1886) | that Common Room shall pay rent for the | rooms now used by it as Drawing-room, &c. | [*A line: the text follows*]

[Oxford, printed by E. Baxter]: (1886): (two) 8°: pp. 4. CONTENTS: p. 1, the title: 1–4, the Remarks, signed 'C. L. Dodgson', 'Ch. Ch., May 27, 1886.' Issued without covers.

A purely domestic affair about the rent of rooms used by the Common Room, and who should pay for it. Incidentally Dodgson mentions that there were 600 members of Common Room, i.e. presumably all Masters of Arts of the House, for the Governing Body consisted of some two dozen only, and the *resident* M.A.s may have been fifty or so.

Williams, ii. 52 (p. 105); *Parrish Catalogue*, p. 90; *Collingwood*, p. 439: F. Madan; Christ Church.

186. *Observations on Mr. Sampson's new proposals, etc.* (1886) [163

OBSERVATIONS | on (1) Mr. Sampson's new proposal (to be | brought before Common Room on June 18, | 1886) . . . [about the Governing Body paying rent for its use of Common Room]; (2) certain recent proceedings of the Wine-| Committee. | [*A thin line, and the text follows.*]

(Oxford, printed by E. Baxter: 1886): (six) 8°: pp. 10+[2]. CONTENTS: p. 1, the title: 1–10, the piece, in two sections, signed 'C. L. Dodgson', 'Ch. Ch., June 10. 1886'. At the foot of p. 10 is 'Baxter, printer, Oxford.' Issued without covers.

More about the Governing Body paying, or not paying, £10 to the Common Room for, or not for, a remuneration of the Common Room servant; and more about the supply of wine outside the Room. The entire code of 'Rules for the wine-Committee' framed on 28 Feb. 1884 is quoted on pp. 4–5.

Williams, ii. 53 (p. 105); *Parrish Catalogue*, p. 20; *Collingwood*, p. 440: F. Madan; Christ Church.

187. *Election of Proctors* (1886) [159

SUGGESTIONS || AS TO THE || ELECTIONS OF PROCTORS | BY | C. L. DODGSON | *Student of Ch. Ch.*

Oxford (Printed by Baxter): 1886: (six) 4°: pp. 10+[2]. CONTENTS: p. 1, the title: 3, introduction signed 'C. L. Dodgson', dated 'Ch. Ch. April 1886': 4–10, the piece, in eight sections: 10, 'Baxter, Printer, Oxford'. Issued without covers.

An enlarged, final and exhaustive (not to say exhausting) form of the 1885 suggestion, issued in view of a statute to be proposed to Congregation in May 1886, giving a thirty-year cycle. This finally passed Congregation on 18 May by 46 to 17, but was rejected in Convocation on 1 June by 44 to 29. The comedy initiated in 1885 was fairly played out. At last in 1887 a statute embodying simple rotation of Colleges passed wearily through Congregation on 25 Jan. by 51 to 22, and through Convocation on 8 Feb. by 150 to 53. After the present pamphlet Dodgson took no part in the contest.

Williams, ii. 49 (p. 104); *Parrish Catalogue*, p. 89; *Collingwood*, p. 439: Bodleian, Christ Church, Oxford.

188-91. Papers on Logic (1886)   [165-8

First paper on Logic. 8°: pp. 2, printed on both sides. Five problems are presented. Known from Collingwood, also from the Hatch sale: owned by Mr. Parrish. [165]
Second paper on Logic. Assumed to exist. [166]
Third paper on Logic. Assumed to exist. [167]
Fourth paper on Logic. Assumed to exist: 8°: pp. 4, three pages printed. Known only from Collingwood. [168]

The first part of a series of nine octavo papers for use in teaching Logic. Problems or examples are presented, often in the form of 'Sets of Premisses' (often very humorous), from which correct conclusions have to be drawn. Collingwood records that all these papers were printed by E. Baxter at Oxford. They are rare. See Nos. 173-5, 211-14.

Williams, ii. 54 (p. 306, Nos. 1, 4); *Parrish Catalogue*, p. 106 (No. 1); *Collingwood*, p. 440 (Nos. 1, 4); see above.

Only the fourth has specific mention in *Diaries*, but the relevant entries run as follows:

7 June 1886: 'Went to Lady Margaret Hall and lectured for about an hour on Logic, to about twenty-five young ladies. . . .'

14 June 1886: 'Gave second lecture at Lady Margaret Hall.'

21 June 1886: 'Gave third lecture on Logic at Lady Margaret Hall: presented copies of my *Fourth Paper* (50 sets of premisses).'

192. Circular about Situations (1886)

Madan adds (*Supplement*, 1935, p. 9) the following: 'A printed circular, dated May 1886, beginning "kindly excuse this being in print". Dodgson hopes to find a governess for some nieces, and situations for two persons whose capacities he describes. The only copy known is owned by Mr. S. H. Williams, and is printed on both sides of an octavo leaf.'

193. Game of Logic (1886) (First, Private, Edition)   [164

The Game | of | Logic | by | Lewis Carroll | Price three shillings |
London | Macmillan and Co. | and New York. | 1886. | All rights reserved. |
8°: pp. [xii]+96: p. [i] the half-title | The Game of Logic. |: [ii] blank: [iii]
blank: [iv] frontispiece, consisting of two diagrams: [v] the title as above:
[vi] blank: [vii] three verses headed | To my Child Friend |: [viii] blank: [ix]
the preface: [x] blank: [xi] contents: [xii] a small light-lined square in the
centre, containing 'Nota Bene' over seven lines: 1–96, the text. At the bottom
of p. 96 is | The End. |
    The copy from which the above collation was made was unbound, uncut
and unopened, though folded and marked for the binder. When found bound
there are four unnumbered pages at the end, as follows: p. [1] Turn over | at
the bottom right-hand corner: [2–3] have advertisements of the works of
Lewis Carroll (their first occurrence): [4] blank.   S. H. W.

A mystery edition, which is rarer than would be expected. Printed
by E. Baxter at Oxford, and the first work of any size attempted
by Baxter, for Dodgson, it seems to have failed to reach Dodgson's
standard, and was apparently condemned by him before public issue.
One copy of the sheets of this folded and ready-to-be-bound item
has been seen, which about 1924 was in Mr. Kashnor the bookseller's hands in London. This issue was passed for press by Dodgson
on 22 Dec. 1886, and only a few copies are known, one being in
the Parrish Collection, bound in the original red cloth. There is a
facsimile of the title-page in the *Parrish Catalogue*, p. 31. This edition
is rare. With it, and as part of it, was an envelope dated 1886, containing a card and nine counters, which will be found fully described
under No. **170** (1887), the second edition of the Game.
    The game is, as a game for children of ordinary capacity, a failure.
In the first chapter (36 pages) the child (for the style is adapted to
children) studies Propositions, Syllogisms, and Failures(!), and by
the end he is expected to understand (p. 77) 'N.B. These are not
legitimate Premisses, since the conclusion is really part of the second
Premiss.' It is in fact an attempt to make formal deductive logic
clear by diagrams, symbols, counters, and plain words, illustrated
by countless examples and tests. A schoolboy might understand the
game, but would certainly not be amused by anything except the
examples. He would prefer 'Barbara, Celarent'. The usual vein of
humour, however, runs through the whole book, with excellent
effect, but as in *Sylvie and Bruno* (at this time in preparation) it is
too light to bear the superstructure.   F. M.
    For the second edition, printed by Clay, see No. **177** (1887).

Williams, i. 53 (p. 66); *Parrish Catalogue*, p. 30, cf. 29–31: Harvard (2 copies),
Huntington, S. H. Williams.

The 'mystery' of this edition is explained by the following *Diary* entry:

5 Dec. 1886: 'The printing of *The Game of Logic* (by Baxter at Oxford) has not been a success: and I wrote today to Macmillan my decision to have it printed again by Clay, for England, and send these 500 to America—just what happened in '65 with *Alice*, when the first 2000, done at the University Press, turned out so bad that I condemned them to the same fate.'

In his letter to Macmillan, Dodgson says 'they will do very well for the Americans, who ought not to be very particular as to *quality*, as they insist on having books for very cheap' [*sic*]. He adds: 'I would rather that these Oxford copies were not sold in England *at all*. . . . They must not begin to be sold in America until the English Edition is ready.'

As, however, he concludes: 'I would still like the 50 copies bound, as already ordered', this edition stands, as in Madan's heading, as 'First, Private, Edition'. Presumably the American edition can be described as 'Second (First Published) Issue of the First Edition' and the 1887 English Edition as 'Second (First Published) Edition'.

194. *Alice's Adventures Under Ground* (1886)   [158

ALICE'S ADVENTURES | UNDER GROUND ‖ *BEING A FACSI-MILE OF THE* | *ORIGINAL MS. BOOK* | *AFTERWARDS DEVELOPED INTO* | 'ALICE'S ADVENTURES IN WONDERLAND' | *BY* | LEWIS CARROLL ‖ *WITH THIRTY-SEVEN ILLUSTRATIONS BY THE AUTHOR* ‖

Price four shillings: London, Macmillan and Co., and New York: 1886: 8°: size $7\frac{3}{10} \times 4\frac{4}{5}$ in.: pp. xvi+91+[9]: signn. 1-7⁸, [8]²: CONTENTS:¹ p. i, the half-title, | Alice's adventures | under ground. | [ii] blank: iii, the title as above, and at the foot '[The Right of Translation and Reproduction is Reserved.]': iv, the imprint, Richard Clay and Sons, London and Bungay.: v, introduction, headed by 'Who will riddle etc.' in Gothic type, and followed by twenty-one lines in italics: vi, introduction continued: vii, introduction continued: viii, introduction concluded, ending with 'Lewis Carroll' and the date 'Dec. 1886': ix, postscript five lines in italics, then 'P.P.S.,' three lines in italics followed by a verse of four lines: x, blank: xi, the contents: xii, blank: xiii, pictorial title 'Alice's | Adventures | under | Ground'. |: xiv, blank: xv, Pictorial Dedication | A | Christmas Gift | to | a Dear Child | in Memory | of | a Summer Day. |: xvi, blank: 1–90, the text; 91, blank except for | '[Turn over.' | at the bottom right-hand corner: [1] Blank: [2] 'An Easter Greeting' beginning 'Dear Child' and ending 'day': [3] 'An Easter Greeting' continued beginning 'first' and ending 'air': [4] 'An Easter Greeting' concluded, beginning '—and' and ending 'Easter, 1876.' Signed Lewis Carroll: [5] 'Christmas Greetings From a Fairy to a child', five verses Christmas 1867 signed Lewis Carroll. with imprint at the bottom of the page, Richard Clay and Sons, London and Bungay.: [6] blank except for | Turn over | at the bottom right-hand corner:

XIII. Four trial title-pages of *Alice's Adventures*, 1864

XIV. ALICE GROWING

One of Lewis Carroll's own illustrations. From *Alice's Adventures Under Ground,* 1886

[7 and 8] Macmillan's advertisements of Lewis Carroll's works: [9] blank: grey end-papers.

Issued in red cloth (Miss Alice Liddell's copy was bound in white vellum). Gold lettering in script along the back | Alice's Adventures under ground | The front cover has three gold lines around the border, and in the centre is | Alice's | Adventures | Under | Ground | in script letters. The back cover has three gold lines around the border, and three circular lines in the centre containing a picture of the Mock Turtle. All edges gilt. Some copies have white end-papers and are mostly in mint condition; they appear (like some copies of the Italian Alice) to be remainder sheets, recently put into covers.

S. H. W.

A most interesting volume, consisting of a facsimile of the first draft of *Alice's Adventures* in the Author's hand, and bearing thirty-seven illustrations (fourteen of which are full-page) by him. There are about 12,715 words as compared with more than 26,708 in the fuller form which was published.

The Evolution. The tale of Alice was told first, as is well known (see No. **30** above), during a river expedition at Oxford in 1862. Dodgson even then seems to have promised Miss Alice Liddell to write out the story, which he did, inserting his own illustrations. The further elaboration to nearly twice the size, with the famous Tenniel pictures, has been described already. Dodgson had 'no idea of publication' when he wrote this book in the first form, between July 1862 and Feb. 1863 (*The Times*, 4 Apr. 1928).

Production. On 11 Nov. 1886, the author wrote to Miss Liddell (now Mrs. Hargreaves) 'I have had almost as many adventures in getting that unfortunate facsimile finished, *Above* ground, as your namesake had *Under* it!'. This refers to the refusal of a good London zincographer to photograph the MS. unless it were sent to town. The next photographer took the photographs in Oxford, but late in 1885 levanted with the negatives of the last twenty-two pages, but zinc blocks from the other negatives had already been sent in for all the rest. At last eight more blocks came, in Apr. 1886, but it needed a legal summons, and Dodgson's personal appearance in the witness-box, to extract the last fourteen negatives from which blocks were made. On 17 Dec. 1886 Dodgson received his first copy.

[The first—and only—edition was of 5,000 copies, according to a letter from Dodgson to Macmillan of 21 Nov. 1886. He had suggested 500 on 7 Oct., and agreed to 1,000 on 28 Oct.]

Notes. The preface is largely serious, quoting testimonies chiefly from a letter from Mrs. Feilden (*The Times*, 7 Apr. 1928) of the use of Dodgson's books in Nursing Homes (where the Easter Greeting of the 'Alice-man' was especially welcome). The profits of the book were to go to Hospitals for sick children. The dedication is clearly to Miss Alice Liddell. The illustrations gave the author much trouble. He had freely illustrated the little magazines of his youth, but had neither the talent (as Ruskin told him) nor the technical training for producing first-rate work, and fanciful illustrations (such as were here needed) taxed the powers even of the best Victorian artists. However, he boldly faced all his difficulties, and produced designs and drawings of considerable interest, if not value. They indicate his idea of the scenes, and he is known to have borrowed an illustrated Natural History from the Dean of Christ Church, Dr. Liddell, to give him ideas for animals and insects. In spite of some inevitable similarities, it may be doubted whether Tenniel derived any ideas directly from this book, though he may have seen it. In a presentation copy of this book Dodgson writes in a letter of 21 June 1889 that it 'has pictures by the author, but they are very badly drawn, I never learned drawing'. The reproduction of the MS. is quite good for the date. The title, dedication, and ornamental headings for the four chapters seem to be all in Dodgson's hand. Facsimiles of the printed and ornamental titles are in Williams's *Bibliography* (1924) at pp. 64, 63.

The episodes of most of the fuller form occur here in the same order, but though the actual words of the MS. are often made use of, there are numerous changes, much is interpolated, some parts are left out, and some whole new episodes introduced. The lettering on the mouse's twisted tail (p. 28 of the facsimile) is entirely different. The episode of the Gryphon and Mock Turtle is a good example of all these points. The trend of the change is perhaps away from mere child's play, towards more advanced and reasoned ingenuity.

The *Easter Greeting* is of the type of No. 7 (see above, 1876), and the *Christmas Greetings* are still in very small type.

The only known point in which the facsimile differs from the MS. is that the MS. has at the end a photograph by Dodgson of Miss Liddell, and the absence of this in the reproduction 'necessitated the re-writing of the last line' (Sotheby's Auction Catalogue, 3 Apr. 1928, lot 319): and it is true that the word 'happy' in that line looks as if it were faked, and other words may have been removed from the negative. See Plate XI.

Mr. Parrish owns a little pamphlet on the history of the MS., issued by the New York Public Library in 1928, entitled 'A Christmas Gift to a Dear Child'.

Supplement (p. 8) adds: 'The title-page bears "Alice in Wonderland The Manuscript and its Story. By R. W. G. Vail. New York,

The New York Public Library": 1928: (four) 8°: pp. 8+3 leaves bearing 5 illustrations+parchment covers.'

Owners, prices, &c. The original MS. was in a Sotheby Book-auction on 3 Apr. 1928, and fetched £15,400, the purchaser being Dr. Rosenbach of Philadelphia. This is a record price for a book at an auction in the United Kingdom. The book was offered by the purchaser to the British Museum for the same sum—an offer very properly not accepted—was then exhibited in the Philadelphia Free Library, and finally resold in Oct. 1928 (with two copies of the first edition of *Alice*) to Eldridge R. Johnson of Morestown, New Jersey, for £30,000 (*Daily Mail*, 16 Oct. 1928). The *New York Times* of 25 Mar. 1928, in a long article on the book, presents a portrait of a spectacled cleric not in the least like Dodgson.   F. M.

Madan adds (*Supplement*, p. 9) that 'the spectacled cleric is Father H. M. Benson!'

The Preface was written on 13 July 1885, according to the *Diaries*.

The original *Alice* MS. was bought for $50,000 in 1948 and pre-sented to the British Museum by American donors 'who wished to show their appreciation of the courage of these islands in protecting liberty during two great wars'. See *The Times*, 15 Nov. 1948.

Dodgson's original illustrations to *Alice's Adventures Under Ground* were used as illustrations to *Alice's Adventures in Wonderland* in the volume (number 836) of Everyman's Library first published in 1929, with an introduction by Ernest Rhys, under the title of *Alice in Wonderland, Through the Looking-Glass, &c.* The Introduction con-tains a facsimile of the Mouse's Tail, and the penultimate paragraph is quoted; but the discrepancies between illustrations and text are not fully explained.

The reissue (of *Wonderland* alone) in Dent's Everyman Paperbacks in 1961 contains a new Introductory Note about the illustrations.

There seems to have been a reprint by Macmillan in America in 1932, according to the Library of Congress Catalog.

195. Savile Clarke's Alice (1886)   [702-4

Alice in Wonderland. A Dream Play for Children, in two Acts. Founded upon Mr. Lewis Carroll's 'Alice's Adventures in Wonder-land', and 'Through the Looking-Glass', with the express sanction of the Author. By H. Savile Clarke. Music by Walter Slaughter. London . . . at 'The Court Circular' Office . . .: 1886: 8°: pp. 54+ [2]. Issued in brown paper wrappers, lettered and decorated, with-out the music, but with some Tenniel illustrations.

With advertisements on the inside of both wrappers. The first wrapper bears 'First edition under revision' and 'Price One Shilling'. There are Dedication Verses to Lewis Carroll by 'H. S. C.', Christmas 1886. Mrs. Ffooks owns a copy.

Mr. Parrish possesses this and editions of 1888 [703] and 1889 [704]. The 1889 edition has changes and omits the Verses. See the *Parrish Catalogue*, p. 125 (all three issues): the Library of Congress possesses a 1906 edition (London, Ascherberg: 4^0: p. 90): see under 1906.

This operetta was composed and issued with Dodgson's approval: see Collingwood's *Life*, p. 254. Phœbe Carlo played Alice. For Miss Whitehead's circular 'flimsy' see no. 705. Mrs. Ffooks possesses a souvenir of the Garrick Theatre performance, with a small photograph of Dodgson on it.

Dodgson's own special copy with his annotations on the performance was sold by Messrs. Parker of Oxford in 1898.

Mr. W. T. Spencer, bookseller, of New Oxford Street, London, owns 97 letters (1886-90) from Dodgson to Mr. Savile Clarke and Miss Kitty Clarke, concerning this dramatization, for which in 1929 he was asking £500.

It may be noted that 'Flowerland', one of the two supplementary songs mentioned above, and in the present volume anonymous, was issued separately in 1907 as a 'Song from Alice in Wonderland', but it was not written by Dodgson. The first words are 'Flow'rs awake from out your long repose', and the music of both songs is by W. Slaughter.   F. M.

Madan places this item in an Appendix among 'Dramatizations, &c.', but it should more properly be here as it contains first publication of material by Dodgson himself.

The bibliography of this Play is obscure and could only be contemplated in detail after collation of all available copies both in England and America—which I cannot attempt. MS. notes in a copy of the *Handbook* now in the possession of Mr. Derek Hudson give four variants as follows:

1. 'My 1886 1st Issue has no "First Edition under Revision", on cover, so probably earlier.'

2. 'Also 1886 with "First Edition under Revision" on front, different inside, not printed on back of illustrations, parts cut out, only one advert. at end on inside cover.'

3. 'My 1889 cover has 1888 title page. Identical inside.'

4. '1888 and 9, no verses.'

A copy in my possession has title-page as described by Madan—as far as 'Walter Slaughter', but then 'Performed at the Opera

Comique Theatre under the Management | of Mr. ARTHUR ELIOT'—
[this was the revival opening on 22 Dec. 1898]. No publisher is
given, but the imprint is at the foot of the page: 'Printed by Richard
Clay and Sons, Limited | London and Bungay' [all in capitals]. It
is not dated, but would be 1898. It consists of the songs only—and
they are not complete—with six Tenniel illustrations.

Dodgson gave his consent for Henry Savile Clarke to make his
version on 2 Sept. 1886. On 30 Oct. 1886 he records: 'On my way
through London I called on Mr. Savile Clarke . . . I had a long talk
about the play of *Alice in Wonderland.*' On 27 Oct. 1886 he had
written to Macmillan to supply Savile Clarke with pictures: 'Please
have electros done for him of any he likes to order.'

On 9 Nov. 1886 Dodgson was instructing Macmillan to print
5,000 of the book *Alice's Adventures in Wonderland*—'when title-sheet,
mouse's tale, and pp. 159 etc., have been corrected'. The first correction was to add the price; the second was typographical; but
the third was the substitution (and consequent rearranging of
several pages) of the 16-line version of ' 'Tis the voice of the Lobster'
for that of six lines in all previous editions. For this reprint (the
seventy-ninth thousand) he wrote the special Preface: 'As Alice is
about to appear on the Stage, and as the lines beginning " 'Tis the
voice of the Lobster" were found to be too fragmentary for
dramatic purposes, four lines have been added to the first stanza,
and six to the second, while the Oyster has been developed into a
Panther.'

It is not certain whether this edition came out before or after the
first publication of the Play—which contained the complete version
of the poem.

On 30 Dec. 1886 Dodgson saw a performance of the play (the
first was on 23 Dec.) and noted that 'The second act was flat . . .
the "Walrus etc." had no definite finale.'

On 3 Jan. 1887 he noted in the *Diaries*: 'To town, to talk with
Mr. Savile Clarke about the Play. I had written a finale, which he
approved, for "Walrus, etc.", bringing in three ghosts of oysters.'

The finale to 'The Walrus and the Carpenter' is reprinted in my
notes to the *Diaries* (pp. 446–7): I have been unable to discover in
which edition of the Play (or the songs) it was first published.
Possibly earlier editions contain the stanza of six lines sung by Ghost
of First Oyster but not that by Ghost of Second Oyster. Miss Empsie
Bowman, who played Dormouse and Ghost of Second Oyster in
the 1888 revival, told me that Dodgson was so sorry that she had
no lines in her second part that he wrote the stanza specially for

her—and she was still able to sing it word-perfect sixty years later. Subsequent research showed that it is, in fact, included in later reprints, and that I had not as I thought (see *The Story of Lewis Carroll*, 1949, p. 127) rescued this stanza from oblivion!

So far as can be ascertained the London productions of the play (with actress who played Alice) have been as follows:

23 Dec. 1886—Prince of Wales Theatre (Phoebe Carlo).
26 Dec. 1888—Globe Theatre (Isa Bowman).
22 Dec. 1898—Opéra Comique (Phyllis Beadon).
    Dec. 1899—Opéra Comique (Rose Hearne).
19 Dec. 1900—Vaudeville Theatre (Ellaline Terriss).
    Dec. 1906—Prince of Wales Theatre (Marie Studholme).
23 Dec. 1907—Apollo Theatre (Maidie Andrews).
27 Dec. 1909—Royal Court Theatre (Ivy Sawyer).
26 Dec. 1910—Savoy Theatre (Ivy Sawyer).
23 Dec. 1913—Comedy Theatre (Cora Goffin).
26 Dec. 1914—Savoy Theatre (Ivy Sawyer).
24 Dec. 1915—Duke of York's Theatre (Ivy Sawyer).
26 Dec. 1916—Savoy Theatre (Vera Hamilton).
26 Dec. 1917—Savoy Theatre (Estelle Dudley).
27 Dec. 1920—Victoria Palace (Phyllis Griffiths).
26 Dec. 1921—Garrick Theatre (Phyllis Griffiths).
26 Dec. 1922—Royal Court Theatre (Evelyn Joyce).
20 Dec. 1926—Golders Green (Gwen Stella).
23 Dec. 1927—Savoy Theatre (Myrtle Peter).
22 Dec. 1930—Savoy Theatre (Joy Blackwood).

Later revivals were in new versions, by Nancy Price, A. A. Milne, Clemence Dane, &c. 'Alice' in these has been played on various occasions by such famous actresses as Joyce Redman (1938), Roma Beaumont (1943), and Peggy Cummins (1944).   R. L. G.

1887

196. *Game of Logic* (1887)   [170ᵃ

THE GAME | OF | LOGIC ||| BY | LEWIS CARROLL. |||| *PRICE THREE SHILLINGS* |.

London Macmillan and Co. and New York: 1887: 8°: size $7\frac{1}{4} \times 4\frac{15}{16}$ in.: pp. [12]+96+[4]: signn. [A]⁶, B-G⁸ [H]²: CONTENTS: p. [1] the half-title: [4] frontispiece consisting of two diagrams, one occupying the upper half of the page, the other, the right-hand side of the lower half of the page, the left-hand side of the lower half having | Colours for | counters. | [*a thin line*: then six lines over a thin line]: [5] the title as above: [6] imprint of | Richard Clay and Sons, | London and Bungay. | in the centre: [7] three six-line verses headed by | To my Child Friend.: | [8] | Nota Bene | over fourteen lines, enclosed in a thin-line square: [9] the preface: [11] contents: 1–96, the text: [1] blank, except for | [Turn over | at the bottom right-hand corner: [2-3] advertisements of the works of Lewis Carroll. Dark grey end-papers.

Issued in red cloth. Along the back is | The Game of Logic | in gold. The front cover has on the upper half | The | Game | of | Logic | in gold script. The back cover is blank. All edges cut and plain. The reader will notice slight differences of imprint and arrangement from No. 164 (1886).

Accompanying this book there should be an envelope (170ᵇ), containing a card diagram (170ᶜ) and nine counters (170ᵈ), four red and five grey. The size of the envelope is $7 \times 4\frac{1}{8}$ in. The front of the envelope is lettered vertically | The Game | of | Logic | by | Lewis Carroll | Price of book | (with Envelope containing board and nine counters) | Three shillings | Price of envelope, &c. | three pence | [the last 18 words are also on the title-page, above]: London | Macmillan and Co. | and New York | 1887 |. The size of the board contained in the envelope is $6\frac{5}{16} \times 4\frac{1}{16}$ in., and it is lettered on the one side exactly as the front of the envelope: on the other side of the board are two diagrams, one occupying nearly the whole of the upper two-thirds of the board, while the other diagram appears in the right-hand half of the remaining third of the board, and the left-hand half has | The Game | of | Logic. | [line] | Instructions for playing | the game will be found in the accompanying book. | [line]. The diameter of the counters is $\frac{3}{4}$ in.

Whatever reason Mr. Dodgson had for superseding the first edition of this book, he evidently had no occasion to re-issue the envelope with the card and counters (dated 1886), for they were issued with this second edition, and although I am assured that there are envelopes and cards bearing the date 1887, I have never seen one.

[I possess two copies of the card (though not the envelope) both dated 1887, which were given to me with a copy of the book by the late Miss Caroline J. M. Hubback, who was one of Dodgson's pupils at the Oxford High School in 1887. R. L. G.]

This second edition is, as with Alice's Adventures, dated a year later than the true first edition: it is an entire reprint by Clay and Sons, of E. Baxter's Oxford work (see what has been noted under the first edition of 1886, No. 164), and was speedily made, for the author's own copy reached him on 22 Feb. 1887.

The game has been described under No. 164. There are three chapters, 'New Lamps for old', 'Cross questions', and 'Hit or miss'; the last, like the papers on Logic (Nos. 165-8, &c., 1886, &c.), containing tricky premisses from which conclusions have to be drawn. The 'Nota bene' invites suggestions, and after the advertisements at the end come notes of the discount allowed for the book, and a note of the separate issue of the Easter Greeting at a penny. A facsimile of the title of the second edition, as well as of the first, is given at p. 33 of the Parrish Catalogue. The diagrams are suited, in conjunction with red counters (one or more objects) or grey counters (no objects) placed on them, to express various kinds of logical statement. *Symbolic Logic* No. **240** (1896) is a development of this idea.

There is considerable change in the new edition in detail, such as, in the syllogisms, 'New cakes are nice' takes the place of 'Red apples are ripe' in Chapter 1, and in Chapter 4 the text and diagrams vary considerably.

Published 21 Feb. 1887 (*Diaries*). This edition was of 500 (letter to Macmillan: n.d. [*c*. 20 Dec. 1886]).

It was reprinted in 1958 in the *Mathematical Recreations of Lewis Carroll*, vol. i. See No. *318*.

197. Nature (1887–98)

Dodgson made three contributions to *Nature*, as follows:

1. 'To Find the Day of the Week for Any Given Date.' [Written 8 Mar. 1887.] Vol. xxxv, p. 517. 31 Mar. 1887.
2. 'Brief Method of Dividing a Given Number by 9 or 11.' [Written 28 Sept. 1897]. Vol. lvi, pp. 565–6. 14 Oct. 1897.
3. 'Abridged Long Division.' [Written 21 Dec. 1897: this is his last work]. Vol. lvii, pp. 269–71. 20 Jan. 1898.

198-200. Papers on Logic (1887)   [**173-5**

Fifth paper on Logic. 8°: pp. 4, all printed on. Dated May, 1887. [**173**]
Sixth paper on Logic. Dated June, 1887. [**174**]
Seventh paper on Logic. Assumed to exist. Date uncertain (1887?). [**175**]

For preceding papers see Nos. **165–8** (1886), and for subsequent papers see Nos. **211–14** (1892).

Williams, ii. 56, 57 (p. 106; Nos. 5–6); *Parrish Catalogue*, p. 108 (Nos. 5–6); *Collingwood*, p. 440 (Nos. 5–6): F. Madan (Nos. 5–6).

Though he does not mention the papers, they must have been printed for the following occasion:

11 May 1887. 'Gave first lecture at the High School, on *The Game of Logic*.' There were further lectures in May and June.

201-2. Questions in Logic (1887)   [**176-7**

Questions in Logic. Folio, pp. 4, all printed on. The date is supplied by Collingwood's *Life*. [**176**]
—— Another issue. Folio, pp. 8, all printed on. The date is perhaps doubtful. Both these pieces are very rare. [**177**]

Williams, ii. 58 (p. 106, first issue only); *Parrish Catalogue*, pp. 107–8; *Collingwood*, p. 440 (first issue only).

Presumably printed for use at the Oxford High School during his lectures in May and June 1887—but neither is mentioned in the *Diaries*.

203. *Alice on the Stage* (1887)   [171 ⁻

'Alice' on the Stage. By Lewis Carroll.

A paper of six pages so entitled, in the *Theatre* for Apr. 1887, beginning 'Look here', is reprinted in the *Lewis Carroll Picture Book* (1899) at pp. 163–74, and criticizes Savile Clarke's dramatization of *Alice*. Incidentally Dodgson recounts the origin of *Alice* and of the *Snark* (pp. 165, 167). In an 'appreciation' (in Pater's sense) he singles out Mr. Sydney Harcourt (the Hatter and Tweedledum), Miss Phœbe Carlo (as Alice), and Miss Dorothy d'Alcourt (the Dormouse) as specially successful. The most interesting part of the article is his conception of Alice, the White Rabbit, the Queen of Hearts, the Red Queen, and the White Queen, in character sketches, apart from what they said or did on the stage.

Not reprinted in *Nonesuch* (nor anywhere else, except *L.C.P.B.*).

204. *Children in Theatres* (1887)   [172

CHILDREN IN THEATRES.

An offprint in two columns of a letter to the *St. James's Gazette*, signed 'Lewis Carroll' and dated 16 July, beginning, 'Sir, In your Gazette of this day [16 July] I see', and occupying 87 lines. Dodgson attempts to show that at least three little girls on the stage, whom he knew, were still happy and healthy, and that a recent meeting at South Kensington to protest against children under ten being allowed to act on the stage was a mistaken move. The date is probably 1887 if Savile Clarke's dramatization of *Alice's Adventures* was then being played at Brighton, to which reference is made in the letter. Some of the letter is printed in Collingwood's *Life and Letters* at pp. 180–1. Mr. Parrish owns the only copy known of this offprint.

Williams, i. 55 (p. 68); *Parrish Catalogue*, p. 34; *Collingwood*, p. 180.

The letter appeared in the *St. James's Gazette* (145) for 19 July 1887. I have reprinted nearly the whole in *Diaries*, pp. 452–3. Madan adds in *Supplement*, p. 9: 'No doubt, I am informed, the "three children", are Miss Isa Bowman and two of her sisters.' This is a mistake which I repeated in *Notes and Queries*, 7 Apr. 1945 and with modifications (Miss Isa Bowman assured me that one of her sisters was of the trio) in *The Story of Lewis Carroll* (1949), pp. 127–8. But the entries in the *Diaries* for 15 and 16 July 1887 give the true facts:

15 July: 'To Brighton . . . To Mrs. Carlo's, and saw her and Mrs. d'Albuquerque, Phoebe, Dorothy, and also Lizzie Carlo, whom I added to my already-two-large party [Dodgson had invited Phoebe and Dorothy—and he always insisted that one child-friend made a party, and even two made too large a party]. We first drove to Henrietta's lodgings where the children got some strawberries. Then to the Smiths, and had a short time with Mrs. Smith, Gracie and Constance; but I wanted the children to see Miss Louey Webb, so we went on the Pier, for an hour, and returned. Then gave my little charges "High tea", and I got them home again at 7 p.m. having had five hours of their company. . . .'

16 July: '*The St. James's Gazette* has an account of a large ladies' meeting "to prevent children under 10 acting in theatres". Whereupon I wrote a letter to the Editor with an account of yesterday.'

R. L. G.

205. *Four Seasons* (1887)

This was the original title for *Sylvie and Bruno*, and under it Dodgson sent 'Bruno's Revenge' and some of the verses to Macmillan on 6 Aug. 1887: he received proofs on 12 Aug. 1887.

One sheet survives among the family papers, which Miss F. Menella Dodgson has allowed me to examine. It consists of the verses 'Little Birds' finally published in *Sylvie and Bruno Concluded* (1893), Chapter XXIII. The poem contains an additional stanza, omitted from the book so that what remained might fit into the frames supplied by Furniss's illustrations—and for this reason I include *Four Seasons* as an item here.

The missing stanza was published for the first time in my notes to the *Diaries* (pp. 453–4), and may be found in its place in the complete poem in *The Book of Nonsense* (1956), pp. 70–73. See item 317.

1888

206. *To my Child-Friend* (1888)   [178

To my Child-Friend | [*A line, then the poem.*]

[No place or date, but 1888?]: (one) 8°: printed on one side only.

A graceful poem of eighteen lines, entitled as above, beginning 'I charm in vain'. This was prefixed as a dedication to the *Game of*

Logic (No. **164**, 1886). The question is, whether this leaflet was reprinted in the *Game*, or here from it. Collingwood thinks the former. The only difference is that in lines 6 (twice), 12, 18 'F' in the *Game* is replaced by 'f' in this leaflet. If the leaflet is prior, then Dodgson inserted it without any relevance in the *Game*. If, however, he had written the poem recently and wished to put it into print, he may have seized the opportunity, in spite of irrelevance, and later reprinted it separately. It is almost decisive that on the back of the only copy known (in the possession of Mr. Parrish) there is a note 'Correspondence references.' Wilcox. W. M. 61961.' This of course refers to Dodgson's Register of letters, &c., and the number points clearly to May or June 1888, but this is the only case in which the number does not stand alone, out of more than sixty examples noted.

The name of the 'Child-Friend' may be found by taking the second letter of each of the eighteen lines. Climene Mary Holiday was the niece of Henry Holiday, one of Dodgson's illustrators. Very rare.   F. M.

Williams, i. 77 (p. 87); *Parrish Catalogue*, p. 11; *Collingwood*, p. 443.

207. *Memoria Technica* (1888)   [**179**

Memoria Technica | [*an ornamental line*: then nineteen lines of text.]

[Oxford]: Cyclostyled: 1888: (two) 8°: pp. [4]. CONTENTS: p. [1] the title: [1–3] the piece in italic script, dated at the end: June, 1888.

This anonymous piece is Dodgson's modification of Dr. Richard Grey's system, first published in 1730, and lastly in 1861, by which dates are fixed in the memory by the last letters of the fact to be dated being altered into letters representing numbers. Dodgson represents 1–9, 0 by two alternative consonants each, and fills in with vowels to make a word. Thus the Discovery of America was in 1492. The 1 may be disregarded; 4, 9, 2 can be represented by *f, n, d* (or *q, g, w*): so you compose a rhyme, '| Columbus sailed the world around | Until America was FOUND.' | The whole is reprinted in Collingwood's *Life*, pp. 268–9, where the author remarks that Dodgson had a 'wonderfully good memory except for faces and dates'!

Williams, ii. 60 (p. 107); *Parrish Catalogue*, p. 108; *Collingwood*, pp. 267–70, 440: Bodleian, Harvard.

See No. *120* above.

208. *The Stage* (1888)   [180

The Stage and the Spirit of Reverence. By Lewis Carroll.

An article in the *Theatre* for June 1888, beginning 'This article is not going to be a sermon in disguise', is reprinted entire in the *Lewis Carroll Picture Book* (1889) at pp. 175–95. An interesting part is Dodgson's account of several plays he had seen: at the end he suggests that the parable of the Prodigal Son might well form the basis of a drama.

This article (sent to the editor on 4 May 1888) is not reprinted in *Nonesuch*, nor apparently anywhere else except *L.C.P.B.*

209. *Lesson in Latin* (1888)   [181

A poem of twenty-one lines in the *Jabberwock*, vol. ii, no. 5, June 1888 (Boston, U.S.A.), is so entitled, and begins 'Our Latin Books, in motley row' (p. 2). The point turns on the Latin words *amarĕ* and *amarē*, and ends '| Our Latin lesson is complete: | We've learned that Love is bitter-sweet! | Lewis Carroll.' The *Jabberwock* was published monthly by the Fourth Class, '91, of the Girls' Latin School, Boston. The editor mentions that she had received three letters from Lewis Carroll, one giving permission to use the title, and explaining the word, a second objecting to an anecdote printed in the paper, and a third (printed by the editor on p. 2), dated 17 May 1888, and typewritten, enclosing the poem, which he styles a lump of sugar after the black draught of remonstrance. The whole number is only one quarto leaf, two pages, in double columns. The poem is reprinted in *Three Sunsets* (1898), Collingwood's *Life*, p. 276, and *Further Nonsense*, p. 46.

Williams, iii. 17 (p. 120); *Collingwood*, p. 276, cf. 275: M. L. Parrish, F. Madan.

Also reprinted in *Collected Verse* (1932), p. 439, *Nonesuch*, pp. 976–7 (876–7), &c.

210. *Curiosa Mathematica. Part I* (1888)   [182

𝕮𝖚𝖗𝖎𝖔𝖘𝖆 𝕸𝖆𝖙𝖍𝖊𝖒𝖆𝖙𝖎𝖈𝖆 | *PART I* | A NEW THEORY || OF | PARALLELS || BY | CHARLES L. DODGSON, M.A. | *Student and late Mathematical Lecturer* | *of Christ Church, Oxford* ||

Price two shillings. London Macmillan and Co.: 1888: 8°: pp. xxiii+[1]+ 63+[5]: signn. a⁸, b⁴, B–E⁸, [F].¹ CONTENTS: p. iii, the half-title: iv, a Macmillan mark: vi, a large pentagon and circumscribed dotted circle with letterpress: vii, the title; at the foot is '[All rights reserved]': viii, 'Oxford Horace Hart, Printer to the University': ix–xviii, the preface, signed 'C. L. D.', 'Ch. Ch., Oxford. July 1888.': xix–xxiii, the contents: 1–34, the New Theory:

35–63, four appendices, with half-title, and p. 36 blank: 63, '[Turn over.': [1] blank: [2] advertisements of six works by Dodgson. Issued in light grey cloth, with black lettering on the back, and on the front and back covers.

A scientific attempt to improve Euclid's 12th Axiom about two lines unequally inclined to a transversal, compared with his 35th Definition (of Parallel Lines) and certain Propositions. Dodgson spent a vast amount of time in this investigation, as can be seen from a large collection of his mathematical papers which has survived. In this long and exact inquiry he has imbedded an investigation into circles with inscribed and circumscribed hexagons, as one of his methods of confuting Circle-Squarers. The amusing preface shows that in his task of meeting and defeating that particular band of cranks the mantle of Augustus De Morgan (who died in 1871) descended on Dodgson's shoulders. He finds room also for a piece of would-be verse beginning 'I have wandered' (which had not before been printed and is worthy of a place in Wyndham Lewis's *Stuffed Owl*) (p. 61), and for a 'Will-o-the-wisp' of his own (p. 62). A presentation copy dated Aug. 1888 is known.

The second edition was issued in 1889, the third in 1890, the fourth in 1895, each with changes and replies to critics. In and after the third, the frontispiece and allied figures bear a tetragon instead of a hexagon.

The second part of Curiosa Mathematica is *Pillow-problems*, see No. 220 (1893).

The *Diaries* for 8 Apr. 1888 give 'I have nearly completed my *New Theory of Parallels*'.

A letter to Macmillan on 6 July 1888 says: 'I have now passed the whole of this book for "Press", and have told them to print 250 copies, on toned paper, and to send you 100.'

211. *Seven Diagrams* (1888)   [183

Seven diagrams, on seven octavo leaves, printed on one side only, believed to be used in *Symbolic Logic* (No. 240 below). They begin respectively: No x are m: x_0y_1: $B—By—y$: (a variety of the last): Not all x are y: (a variety of the last): No x are m (a variety of the first). These seven sheets, the only copies known, are in the collection of Mr. Parrish. They bear Dodgson's correspondence number 59584, which seems to indicate early in 1888.

Parrish Catalogue, p. 111.

1889

212. *Alice's Adventures* (In Shorthand: 1889)   [184

[Alice's Adventures in Wonderland, chapter VII, in Callendar's Cursive Shorthand: one of the series of 'Reading Practices in Cursive Shorthand; facsimiles of actual writing. By Hugh L. Callendar, M.A. Fellow of Trinity College, Cambridge.'

London, C. J. Clay and Sons: 1889: eight 12° pages of shorthand, with grey wrapper, bearing the title of the series, Remarks, Advertisements, &c., in English: price 3 pence.

The first shorthand edition of any part of Dodgson's works. Chapter VII contains the Mad Hatter's Tea-party.

213. *Common Room Meetings* (1889)   [190

MEETING OF COMMON ROOM. | Thursday, March 7, 1889, at 1.30 p.m. |

[Oxford]: 1889: folio: pp. 8.

Agenda for a Meeting of the Christ Church Common Room. On p. 6 'Eligeni' is a misprint for 'eligendi', persons to be elected selectors of wine. On p. 8 are 'Apagenda', things not to be submitted to the Meeting. Signed 'C. L. Dodgson, Curator' [190ª]. Sir H. Hartley has a similar notice of 28 Feb. 1884.

Christ Church, Oxford.

SPECIAL MEETING OF COMMON ROOM. | Thursday, May 9, 1889, at 1.30 p.m. |

[Oxford]: 1889: folio: pp. 4.

Agenda for a Meeting, as next above. Signed 'C. L. Dodgson, Curator' [190ᵇ].

Christ Church Library.

——Other Agenda papers are extant for Meetings on 20 Feb. 1890 (4 folio pages signed as before); 12 Feb. 1891 (2 folio pages, signed as before); 13 Feb. 1892 (signed as before); and 3 Mar. 1892 (a desire to resign the Curatorship, signed as before). On all these six papers the words 'For Members of Common Room only' are printed at the head. [190ᶜ⁻ᶠ].

Christ Church Library.

[191

SPECIAL MEETING OF COMMON ROOM. | Friday, May 17, 1889, | at 1.30 p.m., | [To receive the resignation of the present Curator.] |

[Oxford]: (1889): (one): obl. 12°: printed on one side only.

A notice addressed to Members of the Christ Church Common Room at Oxford. It is signed 'C. L. Dodgson, Curator'. 'Ch. Ch., May 10, 1889', and in the upper left corner is 'For Members of Common Room only.]': it convenes a meeting, and Dodgson emphatically declares that he will thereat resign the Curatorship, after six years' tenancy, in view of the rejection of certain proposals on 9 May. He was, however, induced to retain the office till 1892.

The only copy known is owned by Mr. Parrish.

F. M.

Parrish Catalogue, p. 91; with facsimile on p. 92.

There are copies of all these in Christ Church Library. Strictly speaking, the above entries could have been omitted here, as I have listed the items with the other Common Room Meetings under No. *161* above.

214. *Stage Children* (1889)   [189

A letter thus headed, by Lewis Carroll, is in the *Theatre* for Sept. 1889, according to the *Oxford Art Agency Sale* of Carrolliana in 1898, art. 395, describing Dodgson's own copy with his notes.

F. M.

The letter was first published in the *Sunday Times* on 4 Aug. 1889, and reprinted in the *Theatre*, Sept. 1889.

It is quoted in my notes to *Diaries*, p. 473, and in my article 'Lewis Carroll and Stage Children" in the *Stage*, 21 Oct. 1954.

R. L. G.

215. *Nursery Alice* (1889)   [185ᵃ

THE NURSERY 'ALICE' ‖ *CONTAINING TWENTY COLOURED ENLARGEMENTS* │ *FROM* │ *TENNIEL'S ILLUSTRATIONS* │ *TO* │ 'ALICE'S ADVENTURES IN WONDERLAND' │ *WITH TEXT ADAPTED TO NURSERY READERS* │ BY │ LEWIS CARROLL ‖ *THE COVER DESIGNED AND COLOURED* │ BY │ E. GERTRUDE THOMSON ‖│

London Macmillan and Co.: 1889: 4°: size 10×7¾ in.: pp. [12]+56+[8]: signn. [A]⁶, B–H, [I]⁴. CONTENTS: p. [1] the half-title │ The Nursery Alice.│: [4] frontispiece: [5] the title as above, at the head 'People's Edition │ Price Two Shillings.' and at the foot '[All rights reserved]': p. [6] the imprint, in the centre │ London │ Engraved and Printed │ by │ Edmund Evans │: p. [7] two stanzas, 16 lines, in black-letter, headed by │ A Nursery Darling │ , above and below the two stanzas are double lines: [9–10] preface, with date at end, │ │ Easter-tide, 1889. │ [11] contents, in 14 chapters: 1–56, the text: [1] blank, except for │ [Turn over. │ at the bottom right-hand corner: [2–4] 'An Easter Greeting', signed 'Lewis Carroll': [5] 'Christmas Greetings', signed Lewis Carroll: [6–8] Macmillan's advertisements of the works of Lewis Carroll.

Issued with orange-coloured end-papers, and glazed in yellow paper boards. The spine is blank. The front cover has | The | Nursery | 'Alice' | and a pictorial design of Alice asleep, and dreaming beneath a tree, signed 'E. G. Thomson—'. The back cover has a picture of the March Hare in the centre, and the initials 'E. G. T.' All edges cut and plain.

In an interesting preface Lewis Carroll states that *Alice's Adventures* has been read by 'children' from five to an age which he will not mention. He wishes it to be 'read, to be cooed over, to be dogs' eared, to be rumpled, to be kissed' by children from nought to five. He therefore rewrites parts of it in a simpler and much abbreviated form, but in as many as sixteen chapters. It begins with 'Once upon a time, there was a little girl called Alice, and she had a very curious dream.' The attraction for 'children' above four, lies in the coloured mechanical enlargements of twenty of the Tenniel illustrations (two full-page), for these were submitted to Tenniel for approval of the colours. The type also is large. The second letters of each line of the dedicatory verses give the name of the dedicatee, Marie Vander Gucht. Dodgson received his first copy on 19 Oct. 1889, and distributed 121 presentation copies. This first edition is not common. An uncoloured early copy with 'Price three Shillings' was presented on 13 Aug. 1889 [185ᵇ]. The notes at the end include two 'cautions to readers' referring to 'The Land of Idleness' and 'From Nowhere to the North Pole'.

Mrs. Milner informs me that in *The Lady* for 24 Mar. 1892, is a letter from Dodgson, stating that in some copies of the *Nursery Alice* (1890) there were some imperfections of printing, and that consequently the price would be lowered until the stock of such copies was sold out.

In Maggs's Catalogue 548, art. 280, occurs an early form (?) of the first edition, with no 'People's Edition', price two shillings, and differences of colouring, but still dated 1889: this copy was a presentation one from Dodgson on 19 Mar. 1891 [185ᶜ]. Another form has no 'People's Edition' and no price [185ᵈ]. Another has 'Price one Shilling', covering 'Price Three Shillings' [185ᵉ].

216. The second edition [186], issued in glazed white boards, appears to differ only in the date 1890, in the substitution of 'Price four Shillings' above the imprint for 'People's Edition. Price Two Shillings' above the title, and in the Advertisements at the end. Copies also have an inserted printed slip advertising *Sylvie and Bruno.* A presentation copy dated 25 Mar. 1890 is known. This edition is in the British Museum, Bodleian, &c. From a note in No. **216** (1893) we learn that the seventh thousand was then on sale. These were sold at 2s. each, just over cost price, because 'the colours came out a little too bright': the price would be raised again when these had been sold off. In 1898 the book was in its eleventh thousand.

F. M.

Williams, i. 59 (p. 69); *Parrish Catalogue*, p. 37; *Collingwood*, pp. 284, 292, cf. 440: S. H. Williams, Mrs. Ffooks, Harvard. All these references are to the first edition.

I have let the above stand unaltered; but in fact *The Nursery Alice* is another case for careful study by a bibliographer able to collate many copies from collections on both sides of the Atlantic.

Apparently no one (not even Collingwood) knew that the first edition was withdrawn after 10,000 had been printed—because the pictures were too bright (letter to Macmillan 23 June 1889), 500 bound up and sent to America—where it was refused, because the pictures were not bright enough—and reprinted (second issue of the first edition) for Dodgson to receive his first copy on 19 Oct. 1889.

As Collingwood gives 1890 as the date of the first edition, he may have known (but not said) that an edition was withdrawn, and assumed that all copies dated 1889 were of this edition.

Copies dated 1889 have been seen with all sorts of variants from the details given by Madan: my own copy bears the same title-page, but without 'People's Edition Price Two Shillings', with PRICE THREE SHILLINGS printed above the imprint at the foot of the title-page—and then that price cancelled by a small decorated panel printed over it, and above that the words PRICE ONE SHILLING printed in a slightly different shade of brown ink. The back cover has no picture, and the end-papers are white.

Variants dated 1890 have also been recorded.

The letters to Macmillan show that Dodgson had copies (4) without colour bound up in June, and further ones at the time of the reprint (14) in September. Copies sent to him in September were returned as the 'hare' on the back was not central. The first twelve coloured copies received on 19 Oct. 1889 were returned immediately as 'every one cracked to pieces on simply being opened'. A dozen received on 29 Oct. 1889 were 'quite satisfactory'.

In Jan. 1890 Macmillan found an American agent willing to take 1,000 copies of *The Nursery Alice* for which Dodgson was to receive £80.

The new edition, of 10,000 copies, was printed by the end of Feb. 1890, on *white* paper, instead of the 'off-white' (which Dodgson calls 'tinted') of the original edition, and Dodgson directed that it should be published in time for Easter. In July he was giving away copies to 100 hospitals—which may have been drawn from the first edition.

On 13 Dec. 1890 he restated the book's history to Macmillan: 'The *first* impression was over-coloured and condemned *not* to be sold in England: and you got me £75 per 1000, for 4,000 of them from your American Agent', and he asks for accounts for the two impressions, 10,000 each. In Apr. 1891, 500 copies (of first issue) were sold to Australia.

217. *Sylvie and Bruno* (1889)   [187

SYLVIE AND BRUNO ||| BY | LEWIS CARROLL | *WITH FORTY-SIX ILLUSTRATIONS* | *BY* | *HARRY FURNISS* |

Price Three Half-crowns London Macmillan and Co. and New York: 1889: 8°: size $7\frac{3}{16} \times 5$ in.: pp. xxiv+400+[4]: signn. [a]⁴, b, B–Z, Aa–Cc⁸, [Dd]². CONTENTS: p. i, the half-title | Sylvie and Bruno |: ii, Macmillan's monogram in the centre of the page: iv, frontispiece: v, the title as above, and at the foot | *The Right of Translation and Reproduction is Reserved.*|: vi, imprint | Richard Clay and Sons, Limited, | London and Bungay.|: vii, two thin lines over, and also under, three verses in black-letter type, beginning 'Is all our Life, then, but a dream': ix–xxi, the Preface: xxii–xxiii, the contents, in 25 chapters: 1–395, the text: 396–400, the index. At the bottom of p. 400, under a thin line is | Richard Clay and Sons, Limited, London and Bungay. |: pp. [1–3] have a list of the works of Lewis Carroll, with a note about trade-discount, and two 'Cautions to Readers' about the *Land of Idleness* and *From Nowhere* . . .

Issued in red cloth. The back has at the top under three gold lines | Sylvie | and | Bruno |, then an ornamental device, and at the bottom over three gold lines is | Macmillan & Co. | The front cover has three gold lines around the border, and in the centre are three circular gold lines, enclosing the head of Sylvie. The back cover is the same except that the head within the circular gold lines is that of Bruno. All edges gilt. Some copies were bound (presumably for presentation) in green cloth, and at least one in white decorated in gold, with the illustration on p. 307 repeated on the front cover. These copies omit the three pages of advertisement at the end of the book.

Evolution. The Preface reminds us that the fourteenth and fifteenth chapters ('Fairy-Sylvie' and 'Bruno's Revenge') are a reprint, with a few alterations, of No. 42 (1867) in *Aunt Judy's Magazine* (where it was illustrated by one rather Victorian drawing by F. Gilbert). This fairy story suggested to Dodgson in 1874 (corrected in the Preface to vol. ii to 1873) the idea of a longer story, of which it should be a nucleus. From then he jotted down at odd moments ideas, fragments of dialogues, and at least two dream suggestions. Lastly for about ten years he arranged a patchwork of the mass of these notes to see what connected thread they seem to indicate— and wrote it, incorporating the notes. In the story he has tried to be original, for *Alice* had been so freely imitated that some originality was necessary. Dodgson's own private account of the construction is contained in a letter of 28 Aug. 1890, from him to Miss Maud Standen (now Mrs. Ffooks) printed in *Six Letters by Lewis Carroll* (London, 1924, for private distribution), p. 11: 'Last Xmas I brought out Sylvie and Bruno . . . and what I'm now at work at, is "Sylvie and Bruno Concluded". The book had been on hand for about seven years until I had accumulated a chaotic mass of fragments (I can't write a story straight on!): and when I came to arrange and piece them together, I found it had grown so much too big for one volume, that I decided on cutting it in two . . .'

The *Times Literary Supplement*, 19 May 1927, prints a letter from Dodgson to a girl-friend, dated 8 Feb. 1887, in which he says that he is 'passing into the sere & yellow leaf, being turned 55!', and that there is 'another book for children [i.e. *Sylvie and Bruno*], which I am *longing* to get finished: if only the days would contain 24 hours, as they used to do.'

Production. Dodgson was still receiving proofs for correction in Nov. 1889, but a presentation copy is known which was dispatched on 12 Dec. in that year.

Binding. The forms of binding have been noted above.

Notes. Sylvie and Bruno, with its conclusion in 1893, was the last considerable work issued by Dodgson. Though he fully explains in the Preface (pp. xvi-xx) the principles on which he introduces many solemn pages into his fairy tale, the serious subjects of life and science cannot be thus inserted without marring the effect of the whole. This mixture, which is repeated in *Sylvie and Bruno Concluded* (1893) led the publisher after Dodgson's death to issue a smaller volume, the *Story of Sylvie and Bruno* (1904), in which the heavier parts are omitted. Somehow the light and airy touch of *Alice* is wanting, but there is plenty of amusing incident and entertaining verse. There is hardly any plot: Sylvie and Bruno, after living with a Warden, Sub-Warden, Professor, Beggar, Gardener, Uggug (the young artist) and others, are conducted by the Gardener into Elfland, ride on a lion, visit Dogland, and so on. There are five songs, which are attractive: I. The Gardener, eight stanzas of the form 'He thought he saw. . . . He found it was . . .', see index under Gardener; II. Peter and Paul (beginning 'Peter is poor', p. 143); III. A fairy song 'Rise, oh, rise! The daylight dies' (from the 'nucleus', see above, which occupies pp. 190-221), p. 215, with the music; IV. 'There be three badgers', p. 247; V. 'He stept so lightly', p. 291. Chapter 18 is entitled 'Queer Street, number forty'. The book has never been so popular as *Alice* and the *Looking-Glass*. Its thirteenth thousand was in 1898.

The forty illustrations (ten full-page) are rightly described by Dodgson (preface, p. ix) as wonderful. Though not so inspired as Tenniel's, they are very clever and serve their purpose admirably, both in the fanciful and the realistic parts: take pp. 48, 62, 229, 249, 380 as specimens. One small drawing at p. 77 is by Miss Alice Havers. I have the best reasons for knowing that Furniss's charges for his drawings were: whole page twenty guineas, three-quarter page fifteen guineas, quarter-page seven guineas, and five guineas as a minimum. Furniss was a rapid draughtsman, and Dodgson an exacting critic, and it is stated that at a time when the illustrations were needed for printing, Dodgson called on Furniss to see what they were like. Furniss took Dodgson to the door of his studio, and he then said 'Now, Mr. Dodgson, you must understand that I am a peculiar person. You can of course see the drawings I have already made, but if you criticize one of them, I shall certainly tear them up and do no more. When they are finished you may criticize them as much as you please.' Dodgson stammered out 'Well—of course— if you put it that way—I'd rather leave them to-day.' Furniss told my informant that at the time he hadn't even begun one single drawing! His daughter Margaret was his model for Sylvie. But this story does not square with Collingwood's *Life*, p. 259. Dodgson's own attempted illustrations, sixteen in number, were offered for sale by an Art agency in Oxford in 1898 for £50, and another illustrating the 'nucleus' is reproduced in *The Times* of 3 Apr. 1898. The correspondence between Dodgson and Furniss, including sixty-eight letters from the former and the original drawings by the latter, was sold in New York on 13 May 1930 for £340. An interesting account by Furniss of his dealings with Dodgson will be found in Collingwood's *Life and Letters of Lewis Carroll* (1898), pp. 319-20.

The dedicatee can be found by taking the initial letters of the lines of the little poem which follows the title—namely Miss Isa Bowman; the lines begin 'Is all our life, then,': *or* by taking the first three letters of each stanza—a new kind of double acrostic.

A copy dated 1890 is at Harvard [**188**].

The Continuation was issued in 1893 (see No. **216**) and the Abridgment in 1904 (No. **585**). Miss H. B. Griffiths dramatized the book in 1896 (No. **712**). F. M.

(The dramatization mentioned above seems never to have been either acted or printed; nor has one made by the present writer in 1945!)

The book grew out of 'Bruno's Revenge' (1867) which Dodgson was accustomed to tell to children. On 2 Jan. 1873, when he was staying at Hatfield, he noted: 'The morning began with another story-telling . . . I gave them [the Cecil children] a new chapter of *Sylvie and Bruno*, which I had devised since the story-telling on Tuesday which I must write out before I forget it.' And next day: 'I had thought of a few more incidents for *Sylvie and Bruno*, and gave them another chapter, which took nearly an hour.'

He was telling 'some more of Prince Uggug' on 1 Jan. 1875; 'Little Foxes' on 12 Sept. 1877; 'Bruno's Picnic' on 12 Jan. 1878; and 'Bruno and the Foxes' on 22 Apr. 1878, to various groups of children.

On 31 July 1882 he 'at last made another start with *Sylvie and Bruno*', and had got far enough to mention it to Macmillan on 23 Nov. 1886 as likely to be 'about as large as the two *Alices* together', and hoped to have it out in 1888.

On 30 Nov. 1888 he decided to publish it in two parts.

R. L. G.

1890

218. *Circular Billiards* (1890)   [192ᵃ⁻ᶜ

CIRCULAR BILLIARDS, | FOR TWO PLAYERS | *INVENTED IN* 1889, *BY* | LEWIS CARROLL. | [*a thin line: text follows*].

[Oxford?]: [1890]: (one) 8°: size $8\frac{7}{16} \times 5\frac{1}{4}$ in.: a single sheet printed on both sides. P. [1] has the heading or title as above, then follow three lines of text | [*thin line*] | Rules | [*in black-letter type*], then six rules, the first occupying two lines, the second one line, the third two lines, the fourth one line, the fifth five lines, and the sixth one line. At the bottom in the right-hand corner is | [P.T.O.] |: [2] | Remarks | [*in black-letter type: three paragraphs of 4, 2, and 2 lines respectively*] | Table of Scores | [*five lines within a thin line rectangle. (Size of rectangle, $2\frac{7}{16} \times 2\frac{3}{16}$ in.)*].   [192ᵃ]

Second Issue.

The second issue is the same as the first, except for variation in the length of the first two rules, the first having 4 lines instead of 2, and the second 3 lines instead of 1.   [192ᵇ]

Third Issue.

This issue differs from both the preceding issues in the length of the rules, the Remarks, and the Table of Scores.

The differences are: Rule i, 3 lines: Rule ii, 1 line: Rule iii, 2 lines: Rule iv, 1 line: Rule v, 7 lines: Rule vi, 1 line.

The three paragraphs under | Remarks | on the verso are of 4, 4, and 2 lines respectively. And under the | Table of Scores | are 11 lines. [191ᶜ] All these issues may be found on a rough thick paper, tinted brown, or on a smooth thin white one.

The three issues of the first edition of this rare item bear only the date of invention (1889), but were published in 1890, and I have had difficulty in placing them in what I conceive to be their chronological order within the latter year. My reasons for placing them as above are as follows: Firstly, the first and second issues as I have placed them have in common the same paragraph over | Rule | i.e. 'the table is circular, with a cushion all around it, no pockets, and their white spots arranged in an equilateral triangle'. In the third issue the paragraph reads 'and has neither pockets nor spots' a clear rescinding of the paragraph in the first and second issues, because this negative sentence would have been unnecessary had there not been some previous mention of pockets and spots. This seems to me to settle the question of the third issue, but leaves that of prior issue between the other two forms.

Now there is nothing so far as I can see in these two forms to indicate which was issued first, and I must have left it so, but for the fact that fortunately the two copies from which I made the above collations were Lewis Carroll's own copies, and bore in the upper right-hand corner his filing numbers in violet ink, the one being 69575, and the other 69614, and therefore I assume the earlier number to be the earlier issue, hence the order I have given them.

The game is a simple arrangement for playing billiards on a circular table, with cushions and no pockets or spots. The six rules chiefly concern the scoring, a cannon counting two, and every cushion struck in the course of a cannon, one or two, and so on.

The Remarks (p. 2) point out the curious rebound off a curved cushion, and illustrate the eleven possible methods of scoring with a table.   S. H. W.

Williams, i. 59 (p. 70; 2nd and 3rd); *Parrish Catalogue*, p. 35 (2nd); *Collingwood*, p. 440 (2 edd.): Bodleian (3rd), Harvard (2nd and other issues), S. H. Williams (3rd), F. Madan and Sir H. Hartley (2nd and 3rd).

Circular Billiards (never reprinted) was not, as I thought (*Lewis Carroll*, 1960, p. 68), merely noologistic. Miss F. Menella Dodgson tells me that the table was made and used, and is still in existence.
                                                          R. L. G.

219. *Registration of Parcels* (1890)   [201

A folio official Report dated 1890, consisting of six leaves, being a report of the Postmaster-General on the above subject. Of eight paragraphs No. 1 is an extract from a letter of the Rev. C. L. Dodgson, dated 30 Dec. 1889.

I am officially informed that this report is a confidential document, and was never placed on sale to the public.

F. M.

Parrish Catalogue, p. 93.

220. *Stranger Circular* (1890) [197

(The Stranger Circular. A leaflet of Disavowal sent by Mr. Dodgson to people who wrote to him about his 'Lewis Carroll' books, addressing the envelope to the Rev. C. L. Dodgson.)

Oxford: Printed by Sheppard. 1890.

At one time, for some reason or other, Mr. Dodgson, while not denying that the books issued under the name of Lewis Carroll were written by himself, would not admit that this was so: and I imagine that this circular was a protest to people who, innocent of any desire to give offence, wrote to him as Lewis Carroll.

An instance of his desire not to be known under any other name than his own may be found in the *Dictionary of English Authors* (1897) by Mr. Farquharson Sharp, where under 'Dodgson (Charles Lutwidge)' is a footnote which says 'It should be noted that Mr. Dodgson states with reference to this list that he "neither claims nor acknowledges any connexion with the books not published under his name".'

This peculiar attitude of Mr. Dodgson was further confirmed in a letter which I received from the late Canon Egerton Leigh of Richmond, Yorks., in which he said '. . . agreeable to this when Mrs. Thomas Arnold introduced him to me as the author of "Alice in Wonderland" he looked annoyed and shut up at once'.

This is a rare item and I have only heard of one copy and that was sold at Sotheby's in June 1927. The text is as follows:

'Mr. Dodgson is so frequently addressed by strangers on the quite unauthorized assumption that he claims, or at any rate acknowledges the authorship of books not published under his name, that he has found it necessary to print this, once for all, as an answer to all such applications. He neither claims nor acknowledges any connection with any pseudonym, or with any book that is not published under his own name. Having therefore no claim to retain, or even to read the enclosed, he returns it for the convenience of the writer who has thus misaddressed it.'

S.H.W.

Dodgson wrote several times to Macmillan, asking him to *write* to such correspondents. The last such request was made on 20 Jan. 1890—so it may be assumed that he had the Stranger Circular printed shortly after.

221. *Circular to Hospitals* (1890)   [198

A letter beginning 'Dear Sir,' and signed 'Lewis Carroll', dated Messrs. Macmillan and Co., London, 1890, printed on both sides of a single 4° leaf (size $7\frac{7}{16} \times 9\frac{1}{4}$ in.) and addressed 'To the Resident Managers of the . . .', states the writer's wish to present copies of *Alice's Adventures, Through the Looking-Glass,* and the *Nursery Alice* for use in Hospitals and Homes. On the verso are questions to ascertain the suitability of the institutions [198a].

There are two forms, one of which is printed at Oxford by Sheppard, and inserts the word 'sick' before 'children' in three paragraphs of the Questions, and is presumably the later [198b].

Williams, i. 64 (p. 75); *Parrish Catalogue,* p. 50 (both forms); *Collingwood,* p. 441: Williams . . . form.

222. *List of Institutions* (1890)   [199

List of Institutions to which the preceding item was to be sent. Oxford: Printed by Sheppard . . . 1890.

So in Collingwood's *Life and Letters,* p. 441, but no copy is at present known.

Williams, i. 65 (p. 75).

On 20 July 1890 Dodgson wrote to Macmillan 'I have asked Messrs. Parker to send you all the "Hospital" copies of *Alice* and *Looking-Glass,* that are left, in order that you may send them round along with *The Nursery Alice.* There are some 20 or 30 answers to the Circular yet to come in: but there is no need to wait, for all to come in, before we begin sending round. I will send you, very soon, a list of about 100 Hospitals and Homes, for whom parcels are to be made up.'

[Dr. Warren Weaver owns the only known copy of this item].

223-5. *Eight or Nine Wise Words* (1890) (With Stamp case and Envelope)   [193, 194, 195

EIGHT OR NINE | WISE WORDS | ABOUT | LETTER-WRITING || BY | *LEWIS CARROLL* ||

Emberlin and Son, 4, Magdalen Street Oxford: 1890: (eights) 24°: pp. 40+ [4]: signn. [π], [$\pi^\star$]8, [$\pi^{\star\star}$]4, not counting the covers. CONTENTS: p. 1, title, within double lines intersecting at the corners, 1-2 forming the front cover: 2, 'Oxford: Printed by George Sheppard': 3, the contents, in 5 sections: 5-33, the Wise Words: 35-40, Macmillan's advertisements of Lewis Carroll's works, with two notes about discount, &c., and two Cautions to Readers (see No.

187): 40, 'Sheppard, Printer Oxford': [1-4] blank, 3-4 forming the back cover. A stitched pamphlet.

A small but excellent work, full of sound sense and humour. It may be abbreviated as follows: § 1. Many are the uses of Stamp-Cases. §§ 2-4. In letter writing first address your envelope, then on the letter put your full address and full date, write legibly, read your correspondent's last letter, answer a severe note by one *less* severe, &c. § 5. Keep a Register, in chronological order, of all letters received or answered, assigning a running number to each successively. (Dodgson kept one from 1 Jan. 1861 to 8 Jan. 1898. The numbers ran from 1 to nearly 100,000, with some gaps: the scheme is full of technical facilities for cross-reference.) The consecutive entries form a tangled tale indeed: one thread of the tangle recounts how Mr. and Mrs. Jones presented Dodgson with a 'white elephant', which Dodgson skilfully diverted at the Oxford station to the London Zoological Gardens. The Directors after an interval return thanks to Dodgson for a case of one dozen of admirable port, consumed at the Directors' banquet. Letter from Dodgson to Aunt Jemima Jones. 'Why call a dozen of port a white elephant?' Answer, 'It was a joke.' It is odd that Dodgson the mathematician should call the wise words 'Eight or nine', giving in some sense the impression of precision, and in some sense of doubt, for the rules are precisely nine or thirteen, and the sections (in the first edition) five. No doubt copies of the *Wise Words* were given and circulated without the Stamp Case and Envelope (see below), when there was occasion.

The *Wise Words* are connected with, and in some sense an advertisement of a Wonderland Stamp Case, and a pink envelope containing both. There appear to be eight editions of the *Words*, and three each of the *Stamp Case* and the *Envelope*, the differences between all the issues being slight.

The *Stamp Case* [194] consists of a detachable cover of cardboard [194*], into which slips the stamp-holder itself, which is made of stiff paper backed with canvas. This inner case [194**] itself measures $5\frac{9}{16} \times 3\frac{7}{8}$ in., folded once and exhibiting twelve little sewn pockets to hold twelve stamps from $\frac{1}{2}d.$ to $1s.$ in value. The case and cover each bear two coloured pictures of Alice, and are so arranged as to form two 'Surprises', for on pulling out the case, the cover picture of Alice holding the Duchess's baby turns into Alice holding the pig, and on the other side the Cheshire Cat, whole and entire, turns into the well-known residual smile of that quadruped. The four coloured pictures in the Stamp-case do not differ from beginning to end. A few known copies are fitted, as Dodgson suggested, with actual stamps of each indicated value.

The *Envelope* [195] needs no special description; its size is $4\frac{5}{8} \times 3\frac{1}{2}$ in. with a flap. The idea of it and its contents seems to have first occurred to Dodgson on 29 Oct. 1888.

Stamp Case, 1890. In *The Lady*, 7 Apr. 1892 there is an account, as Mrs. Milner informs me, of Dodgson's invention of the Stamp Case, and his practical need of it, from his own pen. Unfortunately in some descriptions the outer Stamp Case is called an Envelope—which causes confusion.

The Stamp Case invented in 1889 is apparently the oldest of the three parts, and led to the *Wise Words*, for Mr. Parrish owns an early Stamp Case, of which the presentation is dated Mar. 1890, whereas the earliest known presentation of the *Wise Words* was 8 June 1890, and of the set of three, 31 July 1890 (The Kern copy).

The successive editions of the three parts together may be numbered 1–8, and the early separate issue of the Stamp Case 0.

0. *Stamp-Case* [first edition]. In this, the space above the cat in the cover or outer case is blank, and the space below bears 'Price one shilling' (*Parrish Catalogue*, pp. 38, 50 and plates xiii, xv*, xv**, xv***). Mr. Parrish has a copy presented by Lewis Carroll to his sister Louisa F. Dodgson in Mar. 1890, and Quaritch (Cat. 435 [1930], art. 51) another presented in the same month. This rare issue seems to have been distributed *before* the formal publication with the *Envelope* and *Wise Words*.

1. *Wise Words* [first edition], as above described. The earliest known presentation is dated 18 June 1890. The contents are in five sections (*Parrish Catalogue*, p. 38, with a proof on p. 37).

Stamp case [second edition]. In the outer case the space above the cat bears '(Published by Emberlin and Son, 4 Magdalen Street, Oxford)': and the space below 'Price one Shilling. (post-free, 13*d*.)' *Parrish Catalogue*, p. 50, and Plate XIV.

Envelope [first edition]. Pink, opening at the side: on the back is ' "The Wonderland" Postage Stamp-Case. invented by Lewis Carroll, Oct. 29, 1888', and five lines of description, the second line ending 'Coloured', with prices. On the flap is the publisher's name and address (*Parrish Catalogue*, p. 39, and Plate X).

2. *Wise Words*. Second edition (on the title), with date 1890, otherwise almost as No. 1, except that in p. 3 the contents are in only four sections, p. 4 has an advertisement of the Stamp Case, and the text ends on p. 34; on p. 35 is '[Turn over', and on pp. 36–

41 advertisements, &c. A presentation copy is known dated 1 Oct. 1890.

Stamp Case [second edition], as in No. 1.

Envelope [first edition], as in No. 1, but opening at the end.

3. *Wise Words*. Third edition (on the title), with date 1891. As No. 2, except that on p. 2 Sheppard adds his address, '1. Walton Crescent'.

Stamp Case [second edition], as No. 1.

Envelope [first edition?], as No. 1, opening at the end. (?)

4. *Wise Words*. Fourth edition (on the title), with date 1891. As No. 3.

Stamp Case [third edition?] with the post-free price ($13d.$) preceding the ordinary price ($1s.$), see Plate XV of the *Parrish Catalogue*.

Envelope [second edition]. In the description the second line ends 'Pic-' and the envelope opens at the end, not side: see Plate XI (*Parrish Catalogue*). The prices are now for 1 copy, 2–3, 4, 5–15, and every subsequent 15.

5. *Wise Words*, fifth edition (on the title), with date 1897. As No. 3.

Stamp Case [third edition], as No. 4.

Envelope [second edition], as No. 4.

6. *Wise Words* [sixth edition], with date '1890', really probably early in 1908.

This is a reprint, date and all, of No. 1 with some late features which show that it was probably issued early in 1908. The Sheppard imprint on p. 2 is omitted; p. 5 ends 'and' not 'turned', &c. The text ends on p. 35, not 33: after Macmillan's Advertisements on pp. 38–39 comes Chatto & Windus's advertisement of 'Feeding the Mind' (1907). This reprint (naturally) restores the old division of the book into five chapters or sections, instead of four.

I have seen a copy of this reprint owned by Mrs. S. Masefield of Cheadle, in which after p. 35 occur no advertisements, but three blank pages, the last two being the back cover. It bears 'With love from D. A. C. for Jan. 21. 08' (not in Dodgson's hand), and is probably an early form, before advertisements had been decided on. It may be called 6*.

Stamp-Case [third edition], as No. 4.

Envelope [third edition]. The second line of the description ends 'Pictorial'. The prices are for 1–4 copies, 8, 15, and every subsequent 15.

7. *Wise Words* [seventh edition], dated, and probably issued later in 1908 than No. 6, from which it differs in at least two points. It

inserts on the title at the foot 'London: Simpkin Marshall & Co., Ltd.', on p. 2 is 'FIRST PUBLISHED 1890' within bounding lines; otherwise it is practically identical. As this note of first publishing occurs in the current edition, the eighth, of the *Wise Words*, this No. 7 would seem to be later than No. 6. It may be presumed that after No. 6 had come out, Messrs. Simpkin Marshall insisted on their name appearing on the title-page, but subsequently Emberlin arranged to omit it.

Stamp Case [third edition] as No. 4.

Envelope [third edition] as No. 6.

8. *Wise Words* [eighth edition], probably issued about 1910 to 1915, and still to be purchased from Messrs. Emberlin, Broad Street, Oxford. It differs in no discernible respect from No. 7, except as being undated, and that it omits mention of Simpkin Marshall on the title-page.   F. M.

Williams, i. 60 (p. 72, Stamp case and Envelope), and i. 61 (p. 74, Wise Words); *Parrish Catalogue*, pp. 37–50, with 10 facsimiles; *Collingwood*, pp. 277–8, 441. Mr. Parrish owns all the editions, and has perhaps the only complete set to be found. It is too complicated a matter to record other ownerships, as the parts often become separated. No set approaches Mr. Parrish's. Christ Church has the fifth edition of the *Wise Words*.

The *Diaries* tell us that the Wonderland Stamp Case was invented on 29 Oct. 1888; and that Messrs. Emberlin began sale after receiving 75 stamp cases, 150 *Wise Words*, and 950 envelopes on 2 July 1890. They were still selling them in 1944 at the original price of 1s. (a search was made, at my request, a year or so earlier, and a number were found in the cellar), some with envelopes and some without. . . . When I went again in 1950 to their new shop in the Turl I was offered two for £5.

Eight or Nine Wise Words was reprinted in *Letters to Child-Friends* (1933), pp. 247–64 (see No. *311*); and also in *Nonesuch*, pp. 1211–25 (1091–1104).

A photograph of the Stamp Case with cover appears in *Diaries*, facing p. 519.   R. L. G.

226. *Circular to Stationers* (1890)   [196

(A circular asking friends to send addresses of stationers likely to sell the 'new Stamp-Case' and '8 or 9 Wise Words')

[Oxford, printed by Sheppard]: (1890): 8°: pp. [4], 1–2, 4 blank.

Anonymous: dated 'Ch. Ch., Oxford.   1890'; beginning 'Would you kindly furnish me'. The only copy known, sent to

Miss Thomson by 'C. L. Dodgson', 31 July 1890, is owned by Mr. M. L. Parrish, of Philadelphia.

Williams, i. 62 (p. 74); *Collingwood*, p. 441: M. L. Parrish.

A photograph of this copy appears in *Diaries*, facing p. 534.

227. *Eight Hours Movement* (1890) [200

A letter on this proposal to reduce workmen's hours of labour to eight a day appeared in the London *Standard* of 18 Aug. 1890, and is reprinted in Collingwood's *Life* (1898), p. 293. It is signed 'Lewis Carroll', and proposes payment per hour, and voluntary hours. The first words are 'Sir, Supposing it were the custom'.

The Golden Flower (1890)

In his *Supplement* (1935), p. 9, Madan directs: '*At end of* 1890 add: The Golden Flower. It contains the first appearance of "Light in the East", 1890.' But search has produced a copy of the book in question: THE GOLDEN | FLOWER CHRYSANTHEMUM | ... Copyright 1890 by L. Prang & Co. Boston, U.S.A. It contains three poems signed 'Louis Carroll', namely:

Pp. 13-14. 'The Princess Golden Flower, Chrysanthemum' of 64 lines, beginning: 'Beyond the "Golden Gate" where sinks the sun.'

P. 25. 'Medusa · Grace' of 14 lines, beginning 'Sweet child with unkempt hair, art thou my child'.

P. 69. 'Light in the East' of 24 lines, beginning 'Flower of Neesima, so passing fair.'

They bear no resemblance whatsoever to the works of Charles Lutwidge Dodgson.   R. L. G.

1891

228. *Postal Problem* (1891) [202

A POSTAL PROBLEM | June, 1891. | [*a line: then* 25 *lines of text.*]

No place: (1891): (two) 4°: pp. [4]: only pp. [2-3] bear printed matter.

A questionnaire based on the rule for commissions chargeable on overdue Postal Orders, which is here quoted from the Post Office Guide, and which Dodgson regards as ambiguous. There are sixteen questions and space for answers, and for a signature and date of the replies. The piece is anonymous, but anyone who received the paper would know the origin of its amusing subtleties, full of pitfalls. The Postmaster-General (Henry Cecil Raikes, $d.$ 24 Aug. 1891) was, I am informed, a cousin of Dodgson. This is a rare piece.

Williams, ii. 62 (p. 107); *Parrish Catalogue*, p. 108; *Collingwood*, p. 441: Bodleian.

On 1 June 1891 Dodgson wrote in his *Diaries*: 'Got answer, about my Postal Problem, from Judge Denman and Sir Richard Harington, differing from each other, and from Giffard, who is a Q.C.! Sent MS. for a set of sixteen questions on it, to be printed, to be filled in by my friends. It is a very curious verbal puzzle.'

Reprinted (with Supplement) in *Nonesuch*, pp. 1280–2 (1153–5).

229. *Postal Problem—Supplement* (1891)   [203

A Postal Problem. | June, 1891. | [*a line*] SUPPLEMENT | [*a line: then 17 lines of text.*]

No place: (1891): (one) 4°: pp. [2]: printed only on p. [1].

A reprint of the Rule in diagram form, to show its grammatical construction, marked with Dodgson's correspondence number 74529. Anonymous and rare.

Williams, ii. 63 (p. 107); *Parrish Catalogue*, p. 109; *Collingwood*, p. 441.

230. *The Lady* (1891–2)

Dodgson's contributions to this periodical, as listed in the Catalogue of the Harcourt Amory Collection (1932), were as follows:

1891–1892. July 2–June 2. Syzygies.
1891. October 29. Invention of writing in the dark.
1892. January 7. A New Code of Rules.
1892. March 24. [Under 'Things to talk about']
    For All Writers of Letters: The Postage Stamp Case, and Eight or Nine Words about Letter Writing.
    For All Lovers of Children: Offers to send The Nursery Alice, which was suppressed, to Hospitals that have not received a copy.
    For All Wrestlers of Syzygies.

231. *Syzygies* (1891)   [204

SYZYGIES. | [*line*] | A WORD-PUZZLE. | BY LEWIS CARROLL. | [*line*] | [*Reprinted, with additions, from* 'THE LADY' *for* | July 30, 1891.] | [*line*]

No place or date: (1891): (two) 12°: pp. [4]. CONTENTS: p. [1] title, as above: [1–4] Notes, 'Rules', 'Specimen Chains', and conditions of a (first) prize competition, Aug. 6–Dec. 3 (1891). The four Rules occupy 13, 3, 6, and 6 lines respectively. The first begins 'When two words'.

A rare offprint, antedating the next edition of this game by two years. Mrs. Florence Milner has found that in *The Lady* for 30 July 1891, and for some months following there is correspondence from Lewis Carroll about this game; and he organized competitions in its columns. For an account of the game see No. **217** (1893).

Mrs. Ffooks has a copy.

Dodgson 'completed *Syzygies* and sent to *Vanity Fair*' on 14 Apr. 1891 (*Diaries*). Apparently this was returned, for he sent it to *The Lady* (see No. *230* above) on 2 July, and it appeared there on 23 July.

232. Scoring Papers (1891) [205

A letter of Dodgson to his printer George Sheppard, of Oxford, dated 9 Aug. 1891, asks Sheppard to send him 100 Syzygies Competitors' Scoring Papers (and on 31 Aug. 250 more). Nothing more is known of these.

233. Play-Bills (1891–2) [206

A letter of Dodgson to his printer George Sheppard, of Oxford, dated 10 Nov. 1891, states that he wants 'some play-bills for some friends' with 'plenty of variety of ornamental type to make them look handsome'. On 14 Apr. 1892 the Play-bills were still standing in type.

Nothing more is known of these.

[But surely this refers to the following item. As there may have been a bill in the sense of 'poster' or 'hand-out' as well, I have numbered it as a separate item.]

234. Royal Cowper Theatre, Fulham (1891) [859

Royal Cowper Theatre, Fulham. Sole Lessee and Manageress, Miss Isa Bowman. December, 1891. . . . A four-page octavo Programme of four short Plays (Little Bo-peep, Unworthy Love, Punchinelli, and Fanny), entirely played by the Bowman family (Empsie, Maggie, Nellie, and a brother Charles, with Miss Jane Wythe), who were child-friends of Dodgson, who certainly corrected, if he did not write, at least the framework of the programme. Proofs corrected by him are on p. 5 of Messrs. James Parker & Co.'s (Oxford) Catalogue of books, 1898, now owned by Sir H. Hartley.

Williams, Add. B. 2 (p. 135); *Parrish Catalogue*, p. 128: Bodleian.

235. Christt Church Circular [207

A circular addressed to the Governing Body of Christ Church, Oxford, about the proposal to invite M.A.s to dine at High Table ... 1891.

So in Collingwood's *Life*, p. 441. It appears to have been a small two-leaf piece, of which Mr. Parrish owns the second leaf.

Williams, ii. 61 (p. 107); *Collingwood*, p. 441.

No copy has yet been found—even among the new material discovered at Christ Church in 1952.

1892

236. Circular about Curatorship (1892) [208

A circular about Resignation of Curatorship. Oxford: Printed by Sheppard . . . 1892.

So in Collingwood's *Life* (1898), p. 441, but no copy is known at present. Dodgson vacated the Curatorship of Common Room at Christ Church in, or shortly before, Aug. 1892.   F. M.

Dodgson ceased to be Curator of Common Room on 26 Apr. 1892, judging from the *Diary* entry for that date.

The *Circular* is fortunately among the Common Room Papers discovered by Duncan Black in 1952, and by kind permission of the Librarian I have been allowed to make a description of it.

For Members of Common Room only.] [Sic; with heavy rule under it] ||MEETING OF COMMON ROOM. | Thursday, March the 3rd, 1892, at 1.30 p.m. | [short rule] | [Quotations of two lines] | [short rules] |
[Followed by 18 lines of text, beginning:]
It is my earnest wish to be permitted to resign, at the next | Audit-Meeting, the Office of Curator, with which Common Room | did me the honour of entrusting me nine years ago. |
[At foot of page on right] [P.T.O. [sic]
[On verso 13 lines of text and verse quotation of 6 lines. Then] [Heavy rule] | [to right of centre] C. L. DODGSON, *Curator*. [at left below text] *Feb.* 13, 1892.
There is no imprint. A single sheet of paper $8\frac{1}{4} \times 6\frac{3}{4}$ in., printed on both sides.

This was apparently the 'sort of farewell address on resigning the Curatorship, as I hope to do at that Meeting [3 Mar.]' which Dodgson notes that he is printing on 9 Feb. 1892 (*Diaries*). It was reprinted on pp. 252-3 of Derek Hudson's *Lewis Carroll* (1954). See XXV, below.   R. L. G.

237. *Curiosissima Curatoria* (1892)   [209

|| CURIOSISSIMA | CURATORIA ||| BY | 'RUDE DONATUS' ||
[Motto:—Hæc olim meminisse juvabit] || At the head is:—'Printed
for private circulation', underlined.

Oxford: printed by G. Sheppard: 1892: 8°: pp. [8]+47+[1]: signn. [A]^4,
B–D^8. Grey paper wrappers, the front one bearing the title repeated. CON-
TENTS: p. [1] the half-title: [3] the title: [5-6] the preface, signed 'C. L.
Dodgson, Ex-Curator,', 'Ch. Ch. August, 1892.': [7-8] the contents, in two
chapters and 25 sections: 1-47, the work. An erratum slip precedes p. [1].

A 'Curatorial parting gift' from the Curator of the Christ Church
Common Room at Oxford, on his resignation in, or shortly before,
Aug. 1892, after nine years' service from 8 Dec. 1882. Most of the
Resolutions passed by Common Room and its Committees between
1859 and 1892 are recorded, and a great deal of interesting and solid
information is given, some details reaching back to 1818, and in
one case to 1797. The humour is generally latent, but examples are
well drawn out in the preface, such as that the average time taken·
by a Hot-dish Committee in not drawing up a report, is six years.
The subjects are generally the qualifications of Members, the fees,
the books and newspapers provided, the wine, and finance. Afternoon tea was introduced early in 1884.   F. M.

Seventy-five copies were printed, but are now quite rarities.

Williams, ii. 66 (p. 108); *Parrish Catalogue*, p. 94; *Collingwood*, p. 441: Bodleian, Harvard, Huntington, F. Madan.

Christ Church (10 copies discovered 1952).

238. *'Unparliamentary' Words* (1892)   [210

A circular about 'unparliamentary' words used by some competitors
in the 'Syzygies' competition in *The Lady*. Oxford: Printed by
Sheppard . . . 1892.

So in Collingwood's *Life and Letters* (1898), p. 441, but no copy
is at present known.

239-42. *Papers on Logic* (1892)   [211-14

Eighth Paper on Logic. Pp. 2: printed on both sides: dated Nov.
1892. [211]
Eighth and Ninth Papers on Logic. Notes. Pp. 4, all printed on:
dated Nov. 1892: probably given out with the preceding item.
[212]
Ninth Paper on Logic. Pp. 4, all printed on: dated Nov. 1892. [213]

Eighth Paper on Logic. Pp. 2, printed on both sides: dated Dec. 1892: Second issue, see above, with one page altered. [214]

The preceding four items were, according to Collingwood, printed at Oxford by Sheppard. For the earlier papers on Logic see Nos. 165-8, 173-5 (1887). All are now rare: the ninth is the last in the series.

Williams, ii. 67, 69, 68 (p. 108); Parrish Catalogue, pp. 109, 109, 110, 109; Collingwood, p. 442: Christ Church (211, 212), Harvard (213), F. Madan (211-13).

243. *Challenge to Logicians* (1892)   [215

An octavo leaf printed on one side only, dated Oct. 1892, and signed 'C. L. Dodgson'. Eleven propositions are given, from which it is possible to prove that 'if some a are b, and if some e are not f, no c are d'. The only copy known is at Christ Church, Oxford.

Williams, ii. 70 (p. 108): Christ Church, Oxford.

[Madan notes in *Supplement* (p. 10) to add here that 'Mr. Athelstan Riley wrote to the *Observer* in Jan. 1932 that a letter from Dodgson was printed in the *Pall Mall Gazette* (probably early in the nineties) reviewing a book on Logic by Mr. W. E. Gladstone, who was then Prime Minister (1892-4?). It seemed a genuine review to Mr. Riley till he came to a suggested advantage of a fourth term in a syllogism —which perhaps implies that the whole review was satirical and the book imaginary.'

This 'review' has not been traced, and seems unlikely to be by Dodgson—certainly at this date. He ceased writing to the *P.M.G.* after 1877, and even instructed Macmillan not to send *Sylvie and Bruno* to that periodical for review.]

1893

244. *Syzygies and Lanrick* (1893)   [217

SYZYGIES | AND | LANRICK | *A WORD-PUZZLE AND A GAME* | FOR *TWO PLAYERS* ||| BY | LEWIS CARROLL |||

Price sixpence Post-free sevenpence London 'The Lady' Office 39 Bedford Street, Strand: 1893: (sixteen) 8°: size $7\frac{1}{10} \times 4\frac{7}{10}$ in.: pp. 6+[2]+26+[6]: signn. A2 on p. 1, A3 on p. 9. CONTENTS: p. 1, the half-title, | Syzygies | and | Lanrick |: 3, the title as above: 4, imprint | Richard Clay and Sons, Limited, | London and Bungay. |: 5-6, preface: followed by date at the bottom | Dec. 1892. |: [1] contents: 1-16, Syzygies: 17-26, Lanrick: [1-4] Macmillan's advertisements of the works of Lewis Carroll, the last page bearing a facsimile page of *Alice's Adventures under Ground*.

A stitched pamphlet issued in wrappers, pale grey in colour, the first page of the wrapper being lettered as the title-page. All edges cut and plain.

A 'full-dress' account of the two games, and part of a projected 'Original Games and Puzzles'. Syzygies was first published, and reprinted separately, in 1891 (see No. 204). The first trace of it is in *The Lady*, 23 July 1891. The tournament which ensued lasted till 26 May 1892.

The Συζυγίαι or Yokings are a set of one or more letters common to both the words yoked, and the yokings connect two given words by means of links, the whole series forming a chain. Thus, given 'Walrus' and 'Carpenter' they can be connected by walrus, peruse, harper, carpenter, not wholly unlike Doublets (No. 105). The whole of the elaborate rules and examples are reprinted in Collingwood's *Lewis Carroll Picture Book*, 1899. They are hardly adapted for popular use.

Lanrick requires a chess or draughts board, eight men of one colour and eight of another, each with the move power of a Queen in Chess. They have to fight their way into one or more rendezvous, 'close' or 'open', and the moves are of limited length. The name is from a passage of Scott's *Lady of the Lake*.   F. M.

The game of Syzygies does not appear to have been published before 1891. The only reference that I can find to it is in Mr. Collingwood's *Life and Letters* on p. 209, where an extract from Mr. Dodgson's diary is given as follows: 'Dec. 12 (1879). Invented a new way of working one word into another. I think of calling it Syzygies.'

With regard to the game of 'Lanrick', according to Mr. Collingwood, it was published separately by the University Press, Oxford, in 1881, but in the Preface of the above pamphlet, dated Dec. 1892, Lewis Carroll says, 'I have taken this opportunity to publish the rules for Lanrick, in order to make the game known, rather sooner than it would otherwise be . . . &c.' Farther on in the Preface he says that the first version of the rules was written, not published, on 26 Dec. 1878. As a fact 'Lanrick' was first published in Dec. 1880, on p. 614 of the *Monthly Packet*; see also p. 303 of that periodical for Mar. 1881, and p. 611 of June 1881. A second edition of the rules is at p. 198 of August 1881, and a third edition at p.512 of Nov. 1881—all in connexion with a *Tangled Tale* (see No. 144).   S. H. W.

The present is the fourth edition of the Rules, and is reprinted with Syzygies by Collingwood. The advertisements are nearly as in *Sylvie and Bruno Concluded*, but earlier in date.

Following the advertisements on p. 29 are some reprinted

'cautions'. Lewis Carroll disclaims 'The Land of Idleness', and vindicates the originality of *Alice's Adventures*: see No. 187.

Williams, i. 67 (p. 77); *Parrish Catalogue*, p. 52; *Collingwood*, p. 442: Christ Church, Oxford; Harvard, Huntington, &c.

In *Diaries* Dodgson notes on 21 Jan. 1893: 'Have got through the press the *Syzygies and Lanrick* pamphlet; and on the 14th told Clay to work off 250 copies.'

245. *Syzygies and Lanrick.* (Second Edition)   [218

——Second Edition, 1893.

The only changes appear to be these: the covers are light pink; on the title-page after 'Lewis Carroll' follows 'Second Edition. Printed for private circulation. Feb. 1893.' and no more. The same change is made on the front cover. The Preface and Syzygies are unchanged. In 'Lanrick' a few changes occur on pp. 17, 20, 21, 22. The rest is identical with the first edition. It is from this edition that Collingwood reprinted both games in the *Lewis Carroll Picture Book* (1899), p. 228. Rare.

Professor J. A. Stewart of Oxford owns a copy. [Now in the Parrish Collection.]

246. *Curiosa Mathematica* (1893)   [220

Curiosa Mathematica | *PART II* | PILLOW-PROBLEMS | *THOUGHT OUT DURING* | *SLEEPLESS NIGHTS* || BY | CHARLES L. DODGSON, M.A. | *Student and late Mathematical Lecturer* | *of Christ Church, Oxford* |||

Price two shillings London Macmillan and Co.: 1893: 8°: pp. xiv+[2]+, 109+[3]: signn. [A] B–H⁸. CONTENTS: p. i, the half-title: iv, a diagram: v the title with '[All rights reserved.]' at the foot: vi, 'Oxford Horace Hart, Printer to the University': vii–xiv, the Introduction, dated 'Ch. Ch., Oxford, May, 1893.': xv, the Contents and Subjects: 1–18, Questions: 19–27, Answers: 28–109, Solutions: [2] Advertisement of works by C. L. Dodgson. In grey cloth, with diagram and part of the title lettered in black on the front cover and back.

A set of seventy-two problems, chiefly in Algebra, Plane Geometry or Trigonometry, almost all mentally worked out in the night, without a word or line put on paper till the daylight came. Some are dated from 1874 to 1891. The Introduction describes the method of calculation, and states that Dodgson generally wrote the answer first, then the question and solution! He could distinctly visualize complicated diagrams in the dark, such as the frontispiece, for which see p. 100. of the book. He published the problems to encourage the pastime as a means of avoiding undesired thought by concentration on a subject. Mr. Parrish's copy bears a presentation date of 'July 8, 1893'. Rare.

For Part I of the *Curiosa* see No. **182**, and for a second edition of Part II, the next item [**221ᵃ**]. There was a third edition in 1894 [**221ᵇ**], and a fourth in 1895 [**221ᶜ**].

Williams, ii. 71 (p. 109; 2nd ed.); *Parrish Catalogue*, p. 95 (2nd ed.); *Collingwood*, p. 442, edd. 1–4: Huntington, F. Madan (1st ed.), Harvard (3rd ed.), British Museum (2nd and 4th edd.), Bodleian (2nd ed.).

There are no Macmillan letters available for the period covering publication of this book. Dodgson notes in *Diaries* (21 Jan. 1893) that during his month's holiday at Guildford 'I got into the printers' hands the rest of the MS. of *Pillow Problems*'. But no date of publication is given.

Pillow Problems is reprinted in *Mathematical Recreations of Lewis Carroll*, 1958. (See No. *318* below.) The fourth edition being used.

247. Curiosa Mathematica (1893) (Second Edition)   [**221ᵃ**

——Pillow Problems, second edition, 1893.

As preceding item, substituting 'wakeful hours' for 'sleepless nights', and adding | SECOND EDITION | on the title, above the price. Before the introduction are inserted three pages of 'Preface to second edition', dated 'Ch. Ch., Oxford. September, 1893.', occupying pp. vii–ix, so that the prefatory matter is pp. xvii+[3], signn. [a]⁸, b². The rest of the book is very slightly altered. Dodgson explains that his 'sleepless nights' were not due to insomnia, from which he 'never suffered', but usually to 'luxurious idleness in the preceding day'; he now 'allays the anxiety of kind friends'.

Mr. Parrish's presentation copy is dated on the half-title, Oct. 3, 1893.   F. M.

This edition was ready shortly after 16 Aug. 1893 when Dodgson wrote to Macmillan that no more copies of the first edition were to be supplied, and that unsold copies in the hands of agents were to be recalled: 'supply, instead of them, copies of the new edition, as soon as you get it.

'The improvements in the 2nd edition are so important, that any purchaser of the book might reasonably consider he had been very hardly dealt with, if, with the new edition on the point of appearing, he was allowed to buy a copy of the inferior edition.'

The fourth edition (1895) has a new Preface of just over a page.

248. Second-hand Books (1893)   [222

SECOND-HAND BOOKS. | (1893).

An $8°$ circular: size $7\frac{1}{16} \times 4\frac{7}{16}$ in.: pp. [4]: as follows: p. [1] the text: [2] blank: [3] the remainder of the text: [4] blank. This circular is addressed to booksellers, mentioning six volumes which Dodgson wishes to secure. One is Inman's *Preservation of Health*, see p. 106. The letter is dated Ch. Ch., May 1, 1893, and begs the booksellers to discontinue sending him their catalogues more than once a year, as Dodgson has 'more books on his shelves than he has any chance of ever being able to read'. He enclosed an envelope addressed to himself at 7 Lushington Road, Eastbourne. Rare: a copy was in the Kern sale in New York in 1929.

Williams, ii. 69 (p. 109); *Parrish Catalogue*, p. 95.

249. Advertisement about Through the Looking-Glass
(1893)   [219

ADVERTISEMENT. | [30 *lines of text follow*].

An octavo leaf, so headed, printed on one side only, beginning 'For over twenty-five years', and signed 'Lewis Carroll', 'Christmas, 1893'.

Dodgson is deeply annoyed to find that in the 60th thousand of *Through the Looking-Glass* 'most of the pictures have failed so much, in the printing, as to make the book not worth buying'. He therefore begs owners to return them for exchange. The returned copies will be given away to 'Mechanics' Institutes, Village Reading-Rooms,' &c. The Advertisement is reprinted in the *Bibliography* (1924) on pp. 78–9.

It is an ordinary composition enough, but interesting on account of its rarity, and also because it so finely illustrates the character of Lewis Carroll, both the almost meticulous care and pride in his work and its production, and also his generosity and thought for the poorer members of his public, who could not afford to buy his books. It will be remembered that the People's Edition of the *Alice* books (see p. 30) was issued at a loss to the author, 'Rather than', as he says in the preface, 'let the little ones for whom it was written go without it.'   S. H.W.

This is not as rare as Williams suggests. Copies were inserted in most, if not all copies of *Sylvie and Bruno Concluded*—the first edition of which was still obtainable new in 1939. The fly-leaf 'Advertisement' is often still to be found in copies of the book.

It was also published in the 'Agony Column' of *The Times* on 2 Dec. 1893.

250. *Sylvie and Bruno Concluded* (1893)   [216

SYLVIE AND BRUNO | CONCLUDED ‖ BY | LEWIS CAR-ROLL | *WITH FORTY-SIX ILLUSTRATIONS* | *BY* | *HARRY FURNISS* ‖

Price Three half-crowns London Macmillan and Co. and New York: 1893: 8°: size $7\frac{3}{16} \times 4\frac{15}{16}$ in.: pp. xxxii+423+[9]: signn. [*a*], *b*, B–Z, AA–DD⁸, EE, [FF]⁴. CONTENTS: p. i, the half-title, | Sylvie and Bruno | Concluded |: ii, Macmillan's monogram in the centre of the page: iv, frontispiece: v, the title as above, and at foot | *The Right of Translation and Reproduction is Reserved.*|: vi, imprint, | Richard Clay and Sons, Limited | London and Bungay. | vii, eleven lines of verse to Sylvie and Bruno in black-letter type, with two small rules above and below: ix–xxiii, Preface, which is dated | Christmas, 1893. | at the bottom left-hand corner of p. xxiii: xxvi–xxvii, contents: xxviii–xxix, list of Illustrations to vol. i: xxx–xxxi, illustrations to vol. ii: 1–411, the text: 413–423 Index: an imprint | Richard Clay and Sons, Limited, London and Bungay. | at the bottom of the page: [2] blank, except for | [Turn over. | at the bottom right-hand corner: [3–6] advertisement of the works of Lewis Carroll: [7] facsimile of a page from *Alice's Adventures under Ground*. Issued in red cloth generally, but green and even white (for presentation) are sometimes found. On the back of the cover are found three gold lines at the top then | Sylvie | and | Bruno | Concluded | then an ornamental device, and at the bottom of the cover three gold lines. The front cover has three gold lines around the border, and three circular lines in the centre containing a picture of the Professor. The back cover is the same except that the head within the three circular lines is that of the Chancellor. All edges gilt. There is an error in the table of contents; chapter 8 is given as at page 110, instead of 113, also in the fourth line of the preface it is stated that the 'locket' is on page 405, instead of 409.

The second part of *Sylvie and Bruno* (1889) came out on 29 Dec. 1893, and is written in the same style as the first, being in fact a succession of scenes with slight connexion or sequence, such as Bruno's lessons, Fairy Music, Bruno's Picnic, the Professor's Lecture, The Pig-tale. There is more of serious tone than before, and some real tragedy (Arthur Forester's death), but the humour is well sustained, even when the subject is Accelerated Velocity or Political Dichotomy, and the songs and illustrations show no falling off. The number of *Dramatis Personae* is smaller, but Mein Herr is intro-duced. The social situations are as Victorian as ever, and the Uni-versity 'Cub-Hunt' (p. 187) very good fooling. The songs are: | 'King Fisher courted Lady Bird | Sing Beans, sing bones, sing butterflies |' (p. 14); 'Matilda Jane, you never look', of a doll p. 76); 'What Tottles meant', beginning 'One thousand pounds per annum' (pp. 195, 201, 209, 248); 'In stature the Manlet was dwarfish'

(p. 265); 'Say, what is the spell', a fine piece (pp. 305, 411); 'He thought he saw an Argument. . . . And found it was . . .' (pp. 319, 335); 'Little Birds are singing' or 'There was a pig that sat alone' (pp. 364, 371, 377), cleverly illustrated. The other more noteworthy illustrations are at pp. 51, 63, 83, 88 (in all of which shadowy forms are effectively employed) and pp. 236, 367, 388.

The Preface is of great interest, for Dodgson defines the limitations under which he conceives of fairies, their powers and forms, and of psychical states of human beings, showing how carefully chastened his apparently riotous imagination was. He also describes his method of compiling the story, selects 'Bruno's Picnic' as eminently suitable for recitation, and discusses the treatment of religious subjects, especially sermons and ritual. The Index covers both volumes. Among the advertisements at the end are notes of three works in preparation: *Symbolic Logic* in three parts, of which only Part I ever saw the light; *Original Games and Puzzles*, and *The Valley of the Shadow of Death*, the latter two illustrated by Miss E. G. Thomson, the last a reprint of the serious part of *Phantasmagoria*; but neither came out. The last page of advertisement is a facsimile, see above.

A poem of sixteen lines, beginning 'Matilda Jane, you never look', printed in Messrs. Maggs Brothers' Catalogue 511 (1928) at p. 78, accompanied a copy of *Alice's Adventures*, in French, presented by Dodgson to Mrs. Holiday on 7 June 1870, and is addressed to a doll named Matilda Jane, reminding her that though 'deaf & dumb & blind' she is loved. It was subsequently incorporated in the present volume (1893) at p. 76.

The third letters of each line of the introductory poem reveal the name of the dedicatee, Miss Enid Stevens.

This volume was one of those presented by Dodgson to Mechanics' Institutes' Lending Libraries.   F. M.

1894

251. Circular about 'Through the Looking-Glass' (1894)

[223

[A circular asking for a return of inferior copies of the sixtieth thousand of *Through the Looking-Glass*.]

Printed on both sides of a quarto leaf: 1894: 8°: size $9\frac{3}{16} \times 7\frac{7}{16}$ in.

A second edition of No. *249* (1893), with Macmillan's address and date in the upper right-hand corner, beginning 'Dear Sir or Madam, for over 25 years', and signed 'Lewis Carroll'. The text of the first page is as No. *249*, omitting the last paragraph (about communicating with readers by advertising in the newspapers), but substituting another about filling details on the second page. It is addressed 'To the Resident Manager of the . . .'. On the second page are six questions about the institution addressed, to ensure its suitability by the replies.

Williams, ii. 77 (p. 110); *Parrish Catalogue*, p. 53: F. Madan.

252. *The Times* (*6 March 1894*)

On page 1, column 3 of *The Times* of 6 Mar. 1894 appeared an announcement, headed 'THROUGH THE LOOKING-GLASS' beginning: 'Mr. Lewis Carroll advertised on Dec. 2, 1893 that the sixtieth thousand was withdrawn from sale, as some of the pictures had failed in the printing, and that he would present them to mechanics' institutes,' &c.

Dodgson notes that many applications have been received, but as frequently the necessary information was not supplied 'it will be necessary to send a circular to them' [i.e. No. *251* above].

This business concluded, Dodgson proceeds to give the rules for *Co-operative Backgammon*.

He notes in *Diaries* on 17 Feb. 1894: 'Invented *Co-operative Backgammon*', and I have printed the relative paragraph from the notice in *The Times* on p. 509 of *The Diaries*.

Dodgson concludes the notice: 'If at any future time Mr. Lewis Carroll should wish to communicate anything to his readers, he will do so by advertising in the "Agony" column of some of the daily papers on the first Tuesday in the month.'

The original draft MS. of this was given by Dodgson to his childfriend Edith Lucy, and was lent to me by the kindness of her son Mr. Terence Greenidge the actor. On the back is written: '29, Bedford Street, 25 Feb: '94. Mr. Lewis Carroll presents his compliments to editors of *Times, Standard, Daily News, Daily Telegraph*', and asks for the advertisement to be published in 'Agony' column 'on Tuesday, March 6th—*no other day will suit his purpose*'. He asks for price and proofs.

R. L. G.

253. Symbolic Logic. Premisses (1894)   [**224**

Symbolic Logic | Specimen-Syllogisms. | Premisses. |
A single octavo sheet (size $8\frac{3}{4} \times 5\frac{5}{8}$ in.), dated Feb. 1894: printed
on both sides. Mr. Parrish possesses the only copy known. The
treatise on 'Symbolic Logic Part I.' did not come out till 1896 (No.
240). Anonymous, rare.

Williams, ii. 75 (p. 109): *Parrish Catalogue,* p. 110.

254–5. Symbolic Logic. Conclusions (1894)   [**225, 226**

Symbolic Logic. | Specimen-Syllogisms | Conclusions. |
A single octavo sheet (size $8\frac{3}{4} \times 5\frac{5}{8}$ in.), dated Feb. 1894; printed
on both sides. The only copy known, Mr. Parrish's, inserts 'second
edition' after the word Syllogisms [**226**]. Anonymous. No copy of
the first edition is known.

Williams, ii. 76 (p. 110); *Parrish Catalogue,* p. 110 (both 2nd ed.).

256. Symbolic Logic. Questions I (1894)   [**227**

Symbolic Logic. Questions I.
A single octavo leaf (size $8\frac{11}{16} \times 5\frac{3}{8}$ in.), dated Feb. 1894. Printed
on one side only. Mr. Parrish owns the only copy known. Anony-
mous. Rare.

Parrish Catalogue, p. 111.

257. Symbolic Logic. Questions II (1894)   [**228**

Symbolic Logic. Questions II.
A single octavo leaf (size $8\frac{3}{4} \times 5\frac{11}{16}$ in.), dated Feb. 1894. Printed
on both sides. Mr. Parrish owns the only copy known. Anonymous.
Rare.

Parrish Catalogue, p. 111.

Dodgson notes on 15 Feb. 1894 (*Diaries*): 'Came to an important
decision about *Symbolic Logic*—to give up the quarto size, in which
some has been set up, and adopt a page to range with *The Game
of Logic.* This will, I think, give the book a far better chance of
selling.'

As the above 'octavo' sheets are all larger than the final book
(and than *The Game of Logic*) they may be specimens of Dodgson's
original 'quarto size'.

258. Disputed Point in Logic (A: 1894)   [**229**

A DISPUTED POINT IN LOGIC | [*a line, then 24 lines of text.*]
A double octavo leaf (size $8\frac{13}{16} \times 5\frac{5}{8}$ in.), dated | [April 1894.] |:
pp. [4], of which pp. [1] and [4] are blank, p. 2 is not numbered,
and p. 3 is numbered 2. Anonymous, beginning 'There are two
propositions, *A* and *B*.'
This is a problem in hypotheticals, and part of a keen dispute
between Nemo (Dodgson) and Outis (Professor John Cook Wilson),
both pseudonyms of course meaning 'Nobody', a disguise dating
back to Homer's *Odyssey*, in which Odysseus called himself Οὖτις,
to deceive the blind Polyphemus, in the ninth book of that work.
The first paper bears a statement of the point, Nemo's argument,
Outis's reply, and Nemo's rejoinder; all wholly in Wilson's own
words (see Collingwood's *Life and Letters*, p. 324), but printed by
Dodgson. In Mr. Parrish's copy near the foot of the first printed
page (p. 2) 'not contradictories' is altered to 'incompatible', and
'contradictories' to 'compatible'. Rare. See next item.

Parrish Catalogue, p. 112.

Dodgson notes on 31 Mar. 1894 (*Diaries*): 'Have just got printed,
as a leaflet, *A Disputed Point in Logic*—the point Prof. Wilson and I
have been arguing so long. The paper is *wholly* in his own words,
and puts the point very clearly. I think of submitting it to all my
logical friends.'

259. Disputed Point in Logic (B: 1894)   [**230**

A DISPUTED POINT IN LOGIC | [*a line, then 25 lines of text.*]
A double octavo leaf (size $8\frac{11}{16} \times 5\frac{5}{8}$ in.), pp. [4]: printed on the
second and third pages, with p. '2' on the third page, dated | [May.
1. 1894. |. Anonymous, beginning 'There are three men in a house,
Allen, Brown and Carr.'
This second form is a very neat recasting of the preceding April
paper in terms of a story of Carr, Allen, and Brown (see No. **232**
below, for the whole story in literary form), with statement, argument, reply and rejoinder precisely repeated, 'mutatis mutandis'.
This, of course, is wholly by Dodgson, and greatly clarifies the
problem. Rare.

Williams, ii. 73 (p. 109); *Parrish Catalogue*, p. 112; *Collingwood*, p. 442: Christ
Church, Oxford.

260. *Theorem in Logic* (C: 1894)   [231

A THEOREM IN LOGIC.

A single octavo leaf (size $8\frac{11}{16} \times 5\frac{5}{8}$ in.), printed on one side only, undated and anonymous, but issued in June (?) 1894.

A purely mathematical problem in hypotheticals (with an algebraical example), beginning 'There are three propositions, A, B, and C.' The correspondence number in the Parrish copy (87515) indicates June 1894 as the probable date of this third piece. Only one copy is known. Rare.

Parrish Catalogue, p. 110.

(Possibly the 'curious problems on the plan of "lying" dilemma. E.g. "A. says B. lies; B. says C. lies; C. says A. and B. lie". Answer: "A. and C. lie; B. speaks truly" '—which Dodgson noted on 27 May 1894 that he had 'worked out in the last few days'.)

261. *Logical Paradox* (D: 1894)   [232

A LOGICAL PARADOX. | [Offprinted from *Mind*, a quarterly Review of Psychology and Philosophy. By Lewis Carroll.

A four-page offprint (size $8\frac{5}{16} \times 5\frac{1}{2}$ in.), from *Mind*, N.S. iii (1894), July, pp. 436–8, the first page bearing only the above title.

The article begins 'What, *nothing* to do?' A humorous problem, involving hypotheticals, in the form of the short story about Carr, Allen, and Brown being in or out of the house (see No. 230 above), followed by a note on the problem. The problem in this fourth piece is answered by A. Sidgwick and W. E. Johnson in *Mind*, iii, pp. 582, 583, and again by both in iv (1895), p. 143. The puzzle is reprinted in Collingwood's *Lewis Carroll Picture Book* (1899), pp. 312–16, and was intended to form part of *Symbolic Logic*, Part 2, Book viii (never published). Rare.

Williams, i. 70 (p. 80); *Parrish Catalogue*, p. 53: Christ Church, Oxford, Harvard.

On 4 May 1894 Dodgson noted (*Diaries*): 'Yesterday I wrote out the "Allen & Co." paradox in form of a dialogue for *Mind*.'

262. *Logical Puzzle* (E: 1894)   [233

A LOGICAL PUZZLE.

A double octavo leaf (size $8\frac{3}{4} \times 5\frac{11}{16}$ in.), printed on all four pages. Dated | [September, 1894] | . Anonymous. This fifth and last piece is a resumption of the logical arguments between Nemo and Outis (see above, No. 229), still on the subject of hypotheticals. Rare.

Williams, ii. 74 (p. 109); *Parrish Catalogue*, p. 112: Christ Church, Oxford.

263. *What the Tortoise said to Achilles* (1894)   [234

WHAT THE TORTOISE SAID | TO ACHILLES. | [*a short line*] | [Reprinted from *Mind* for December, 1894.] | [*A short line, and then part of the text.*]

A double octavo leaf: size $8\frac{7}{8} \times 5\frac{9}{16}$ in.: pp. [4], consisting of p. [1] the title as above, followed by 25 lines of text: [2–4] the rest of the text, ending '*A Kill-ease!*', followed by an ornamental line: printed presumably in December, 1894.

Anonymous, beginning 'Achilles had overtaken the Tortoise, and had seated himself comfortably on its back'. A dialogue (involving hypotheticals once more) between Achilles and the Tortoise, when the race was over; in which the latter has his revenge on the stolid warrior, supplying him with an endless concatenation of conditional conclusions. It overflows with humour and puns; the depraved character of the latter can be gathered from the last sentence, in which, in view of the high educational value of Achilles, the Tortoise entreats that his victim should rename himself Taught-us, and the weary athlete consents with a last hypothetical, namely, if the tortoise will kindly re-name itself A-kill-ease. The reference to the original printing, which does not differ in text, is *Mind*, N.S. iv (1895), pp. 278–80. Mr. Parrish owns the original manuscript of this piece. It is reprinted in *Nonesuch*, pp. 1225–30 (1104–8).

Williams, i. 69 (p. 80); *Parrish Catalogue*, p. 113; *Collingwood*, p. 442: Harvard, F. Madan.

1895

264. *Three Problems* (1895)   [237

'Three problems by ŒDIPUS (LEWIS CARROLL himself) (on the cube and fifth root of 2; on the circle and inscribed polygons; on the tri-section of an angle): with the initials of Lewis Carroll and date: 4to cloth, £- 10s. 1895.'

So in the catalogue of a portion of the collection formed by the late 'Lewis Carroll' and offered for sale at the Art and Antique Agency, 41 High Street, Oxford (in 1898), art. 102. This *may* be in manuscript; at any rate no copy is at present known.

[There is no mention of this in *Diaries*, nor has any other copy—or reference —turned up. It seems unlikely to be by Dodgson.]

265-6. Logical Nomenclature, Desiderata (1895)   [**236, 235**

LOGICAL NOMENCLATURE. | *Desiderata* | [*a short line: then the text follows*].

A single octavo leaf, printed on one side only, dated June 1895. Anonymous, beginning 'In each of the following sets': here called the *B*-form No. **236**.

A list of eight cases in which logical positions need a distinctive name, with suggested choices of terms; e.g. '(6). A proposition, offered as the conclusion of an inverted argument may be called [inconvenient, incorrect, unlawful . . . etc.]'

——There is an earlier form of this piece [*A*: **235**], with similar title, date, and commencement, in which the letterpress occupies both sides of the leaf, and four humorous 'Fallacies' follow the eight points of the *B*-form [**236**], here given as six. The four 'fallacies'—for which new names are requested—are really three, for a second 'Books in my bookcase' is only an *a fortiori* argument. The reasons for regarding this longer form as the earlier are:

I. It is more prolix, inferior in style, written *currente calamo*, just as a draft would be.

II. It is involved, the parts being 1, 2, 3 (1), 3 (2), 4 (3), 4 (4), then 1-4 again, whereas *B* is clear-cut, neat and direct, in eight divisions (1-8).

III. The 'Fallacies' in *A* are amusing, rather than businesslike, and not all are fallacies, so Dodgson probably omitted them, rather than added them.

IV. *B* bears the correspondence marks 90133, 90104 in Dodgson's register, and was actually sent out with a request for a reply.

V. The type of *A* is careless, for '(3)' and '(4)' are both divisions and subdivisions, see above. Moreover, the need of an autograph correction in *B* (1) of 'soldier' to 'a soldier' seems due to his copying 'soldiers' from *A* in the first instance.

Both forms are rare, *A* very rare; in fact *A* is perhaps a unique proof in Mr. Parrish's possession. *B* is in Christ Church Library and in Mr. S. H. Williams's Collection.   F. M.

Williams, ii. 78 (p. 110: B): M. L. Parrish (A); Christ Church, Oxford (B); S. H. Williams (B).

267. Fascinating Mental Recreation (1895)   [**238**

A FASCINATING MENTAL RECREATION | FOR THE YOUNG. | SYMBOLIC LOGIC. | BY | LEWIS CARROLL. | PART I. ELEMENTARY. | [*a thin line*] |

29, Bedford Street, | Covent Garden, | *November*, 1895. | Dear Madam, or Sir, | [then 22 lines of text beginning 'Any one' and ending 'meaning'.]

(London): (1895): (four) 12°: size $6\frac{3}{4} \times 4\frac{1}{2}$ in.: pp. 7+[1]. CONTENTS: p. 1, the title, as above: 1-4, the letter, ending | Your obedient servant, | Lewis Carroll. | : 4, a short postscript | P.S. The book is nearly all in type, and will, I *hope*, be | ready for delivery by Christmas. | : 5-7, Macmillan's advertisements of Lewis Carroll's works. A stitched pamphlet issued without wrappers, on white wove paper. The three pages of advertisements are paged at the bottom.

An Advertisement, pure and simple, or Prospectus, to promote the sale of 'Symbolic Logic, Part I. shortly to be published.' Dodgson claims a high place for Symbolic Logic as a recreation; it is a cricketground compared with the treadmill of ordinary Formal Logic; it is an 'Open Sesame!' to a treasure-house, for students from 12 to 20 years of age and even for children. A copy seen has 'by Christmas', on p. 4, deleted and 'in January' writtten in; and another copy has these corrections and 'nearly all' deleted, and 'by Feb. 8' inserted, all in the author's hand.

Williams, i. 71 (p. 80); *Parrish Catalogue*, p. 54; *Collingwood*, p. 442: Bodleian, Harvard.

On 5 Aug. 1895 Dodgson was arranging to have 20,000 copies of this 8-page circular sent by Macmillan's with their catalogues to schools, &c.

There seems, however, to have been another form of advertisement, if a rather cryptic remark in a letter to Macmillan of 14 May 1895 really refers to *Symbolic Logic*: 'It was not worth while setting up the short description a second time as I shall circulate the longer one among my friends. Still, as it is done, it would be a pity not to utilise it as a leaflet. It had better be on one page, I think.'

268. ——A Fascinating Mental Recreation. Symbolic Logic [etc., exactly as No. **238**, but dated May 1896, and with additional paragraphs on pp. 3 and 4, and the Postscript on p. 4 omitted.] A second edition [**239**].

Williams, under i. 71 (p. 81); *Parrish Catalogue*, p. 54.

269. Eternal Punishment (1897 ?1895)   [253

Six galley-slip proofs of a paper by Dodgson on Eternal Punishment, intended to be part of a volume of Essays on religious difficulties, are owned by Mr. Parrish. They are dated by the printers

28 Oct. 1897, and are reprinted by Collingwood in his *Lewis Carroll Picture Book* (1889) at pp. 345–55. Dodgson states with clearness the difficulties of the subject, and appears to lean to the opinion that 'eternal' is a mistranslation in the New Testament, and that the original word (presumably αἰώνιος) implies punishment of unknown duration (as several divines believe). The slips were Lot 499 in the Hatch sale at Hodgson's on 18 Dec. 1924. For a later separate edition see No. **609**★ below.

There are earlier traces of this piece. Collingwood (*Life*, p. 76) testifies that Dodgson preached before the University on the subject, and on 11 July 1895 (ibid., pp. 326–7) he sent to his brother an article on 'Eternal Punishment' and discussed the subject in his covering letter.

Parrish Catalogue, p. 56; cf. *Williams*, p. 85; *Collingwood*, pp. 76, 325.

In spite of the printer's date given above, it seems probable that this item was printed in 1895. Dodgson says (*Diaries*) on 20 June 1895: 'Today I have made a beginning of the work of getting *Solvent Principles* into type, by sending to Clay the MS. on "Eternal Punishment".' Thus he would have the article in 'proof' to send to Bertram Collingwood on 11 July, as quoted above.

The only reference to *Solvent Principles* in the (available) letters to Macmillan was on 14 May 1895 when, without naming it, he speaks of 'another book. . . . It will be an attempt to treat some of the religious difficulties of the day from a logical point of view'.

It is a pity that Dodgson did not live to complete this volume. Some excellent salvage from it is printed in the Appendixes to my edition of the *Diaries*.

R. L. G.

The reprint from *L.C.P.B.* is described by Madan as follows:

Undated.

Great Religious Difficulty (*undated*)   [609★

For Private Circulation. A Great Religious Difficulty. A Paper by the Rev. C. L. Dodgson ('Lewis Carroll'). Reprinted from 'The Lewis Carroll Picture Book' by Permission of the Publisher, T. Fisher Unwin, 11 Paternoster Buildings, London. (No place or date: 12°, pp. 1–16 and wrapper.) A reprint of 'Eternal Punishment' (No. **253**), an Essay on pp. 345–55 of the Picture Book. A copy is owned by the Dodgson family. Rare.

1896

270. *Symbolic Logic* (1896)   (First Edition)   [240ᵃ⁻ᵈ

SYMBOLIC LOGIC | *PART I* | ELEMENTARY | BY | LEWIS CARROLL ||||

Price two shillings London Macmillan and Co. and New York: 1896: (eights) 12°: size $6\frac{11}{16} \times 4\frac{5}{8}$ in.: pp. xxxi+[1]+188+4: signn. [a], b, A–N⁸. CONTENTS: p. i, the half-title | Symbolic Logic |: iv has the following | A Syllogism worked out. | over a thin rule, then four lines of prose over a double rule, after which come | The Premisses separately |, a thin rule, two diagrams and two thin rules, then | The Premisses combined. | and a thin rule, a diagram and a double rule followed by | The Conclusion. | and a thin line, a diagram and two lines of prose—the whole in black-letter type, and within a double-rule border, the ends of which overlap: v, the title as above, and at foot 'All rights reserved': vi, the imprint, | Richard Clay and Sons, Limited, | London and Bungay. | vii, | Advertisement. | i.e. notes addressed to readers, four paragraphs over a thin rule: ix, dedication. | Dedicated | to | the Memory | of Aristotle | xi–xiii, Introduction, signed 'L. C.', '1896': xv–xxxi, Contents, in 8 books, Appendix and Index: 1–184, the text: 185–8, the Index: 1, blank, except for | [Turn over. | in the bottom right-hand corner: 2–4, Macmillan's advertisements of the works of Lewis Carroll. Preceding page 1 of the text should be a slip of corrections dated Feb. 24, 1896.

Issued in brown cloth, with white end-papers. The back is blank. The front cover has two horizontal lines at the top, and two at the bottom, the inner lines being of double thickness. The remainder of the front cover is taken up with | Symbolic | Logic | Part I Elementary | Lewis Carroll |. The back cover is quite blank. All three edges are sprinkled, and are cut level with the edges of the covers.

The subject of this work is related to several items already dealt with in the present volume.

The second and third editions were also issued in 1896, and the fourth in 1897, but there are no more. Christ Church Library has corrections of this book on several separate leaves, and also a copy of Book VIII bound separately in red paper wrappers, with many variations.

The first part of *Symbolic Logic* (which was intended to consist of three parts, Elementary, Advanced, and Transcendental) is a development of the *Game of Logic* (No. 164: 1886) and a great advance on it. It is a serious attempt to popularize Formal Logic and accuracy of thought, largely by the use of diagrams. The smaller and larger diagrams of the *Game* become biliteral, triliteral, &c., up to octoliteral, but the treatise does not extend beyond Syllogisms and Sorites. Even Hypotheticals and Dilemmas were left for the second part. When X (and $X' = $ not-X) and Y (and $Y' = $ not-y) are used as classes, they fit into a biliteral diagram; when m (and m') is added, into a triliteral, and so on. By a 'method of Subscripts' ($x_1 =$ some x exist; $xy_1 =$ some xy exist; $x_0 =$ no x exist), and with the help of their symbols and ¶ (= 'would, if true, prove'), a Syllogism can be succinctly expressed. There are plenty of quaint examples, answers and solutions, and an Appendix addressed to teachers (pp. 165–8), in which occur some foretastes of Parts II and III, including some hypothetical problems.

The novelty of method and the fame of the author secured a considerable vogue for this book, but there is no royal road to or through Logic. Dodgson, however, attached special value to this book, if, as he hoped, it would lead to clearer judgements in people who thought at all: and regarded it as 'work for God', referring especially to the (unpublished) second part, see Collingwood's *Life and Letters*, pp. 330–1.

Presentation copies dated 22 Feb. 1896 are known. A slip of corrections dated 24 Feb. 1896 later precedes p. 1 of the text. In the second edition (No. **240**b: 1896), of which a presentation copy dated 13 June 1896 is known, a few changes are made, including the correction of one 'splendid' and one 'terrible' mistake; the new Preface is dated 11 May 1896, and its two pages occupy the place of the dedication and next (blank) page. The work now occupies pp. 1–192+4, signn. A–N⁸. To the 'advertisement' is now added a sentence worth quoting in full:

'P.S. I take the opportunity of giving what publicity I can to my contradiction of a silly story, which has been going the round of the papers, about my having presented certain books to her Majesty the Queen. It is so constantly repeated, and is such an absolute fiction, that I think it worth while to state, once for all, that it is utterly false in every particular: nothing even resembling it has ever occurred.'

The story, of course, was that the Queen after reading 'Alice' had expressed a desire to receive his next work—which was presumably the 'Condensation of Determinants'!

The third edition (second thousand, No. **240**c: 1896) with a preface dated 20 July 1896, incorporated the new matter of the second edition, but makes little or no further change in pagination or otherwise. It adds one clause to the advertisement, to the effect that an envelope with two diagrams and nine counters (No. **241**) can be purchased.

The fourth edition (second thousand, No. **240**d: 1897) with Preface dated Christmas, 1896, has been altered in the Sorites examples, and the Appendix exhibits nine instead of four examples, the 'Five

Liars' being suppressed and six new examples added, including 'Jack Sprat could eat no fat, etc.' The work now occupies 199 pages.

F. M.

Williams, i. 72 (p. 81); *Parrish Catalogue*, p. 56 (1st ed., and addenda to Part I, 2nd ed.); *Collingwood*, pp. 332, 442: British Museum (1, 2, 3, 4 edd.), Bodleian (2, 3, 4 edd.), Christ Church, Oxford (1st ed.), Professor J. A. Stewart (1st ed.), Mrs. Ffooks (1st ed.).

271. *Symbolic Logic* (Card and Counters) (1896) [241

TO BE USED WITH | SYMBOLIC LOGIC | PART I | ELEMENTARY | BY | LEWIS CARROLL | [A thin line, then a note about the card, diagrams and counters]: then a thin line.

Price Threepence. London Macmillan and Co., Ltd. New York: The Macmillan Co.: 1896: (four) 8°: pp. [8]. CONTENTS: pp. [1–2] Biliteral Diagram; Tables I–III: [3–7] Triliteral Diagram; Tables IV–VIII. A stitched pamphlet.

Accompanying this piece is an envelope dated 1896 containing a card with two diagrams and nine counters, four red, and five grey. These two items (pamphlet and envelope) accompany the third and fourth editions of *Symbolic Logic*, but were perhaps provided from the first for use with the book. Rare.

Parrish Catalogue, pp. 54–56 (with facsimile of the title-page).

On 1 Feb. 1893 Dodgson made the first reference to his book on Logic in a letter to Macmillan: 'I have been at the book for 20 years or more.'

It was published on 21 Feb. 1896: '500 were printed,' records Dodgson (*Diaries*), 'of which 100 are for me to give away, 100 have been presented to schools etc. (100 more have to be given), and 50 are to go to America. Orders exhaust the rest of the First Edition, and I am correcting press for the Second.' And on 9 Mar.: 'I am adding a note to the Appendix of *Symbolic Logic* in which, anticipating Part II, I try to prove that A and O are *not* Contradictories.'

On 21 May 1896: 'Passed for Press . . . the second edition of *Symbolic Logic*.'

Finally, on 8 Aug. 1896: 'I find I must rewrite, in *Symbolic Logic*, the section on Propositions in A.'

Selections from *Symbolic Logic* are included in *Nonesuch*, pp.1238–65 (1116–40).

The whole book, together with *The Game of Logic*, was reprinted in America by Messrs. Dover in 1958—in *Mathematical Recreations of Lewis Carroll* (No. *318* below), the fourth edition being used (Preface dated Christmas 1896).

272-9. *Diagrams* (1896)   [242-9

Diagrams on paper (about $5 \times 6\frac{1}{2}$ in., printed on one side only) were supplied for such as wished to work out independently the methods and problems of Dodgson's *Symbolic Logic*. Bi literal [No. 242], Triliteral [No. 243], Quadriliteral diagrams [No. 244 (20 on the sheet), used when four classes (such as x, y, m, n) were dealt with]; Quinqueliteral [No. 245] (6 on the sheet) when five were concerned, and so on. Each sheet is headed 'Quadriliteral Diagrams', &c. All seven diagrams (Sexliteral [No. 246], Septiliteral [No. 247], Octoliteral [No. 248]), besides the above; and also 'Tables I–VIII' [No. 249] (pp. 8, dated 1896), were in the Hatch collection, sold at Messrs. Hodgson's London sale on 18 Dec. 1924, lots 498, 505. The precise date of the issues of these diagrams cannot be stated. Some were perhaps earlier than 1896.

Williams, ii. 80–81 (p. 110; four and five), *Parrish Catalogue*, p. 111 (four and five), Bodleian (five), F. Madan and Sir. H. Hartley (four and five).

280. *Circular about Books to Give Away* (1896)

On 29 Dec. 1895 Dodgson wrote to Macmillan: 'I have sent to Messrs. Clay the MS. of an announcement about books to give away.'

This was a new one as it included copies of both volumes of *Sylvie and Bruno* and (possibly) a reference about *Symbolic Logic*— of which only sample copies for schools were to be given.

No copy of this circular has so far been discovered.   R. L. G.

281. *Resident Women Students* (1896)   [250ᵃ⁻ᵇ

RESIDENT WOMEN-STUDENTS. | [*a line, then* 28 *lines of text.*]

(Oxford, printed by G. Sheppard: 1896): (two) 8°: pp. [4]. CONTENTS: p. [1] the title: [1–3; 2 mispaged '3'] the paper, signed 'Charles L. Dodgson' and dated 'Ch. Ch. Mar. 7th. 1896'. At the foot of p. [3] is 'Sheppard, Printer, Oxford': [4] blank.

Part of the long controversy about granting Certificates and Diplomas and finally Degrees of the University of Oxford to women. Dodgson foresaw that residence would soon follow, and he agreed with Canon Liddon that in that case the women themselves would suffer. The proper way out was to petition the Crown to grant a charter for a Women's University, in spite of the un-doubted fact that they did not desire it. 'Even men very often fail to "desire" what is, after all, the best thing for them to have.'

There are two forms of this paper: (A) [No. 250ᵃ] where on pp. [1] and [2] the word 'consequently' is central in the page, and (B) [250ᵇ] where the word is shifted on both pages 1¼ inches to the left—which appears to be an improvement in form. Dodgson had on 11 Mar. 1884 made one of his few speeches in Congregation on the same side.

Williams, ii. 79 (p. 110; A *or* B); *Parrish Catalogue*, p. 96 (A and B); *Colling-wood*, p. 442 (A *or* B), cf. 231: Bodleian, Harvard (A *or* B), Huntington (A *or* B), S. H. Williams (B), F. Madan (A *and* B).

This was published on 7 Mar. 1896, between Debates in Congre-gation on 3 and 10 Mar. on the subject. The motion to admit Women for the B.A. Degree was defeated, also other motions to give them diplomas of any kind.

1897

282. A Mysterious Number (1897)

On p. 269 of *The Lewis Carroll Picture Book* (1899), Collingwood prints this and another numerical problem with the comment: 'I give two numerical curiosities which I believe to have been discovered by Mr. Dodgson.'

The 'curiosity' in question is here headed: 'A Magic Number: 142857.'

This may be the 'number repeating puzzle' which Dodgson mentions in *Diaries* on 26 Jan. 1897 as part of his 'lecture' at the Guildford High School, and is certainly one of the puzzles demon-strated to 'Mr. Allen's School' at St. Leonards on 6 Oct. 1897: 'I did the "goose" on the blackboard. . . . I gave them "C.T." and "M.O.W.S." stories; the saying a lot of figures by *Memoria Technica*; 142857; the reversed £. s. d.'

It has not hitherto been noticed that the '142857' discovery was published anonymously in *Chatterbox*, 1897, No. 6, p. 46—this is the number for the sixth week of the year, which would be early in Feb. 1897.

The wording is not the same as that given by Collingwood but the numerical portion is, of course, identical. If Dodgson had copied the puzzle from *Chatterbox* he would surely have kept both the original name and wording. Unless someone who had heard him describe it 'stole' his discovery, it seems probable that Dodgson was himself the anonymous contributor of the piece in *Chatterbox*.

R. L. G.

283. *Address for Children* (1897) [254

Address by the Rev. C. L. Dodgson (Louis* Carroll) at S. Mary | Magdalen Church (3 P.M. The Children's Service) on Harvest | Thanksgiving Day. |

(Collations taken from the St. Mary Magdalen Church Magazine (St. Leonards-on-Sea), Oct. 1897): 4°: size of letterpress, $5\frac{8}{8} \times 8\frac{1}{4}$ in.: pp. [1–2]: [1] heading as above, beneath 16 lines of 'Occasional Offices and Notices of the Church'; 34 lines of text beginning 'A little girl named Margaret' and ending 'Margaret's little pale face till her cheeks': [2] 59 lines of text beginning 'began to take a faint colour too' and ending 'God's law of Love'; below the last line of the text is 'Mr. Dodgson also twice most kindly addressed our children in the schools'. The sermon tells a story of Florence Nightingale's care for a suffering dog.

I am unable to describe the Church Magazine of this date, as there does not appear to be one in existence. The above collation was made from a page, cut from a copy, in the possession of the Brassey Institute, Hastings, whose librarian, Mr. Ruskin Butterfield, kindly allowed me to examine and collate. S. H. W.

The Address was given on 3 Oct. 1897. It was reprinted as a pamphlet (4 pp. octavo) headed LEWIS CARROLL CENTENARY, 1932 with an extract from the *Diaries* for the day in question supplied by Major C. H. W. Dodgson. (See No. *304* below.)

It had already been reprinted on pp. 340–4 of *The Lewis Carroll Picture Book*, 1899.

284. *Divisibility* (1897) [251

BRIEF METHOD OF DIVIDING A GIVEN | NUMBER BY 9 OR 11. |

Two numbered galley-slips forming a reprint from some mathematical periodical of an article by Dodgson, but unsigned and undated (77+46 lines). The methods were discovered by Dodgson, and cannot be stated here shortly, but they involve only subtraction and addition.

The slips begin 'Years ago I had discovered' and 'Right-hand end'. Internal evidence shows that the printing was not before 28 Sept. 1897, and the correspondence number 98281, written on each

---

* So in original *Handbook*, and no copy is available to check.

copy by Dodgson, that it was not later than November or December of that year.

The only sets known of these slips (six sets in all) are owned by Mr. Parrish of Philadelphia, U.S.A. [Mr. Parrish also possesses [No. 252] an undated single leaf of a 'Note on question 7695', concerning a mathematical problem, of which the answer was correct, but the method of arriving at it wrong.]

This is a 'proof' or 'offprint' from *Nature*, vol. lvi, pp. 565–6, 14 Oct. 1897. (See No. *197* above.)

[No. **252** is a proof or offprint from the *Educational Times*, 1 May 1885. See No. *136* above.]

285. *Lost Plum Cake* (1897) [255

THE LOST PLUM CAKE | *A TALE FOR TINY BOYS* | BY | E. G. WILCOX | (*Mrs. Egerton Allen*) | AUTHOR OF 'LITTLE HUMPHREY'S | ADVENTURE' AND 'EVIE' | *WITH NINE ILLUSTRATIONS* | BY | E. L. SHUTE. |

Price one shilling net London Macmillan and Co., Limited New York: The Macmillan Company: 1897: (eights) 12°: pp. xvi+101+[3]: Signn. [A], B–G⁸, H⁴. CONTENTS: p. i, the half-title. | The Lost Plum Cake |: ii, | Oxford | Horace Hart, Printer to the University |: iv, frontispiece: v, the title, as above, and at foot 'All rights reserved': vii–xi, the introduction, signed 'Lewis Carroll', and dated | Christmas 1897. |: xiii, the preface, signed E. G. A., May 1896: xiv, the contents: xv, a list of the illustrations: 1–101, the text: [2] a list of the works of E. G. Wilcox. Issued in a red cardboard cover with a gilt design on the front.

Lovers of Lewis Carroll will feel a sad interest in the Introduction to *The Lost Plum Cake*, as it was the last of his writings to appear in print during his life; for it is dated Christmas 1897, and he died on 14 Jan. following. Mrs. Allen was a cousin of Dodgson. In the Introduction he praises the authoress and book, points out the optical illusion connected with the gilt pattern on the red cardboard cover (designed by Miss E. Gertrude Thomson), and writes in favour of children bringing picture-books, such as this one, into church, to be read during the sermon. He had interested himself in the book, giving advice and suggesting incidents, his last letter to the authoress being dated 22 Dec. 1897. The book was first published in Jan. 1898, though dated 1897.

The Lost Plum Cake was 'passed for Press' by Dodgson on 21 May 1896, according to *Diaries*.

1898

286. *Three Sunsets* (1898)   [581

Three Sunsets | and other Poems | by | Lewis Carroll | with twelve fairy-fancies | by | E. Gertrude Thomson.

Price four shillings net: London Macmillan and Co., Limited . . .: 1898: 'All Rights Reserved': (eights, &c.) sm. 4°: pp. [12]+67+[2]+2+[1], signn. A^6, $B-E^8$, $F-G^2$. CONTENTS: p. [1] half-title: [4] frontispiece: [5] title: [6] Richard Clay and Sons, Limited, London and Bungay, the printers: [7] preface, dated Jan. 1898: [9] contents: [11] list of illustrations: 1–67 [1], the poems: [1–2] advertisement.

It is clear that Dodgson allowed himself to issue collections of his poems under new names, although much of the contents had previously been printed. In this case, as the preface shows, nearly the whole of the volume is a reprint of the serious part (Part II) of *Phantasmagoria* (1869), but two there found are not here reprinted (*Lines* and *Christmas Greetings*). The five pieces here added are 'Far away' and 'A Song of Love' from *Sylvie and Bruno*; 'A Lesson in Latin' from the *Jabberwock*, 1888 (No. 209); and two acrostic poems forming *Puck lost and found*, presented to 'Princess Alice' and 'Prince Charlie', 22 and 25 Nov. 1891. Incidentally Dodgson expresses a fear that the limited sale of *Sylvie and Bruno* is due to the necessarily high price. In several cases Dodgson has in this reprint added the dates of composition wanting in *Phantasmagoria*. The engravings are undoubtedly graceful, but have little or no relation to the poems. The full story of them is in Collingwood's *Life*, pp. 193–9; and in Art. 1490 of *Maggs's Catalogue*, 441 (1923) are interesting extracts from eight letters of Dodgson offered for sale, relating to these drawings, 1890–4.

'One cannot read this little volume without feeling that the shadow of some disappointment lay over Lewis Carroll's life. Such I believe to have been the case, and it was this that gave him his wonderful sympathy with all who suffered' (Collingwood's *Life*, p. 355).

[It is worth repeating what Collingwood wrote to Miss F. Menella Dodgson on 3 Feb. 1932 when she had asked him about this passage: 'Nothing I have read in Lewis Carroll's diaries or letters suggested— to the best of my memory—that he had ever had any *affaires de cœur*. I *think* that Aunt Fanny once told me that it was the family's opinion that Uncle Charles had had a disappointment in love. . . . The "shadow" I hinted at had no other basis than what I had heard from Aunt Fanny.'

Dodgson's sisters made the romantic guess (but unlikely in any serious sense) that the Fair Unknown was Ellen Terry.]

Dodgson first wrote to Macmillan about *Three Sunsets* on 20 May 1895. No letters are available for 1897, and there is no reference in *Diaries* for that year. If the Preface bears the actual date of writing, it must have been written during the first week in January and is absolutely the last thing he ever wrote. But it is more likely that he merely corrected and returned the proofs from Guildford at some time between 23 Dec. 1897 and the end of the first week of Jan. 1898.

The above volume was again issued in Feb. 1898, with an addition on the back of the title-page 'First Edition printed February 1898. Reprinted February 1898', but the sheets are identical throughout, except in this particular.

All the poems, as above, were reprinted in *Collected Verse* and *Nonesuch*.

1899

287. Lewis Carroll Picture Book   [583

The Lewis Carroll | Picture Book | a selection from the | unpublished writings | and drawings of Lewis | Carroll, together with | Reprints from scarce and | unacknowledged work | Edited by | Stuart Dodgson Collingwood | B.A. Christ Church, Oxford | Author of | 'The Life and Letters of Lewis Carroll' | Illustrated | [*silhouette of* 'Lewis Carroll. Aged 8.']

London: T. Fisher Unwin, Paternoster Square: [Nov.] 1899: 8°: pp. xv+[1] +375+[1], signn. [π], 1-24⁸, 25⁴: CONTENTS: i, half-title: ii, advertisement of 2 books: iv, frontispiece: v, title: vi, '[All rights reserved]': vii, 'To my Mother': ix–x, preface dated 'The Chestnuts Guildford, July, 1899': xi–xii Contents: xiii–xv, List of Illustrations: 1–371, the work in seven chapters and Appendix: 373–5, Index: [1] 'The Gresham Press, Unwin Brothers, Woking and London'.

An interesting volume, belying the limitations of its chief title. Besides twenty-four illustrations it contains reprints and new matter which make it an indispensable companion of the *Life and Letters* (No. 644). The chapters contain (i) specimens of Lewis Carroll's earliest pieces, including 'Difficulties' about *Where the Day begins*, and about clocks; (ii) Notes by an Oxford Chiel, see No. 80; (iii)

Nos. 171, 180, the two articles about Alice on the Stage; (iv) additional letters to child-friends; (v) fragments of *Curiosa Mathematica*, part 3, about Long Multiplication and Division, with two odd Theorems, the Monkey and Weight problem, and two numerical curiosities; (vi) Games and Puzzles (Castle Croquet, Doublets, Syzygies and Lanrick, also 'A Logical Paradox' (No. 232), a square in 64–65 pieces, &c.): (vii) 'Isa [Bowman's] Visit to Oxford' (1888), the 'Legend of "Scotland" ', the sermon to children at St. Leonards (1897) on Eternal Punishment, and Reminiscences of Dodgson by Professor Frederick York Powell, Henrietta H. Dodgson (his sister), and Canon Duckworth (the Duck of *Alice's Adventures*). The Appendix reprints Hilton's *Vulture and the Husbandman*, the *Jabberwock* in Latin (by H. Dodgson) and German, and a description of Lewis Carroll's study in Christ Church. A chapter on Parodies of *Alice*, promised in the Prospectus, was not printed. The illustrations are chiefly from Lewis Carroll's own photography of well-known persons, child-friends, and comic subjects. Altogether an entertaining volume.

It was first published in the autumn of 1899, at 6s., reissued in November at 3s. 6d., and reprinted in Collins's *Wide World Series* (No. 8, without date) in May 1913, for 7d., a miniature edition.

The following items in *The Lewis Carroll Picture Book* are not included in *Nonesuch*:

Pp. 7–9: Zoological Papers 3—Fishs.
Pp. 15–17: Preface to Mischmasch.
P. 25: Poetry for the Million.
Pp. 163–74: Alice on the Stage.
Pp. 175–95: The Stage and the Spirit of Reverence.
Pp. 240–63: Fragment of *Curiosa Mathematica*, iii.
Pp. 266–9: Six mathematical problems and curiosities.
Pp. 271–7: Castle Croquet.
Pp. 289–303: Syzygies.
Pp. 304–12: Lanrick.
Pp. 312–16: A Logical Paradox.
Pp. 316–18: Four puzzles.
Pp. 321–31: Isa's Visit to Oxford.
Pp. 340–4: Children's Sermon.
Pp. 345–55: Eternal Punishment.

1901

288. *A Visit to Tennyson* (1901)   [584

A Visit to Tennyson. By Lewis Carroll. Illustrations from Photographs.

A short article in the *Strand Magazine*, May 1901 (vol. xxi, No. 125), pp. 543-4: in the form of a letter written by Dodgson to William [Edward Wilcox] on 11 May 1859. Tennyson was at Farringford, Freshwater, I.W., and had framed Dodgson's photographs of the family. The visit was about Easter 1859, and Dodgson mentions that all the books in the shelves nearest to the poet's writing-table were Greek or Latin, that Tennyson often dreamt verses, that he spoke of arguing *a feebliori*, and that the *Lady of Shalott* was from the Italian.

This is reprinted in the first edition of this *Handbook* (1931), pp. 195-8; and in *Diaries* (1953), pp. 143-7.

1904

289. *Story of Sylvie and Bruno* (1904) [585

The story of | Sylvie and Bruno | by | Lewis Carroll | With illustrations by Harry Furniss |

London Macmillan and Co., Limited: New York: the Macmillan Company: 1904: 'All rights reserved': 8°: pp. xii+332, signn. [*a*]⁴, *b*², A–X⁸, Y⁶. CONTENTS: p. i, half-title: ii, the Macmillan mark: iv, frontispiece: v, title: vi 'Richard Clay and Sons, Limited . . .': vii, 6 lines of verse beginning 'Thou delicious Fay': ix, preface, unsigned: xi–xii, Contents: 1–329, the work: 329, printers' imprint: 331–2, advertisement of Lewis Carroll's works.

A note in Mr. Parrish's copy by Louisa F. Dodgson, 19 Mar. 1927, states that this abridgement (containing only the parts concerning the two children *themselves*, and omitting the heavier didactic part and society element) was conceived and carefully carried out by Dodgson's brother Edwin H. Dodgson, when invalided home from Tristan da Cunha. The note is printed in full in the *Parrish Catalogue*, at p. 59. Only a few connecting words here and there are not Lewis Carroll's own. For a subsequent edition see 1913. This abridgement is for many readers the most palatable form of *Sylvie and Bruno*. 'Bruno's Revenge' and most of the songs and illustrations are retained.

1907

290-1. *Feeding the Mind* (1907) [587

Feeding the Mind | by | Lewis Carroll | with a prefatory note by | William H. Draper | [*leaf-ornament*].

London, Chatto & Windus: 1907: (fours) 8°: pp. i–xiii, [xiv], 15–31, [32], signn. [A], B–D⁴. CONTENTS: i, half-title: ii, advt. of two books: iii, title: iv,

'[All rights reserved]': v–xiii, prefatory note, signed W. H. D., November 1907: 15–31, the lecture: 31, 'Billing and Sons, Ltd., Printers, Guildford'. 'Feeding the Mind' and 'Chatto & Windus', on the title-page are printed in red.

A short paper or lecture delivered in Oct. 1884 in the Derbyshire vicarage of Alfreton before a public audience. It is a comparison of feeding the mind with feeding the body in such points as proper food at proper intervals (a 'fat mind'), mastication by thinking over what is read, and mental appetite, all pervaded with quiet humour. Mr. Draper explains that the MS. was handed to him by the author, and occasionally read out at Christmas time to friends. There is a story of a Dean who called at the house and in the presence of others referred to Dodgson as the author of his books, with explosive results. Extracts are also given from the *Eight or nine Wise Words about Letter-writing*.

There is no earlier separate edition, although an advertisement in an '1890' issue of *Eight or Nine Wise Words* seemed to imply it. But the '1890' is a reprint of an old date, and should have been probably '1908', see No. 193 (p. 160, above). The piece did, however, appear at pp. 937–9 of *Harper's Monthly Magazine*, New York, May 1906 (*290*).   [588

The piece was issued at 1s. in grey boards lettered and decorated in red and black with parchment back, or at 2s. in limp brown leather, lettered and decorated in gold.

See *Diaries*, 22 Sept. to 4 Oct. 1884. This charming and characteristic piece seems never to have been reprinted—even in the Nonesuch Omnibus.

1910-20

292. *Love among the Roses* (1910–20)   [590

Love among the Roses.

[Printed in America?]: about 1910–20: one leaf, 8º: printed on one side only: the title is followed by a line, 13 lines of verse, 'Lewis Carroll' and 'January 3rd, 1878'.

The present issue appears to me to be a modern reprint of an acrostic poem written in 1878, and first printed in the *Lewis Carroll Picture Book* (1899) at p. 204. It is, in any case, the first separate printing of it, and presents the true reading of line 2 ('Ask', not 'And'). The first letters of lines form 'Sarah Sinclair'.

Parrish Catalogue, p. 16 (as if of date 1878: the only recorded copy).

Reprinted in *Collected Verse*, p. 328, *Nonesuch*, pp. 933–4 (837–8).

1911

293. *Phantasmagoria* (1911)   [591

Phantasmagoria | and other poems | by | Lewis Carroll | with illustrations | by | Arthur B. Frost.

Macmillan and Co., Limited, St. Martin's Street, London: 1911: (eights) 12°: pp. viii+166+[2]. CONTENTS: p. i, half-title: ii, Macmillan device and addresses: iii, title: iv 'Richard Clay and Sons . . . (London &) Bungay. First published in 1869': v, 'Inscribed to a dear Child . . .' with four 4-line acrostic verses, supplying the name of Gertrude Chataway: vii–viii, contents: 1–166, the work: 166, printers' imprint: [1–2] Advertisements of Lewis Carroll's works.

A reprint of Part I (only) of the 1869 edition, in a miniature edition, omitting the 'Elections to the Hebdomadal Council', as being out of date, and all Part II (the serious poems), and adding Echoes, Téma, A Game of Fives, three out of 'Four Riddles', and Fame's Penny-Trumpet. The prefatory verses (acrostic) are transferred from *The Hunting of the Snark*, to which they properly belong. A reissue of the sheets with very slight formal changes is dated 1919; there were also reissues in July and Oct. 1929, in Macmillan's Cardinal Series.

This reprint is, in fact, from *Rhyme? and Reason?*, giving the revised form of all the verses.

1913

294. *Sylvie and Bruno* (1913)   [592

The | Story of Sylvie & Bruno | (abridged) | By | Lewis Carroll | With Illustrations | by | Harry Furniss [*title on cover*]

Macmillan & Co. Ltd. . . . London: [1913]: (twenty) 8°: pp. 80.

An abridgement of the first abridgement in 1904: issued without date as No. 40 of Macmillan's Children's Classics, price 3½d.; and printed at the Glasgow University Press. The last words are 'went back to Fairyland'. The Bodleian copy was received in Apr. 1913. See *Parrish Catalogue*, p. 60.

1924

295. *Six Letters* (1924)   [593

Six Letters | by | Lewis Carroll | ornament |

'[London, 1924: Printed for Private Distribution.]': 8°: pp. iv+12. CONTENTS: p. i, title: ii, note that 26 copies only were printed, signed 'Wilfred

C 90   O

Partington' and numbered in manuscript: iii–iv, Introductory Note, signed in print 'Wilfred Partington': 1–12, the six letters.

The six letters (dated 1 Sept. 1873, 30 Dec. 1874, 18 Dec. 1877, 14 Apr. 1884, 28 Aug. 1890, and 17 Sept. 1891) are all from Dodgson to Miss Maud Standen, one of his girl-friends, now Mrs. Ffooks, of Kingscote, Dorchester, Dorset, and all are here first printed. They are characteristic and interesting, and describe his stay at Hatfield House (Dec. 1874), give an explanation of strange terms in the *Jabberwocky* (p. 5: uffish, burble), exemplify an 'Anagrammatic Sonnet' (p. 5), give a charade beginning 'They both make a roaring' (p. 6), and explain his 'gift' of a book (p. 9), and his way of composing *Sylvie and Bruno* (p. 11). The astonishing Sonnet has six lines, each composed of four metric feet—and each foot *is* an anagram—it begins, 'As to the war' (oats, wreath). See Part III, No. xv.

Mr. Wilfred G. Partington, the editor of the *Bookman's Journal*, issued this limited edition of twenty-six copies only, by Mrs. Ffooks's permission, in Feb. 1924, each being numbered and signed by him: and the type was used as part of the *Journal* for March (vol. ix, No. 30). So this issue is neither an offprint from the *Journal* nor a reprint, but a fore-print—which is unusual. The first two letters and the sixth were reprinted in the *Dorsetshire Year Book* for 1928. Rare.

Williams, i. 78 (p. 87), *Parrish Catalogue*, p. 61 (no. 18): British Museum, M. L. Parrish, S. H. Williams, F. Madan, Mrs. Ffooks, the editor, &c.

The following extract, originally in another part of the *Handbook*, may suitably be included here.

Anagrams can no further go than an extreme instance composed by Dodgson and printed in that rare booklet *Six Letters by Lewis Carroll* (1924: No. 593 above) at p. 6. He calls it an 'Anagrammatic Sonnet'. It consists of the six lines printed below: each line is composed of four feet, and each of the twenty-four feet is an anagram (!):

As to the war, try elm. I tried.
The wig cast in, I went to ride
'Ring? Yes.' We rang. 'Let's rap.' We don't.
'O shew her wit!' As yet she won't.
Saw eel in Rome. Dry one: he's wet.
I am dry. O forge Th' rogue Why a net?

Dodgson continues: 'To these you may add "abcdefgi", which makes a good compound word—as good a word as "summer-house".'
The first two anagrams are, *oats* and *wreath*: then *big-faced*.

There seems to be no reason for Madan's third anagram, but otherwise it can be worked out as follows:

OATS · WREATH · MYRTLE · TIDIED.
WEIGHT · SCIANT · TWINE · RIOTED.
SYRINGE · GNAWER · PLASTER · WONTED.
WHOSE · WITHER · YEAST · NEW-SHOT.
WEASEL · MOIREN(?) · YONDER · THEWES.
MYRIAD · FOREGO · ROUGETH · HAY WENT.

Strangely enough, however, it is possible to make another poem from this in the same way, with a result that makes nearly as much sense as Dodgson's did:

'So at the raw myrtle it died.
Weight I scant—twine, or tied
In Grey's new rag. Plaster! End tow,
Whose whither at—yes, the snow!
We seal no mire, or deny hew set;
My raid forego? Hot urge—nay whet!'

In both cases the final foot defies proper solution.   R. L. G.

296. *Some rare Carrolliana* (1924)   [594

Some rare | Carolliana | with Notes by | Sidney Herbert Williams, F.S.A. | . . . |

London, printed for private circulation only: 1924: (six) la. 8°: pp. [2]+23+ [1]. CONTENTS: [1] note that 79 copies only were printed, see below: [2] dedication to A. R.: 2, frontispiece: 3, title: 4, 'Printed in Great Britain': 5–23, the Notes and 13 full-page illustrations, signed at end and dated 'St. Leonards-on-Sea. December 8th, 1924.'

The rarities here described and illustrated are almost all from Miss Mary Watson, of St. Leonards-on-Sea, the survivor of three sisters who were girl-friends of Lewis Carroll. Their names were Harriett ('Hartie'), Mary, and Ina, and when he addressed them all together were combined in *Harmarina*. A. R., the dedicatee, first introduced the author to *Alice* and is thus indirectly responsible for the Bibliography of 1924.

The following is a list of the illustrations, in their order, with references to the notes on them. The frontispiece is a collotype, all the rest zincography:

1 (frontispiece, see pp. 20, 23). The Lewis Carroll Biscuit Tin, issued in 1892 by Messrs. Jacob and Co., of Dublin, biscuit-makers: it is decorated in colour with characters from *Alice's Adventures* and *Through the Looking-Glass*. Dodgson himself supervised it, and took 300 of the 50,000 produced, but it is very rare. The makers were Messrs. Hudson of Carlisle.

2 (p. 6). A puzzle in two 4-line stanzas, beginning 'When -a-y and I. a', letters having to be supplied. In facsimile.

3 (p. 7). Eight 4-line stanzas addressed to Miss Mary Watson on Apr. 10, 1871, beginning, 'Three children (their names)', about summer holidays. In facsimile.

4 (p. 9, see p. 8). Part of a picture letter, beginning 'My [*deer*] Ina, Though [*eye*] don't give'.

5 (p. 10, see p. 8). Seven lines of verse, beginning, 'Tell me truly', describing seven flowers.

6 (p. 11). A short letter, beginning, 'Mary dear, Here is a riddle', signed 'Lewis Carroll'. The riddle is in four lines, beginning, 'Dreaming of apples'.

7 (p. 13, see pp. 8, 12). A maze or labyrinth, with letter clues leading to 'Ina'. In facsimile.

8 (pp. 14–15, see pp. 12, 16, 20). Ten small illustrations for a story about pigs, a wolf, and a fox, told by Dodgson to the three children in 1871, and retold by Mary.

9 (p. 17). A letter from Dodgson to Mary, 3 Dec. 1876.

10 (p. 18). A letter from Dodgson to 'Hartie', 13 Dec. 1893.

11 (p. 19). Facsimiles of four trial title-pages for *Alice*, three dated 1864: the order in time is probably (1) in manuscript, (3), (2), (4).

12 (p. 21). A proof of a page, with one illustration, of a projected quarto edition of *Alice*, happily rejected.

13 (p. 22). An elaborate table of details of the 42 Tenniel illustrations of *Alice*: see Plate XII. The originals of 11–13 are owned by the Dean of Christ Church, who also kindly allows us to use Plate I.

Of the seventy-nine (signed) copies, four are on hand-made paper; all are numbered in manuscript. The ordinary copies (5–79) are bound in stiff grey boards, and the title is printed on the front cover. The book was issued at Christmas 1924.

Parrish Catalogue, p. 137 (two copies, nos. 2 and 28): British Museum, Bodleian, Harvard, &c.

The letters numbered 4 and 9 above are included in *Letters to Child-Friends* (1933). See No. *311*.

The verses numbered 2 and 3 above are included in *Collected Verse* and *Nonesuch*. Number 6 above is the riddle from *Puzzles from Wonderland*, included in both collections.

No. 5 (Verses) and No. 10 (Letter) do not seem to have been reprinted in any other collection.

1925

297. *Novelty and Romancement* (1925)   [596

Novelty and Romancement | A Story by Lewis Carroll | . . . |
With an Introduction by | Randolph Edgar | [*ornament*] |

Boston [U.S.A.] B.J. Brimmer Company: Nineteen twenty-five [February]:
printed (p. 4) by 'Wright & Potter Printing Company Boston': (eights) sm.
4°: pp. 55+[1].

The introduction (pp. 11–16) recounts that this short prose piece,
in which the point is that Romancement can be broken into Roman
cement, was printed in the *Train* in 1856 (see No. 9, i.e. *14*) and
is perhaps the only short story written by Lewis Carroll, except
Bruno's Revenge. Mr. Edgar tells the story of Queen Victoria and
Dodgson's books, with the denial of its truth, and believes that
Some Popular Fallacies about Vivisection (No. 87 above) is not Dodgson's. The story occupies pp. 21–55, and is in large type.

Parrish Catalogue, p. 61.

1926

298. *Further Nonsense Verse* (1926)   [600

Further Nonsense | Verse and Prose | by | Lewis Carroll | (edited
by Langford Reed) | Illustrated by | H. M. Bateman | [engraving
of man and two clocks] |

T. Fisher Unwin Ltd. London: Adelphi Terrace: (1926): (eights) 4°: pp.
127+[1]+4 illustrations from photographs, full page, and 16 in the text by
Bateman (one repeated on the title-page). Printed (see p. 4) by Billing and
Sons, Ltd., Guildford and Esher.

Mr. Langford Reed has collected thirty-five pieces by Dodgson,
written in his lighter style, and contributed an introductory life and
estimate of the writer (whom he calls the King of Nonsense Literature), and also notes and settings for many of the pieces, making
up a readable and interesting volume, with some new matter. The
full-page illustrations are from Collingwood's *Life* (1898), pp. 18,
176 (portrait), 346, 366, the portrait forming a frontispiece. About
half the volume is in prose. Mr. Reed deserves credit for having
rescued from oblivion (at pp. 31, 66) two of Dodgson's earliest
efforts, printed in the *Whitby Gazette* in 1854. He also prints

extracts from the *Rectory Umbrella* (a manuscript magazine of about 1850) at pp. 36, 48, 54, 89, 94, 97; 'Maggie's Visit to Oxford', and the like; and winds up with anecdotes of Lewis Carroll. The *differentia* of this book is the large proportion of items *not* drawn from Dodgson's larger books, and the illustrations, but the title might have been bettered.

It is, in fact, a companion volume to Langford Reed's *Nonsense Verses: An Anthology* [1925], by various writers, but including five pieces by Lewis Carroll from more usual sources.

1928

299. *Tour in 1867* (1928)   [601

Tour in 1867 | by | C. L. Dodgson | Ch. Ch., Oxford | from the | original manuscript in the collection of | M. L. Parrish, Esq. Pine Valley, New Jersey |

Philadelphia privately printed. 1928.: 8°: pp. [6]+64+[7]. The first four and the last seven pages are blank, the title-page and preceding leaf being an insertion after the first leaf of the first sheet. '(Sixty-six copies of this book have been printed)'.

A diary by Dodgson of a continental tour in company with Canon Liddon, through Brussels, Cologne, Berlin, and Königsberg, to St. Petersburg and Moscow, returning by Warsaw, Breslau, Dresden, and Paris, 12 July–14 Sept. 1867. In a sense this is an ordinary record of what was seen and done, and there is not much of Lewis Carroll in it, but the characters and opinions of the two men are well exemplified, the long Russian part is quite valuable, and the incidents excellently described. Pp. 1–2, 22, 29, 32, 49, 52–3, and 60 may be said to contain the Carrollian part. Mr. Parrish is to be thanked for this addition to our knowledge of Dodgson's tastes and views, and of his methods of meeting the discomforts of continental travel in the sixties.

This rare little volume is bound in red grained leather, lettered on the back 'Tour in 1867—Lewis Carroll', and enclosed in a red cardboard case. The two notebooks (93 and 30 pages) containing the original record, in Dodgson's hand, are described in the *Parrish Catalogue* at p. 119, but there are few copies of the printed issue on this side of the Atlantic.

Christ Church, Oxford, M. L. Parrish, S. H. Williams, F. Madan, &c.

The Russian Tour was first published in 1935. See No. *312* below.

1929

300. *Collected Verse* (1929)   [605

The | Collected Verse of | Lewis Carroll | With an Introduction by | John Francis McDermott | [*ornament*] |

E. P. Dutton & Co., Inc. New York: (1929): 8°: pp. [2]+xxxviii+228+ [4]. CONTENTS: p. i, half-title: iii, title within ornamental border: iv, note about copyright and date of issue: v–vii, Preface: ix–xii, Contents: xiii–xxxviii, Introduction: 1–183, the Verses: 185–224, Appendixes: 225–8, indexes of titles and first words. Binding, half-blue cloth with black lettering on gold labels.

Professor McDermott of Washington University, St. Louis, U.S.A., has collected the verse pieces in *Alice, Through the Looking-Glass,* the *Snark* (all), *Rhyme? and Reason?* (all), and *Sylvie and Bruno* (both parts), and added to them two prose pieces and some early versions of poems (App. B–D), and a short Bibliography, and lists of titles and incipits. The Introduction is a critical essay on the author and his works, in which the Hyde-and-Jekyll duality of Dodgson is, it may be thought, over-emphasized. It dwells on Dodgson's methods of parody and satire, and concludes that the *Snark* is 'a solemn mockery of life, a general human satire of all life'. Incidentally it gives a clue to the originals which are here parodied.

But see the much fuller *Collected Verse* published by Macmillan, London, in 1932. No. *306* below.

1930

301. *A Christmas Carroll* (1930)

A | CHRISTMAS | CARROLL

'A leaflet (pp. 4) in red paper cover (printed at Edinburgh by Pillans and Wilson). 50 copies printed for Mr. Hugh Sharp at Christmas, 1930. It contains a facsimile of an acrostic poem of twelve lines, beginning "Maiden, though thy heart may quail", written in a copy of the *Snark* presented by Dodgson to Miss "Marion B. Terry" on August 16, 1876.'

So Madan in *Supplement* (p. 13), 1935.

It is bound in red paper wrappers, front blocked in centre with holly wreath in gold round title as above. Back blank. Size $8\frac{1}{16} \times 5$ inches. Collation: [1] Blank; [2] Title; description of contents; [3] Text; [4] Imprint. Reprinted in *Collected Verse* (1932), p. 326; *Nonesuch*, pp. 932–3 (836).

1931

302. Handbook of the Literature of the Rev. C. L. Dodgson (1931)

See No. X below for full description.

The following items by Dodgson were included as Part III:

1. A Visit to Tennyson. *Strand Magazine*, May 1891.
2. Little Maidens. *Sotheby's Sale Catalogue*, 3 Apr. 1928. [*Nonesuch*, &c.]
3. Prologue to Play (1871). [*Nineteenth Century*, Feb. 1932. *Nonesuch*, &c.]
4. Jabberwocky—in English, German, Latin, and Greek.
5. Two Thieves. *Sotheby's Sale Catalogue*, 23 July 1929. [*Nonesuch*, &c.]
6. Prologue to Play (1873). *Strand Magazine*, Apr. 1898. [*Nonesuch*, &c.]
7. Letter to Miss May Parish (1879). *Edgar Wells's Catalogue*, 9 Mar. 1925.
8. Two Poems to Rachael Daniel. The second in *The Garland of Rachael* (1881). Both in *Nonesuch*, &c.
9. Dreamland. *Aunt Judy's Magazine*, July 1882. [*Nonesuch*, &c.]
10. Rhyme? and Reason? [*Verses*]. *Sotheby's Catalogue*, 23 July 1929. [*Nonesuch*, &c.]
11. Copula in a Syllogism. *Parrish Catalogue*, p. 87 (1928).
12. Maggie B——. *Maggs's Catalogue*, 559, 1931. [*Nonesuch*, &c.]
13. What the Tortoise said to Achilles. *Mind*, Dec. 1894. [*Nonesuch*, &c.]
14. Children in Church. *The Lost Plum Cake*, 1897. [*Nonesuch*, &c.]
15. Anagrams. (See No. *295*.)
16. Riddles, Charade, &c.
17. The Rev. C. L. Dodgson's Will, dated 4 Nov. 1871. (See Miscellanea below.)

303. To M.A.B. (1931)

Pamphlet, one leaf folded to make four pages (as No. *301*). Bound in blue cardboard folder. Front, double rule; Alice and Pig in three circles; signature of Alice Pleasance Hargreaves—all in gold. Back and inner covers blank.

Collation: p. [1] blank; [2] FROM | HUGH SHARP | WITH | BEST WISHES | [decoration] || HILL OF TARVIT, CUPAR-FIFE | XMAS 1931 || *Facsimile of a poem inscribed by the Author on the fly-leaf | of a copy of 'Alice's Adventures in Wonderland', 1866. | The signature upon the front cover is that of the original Alice | 'M.A.B.' was Miss Marion Terry, to whom | the book was presented |*
[3] Facsimile of 'To M.A.B.' Twelve lines.
[4] At foot: 50 copies | Printed by Pillans and Wilson, Edinburgh.

Included in *Collected Verse* (1932), p. 325; *Nonesuch*, p. 932 (836), &c.

1932

304. Children's Sermon (1932)

From the Rev. P. GORDON DUFF, Rector of | S. Mary Magdalen's, St. Leonards-on-Sea. | Reprinted with permission. | [These three lines in italic, underlined, in top left-hand corner of p. [1]]. LEWIS CARROLL CENTENARY, 1932 | [six-line extract from Diary with note thanking Major C. H. W. Dodgson] | ADDRESS BY THE REV. C. L. DODGSON (LEWIS | CARROLL) AT S. MARY MAG-DALEN CHURCH, ST. | LEONARDS-ON-SEA (3 P.M., THE CHILDREN'S | SERVICE), ON HARVEST THANKSGIVING DAY, | OCTOBER 3RD, 1897.

Single, unbound sheet making four pages (un-numbered), size $8\frac{1}{4} \times 5\frac{3}{4}$ in.

A reprint of No. 283 (with the addition of the Diary entry not previously published) from The St. Mary Magdalen Church Magazine of Oct. 1897. The address had also been reprinted in L.C.P.B., pp. 340–4. It is not included in Nonesuch.

305. Lewis Carroll Centenary Catalogue (1932)

THE | LEWIS CARROLL | CENTENARY | IN LONDON | 1932 | Including a Catalogue of the Ex- | hibition, with Notes; an Essay on | Dodgson's Illustrators by Harold | Hartley; and additional literary | pieces (chiefly unpublished). With | six illustrations || EDITED BY | FALCONER MADAN

London, The Old Court House, Messrs. J. & E. Bumpus Ltd., 350 Oxford Street, W.1. 1932.

Issued in white cloth over boards, end-paper white.

Limited to 400 numbered copies—(certificate of Issue on p. [iv]).

8vo. Size $5 \times 7\frac{1}{2}$ in. pp. [xx]+140. Six plates tipped in, one as Frontispiece and the rest at the end.

It was published on 28 June 1932. A page of Corrigenda was tipped in before page 1. (Madan notes in his own copy: 'late July 1932'). At the same time a gathering of 'Additional Exhibits' was tipped in between pp. 108 and 109, numbered [blank], 108a to 108g.

This Special Edition cost 5s. The ordinary edition at 1s. was paper-bound, and did not include the 'Literary Pieces' or any illustrations except the frontis-piece. Its title-page ran: Lewis Carroll | Centenary Exhibition | London: 29 June–31 July, 1932 | [line] | CATALOGUE | By FALCONER MADAN | With Illustration and Notes, and | an Essay by HAROLD HARTLEY | on Dodgson's Illustrators.

There was a corrected reprint of the Catalogue, but not of the Special Edition.

The LITERARY PIECES (in the Special Edition only) are as follows:

I. EXAMPLES OF DODGSON'S EARLIEST WRITINGS.

    A. *Horrors*. (Here first published from the *Rectory Magazine*, but included in *Collected Verse* the same year.)

    B. *Musings on Milk*. (Prose.) (First and only publication: from the *Rectory Magazine*.

II. THE JABBERWOCKY IN FRENCH. By Frank L. Warrin. (From *The New Yorker*, 10 Jan. 1931.)

III. SIMPLE FACTS ABOUT CIRCLE-SQUARING. By C. L. Dodgson, 1882. Pp. 121-2: Preface signed F. M. Pp. 122-5: Dodgson's 'Chapter I: Introductory', dated 20 April 1882, from the MS. in the Parrish Collection.

IV. A DOUBLE ACROSTIC. By C. L. Dodgson. ('*Supplied by Miss E. M. Argles*'). Pp. 126-7. In 36 lines of verse; here first printed, but included in *Collected Verse*, &c.

V. LEWIS CARROLL. By E. V. Lucas. Poem of 36 lines reprinted from the *Sketch*, 1898.

VI. LETTERS AND MISCELLANEA.

    Ten letters from Dodgson printed wholly or in part, apparently all for the first time; the 'Madrigal' to May Forshall ('He shouts amain . . .') included later the same year in *Collected Verse*; and two short quotations about Dodgson.

306. Collected Verse (1932)

THE | COLLECTED VERSE | OF | LEWIS CARROLL | (THE REV. CHARLES LUTWIDGE DODGSON) || *With Illustrations by* | SIR JOHN TENNIEL, ARTHUR B. FROST, | HENRY HOLIDAY, HARRY FURNISS, | AND THE AUTHOR

Macmillan and Co., Limited. St. Martin's Street, London 1932.
8vo: size $7\frac{3}{8} \times 5$ in.: pp. xiv+446.
Issued in blue cloth over heavy boards with bevelled edges.
Lettered in gold on spine and front (CLD monogram on latter).

CONTENTS:

I. EARLY VERSE.

My Fairy
Punctuality
Melodies   } From *Useful and Instructive Poetry* (see No. *1*). Here
Brother and Sister } first published.
Facts
Rules and Regulations

Horrors   } From the *Rectory Magazine* (see No. *3*). Here first
Misunderstandings } published.
As it Fell upon a Day

Ye Fattale Cheyse—*Strand Magazine*, Dec. 1898 } From the *Rectory Umbrella*.
Lays of Sorrow: I—   ,,   ,,   ,,   ,, } (See No. *5*)
Lays of Sorrow: II— ,,   ,,   ,,   ,,

The Two Brothers—*Lewis Carroll Picture Book*, 1899
The Lady of the Ladle—*The Whitby Gazette*, 31 Aug. 1854
She's All My Fancy Painted Him—*Comic Times*, 8 Sept. 1855
Photography Extraordinary—*Comic Times*, 3 Nov. 1855
The Palace of Humbug—*The Oxford Critic*, 29 May 1857
} From *Misch-masch*. (See No. 6)

The Mouse's Tale—*Alice's Adventures Underground*, 1886.
The Mock Turtle's Song—*Alice's Adventures Underground*, 1886.
Upon the Lonely Moor—*The Train*, Oct. 1856.
Miss Jones—(Here first published from MS.)

2. FROM *ALICE'S ADVENTURES IN WONDERLAND*.

3. PUZZLES FROM WONDERLAND.
   Aunt Judy's Magazine, Dec. 1870.

4. FROM *THROUGH THE LOOKING-GLASS*.

5. PROLOGUES TO PLAYS.
Prologue to 'La Guida di Bragia'. *Sotheby's Sale Catalogue*, 14 Nov. 1928.
Prologue [to *Loan of a Lover*, &c. 2 Nov. 1871]—*Nineteenth Century*, Feb. 1932.
Prologue [to *Checkmate*, 14 Feb. 1873]—*Strand Magazine*, Apr. 1898.

6. *PHANTASMAGORIA*
   (All the humorous poems, as included in *Rhyme? and Reason?* See No. 160.)

7. FROM *COLLEGE RHYMES* AND *NOTES BY AN OXFORD CHIEL*.
Ode to Damon—*College Rhymes*, Nov. 1861.
Those Horrid Hurdy-Gurdies!—*College Rhymes*, Nov. 1861.
My Fancy [3 out of 4 stanzas of 'Disillusioned']—*College Rhymes*, June 1862.
The Majesty of Justice—*College Rhymes*, Mar. 1863.
The Elections to the Hebdomadal Council
The Deserted Parks
The New Belfry
The Wandering Burgess
A Bachanalian Ode
Examination Statute
} From *Notes by An Oxford Chiel* (reprinted in *Lewis Carroll Picture Book*). See Nos. *98* and *287*.

8. *THE HUNTING OF THE SNARK*.

9. ACROSTICS, INSCRIPTIONS, AND OTHER VERSES.
'Little maidens, when you look' [1861]—*Sotheby's Sale Catalogue*, 3 Apr. 1928.
'Three little maidens, weary of the rail' [1869]—Collingwood (1898), pp. 418–19.
'I sing a place wherein agree' [1869]—*Lewis Carroll Centenary*, 1932 (Catalogue), pp. 126–7.
'Three little maids, one winter day' [1873]—Collingwood (1898), p. 419.
'When [M]a[r]y and I[n]a . . .' [1869]—*Some Rare Carrolliana* (1924), p. 6.
'Three children, their names are so fearful [1871]—*Some Rare Carrolliana* (1924), p. 7.
'Two thieves went out to steal one day' [1872]—*Sotheby's Sale Catalogue*, 23 July 1929.
'Round the wondrous globe' [   ]—Collingwood (1898), p. 408.
'Maidens, if a maid you meet' [   ]—Collingwood (1898), p. 408.

'Two little girls near London dwell' [1870]—*Collingwood* (1898), pp. 372–3.
'Are you deaf, Father William . .' [1876]—*Collingwood* (1898), pp. 374–5.
'Maidens, if you love the tale' [1876]—*Sotheby's Sale Catalogue*, 23 July 1929.
'Love-lighted eyes, that will not start' [1876]—*Lewis Carroll Picture Book* (1899), p. 209.
'The royal MAB, dethroned, discrowned' [1866]—Privately Printed, 1931. (See No. *103*.)
'Maiden, though thy heart may quail' [1876]—*A Christmas Carroll* (privately printed, 1930. (See No. *101*.)
'He shouts amain, he shouts again' [1877]—*Lewis Carroll Centenary*, 1932, p. 139.
'Seek ye Love, ye fairy-sprites' [1878]—*Lewis Carroll Picture Book* (1899), p. 204.
'Oh pudgy podgy pup!' [1880]—Williams and Madan, *Handbook* (1931) p. 209.
'What hand may wreathe thy natal crown' [1881]—*The Garland of Rachel* (1881), p. 29.
'It is the lawyer's daughter' [1881]—*Lewis Carroll Picture Book* (1899), p. 221.
'Around my lonely hearth tonight' [1878]—*Collingwood* (1898), p. 364.
Dreamland [1882]—*Aunt Judy's Magazine*, July 1882.
To My Pupil—*Dedication to A Tangled Tale*, 1885.
To My Child-Friend—Dedication to *The Game of Logic*, 1886.
'My first lends its aid when I plunge into trade' [   ]—*Collingwood* (1898), p. 378.
'There was a young lady of station' [   ]—*Collingwood* (1898), p. 407.
'I'm EMInent in RHYME' [1883]—*Sotheby's Sale Catalogue*, 23 July 1929.
A Nursery Darling—Dedication to *The Nursery Alice*, 1889.
Maggie's Visit to Oxford—1889—Isa Bowman's *The Story of Lewis Carroll* (1899), pp. 104–9.
'Written by Maggie B—' [1891]—*Maggs's Catalogue*, No. 559, 1931.

10. FROM *SYLVIE AND BRUNO*.

11. FROM *SYLVIE AND BRUNO CONCLUDED*.

12. *THREE SUNSETS AND OTHER POEMS*.

Note: All the poems in *Collected Verse* are included in *Nonesuch*.

307. For the Train (1932)

FOR THE TRAIN | *FIVE POEMS AND A TALE* | BY | LEWIS CARROLL | Being Contributions to 'The Train', 1856–1857, | with the original illustrations by C. H. Bennett | and W. McConnell; together with some Carrollean [*sic*] | Episodes concerning Trains ||| Arranged, with a Preface, by | HUGH J. SCHONFIELD | *Author of 'Letters to Frederick Tennyson,'* etc.

London Denis Archer 6 Old Gloucester Street W.C. 1.
'*First Published January, 1932. Second Impression February, 1932*'
8vo, size 4 $\frac{8}{10}$ × 7 $\frac{3}{10}$. [xvi]+78.

This includes excerpts from the 'Prologue' to the *Train* (not by Dodgson), and the original text of the following poems and story:

Solitude—Mar. 1856.
The Path of Roses—May 1856.
The Three Voices—Nov. 1856.
The Sailor's Wife—Apr. 1857.
Hiawatha's Photographing—Dec. 1857.
Novelty and Romancement—Oct. 1856.

It omits 'Ye Carpette Knighte' (Mar. 1856) and 'Upon the Lonely Moor' (Oct. 1856), both of which were anonymous. 'Some Carrollean Episodes concerning Trains' are taken from Collingwood, *Looking-Glass, Snark,* and *Sylvie and Bruno.*

308. *The Rectory Umbrella and Mischmasch* (1932)

Described as Nos. 5 and 6 above.

309. *Two Letters to Marion* (1932)

TWO LETTERS TO | MARION | from | LEWIS CARROLL 1932 | Douglas Cleverdon | Bristol

Pp. 8. Bound in tissue paper over thick art paper: front as above, back blank.
P. [1] TWO LETTERS | to | MARION | from | *LEWIS CARROLL* | . . . Now in the Possession | of | The Bookshop of | DOUGLAS CLEVERDON | 18 Charlotte Street | Bristol | 1932.
P. [2]. MADE IN ENGLAND.
P. [3]. Note re imprint, decorations, &c. Edn. of 300 copies of which 100 are for sale at 4/-. Certificate of issue, &c.
Pp. [4–5]. Letter dated 28 Oct. 1881.
Pp. [6–7]. Letter dated 8 Feb. 1886.
P. [8]. Imprint: PRINTED IN LONDON | AT THE | FANFARE PRESS. Inserted is a sheet offering the letters for sale at £31/10/-.

The letters were published in *Letters to Child Friends* (1933), Nos. CXXI and CXXIV. They were addressed to Marion Richards.

310. *A Charade* (1932)

The third of Hugh Sharp's Christmas Cards, following *A Christmas Carroll* (1930) and *To M.A.B.* (1931) described above (Nos. *301* and *303*). It consists of a single sheet with the facsimile of the poem reproduced on it; but folded so as to form pages [1] and [4], as of a quarto pamphlet. It is bound in cream card. On p. [1], after the usual wishes from Hugh Sharp, is the description: 'Overleaf is a facsimile of a Charade written for Miss Marion Terry in 1879. It was first printed, with one or two small alterations, in *Rhyme? and*

Reason? four years later.' And on p. [4] the answer, 'Galatea', is followed by the note: "The Poem was written after seeing Miss Marion Terry in Gilbert's *Pygmalion and Galatea.*'

As in the case of the other Christmas Cards, 50 copies were printed by Pillans and Wilson of Edinburgh.

1933

311. Letters to Child-Friends (1933)

A SELECTION | *from the* | LETTERS OF LEWIS CARROLL | (THE REV. CHARLES LUTWIDGE DODGSON) | *to* | HIS CHILD-FRIENDS | *Together with* | 'EIGHT OR NINE WISE WORDS | ABOUT LETTER-WRITING | *Edited* | *With an Introduction and Notes* | *by* | EVELYN M. HATCH || *Facsimile Illustrations and 8 Collotype Plates.*

Macmillan and Co., Limited | St. Martin's Street, London | 1933.
8vo. Bound in blue cloth over boards, uniform with *Collected Verse.* Pp. [2] +xviii+270.

This admirable collection contains one hundred and seventy letters, including 'To All Child-Readers of *Alice's Adventures in Wonderland*' originally printed for Dodgson in 1871. Many of the letters are published here for the first time, but many already included in Collingwood's *Life, Lewis Carroll Picture Book,* biophies by Isa Bowman and Langford Reed, *The Lewis Carroll Centenary* and *Some Rare Carrolliana* reappear also, sometimes in fuller form. Some also had appeared in articles in various periodicals. The Editor, however, gives no references—and an attempt to check them all would involve considerable labour for no definitely complete result.

This book has not been reprinted and is not included in *Nonesuch.* A number of extracts may be found in *The Book of Nonsense* (see No. *317*) below.

A number of sets of verses appear in the Letters: those published for the first time are listed below—none of them are reprinted in *Nonesuch* (nor, so far as I can discover, any other collection):

1. ' "Will you trot a little quicker" said a Lily to a Fox.' 12 lines. *c.* 1868. [Reprinted in *The Book of Nonsense* (1956).]
2. 'I saw a child: even if blind.' *Double Acrostic,* 14 lines. *c.* 1868.
3. ' "No mind!" the little maiden cried.' 20 lines. 1870.
4. 'Thanks, thanks, fair Cousins for your gift.' *Double Acrostic.* 20 lines. 1871.
5. 'They both make a roaring—a roaring all night.' *Riddle.* 15 lines. 1877.
6. 'Two went one day.' 4 lines. 1881.

7. 'Something fails.' 8 lines. 1881.
8. 'To find the eldest of the pets.' *Acrostic Riddle*. 2 lines, &c. 1892.
9. 'My first is a berry.' *Riddle*. 6 lines. 1892.
10. Also two rhymed letters, written as prose (1868 and 1889) of 60 and 28 lines respectively when rearranged as verse.

1935

312. *The Russian Journal, and Other Selections* (1935)

THE RUSSIAN JOURNAL | AND OTHER SELECTIONS FROM THE WORKS | OF LEWIS CARROLL | [line] | EDITED AND WITH AN INTRODUCTION BY | JOHN FRANCIS McDER-MOTT

New York | E. P. Dutton & Co., Inc. [Date on verso, with copyright statement.] 1935.
Large 8vo: $8\frac{9}{16} \times 5\frac{1}{2}$ in. Pp. 252 (followed by 4 blank).
Bound in grey boards.

This is a miscellaneous selection of unusual pieces by Dodgson, and forms a companion volume to the American edition of *Collected Verse* (No. *300*).

The pieces not included in *Nonesuch* are as follows:

Difficulties, I and II. From the *Rectory Umbrella*.
Preface to *Mischmasch*.
Letter to Henrietta and Edwin Dodgson. From *L.C.P.B.*, pp. 198–9.
JOURNAL OF A TOUR IN RUSSIA IN 1867
   First publication of this *Diary*, which had been privately printed in 1928 by M. L. Parrish, the owner of the MS., in an edition of 66 copies. (See No. *299* above.)
Alice on the Stage. From *L.C.P.B.*, pp. 163–74.
A Logical Paradox. From *L.C.P.B.*, pp. 312–16.
Three Puzzles. From *L.C.P.B.*, pp. 268 and 317–18.

1939

313. *The Nonesuch Omnibus* (1939)

[In double panel] THE COMPLETE WORKS OF | Lewis Carroll | WITH AN INTRODUCTION BY | Alexander Woollcott | AND THE ILLUSTRATIONS BY | JOHN TENNIEL |||| LONDON | THE NONESUCH PRESS | NEW YORK · RANDOM HOUSE

8vo. size $7\frac{1}{2} \times 4\frac{3}{4}$ in. Bound in heavy red cloth boards with bevelled edges. Pp. xviii+1294. *Manufactured in the U.S.A.* No date.
The volume was reprinted in 1949 in Great Britain (University Press, Glasgow): title-page as above, but with LONDON | THE NONESUCH LIBRARY at

foot. On verso of title-page is the note: 'First published by the Nonesuch Press November 1939'.

The pagination of the new edition is pp. xvi+1168 (last 3 pp. blank). Contents the same in both, but differently paginated owing to smaller type used in the second.

This volume contains by no means all even of the works signed 'Lewis Carroll', but it is, none the less, the best and fullest single-volume collection so far published.

Besides the complete contents of *Alice's Adventures in Wonderland*, *Through the Looking-Glass*, *Sylvie and Bruno*, *Sylvie and Bruno Concluded* and *Collected Verse*, *A Tangled Tale* and *Notes by An Oxford Chiel*, it contains 'Novelty and Romancement', 'A Photographer's Day Out', 'Wilhelm von Schmitz' (complete version), 'The Legend of Scotland', and 'Eight or Nine Wise Words about Letter-Writing', with a few items reprinted from various places in *L.C.P.B.* There are also selections from *Twelve Months in a Curatorship*, *Three Years in a Curatorship*, and *Symbolic Logic*.

Nothing is printed here for the first time, but the following rare items are of particular interest: 'Resident Women-Students', 'Some Popular Fallacies about Vivisection', 'Lawn Tennis Tournaments', 'What the Tortoise said to Achilles', 'Misch-Masch' [the game], 'Rules for Court Circular', 'A Postal Problem', 'The Alphabet Cipher', and 'Introduction to *The Lost Plum Cake*'.

1943

314. *How the Boots Got Left Behind* (1943)

How The | Boots Got | Left Behind [all so far in red: the rest in black] || A Letter to Mary from | C. L. Dodgson | 'Lewis Carroll'.

The White Knight Press | 1943.

12 pages, size $4\frac{1}{4} \times 6\frac{1}{4}$ in., bound in green cover (better quality manilla), size $4\frac{3}{8} \times 6\frac{1}{4}$ in.

Contents: Pp. [1–2] blank: p. [3] Title-page, as above: p. [4] blank: p. [5] Title repeated, and text begins half-way down the page in the form of a letter: '2, Wellington Square | Hastings | Ap. 12. 1873 | My dear Mary, | . . . pp. [[6–7], actually the only ones numbered—the numbers being 2, 3—Text, signed 'Your affectionate friend | C. L. Dodgson.': p. [8] blank: p. [9], one-third of the way down, reads: 'Twenty-five copies privately printed | for Nathan Van Patten, | Christmas, 1943.' Pp. [10–12] blank. Title on front cover; trade-mark of Chess Knight on back.

I am indebted for the above description to Mr. A. J. Beale of Hersham, Surrey.

The letter does not seem to be published anywhere else. No name is given, but the *Diaries* suggest that the addressee is Mary Crofts. Dodgson was staying with 'The Crofts' at Sevenoaks in early April, 1873, and left them to stay with his Aunt Lucy at Hastings, leaving there for London on 16 Apr.

1953

315. The Diaries of Lewis Carroll (1953)

[In double panel of thick and thin lines] THE *Diaries* OF | LEWIS CARROLL | [line] | *Now first edited and supplemented by* | ROGER LANCELYN GREEN | [star] | *In two Volumes* | VOLUME I [II]

Cassell & Company Ltd. | London | 1953.

(American Edition as the English, but with 'New York | Oxford University Press | 1954', and verso of title-page without list of Cassell's branches, but with '*Copyright 1954* | *Oxford University Press*', and at foot 'Printed in Great Britain'.)

Large Cr. 8vo. Bound in black cloth over boards, with gold lettering on spine. Pp. xxvi+606 (numbered consecutively through both volumes: pp. [viii] of prolegomena in Vol. II). Published 28 Jan. 1954.

The 'supplementary' material, mostly incorporated in the Text in square brackets, as the notes are, contains much hitherto unpublished material (letters, verses, &c.) and many quotations from rare or previously unknown printed sources.

The longer pieces, printed as Appendices, include:

Crundle Castle. (A story from the *Rectory Magazine*.)
Letters to Mrs. Ben Greet about *The Little Squire*. (From Dodgson's rough copy).
Extracts from Letters to an Invalid.
Draft of a Letter to an Agnostic.
Mr. C. and Mr. T. (Story with comic illustration remembered by a child-friend, Mary Burrows, later Mrs. Knyvett.)

Among shorter pieces never before published, or reprinted here for the first time, the following may be noted:

Pp. 21–2. 'Thrillings.' Poem of 20 lines from the *Rectory Magazine*.
Pp. 104–5. 'Where does the Day Begin?' The *Illustrated London News*, 18 Apr. 1857.
Pp. 143–7. A Visit to Tennyson. [Letter.] The *Strand Magazine*, May 1901.
P. 148. 'Prologue' to vol. iii of *College Rhymes*. [This may not be by Dodgson.]
Pp. 161–2. 'Disillusioned'. [Complete poem of 32 lines.] *College Rhymes*, June 1862.
P. 166. 'Endowment of the Greek Professorship.' Oxford 'squib', printed 1861.

C 90   P

P. 189. 'Prologue' to vol. iv of *College Rhymes*. (16 lines of verse.) 1862.
Pp. 275–6. 'The Woodstock Election.' The *Oxford University Herald*, 28 Nov. 1868.
P. 284. Riddle: 'Tell me truly, maidens three'. (7 lines of verse.) *Some Rare Carrolliana* (1924).
Pp. 292–3. ' "No mind," the little maiden cried.' (20 lines.) *Letters to Child-Friends* (1933).
Pp. 314–15. *Arithmetical Croquet*. (Never printed: MS. in Dodgson Papers.) 1889.
P. 351. Acrostic to Edith Denham. (5 lines of verse written 2 Sept. 1876.) *Quaritch's Catalogue*, 672 (1949).
P. 374. 'They both make a roaring—'. *Riddle* (1878). *Letters to Child-Friends* (1933).
Pp. 446–7. Dodgson's additions to Savile Clarke's *Alice* play (1887).
Pp. 452–3. 'Stage Children.' The *St. James's Gazette*, 19 July 1887.
Pp. 453–4. Cancelled stanza of 'Little Birds'. (From a 'proof' in the Dodgson Papers.)
P. 473. 'Stage-Children' from letter in *Sunday Times*, 4 Aug. 1889.
P. 487. Acrostic to Gladys Baly. (10 lines of verse.) The *Christian Science Monitor*, 23 Feb. 1932.
Pp. 501–2. Letter to Mary Collingwood about Child-Friends: 21 Sept. 1893. (Dodgson Papers.)
Pp. 507–8. Letter to Edith Lucy. (From MS. in possession of Mr. John Greenidge.) 1894.
P. 509. *Co-operative Backgammon. The Times*, 6 Mar. 1894.
P. 527. Letter to Mrs. Aubrey-Moore. (From MS. in Miss Aubrey-Moore's collection.)
Pp. 538–9. Letter to Louisa Dodgson (1897). (MS. in Dodgson Papers.)
P. 543. Letter to Mary Collingwood on 5 Jan. 1898. (MS. in Dodgson Papers.)

1954

316. *Useful and Instructive Poetry* (1954)

Dodgson's earliest literary efforts. Described above (No. *1*).

1956

317. *The Book of Nonsense* (1956)

THE BOOK OF | NONSENSE | *by many authors* | CHOSEN AND ARRANGED BY | ROGER LANCELYN GREEN |

Dent's *Children's Illustrated Classics*. 1956.

The Lewis Carroll items included are as follows:

Jabberwocky.
THE HUNTING OF THE SNARK.

She's All My Fancy Painted Him—*Comic Times*, 8 Sept. 1855.
The Lobster. (Version from *Songs from Alice's Adventures*, 1870.)
Dolly's Dogs. (Verses from a letter of 1868. *Letters to Child-Friends*, p. 54.)
The Walrus and the Carpenter.
The Aged, Aged Man.
The Mad Gardener's Song.
Outland Fare.
The King-Fisher Song.
The Pig-Tale.
Little Birds. (With the extra stanza.)

Section V is headed 'LETTERS FROM WONDERLAND, and Other Pieces', and contains extracts or complete texts of 16 Letters from *Letters to Child-Friends*, Collingwood's *Life*, and *L.C.P.B.*; also one letter never collected which appeared in *The Times*, 1 Jan. 1938.

There are also extracts from 'Hints on Etiquette' and 'Feeding the Mind', 3 from *Sylvie and Bruno* and 2 from *Sylvie and Bruno Concluded*; 'Stanza of Anglo-Saxon Poetry' from *Mischmasch*, and four lines of verse from the *St. James's Gazette*, 19 May 1884, never before reprinted but apparently by Dodgson.

1958

318. Mathematical Recreations of Lewis Carroll (1958)

MATHEMATICAL RECREATIONS OF LEWIS CARROLL | SYMBOLIC LOGIC | AND | THE GAME OF LOGIC | [in volume II these three lines read PILLOW PROBLEMS | AND | A TANGLED TALE |] (both books bound as one) || BY LEWIS CARROLL || volume one [two] ||||

Volume I gives DOVER PUBLICATIONS, INC., NEW YORK | AND BERKELEY ENTERPRISES; Volume II only the first line.

Issued in England on 23 Apr. 1959 by Constable & Co., whose label is stuck at foot of title-pages beneath the name of the American publisher. Price 12s. 6d. each volume.

Two volumes. Published by Dover Publications, Inc., New York and Berkeley Enterprises. 1958. Both volumes bound in good quality paper covers.

Volume I reprints *Symbolic Logic*, 4th edition, and *The Game of Logic*, 2nd edition; with a prefatory note by Edmund C. Berkeley. Pp. xxxii+200+96+Advertisements.

Volume II reprints *Pillow Problems*, 4th edition, and *A Tangled Tale*, 1st edition. Pp. xxii+110+152+Advertisements.

All the items are reprinted in full. *A Tangled Tale* contains the original illustrations by Arthur Burdett Frost.

PART II

Notes of Ordinary Editions of C. L. Dodgson's Works Issued from 1898 to 1960, with American Editions of any Date

A

EDITIONS OF *ALICE'S ADVENTURES IN WONDERLAND*, WITH NOTES OF TRANSLATIONS

Prefatory Notes

THE advertisements at the end of *Three Sunsets*, published in the month succeeding Dodgson's death, that is to say in Feb. 1898, enable us to state that at that epoch the circulation of Dodgson's chief works had reached the following number of thousands of copies in Great Britain:

Alice's Adventures, 86.
Do. People's Edition, 70.
Through the Looking-Glass, 61.
Do. People's Edition, 46.
Alice, in French, 2.
Alice Underground, 3.

Nursery Alice, 11.
The Snark, 20.
Rhyme? and Reason?, 6.
Tangled Tale, 4.
Sylvie and Bruno, vol. i, 13.
Do., vol. ii, 3.

By 1911, advertisements in the Miniature Edition of *Phantasmagoria* show that the numbers had risen to:

Alice's Adventures, 91.
Do. People's Edition, 162.
Do. Illustrated Pocket Classics, 321.
Do. Little Folks' Edition, 20.
Do. Miniature Edition, 60.
Through the Looking-Glass, 64.
Do. People's Edition, 105.

Through the Looking-Glass. Illustrated Pocket Classics, 220.
Do. Little Folks' Edition, 10.
Do. Miniature Edition, 30.
Alice Underground, 5.
The Snark, 25.
Do. Miniature Edition, 10.
Rhyme? and Reason?, 8.

From 1898 to 1907 Macmillan still held the exclusive copyright of *Alice's Adventures*, both in Great Britain and in the Colonies, until the usual period of 42 years (1865-1907) ran out, and issued the standard octavo edition in red cloth according to demand, only altering the number of the 'thousand', the 86th having been issued in Nov. 1897: while the People's Edition, first issued in 1887, had reached, as has been noted, its seventieth thousand in Feb. 1898.

1898. In December of this year *Alice* was first issued in Macmillan's (Popular) Sixpenny Series: then twice in 1899, in 1900, 1901, 1902, 1903, 1905, 1906, &c. This edition has all the Tenniel illustrations, and is a thin volume, rather larger than the standard issue ($8\frac{1}{2} \times 5\frac{3}{4}$ in.). Pp. 126: 2s. [258].

1904. *Alice* was published at 2s. in Macmillan's Illustrated Pocket Classics for the Young [259].

1907. Notes of editions of *Alice* and *Through the Looking-Glass* issued together after the copyright of the former expired in 1907 will be found below. The copyright of the latter did not run out till 1948.

The London publishers who foresaw the coming opportunity in 1907, and contemplated the possibility of new illustrations, must each have devoutly hoped that he was the only one in the field. But, as a fact, a large number felt bound to issue an illustrated edition, and must have employed artists for months before, while on the other hand, the artists who were willing to challenge comparison with Tenniel's world-renowned engravings must have felt venturesome. However, plenty came forward, as the following tentative list shows.

The original publishers, Messrs. Macmillan, marked the year by three successive issues of a 'Miniature Edition' of *Alice* in July, September, and December, and subsequent annual issues till 1920 (except 1917), and then occasional reprints. *Through the Looking-Glass* followed suit in Oct. 1908, and thenceforward at intervals: and editions of the two together date from 1911.

English Editions of 'Alice' after the copyright expired in 1907
(42 years after publication)

Date	London publisher	Pagination	Illustrator	Notes
[Oct.] 1907	Chatto & Windus	166+	Millicent Sowerby	8°: 12 cold. plates, &c. Will., p. 133. [261]
[Nov. 1907]	Routledge	168+	T. Maybank	8°: 1 cold.+28 other plates. Will., p. 133. [262]

Date	London publisher	Pagina-tion	Illustrator	Notes
[Nov. 1907]	Heinemann	162+	A. Rackham	8°: 13 cold. plates, &c. Will., p. 133. Also issued in 4° There is a prefatory poem by Austin Dobson. [263
[Nov. 1907]	Cassell	179+	C. Robinson	4°: 8 cold., 112 other plates. Will., p. 134. See 1928. [264
[Nov. 1907]	Nimmo (Edinb.)	159	Alice Ross	12°: 5 cold. plates. Will., p. 134. [265
[Nov. 1907]	Lane	152+	W. H. Walker	8°: 8 cold., 42 (47) other plates. Will., p. 133. 1s. 6d. See below. [266
[Nov. 1907]	Routledge		No plates	8°: price 6d. [267
[Dec.] 1907	Macmillan	196+?	J. Tenniel	sm. 8°: 42 plates. Miniature edition. [267*
[Dec. 1907]	Ward, Lock & Co.	212	No plates?	8°: price 1s. [268
[Dec. 1907]	Stead	120	Brinsley le Fanu	sm. 8°: price 3d.: many plates: 'Books for the Bairns'. See 1926. [269
[1907]	Aldine Co.	61 & 60	Anonymous	8°: 1d. each part: 'edited by Lady Kathleen': many poor engravings: 'Tales for Little People', Nos. 95, 96. [270
1907	Nimmo (Edinb.)	160	A. Ross	12°. [271
[1907?]	Ward, Lock & Co.	94	Blanche Mac-manus	8°: most of the 8 plates are dated 1899: price 6d. [272
[Apr. 1908]	Partridge	184	K. M. R.	8°: 8 plates, six signed 'K. M. R.': perhaps part of 'Everyone's Library'. Will., p. 134. [273
[May 1908]	Collins	198	Anonymous	12°: 1s.: part of 'Illustrated Pocket Classics'. [274
[June 1908]	Nicholson	184		8°: 1s. Published at Wakefield (Yorkshire), but Nicholson had a London Office. [275
[Sept.] 1908	Nelson	160	Anonymous	12°: 1s.: 8 cold. plates ('1328'), weird: a 9th plate on cover is signed 'I. P.' or 'A. R.' [276
[Oct.] 1908	Milne	164+	Bessie Gut-mann	8°: 10 cold. plates, 10 others, and cold. borders to every page. Will., p. 134. [277
[Oct. 1908]	W. Scott, Co.	187+	Walter Hawes	8°: 33 plates, chiefly in text. [278
[Nov. 1908]	Nelson	247	H. Rountree	4°: 92 cold. plates, chiefly in text. Will., p. 134. [279
[Nov. 1908]	Lane			(As Lane above but priced 2s. 6d.) [280
[About 1908]	Milner	216+	R. E. McEune	8°: 1 cold. plate, 21 plain, in text. [281
				282 = 275
[Feb. 1909]	Chambers, Edinburgh	128		8°: 6d. 'Chambers's Supple-mentary Readers.' [283
[Mar. 1909]	G. Pitman	63		la. 8°: 1s. In Pitman's short-hand: 'Shorthand Library', No. 10. [284
[1909]	Sunday School Union	122	J. R. Sinclair	8°: 27 plates, partly in the text. In the English Catalogue placed as June 1910. Will., p. 134. See 1921. [285

Date	London publisher	Pagination	Illustrator	Notes
[Aug. 1910]	R. Tuck	148	Mabel Lucie Attwell	4°: 12 cold. plates and many plain in text. Will., p. 134. [286
[1910]	Partridge	32	K. M. R.	8°: 4 plates: price 1d.: small type: 'Paternoster . . . Popular Stories', No. 19. [287
[1910]	E. Arnold	96	Olive Allen	sm. 8°: 1 plate: price 4d.: 'Every Child's Stories'. It omits the last five paragraphs. [288
1910	Cassell		C. Robinson	[288*
[May 1911]	Ward, Lock & Co.	212	No plates?	8°: price 1s.: perhaps only a reissue in the 'World Library'. See 1920, 1921. [289
[Oct. 1911]	Headley	192	G. Soper	sm. 4°: 24 plates, 6 cold., the rest chiefly in text. Will., p. 134. See 1919, 1923. [290
Oct. 1912]	Everett	156	Emily Overnell	sm. 8°: with cold. frontispiece and title 'Everett's Library'. [291
[1912]		94	Adams	Price 6d. [292
1913	Frowde	157	M. Sowerby	12°: price 1s. 6d.: 8 new cold. plates: issued in Oct. 1912. [293
[Sept. 1913]	Nelson	64	H. Rountree	4°: price 1s.: 8 cold. plates, mounted. [294
1913	Cassell	179+	C. Robinson	sm. 4°: price 3s. 6d.: plates as in 1907. [295
1913	Bell	119+	Alice B. Woodward	8°: 8 full-page engravings, 6 in text. [296
1913	Longmans			[297
[Jan. 1914]	Longmans			12°: price 8d. [298
[Oct. 1914]	Bell	161+	A. B. Woodward	8°: price 2s. 6d.: 8 cold. plates: 'Queen's Treasury Series'. [299
[Dec.] 1914	Lee Warner	131+	Tenniel	la. 8°: prices 15s., &c.: 'Riccardi Press' book, with the original illustrations, four slightly enlarged. [300
[Oct. 1915]	Frowde	199+	A. E. Jackson	4°: price 7s. 6d.: 16 cold. plates, with many others (small) in text. [301
[May 1916]	Kelly	202+	Gordon Robinson	8°: price from 1s.: 6 cold. plates, and 20 others (8 full-page). [302
[Aug. 1916]	Ward, Lock & Co.	332	Margaret W. Tarrant	sm. 4°: price 3s. 6d.: 48 cold. plates. There was a 3rd edit. in 1913. See also 1929. [303
[1918 or 1919]	Nelson	64	H. Rountree	4°: 4 cold. plates. [304
[Nov. 1919]	L. B. Hill	254+	None	16°: price 2s.: frontispiece. 'Langham Booklets for children'. [305
[Dec. 1919]	Headley		G. Soper	8°: price 6s. [306
[1919]	Frowde	199+	A. E. Jackson	4°: 16 cold. plates, with many others (small) in text: a reprint of 1915. [307
Apr. 1920	Harrap	165+	Bessie Pease	8°: price 6s.: 8 cold. plates, 14 other (9 full-pages). [312
[Apr. 1920]	Ward, Lock & Co.	212	No plates?	8°: price 2s. 6d.: see 1911. [308
[Dec. 1920]	Collins	136		8°: price 1s. 6d. [309
[1920]	Nelson?		Richardson	310

ORDINARY EDITIONS, 1898–1960   217

Date	London publisher	Pagination	Illustrator	Notes
1920	Milford	174+		sm. 8°: cold. frontispiece, and some small engravings in text: ed. by 'Herbert Strang': 'H. Strang's Library'. [311
[May 1921]	Ward, Lock & Co.	212	No plates?	8°: price 2s. 'Royal Series'. [313
[June 1921]	R. Tuck	108+	Mabel Lucie Attwell	sm. 4°: price 4s. 6d.: 6 cold. plates, many in text: 'Treasure House Library': Will., p. 134. See 1910. [314
[Sept. 1921]	Collins	190		8°: price 1s. 6d. [315
[Sept. 1921]	L. B. Hill	254+?	None	16°: 'Langham's Booklets...', see 1919. [316
[1921]	R. Tuck		A. L. Bowley	Some plates coloured. See 1927. [317
[May 1922]	Sunday School Union			8°: price 1s. 6d. A reissue of the 1909 edition. [318
[Oct. 1922]	Hodder & Stoughton	181+	Gwynedd M. Hudson	4°: 12 cold. plates and many tinted in text. A fine edition: there was a special issue for Messrs. Boots. The éd. de luxe cost 42s. See 1923, 1927. [319
1922	Macmillan		Tenniel	As the 1911 edition. [320
[1922]	Collins	136+	Charles Pears	4°: 4 cold. plates and 15 others in text. [321
[Sept. 1923]	Hodder & Stoughton		G. M. Hudson	As 1922, a reissue. [322
[1923]	Allen & Unwin	192	G. Soper	8°: price 4s. 6d. See 1911. [323
1923	[At Lund, Sweden]			School edition with notes. [323*
[Sept. 1924]	Warne	184	K. M. R.	8°: price 2s.: 9 plates (1, by George Newsome, cold.) [324
1924	Kellerer, Munich	68		Edited by Alfred Bernhard and Wilfrid Well (Kellerer's English Editions). [325
[Feb. 1925]	Sampson Low	159	None?	8°: price 1s. 6d. [326
May 1925	Nelson	158	H. Rountree	sm. 8°: containing Alice and Bruno's Revenge: with many plain engravings. 'Nelson's English Series', No. 13, with notes by Sir Henry Newbolt, and a portrait from a pen-drawing by E. Gertrude Thompson. [327
[1925]	Harrap		B. Pease	A reprint of the 1920 edition. [328
[Nov. 1926]	Benn	120+	B. le Fanu	sm. 8°: 2 vols.: price 6d. each: many plates: 'Stead's Books for the Bairns', Nos. 142 (pp. 1–62) and 143 (pp. 63–120). See 1907. [329
[1926]	Milford	157+	M. Sowerby	12°: see 1913. [330
[Apr. 1927]	R. Tuck	221	A. L. Bowley	8°: price 3s. 6d.: 6 cold. plates: many others in text: 'The Golden Treasury Library'. [331
[May] 1927	Macmillan	205+	Tenniel	sm. 4°: price 6s.: 16 cold. plates, and many others in text: 'Children's Edition'. See the 1911 edition. [332

Date	London publisher	Pagination	Illustrator	Notes
[Sept. 1927]	Hodder & Stoughton	200	G. M. Hudson	8°: price 10s. 6d. See 1922. [333
[Nov.] 1927	Macmillan	205+	Tenniel	sm. 4°: see above. [334 335 = 462
[1927]			T. Maybank	[336
[Apr.] 1928	Cassell	194	C. Robinson	8°: price 3s. 6d.: 120 plates (8 cold.). See 1907. [337
[June 1928]	Little Blue Book Co.	64+	None?	8°: price 3d.: Little Blue Book Series, No. 67. [338
[July 1928]	Collins			8°: price 1s.: 'Treasure Trove Picture Books.' [339
[Mar. 1929]	Harrap		B. Pease	See 1920. [340
[July] 1929	Macmillan		Tenniel	16°: price 5s. 'Cardinal Series'. Reissued in October 1929. [341
[Sept. 1929]	Black	174	Charles Folkard	8°: price 2s. 6d.: stated to be a reissue [342
[Sept. 1929]	Harrap	164+	B. Pease	8°: see 1920. [343
[Sept. 1929]	Ward, Lock & Co.	175	M. W. Tarrant	4°: price 3s. 6d.: 24 cold. plates. See 1916. [344
[Oct.] 1929	Macmillan	206	Tenniel	8°: price 8s. 6d. (Cardinal Series). [345
1929	Dutton, New York	192	W. Pogany	8°: many original illustrations and elaborate coloured endpapers: bound in purple cloth. [346
[1929]	Pitman		Tenniel	In Pitman's Shorthand (intermediate style): price 2s. [347
1929	Nelson			[348
1929	Milford		A. E. Jackson	[348*
1930	Dutton, N.Y. & Dent, London	192	C. L. Dodgson	16°: ed. by Guy N. Pocock, printed in England: with 16 full and 23 smaller illustrations, including portrait. The Snark is added, and 8 songs: some music on p. 184. King's Treasuries, No. 195. [348*
1931	Collins	135	Harry Rountree	
1932	Macmillan		Tenniel	Centenary Edition (Preface by Hugh Walpole).
1932	Readers' Library PublishingCo.		Hume Henderson	
[1932]	Raphael Tuck		A. L. Bowley	Reprinted 1936.
[1933]	Foulsham			'Two Books in One Library' (with Grimm).
1933	Milford		A. E. Jackson	
[1933]	J. F. Shaw		D. R. Sexton	
1934	Blackie		Charles Folkard	
1934	J. Coker		Bessie Pease	Reprinted 1948.
[1934]	Foulsham		Gil Dyer	
[1936]	Nelson		Helen Munro	
1936	Milford		M. Sowerby	
[1937]	Juvenile Publications		D. R. Sexton	Reprinted 1939.
1937	Macmillan		Tenniel	Children's Classics.
1938	Hodder & Stoughton		Gwynedd M. Hudson	
1938	Collins		R. M. Tovey	

Date	London publisher	Pagination	Illustrator	Notes
[1939]	Collins		Irene Mount-fort	Also 'stills' from the Paramount Film.
[1944]	P. R. Gawthorn		Rene Cloke	Reprinted 1948.
1944	Newman Wolsey			
[1945]	W. H. Cornelius		A. Rado	
1945	Arthur Barron		Harry Riley	
1946	Blue Book Co.		?	Published in South Croydon.
[1946]	Birn Bros.		?	
1946	Puffin Books		John Tenniel	Introduction by Eleanor Graham.
1947	Harrap		Eileen A. Soper	
1948	Allen and Unwin			
1948	Adprint		John Tenniel	With 'additional illustrations'.
[1949]	Ward, Lock & Co.		?	8 illus. in colour. 'New Prize Library.'
[1949]	Heinemann		?	
[1950]	James Brodie		Thomas Maybank	
[1952]	Ward, Lock & Co.		?	20 illus. in colour.
1952	Pan Books		John Tenniel	
[1953]	Nelson		Helen Munro	Nelson Classics.
[1954]	Hamlyn		?	Hamlyn Classics.
[1954]	Blackie		David Walsh	
[1955]	Sunshine Press		?	
1956	Publicity Productions			'Winner Books' No. 14.
1957	W. H. Allen			'Splendour Books' No. 4.
1961	J. M. Dent		C. L. Dodgson	'Everyman Paper-back'. Preface by Roger Lancelyn Green.

Uncertain Date

Readers' Library Publishing Co.	253+	Hume Henderson		[349
		Rea Irwin Dudley Jarrett	See however No. 794. [350 Owned by Mr. M. L. Parrish. [351
Epworth Press (F. A. Sharp)	201+	Gordon Robinson	Apparently a reissue of the 1916 Kelly edition. [352
Collins	62+	T. H. Robinson	Price 2d.: 'Collins' Favourite Library'. [353 There was also a 2nd edition. [354
Hurst [? U.S.A.]	80		8°: (Aunt Virginia Series). [355

American Editions of 'Alice' and 'Through the Looking-Glass' 1866–1960

Until 1891 American publishers could reprint British books without restraint, but after that year only by agreement with British authors and publishers.

The following list has been made possible through most generous and willing help from the Librarian and other officials of the great Library of Congress at Washington, who sent me a long series of cards registering Carrollian literature for the purposes of this present volume. Miss Jean Macalister has also spent much time and labour on a list of 167 British, American, and foreign *Alices*. To both these helpers the sincere gratitude of the two editors is acknowledged and tendered.

For notices of British Colonial editions we have still to wait, the sources of information being so widely scattered and difficult of access. Protection for British authors from unauthorized colonial reprints appears to date from 1847.   F. M.

American Alices

Date	Publisher	Pagination	Illustrator	Notes
1866	N.Y., Appleton	192+	Tenniel	8°. See No. 32 (p. 23). This edition was reproduced in facsimile by Appleton in [1927]. See also Suppl. A. [356
1869	Boston, Lee & Sheppard	192+	Tenniel	8°. Second American ed. [357
1870	Boston, Lee & Sheppard	192+		8°. [358
				[359 *not used*]
1871	Boston, do.			[360
1877	N.Y., Macmillan			[361
1885	N.Y., Munro	199	Tenniel	8°. [362
1885	N.Y., Lovell	191	Tenniel	8°. [363
[188–?]	N.Y., Burt	274+	Tenniel	12°. [364
[188–?]	Chicago, Donohue	190	Tenniel	16°. [365
1890	N.Y., Worthington	190+		[366
1890	Chicago, Belford	168		8°. [367
[189–?]	Chicago, Donohue	182	Tenniel	12°. Perhaps the same as the next but two above. [368
[1893]	N.Y., Crowell	218+	Tenniel	[369
1894	N.Y.			[370
1895	N.Y., Macmillan		Tenniel	12°. [371
1895	N.Y., Maynard	72	Tenniel	12°. Abridged. [372
1895	Philadelphia, Altemus	347		8°. [373
1896	N.Y., Burt	274	Tenniel	12°. [374
1896	N.Y., Hurst			16°. [375
1897	N.Y., Macmillan	192	Tenniel	12°. Reprinted 1898, 1899, 1900, 1901, 1902, 1903, 1904, 1905, 1906, 1908, 1909, 1910. [376

Date	Publisher	Pagination	Illustrator	Notes
1899	Philadelphia, Altemus			sq. 16°. [377
1898	Boston, Lothrop		Tenniel	[378
1898	Boston, De Wolfe		Tenniel	[379
1896	N.Y., Mansfield	121	B. McManus	4°. The first American edition with new illustrations. [380
1899	N.Y., McKiblin	179	Anon.?	12°. [381
1899	N.Y., Wessells	255	B. McManus	4°. [382
1900	Chicago, Conkey	150	Tenniel	12°: the signn. run on through Louisa M. Alcott's *Flower Fables*. [383
[190–?]	Boston, Small	192		12°. [384
1901	N.Y., Harper	192+	P. Newell	8°. See Harper's Magazine, Oct. 1901. There was also a 1902 issue. [385
1902	N.Y., Wessels		B. McManus	[386
1902	Chicago, Rand	192	F. Y. Cory	Edited by Florence Milner. Also issued in 1903. [387
[1902–3?]	N.Y., Street			[388
[1902–3?]	N.Y., Globe Co.			[389
[1902–3?]	N.Y., Hurst			[390
1903	N.Y., Crowell			16°. [391
1904	N.Y., Stokes		M. L. Kirk & Tenniel	8°. [392
1904	N.Y., Macmillan	175+	Tenniel	12°: ed. for school use by C. A. McMurry. [393
1905	N.Y., Burt	274		12°. [394
1906	N.Y., Crowell			[395
1906	N.Y., Harper		P. Newell	[396
1906	N.Y., Putnam		Tenniel	[397

(Editions after the English Copyright had run out in 1907)

1907	Garden City		A. Rackham	8°. [398
[1907?]	Boston, Educational Co.		Tenniel	12°. [399
1907	N.Y., Cassell		C. Robinson	[400
1907	N.Y., Dodge	164+	B. P. Gutmann	8°. [401
1907	N.Y., Lane	152+	W. H. Walker	12°. Also issued in 1911. [402
1908	N.Y., Duffield	166+	M. Sowerby	8°. [403
1908	N.Y., Cassell		C. Robinson	Popular edition. [404
1908	Chicago, Brewer			[405
1909	N.Y., Lane			[406
1909	N.Y., Nelson	160		[407
1909	N.Y., Nelson	247		4°. [408
1910	N.Y., McLoughlin		Tenniel	4°. [409
1910	N.Y., Cassell		C. Robinson	Cheap edition. [410
1910	N.Y., Tuck	148	M. L. Attwell	[411
1910	N.Y., Platt	300		[412
1911	N.Y., Baker	300	G. Soper	[413
n.d.	N.Y., Baker	192	G. Soper	[414
1911	Philad., McKay	179		[415
1911	N.Y., Platt	176	Tenniel	[416
1911	N.Y., Macmillan	175+	Tenniel	12°: edited for schools by C. A. McMurry: issued also in 1916. [417
1911	N.Y., Doran			[418
1911	N.Y., Merrill	187	Tenniel	12°. [419
1911	N.Y., Putnam	160+	Tenniel	12°. [420
1912?	N.Y., Chatterton			[421
1912	N.Y., Crowell			[422

Date	Publisher	Pagination	Illustrator	Notes	
1912?	N.Y., Fenno				[423
1912?	Chicago, Flanagan				[424
1912?	Chicago, International Co.				[425
1912?	Chicago, Reilly				[426
1912?	Nashville, Tenn., S. Wn. Co.		Tenniel		[427
1912?	Chicago, Walter				[428
1912?	Chicago, Donohue				[429
1912	Chicago, Hall			{ 1st Adv. of *Alice*. } { 2nd Adventure. }	[430
1912?	Danesville, N.Y., Owen	32		2nd part of *Alice* only: issued also in 1920.	[431
1913	N.Y., Stokes	247		12°.	[432
1913	N.Y., Macmillan	119+	A. B. Woodward	12°.	[433
1913	N.Y., Longmans	128		12°.	[434
1914	N.Y., Hodder		A. E. Jackson		[435
1914	N.Y., Funk	179	C. Robinson		[436
1914	N.Y., Doran	232+	A. E. Jackson	4°.	[437
1914	N.Y., Macmillan	161	A. B. Woodward		[438
1915	N.Y., Macmillan		Tenniel		[439
1915	N.Y., Grosset	320		8°.	[440
1915	N.Y., Sully	64+		4°.	[441
1916	N.Y., Gabriel	48		8°.	[442
1916	N.Y., Kelly	202	G. Robinson	8°.	[443
1916	N.Y., Dutton	131		8°.	[444
1917	Boston, Ginn	224	O. Herford	8° : ed. by W. J. Long.	[445
1917	N.Y., Crowell				[446
1917	N.Y., Graham				[447
1917	N.Y., Cupples	124	{ J. Greene } { H. Pettes }	8°.	[448
1917	Ling				[449
1917	N.Y., Hurst	80			[450
	N.Y., Gregg	154		16°: Gregg's Shorthand edition.	[451
1918	N.Y., American Book Co.	154	Tenniel	12°: ed. by C. Johnson.	[452
1920	N.Y., Danseville, Owen	32		2nd part of *Alice* only.	[453
1920	Boston, Small		G. Soper	4°.	[454
1921	N.Y., Nelson	160			[455
1922	N.Y., Dodd	181+	G. Hudson	4°. Reissued in 1925 or 1926.	[456
1923	N.Y., Sears			16°.	[457
1923	Philad., Lippincott	240+	{ G. A. Kay } { Tenniel }	8°. Reissued in 1928?	[458
1924	N.Y., Doran	192	G. Soper	8°.	[459
1926	N.Y., Macmillan				[460
1926	Philad., McKay	179+	A. Bowley	12°.	[461
1927	N.Y., Appleton	192	Tenniel	8°. A facsimile of the N.Y. 1866 edition.	[462
1928	Chicago, Whitman	160	Tenniel	4°.	[463
1929	N.Y., Dutton	192	W. Pogany	8°. See No. 346.	
1929	N.Y., Macmillan	200+	Tenniel	12°. The miniature edition, first published in 1907.	[464
1930	Dutton, see No. 348.				
1929?	Chicago, Rand		{ F.C.Cooney } { C. L. Dodgson }	Edited by Florence Milner.	[465

Date	Publisher	Pagination	Illustrator	Notes	
1930?	Boston, Cornhill Co.				[466
1930?	Garden City	216+	A. E. Jackson		[467
1930?	Toronto, McLelland	224	A. L. Bowley		[468
1930	Paris, Black Sun Press		Marie Laurencin	obl. 8°.	[469
n. d.	Rahway, N.J., Mershom Co.				[470
n. d.	N.Y., N.Y. Publishing Co.		Tenniel		[471
n. d.	N.Y., Crowell		After Tenniel	16°.	[472
n. d.	Garden City, Doubleday	232	W. Pogany	16°.	[473
n. d.	Cincinnati South-Western Co.				[474
n. d.	Newark, Graham (N.J.?) (England?)			Excelsior Library.	[475
1931	Garden City Pub. Co., N.Y.		A. E. Jackson		
1932	Limited Editions Club, N.Y.		John Tenniel	Limited to 1,500 copies.	
1932	McLoughlin, Mass.		John Tenniel		
1940	Mount Vernon, N.Y.		John Tenniel		
1941	Heritage Press, N.Y.		John Tenniel		
1942	Doubleday, N.Y.		John Tenniel	Facsimile of 1st edn. Introduction by Kathleen Norris.	
1943	McLoughlin, Mass.		Emma C. McKean		
[1945]	McGraw Hill, N.Y.		John Tenniel		
1946	Random House, N.Y.		John Tenniel		
1948	Chanticleer Press, N.Y.		John Tenniel	16 in colour by Henry Gee.	
1957	Gosset & Dunlap, N.Y.		Maraja		

TRANSLATIONS OF *ALICE'S ADVENTURES*

Alice's Adventures, in Braille

(*Alice's Adventures*, in Braille, transcribed by Margaret A. P. Chamberlain.) Boston, Boston Metropolitan Chapter of the American Red Cross: 1924: 3 volumes, hand-copied. [477
Library of Congress, Washington, U.S.A.

—— another copy, transcribed by Martha K. Thompson. Philadelphia, S.E. Pennsylvania Chapter of the American Red Cross: 1926. [478
Overbrook Library, Penn., U.S.A.

—— another copy, press-brailled at Louisville, Kentucky, U.S.A. (n.d.), is in the Library of Congress. [479

Alice's Adventures, in Chinese [480

A translation by Dr. Y. S. Chao was published at Shanghai, at the Commercial Press of Shanghai, but is now out of print.

'1922, 1927 (abridged), 1931 (5th ed.), 1932. . . . In April 1911 General Ho Chien, Governor-General of the Province of Hunan, issued an edict forbidding the use of the book in schools, since speaking animals were degrading to man. There are in all six Chinese editions, all owned by Mr. Warren Weaver of New York.' Supplement (1935).

Alice's Adventures, in Czecho-Slovak

1931. By Dr. J. Cisař of Brünn in Moldavia.

Alice's Adventures, in Danish

1930. (Copenhagen.)
1875; Philobiblon (1932), Heft 8 and (1933), Heft 7.

Alice's Adventures, in Dutch [481

Alice's Avonturen in het Wonderland Naar het Engelsch van Lewis Carroll Met 40 illustraties van John Tenniel.

Leiden Boekhandel en Drukkerij Voorheen E. J. Brill: (1899): 8°: pp. viii+ 146+[6]. CONTENTS: p. i, half-title: iii, title: iv, imprint: v–vi, preface, dated den Haag, 1899, and signed R. ten Raa: vii, contents: 1–146, the text: [1–6] advertisements.

The first complete Dutch edition: see No. 115 (1881). The frontispiece and illustrations are not counted in the pagination. The two illustrations omitted are the Lobster Quadrille, because the original could not be translated, so that chapter 10 is omitted; and the Mock Turtle's dance. The Mock Turtle is translated Soepsschildpad, the Soup-turtle. The front cover bears a figure of Alice dreaming under a tree, with animals around. The illustrations are larger than in the English edition.

Williams, i. 59 (p. 71), with the mistaken date 1889; Parrish Catalogue, p. 58: British Museum, Mrs. Ffooks.

1920. (Amsterdam)
1924.

Alice's Adventures, in Esperanto [482

La Aventuroj de Alicio en Mirlando de Lewis Carroll. Tradukita de E. L. Kearney, M.A. Ilustrita . . . per dek bildoj de Brinsley Le Fanu.

London (British Esperanto Association): 1910: 8°: pp. xii+132: printed by Turnbull and Spears, Edinburgh: issued in light orange coloured paper wrapper. The ten illustrations were used by permission of the proprietor of Stead's Prose Classics (Books for the Bairns). Rare. I possess a copy.

Alice's Adventures, in French [483

1908. An edition with Rackham's illustrations was published by Hachette in Paris.

—— [Nov.] 1919. An edition was published by Nelson (London) in the 'Modern Studies Series': 8°: pp. 96; price 1s. See No. 51 (1869). This was reissued in 1929, see next item. [484

Mrs. Ffooks.

—— 1929. L'Aventure merveilleuse d'Alice. London, Nelson: 8°: pp. 96 (Modern Studies Series). [485

Mrs. Ffooks.

—— n.d. There is an undated edition issued by Messrs. Momm in Paris, but printed in London: 4°. [486

Library of Congress.

1930. (Paris.) By M. Fayet.

1932. (Paris).

n.d. (Paris.) By M. J. Armond.

1938. (London) Nelson; (Paris) Librairie Grund.

1939. (Imperial Book Company.)

Alice's Adventures, in German

For an 1885 edition, see No. 53 (1869).

Mrs. Ffooks.

—— 1912. Alice im Wunderland. (Illustrated by A. Rackham, translated by Scheu-Riesz): Weimar, Kiepenheuer: 1912: pp. 126.

[487

—— n.d. Alice im Wunderland. (Illustrated by J. W. Roth, translated by R. C. L. Barrett): Nuremberg: n.d.: pp. 158.   [488

1923. (Vienna.) By H. Scheu-Riesz.

1931. (Berlin.)

Alice in Wonderland, in Hebrew   [489

[Alice in Wonderland, in Hebrew, translated from the English by L. Simon.]

Frankfurt a.M.: 1924: 8°: pp. 172+.

Alice's Adventures, in Hungarian

1924. (Budapest.)

Alice's Adventures, in Irish   [489*-

Eaċtrad Eiblís i dTip na nIongantas Padraig ó Caḋla do cuir gaeḋealg ar an sgeul so.

Maunsel agus Roberts, teo. Baile áṫa Cliaṫ [Dublin]: 1922: 8°: pp. viii+147+ [1].

There are 31 illustrations, by K. Verschoyle and 'U. M. H.', 13 of which are full-page, but not of high artistic value. A facsimile of p. 1 (without the plate) is at p. 322 of The Library, 4th S., iv (1924), as a specimen of modern Irish monotype.

Bodleian, &c.

Alice's Adventures, in Italian   [490

Carroll. Alice nel Paese delle Meraviglie. (Biblioteca dei Ragazzi, No. 5.)

Milano: 8°: pp. 266+: with nine coloured illustrations. See No. 68. Mrs. Ffooks.

—— Alice nel paese della Meraviglie di Lewis Carroll. Illustrato da Emma C. Cagli.   [491

Bergamo, Istituto italiano d'Arti grafiche: [1908]: 8°: pp. 157. Boston Public Library, U.S.A.

Alice's Adventures, in Japanese

1928. (Tokyo.)

1929. (Tokyo.) Kenkyusha. [In English and Japanese, with Tenniel's illustrations.]

1930. (Tokyo.)
[There are four translations in the Weaver collection.]

Alice's Adventures, in Norwegian
1903. (Kristiania [Oslo].)

Alice's Adventures, in Polish
1927. (Warsaw.)
1932. (Warsaw.)

Alice's Adventures, in Portuguese
1931. (Sâo Paulo: Brazil.) By M. Lobuto.

Alice's Adventures, in Russian
[Alice's Adventures, in Russian, with Tenniel's illustrations.]
[492

1909: sm. 4°: pp. 185+[3]. Pp. 1–20 are a preface with two portraits of Dodgson.
British Museum.

—— Alice's Adventures, in Russian, translated by V. Sirin. [Vladimir Nabokov, author of Lolita.]
[493

1923: 8°: pp. 114.
New York Public Library, U.S.A.

—— Alice's Adventures, in Russian, translated by A. D'Actil (pseudonym?).
[494

1923: 4°: pp. 131.
New York Public Library, U.S.A.

Alice's Adventures, in shorthand
Alice's Adventures, Chapter VII, in 'Cursive shorthand': New York, Putnam, 1912? See Nos. 284 (1909) and 347 (1929).
[495

—— also in Gregg's Shorthand Classics Series. New York, Gregg Co., 1921 and 1931.
[496

—— also in the Intermediate Pitman's Shorthand. New Era edition. London, Pitman, and New York, Pitman: 1930: pp. 154.   [497

Alice, in Spanish (Catalan)   [498

Lewis Carrol [sic] Alícia en terra de Meravelles Traducció de Josep Carner Il·lustracions de Lola Anglada

Barcelona, Editorial Mentora: [1928?]: la. 8°: pp. 135+[1, with only a design in green]. Bound in white paper on boards, with a coloured picture of Alice in the midst of animals, court cards, &c., signed 'Lola Anglada', on the front outer cover.

Alice's Adventures in Spanish, with the same illustrations as No. 499. Almost every page has a design in green in the margins and the ornamental capitals. The text begins 'Alícia començava de cansar-se'. Both this and No. 499 have 31 lines in a page, but vary in the size of the margins (over 2 in.) of the present volume.

British Museum. Mr. M. L. Parrish owns Nos. 498 and 499.

Alice, in Spanish (Castilian)   [499

Lewis Carroll—Alicia en el Pais de las Maravillas Traducción de Juan Gutierrez Gili Ilustraciones de Lola Anglada.

Barcelona, Editorial Mentora: [1928?]: 8°: pp. 140+[4; 1, text concluded; 3, advt.] Bound in light blue cloth, lettered.

Alice's Adventures in Spanish, with many rather roughly drawn, but spirited, engravings. The text begins 'Alicia empezaba a sentirse cansadisima'. (Second edition, 1931.)

British Museum.

Alice, in Spanish (Castilian)   [500

Alicia en el Pais de las Maravillas por Lewis Carroll.

[at end] Editorial Rivademeyra . . . Madrid: [1922]: folio: pp. [12] see below: bound in paper on boards.

An abridgement of Alice's Adventures in Spanish, truly remarkable in form and illustrations. The inner four leaves are normal, the outer two are each double-size in width and folded into two. Fol. $1a$ is a title and large coloured picture of Alice; $1b$ is the beginning of the text ('Alicia sentada, en un banco del jardin'): $2a+b$ bears a 16-line poem to Alice and a large picture of the Mad Hatter's Tea-party: the text is continued on pp. 3–10, $12a$: $11a+b$ is a large picture of hata Elisi alisikia kwa shida maneno ya wimbo.

Namkaripia mwana wangu,
Nampiga akilia.
Apenda sana pilipili
Na moshi chafu pia.

Mama Mkubwa akamtupia Elisi mtoto mchanga akasema "Mshike wee, maana imenilazimu nijiweke tayari kucheza Kriketi na Malkia

Key G minor.

$\{\ |:\ :\ |\ \tilde{n}\ |\ \dot{r}:d\ |\ \tilde{t}_1:l_1\ |\ se_1:l_1\ |\ \tilde{t}_1,\tilde{t}_1:\tilde{n}_1\ |$
      M - ka - ri - pi - e   mwa-na   wa-ko, Na

$\{\ |\ \dot{d}\cdot l_1\ |\ \dot{r}:\dot{r}\ |\ n_1:n_1\ |\ :n\ |\ f:n\ |\ r:l_1\ |$
   a-ki - en-da   chaf-ya,   A - ten-da   hi - vi

$\{\ |\ \tilde{n},\ \dot{r}\ |\ d:s_1\ |\ l_1:f\ |\ n_1:l_1\ |\ r:-\ |\ d:-\ |$
   ku-sum - bua, Ha - jam - bo,   a - na   af - - ya.

Mzunguwapili." Akatoka chumbani, Mpishi akamtupia sufuria.

Elisi alimshika kwa shida mtoto, maana alikuwa ajinyonganyonga, mwisho akamshika sana kwa mgu wake wa kushoto na sikio la kulia, akamchukua nje mwituni apate kupunga hewa, akasema "Lazima nimpeleke nje, wasimwue kule jikoni. Pole mwanangu, wa mekupiga sana sivyo ? Watu hawa ni wajinga kabisa, hawajui kukutunza." Mtoto aka-

guna kama kujibu, Elisi akamwambia "Usiguna! Si vizuri kuguna kama nguruwe." Yule Mtoto akazidi kuguna, Elisi akamtazama sana kwa mashaka, pua yake yalikuwa kama pua ya nguruwe, na macho yake yalikuwa madogo. Elisi akafikiri ya kuwa ni kwa sababu ya kulia

sana ndipo akavimba pua; akaendelea kutembea akasema "Ukigeuka kabisa kuwa nguruwe, basi wewe si mtoto wa kusuhubiana nawe." Mtoto akaguna tena, Elisi akatulia akamtazama kwa hofu, na ilikuwa hakuna shaka, mtoto alikuwa amekwisha geuka kuwa mtoto wa nguruwe. Elisi akamsimamisha chi-

xv. 'Alice' in Swahili (London, 1940)

the Trial, with Alice on the right: 12*b* is a design, with imprint, &c., at foot. The illustrations in text and full-page are highly coloured and singular, and baffle description. The outer covers bear a floral design, subdued in tone, with title on the front cover.

British Museum.

Alice's Adventures, in Swahili

Elisi Katika Nchi ya Ajabu. 1940. (London.)

Translated by E. V. St. Lo Conan-Davies, and published by Sheldon Press under the auspices of S.P.C.K. See Plate XV.

Alice's Adventures, in Swedish   [501

Alices Märkvärdiga Äventyr | i Underlandet | av | Lewis Carroll | — | till Svenska | av | Joel Söderberg |

Stockholm Magn. Bergvalls Forlag: (1917): 8°: pp. 173+[3, advtt.], with Tenniel's illustrations: printed at the Kungl. Hofboktryckeriet, Stockholm.

The preface to this Swedish translation gives no hint of the author's real name, but quotes from the *Pall Mall Gazette* of 1898 an opinion that *Alice* is more often quoted than any book other than Shakespeare's plays.

British Museum.

The first edition of the above appears to have been published in 1898.

1921. (Helsingfors.)

1923. (Paris.) [A school edition.]

Alice's Adventures, in Welsh

1953.

English editions of 'Alice' with 'Through the Looking-Glass' together, from 1911.

[N.B. *The People's Edition*, 1887, of the two books together, was reprinted by Macmillan many times.]

Date	London publisher	Pagination	Illustrator	Notes
[Oct.] 1911	Macmillan	291+	Tenniel	8°: price 5*s*.: with 92 illustrations (16 cold.).: some copies are stated to be bound in scented cloth. [502
1916	Macmillan		Tenniel	A reprint of 1911. [503
[Oct.] 1921	Macmillan	299+	Tenniel	8°: price 10*s*.: a reprint, with only 8 plates in colour. [504 [505 = 535 which see]

Date	Publisher	Pagination	Illustrator	Notes
[May] 1927	Macmillan		Tenniel	$8°$: price $1s.$ $6d.$: 'Children's Story Books'. [506
[Nov.] 1927	Macmillan	235+	Tenniel	sm. $4°$: price $6s.$: 16 cold. plates, the rest plain: 'Children's Edition'. [507a
[Apr. 1928]	Collins	318+	H. Rountree	sm. $8°$: price $4s.$: 'Illustrated Pocket Classics', No. 296: with 56 illustrations (one cold.), 39 full-page. [507b
[July 1928]	Collins			$16°?$: price $1s.$: 'Tales for the Children'. [507c
Oct. 1928	Collins	{ 135+ 143+ }	H. Rountree	$4°$: price $7s.$ $6d.$: with 8 cold. and many other plates. [507d
Oct. 1928	Macmillan	204	Tenniel	$8°$: 'Macmillan's $2s.$ Library'. [507e
[Dec. 1928]	Collins			$8°$: price $1s.$ $6d$: 'Illustrated School Classics'. [507f
[Sept. 1929]	Dent	336	C. L. Dodgson	$8°$: price $2s.$: 'Everyman's Library.' This includes other comic pieces by Dodgson (*Phantasmagoria*, the *Snark*, and a *Tangled Tale*). In this edition Dodgson's own illustrations of Alice are given, both forms of the *Mouse's Tail*, an *Apologia* for the chess setting of the *Looking-Glass*, and an Introduction by Ernest Rhys. [507g
1934	Hutchinson		M. L. Clements	
1937	Collins		A. H. Watson	Collins Pocket Classics.
1945	Jan Förlag [Stockholm]		Robert Högfeldt	
1948	Studley Press			'Children's Classics'.
[1950]	Blackie			
1954	Allan Wingate		Mervyn Peake	
1954	Dent		John Tenniel	'Children's Illustrated Classics', with 8 of Tenniel's illustrations redrawn in colour by Diana Stanley.
1955	Thames Publishing Co.			
1957	Collins			'Crusader Series'.
1957	Dean			'Dean's Classics'.
1958	Macmillan		John Tenniel	'St. Martin's Library' (paperback).
[1959]				'Tower Classics'.

American editions of 'Alice' with 'Through the Looking-Glass' together, from 1881

Date	Publisher	Pagination	Illustrator	Notes
1881	N.Y., Macmillan		Tenniel	$12°$. [508
1885	N.Y., Macmillan		Tenniel	Separate titles and pagination. So 1889. [509
1895	Philad., Altemus	347+	Tenniel	$8°$. [510

Date	Publisher	Pagination	Illustrator	Notes	
1896	Boston, Caldwell		Tenniel	12°. Two issues (= the Atlanta edition?).	[511
1898	Boston, Lothrop		Tenniel		[512
1898	N.Y., Macmillan				[513
1900	N.Y., Wessels	255+	B. McManus (= Mrs. Mansfield)	4°. Also in 1902, 1904.	[514
1903?	N.Y., Hurst		Tenniel		[515
1903	N.Y., Collier	317+	Tenniel B. Stevens	8°.	[516
1910	N.Y., Caldwell	274+		12°.	[517
1911	Boston, Lothrop			4°.	[518
1911	N.Y., Macmillan	292+	Tenniel		[519
1911	N.Y., Putnam		Tenniel		[520
1912	Philad., McKay	192+		Issued also in 1917.	[521
1912	Philad., Jacobs	335	Tenniel E. P. Abbott	8°.	[522
1912	N.Y., Platt	255	B. McManus	8°.	[523
1912	N.Y., Burt				[524
1912	N.Y., McLoughlin				[525
1912	Chicago, Reilly				[526
1913	N.Y., Macmillan	{192+ 224+}	Tenniel	8°.	[527
1915	N.Y., Grosset	320	Tenniel	8°.	[528
1916	Chicago, Rand	242	M. Winter	8°.	[529
1917	N.Y., Graham				[530
1919	N.Y., Grosset			8°. With scenes from a photoplay.	[531
1921	N.Y., Macmillan	192+ 224	Tenniel	12°. Also issued in 1928. Part also dated 1920. Separate titles and pagination.	[532
1923	N.Y., Macmillan		Tenniel	8°. 'Children's Classics'.	[533
1923	Philad., Winston	319+	Tenniel E. J. Prittie	8°.	[534
1925	N.Y., Boni & Livewright	351+	Tenniel	8°: edited by Alexander Woollcott. This adds the Snark.	[535
1925	N.Y., Grosset	297.		12°: children's edition.	[536
1926	N.Y., Sears	236+		4°.	[537
1928	N.Y., Macmillan	19			[538
n. d.	Newark (N.J.?), Graham (?England)			Jun. Classics Series.	[539
1932	N.Y.		Tenniel		
1937	Platt & Munk, N.Y.		Tenniel		
1945	Racine, Wis.		Linda Card		
1945	World Pub. C., N.Y.		Tenniel	Introduction by May L. Becker.	
1946	Gosset & Dunlap, N.Y.		Tenniel		
1949	N.Y., Harper		L. Weisgard		
1955	Whitman Co., Wis.		Roberta Paflin		
1957	Philad., Winston		Tenniel		
1960	N.Y., Clarkson N. Potter		Tenniel	'The Annotated Alice' (see below).	

THE | ANNOTATED | Alice | ALICE'S ADVENTURES IN WONDERLAND | & | THROUGH THE LOOKING GLASS | BY | LEWIS CARROLL || ILLUSTRATED BY | JOHN TENNIEL || *With an Introduction and Notes by* | MARTIN GARDNER.

Roy. 8vo (no signatures) [folded as 16mo]. $11 \times 8\frac{1}{4}$ in. Pp. 352. Imprint p. [2] *Clarkson N. Potter, Inc.*, Publisher, NEW YORK; [3] title as above; [4] Registration; followed by 'Manufactured in the United States of America by Book Craftsmen Association, Inc., New York. Designed by Sydney Butchkeo.'

Printed in large type with copious annotations in small type in the outer margins (occasionally full-page in double columns). Bound in light fawn cloth lettered in blue.

This magnificent work is the complete apotheosis of Carrollolatry.

B

EDITIONS OF *THROUGH THE LOOKING-GLASS*, WITH NOTES OF TRANSLATIONS

English editions of 'Through the Looking-Glass' from 1914

Date	Publisher	Pagination	Illustrator	Notes
1927	Macmillan		Tenniel	8°: Children's Edition with 16 illus. in colour.
[July] 1929	Macmillan	235+	Tenniel	8°: price 5s.: leather. 'Cardinal Series'. Reissued in Oct. in blue morocco. **[540**
[Oct.] 1929	Macmillan	235+	Tenniel	8°: price 8s. 6d.: leather. **[541**
[1936]	Ward Lock & Co.			
[1937]	Nelson			'Nelson's Classics'.
[1939]	Collins		I. Mountfort	
1948	Puffin Books		John Tenniel	Introduction by Eleanor Graham.
1949	Ward Lock & Co.			New Prize Library.
1950	Max Parrish		John Tenniel	
1950	P. R. Gawthorn		Rene Cloke	
[1953]	Nelson		Helen Munro	'Nelson's Classics'.
1953	Ward, Lock & Co.			
[1954]	Hamlyn			'Hamlyn Classics'.
1958	Mellifont			
1959	W. H. Allen		Maraja	'Splendour Books'.

American editions of 'Through the Looking-Glass' from 1872

Date	Publisher	Pagination	Illustrator	Notes
1872	N.Y. Macmillan		Tenniel	
1872	Boston, Lee & Sheppard	xii+ 224	Tenniel	8°: the first American edition. *Parrish Catalogue*, p. 9. The error in the *Jabberwocky* (*wade* for *wabe*) is here reproduced from the first English edition, on p. 21. **[541***
1872	'London', Lee	xii+ 224	Tenniel	8°: 2nd issue of the foregoing with error corrected, but London instead of Boston in the imprint. **[542**

Date	Publisher	Pagination	Illustrator	Notes	
1885	N.Y., Lowell	224+	Tenniel	8°.	[543
1886	N.Y., Munro	230	Tenniel	8°.	[544
1893	N.Y., Crowell	230+	Tenniel	12°.	[545
1896	N.Y., Burt			12°.	[546
1896	N.Y., Macmillan	224+	Tenniel	12°. Also in 1898, 1899, 1901, 1902, 1907, 1910, 1924, 1928.	[547
1898	N.Y., Hurst			12°.	[548
1899	N.Y., Mansfield & Wessels		B. McManus	4°.	[549
1899	N.Y., McKibbin	192		sq. 16°.	[550
1900	Chicago, Conkey	167			[551
n.d.	Chicago, Conkey			sq. 16°: contains also 'The Sleeping Beauty'.	[552
1900	N.Y., Crowell				[553
1902	N.Y., Harper	211+	P. Newell	8°: decorations by R. M. Wright. Pocket edition.	[554
1903	N.Y., Crowell			Pocket edition.	[555
1904	N.Y., Macmillan		Tenniel	12°: Pocket Classic series.	[556
1905	N.Y., Stokes	271	Tenniel		[557
1906	N.Y., Harper		P. Newell		[558
1907	N.Y., Putnam				[559
1908	N.Y., Macmillan			16°.	[560
1909	N.Y., Dodge	185+	B. Gutmann	8°.	[561
1911	N.Y., Platt	175			[562
1912?	Philad., Altemus				[563
1912?	Boston, Caldwell				[564
1912?	N.Y., Chatterton				[565
1912?	Chicago, Donohue				[566
1912?	Boston, Educatl. Co.				[567
1912?	N.Y., Fenno				[568
1912?	Chicago, Reilly				[569
1912?	Nashville, Tenn., S. Wn. Co.				[570
1917	Chicago, Rand	218	F. Y. Cory	12°: edited by Florence Milner.	[571
1919	Akron (O.), Saalfield Co.				[572
1924	Philad., Jacobs				[573
1929	Philad.		E. J. Prittie		
1929	Philad., Lippincott	235+	{ G. A. Kay / Tenniel }	8°.	[574
1930	Chicago, Whitman	222	Tenniel		[575
n. d.	N.Y., United States Co.	224+	Tenniel	12°: (1871?)	[576
n. d.	N.Y., N.Y. Publ. Co.				[577
n. d.	Philad., McKay			12°.	[578
1931	N.Y., Cheshire House		Franklin Hughes		
1932	Washington		John Tenniel		
1932	N.Y.				
1935	Limited Editions Club, N.Y.		John Tenniel	1,500 copies, signed by Alice Hargreaves.	
[1945]	N.Y., McGraw Hill		John Tenniel		
1946	Random House, N.Y.		John Tenniel	Coloured by Fritz Kredel.	

Through the Looking-Glass, in German   [579

Alice in Spiegelland. Lewis Carroll. Deutsch von Helene Scheu-Riesz. Ausstattung von Uriel Birnbaum.

Wien, Sesam-Verlag: 1923: 8°: pp. 121+.

Boston Public Library, U.S.A.

Through the Looking-Glass, in Czech

1923.

1931.

Through the Looking-Glass, in French

1933.

C

EDITIONS OF OTHER WORKS BY C. L. DODGSON, WITH NOTES OF TRANSLATIONS

American Editions of 'Hunting of the Snark'

Date	Publisher	Pagina-tion	Illustrator	Notes
1876	Boston, Osgood	xiv+86	H. Holiday	24°: 1st American edition: much reduced in size. *Parrish Catalogue*, p. 16. [610
1890	N.Y., Macmillan			12°. [611
1898	N.Y., Macmillan	53	Holiday	8°. Perhaps some dated 1899: issued also in 1908, 1910, 1914, 1927. [612
189-?	N.Y., Burt		Holiday	*Snark* and *Sylvie and Bruno*. [613
1901	N.Y., Burt	205		12°. [614
1903	N.Y., Harper		P. Newell	'And other poems.' Also in 1906. [615
1906	N.Y., Putnam			12°. [616
1909	Philad., Altemus	119+		[617
1927	Yellow Springs, Ohio, Kahoe	56		[618

The Hunting of the Snark, and Other Nonsense Verses. Collector's Presentation Edition, *Peter Pauper Press*; and Mayflower Publishing Co. and Vision Press, New York, 1955.

Hunting of the Snark (1910)   [589

The Hunting | of the Snark | an Agony, | in Eight Fits | By | Lewis Carroll | . . . | with nine Illustrations | by Henry Holiday |

Macmillan and Co., Limited . . . London: 1910: (eights) 12°: pp. xii+[2]+ 83+[3]: on the second p. 1 is 'Printed . . . by Richard Clay and Sons, Limited . . . (London) and Bungay . . .'.

This pocket edition was reprinted in 1910, 1911, 1913, 1916, 1920, &c. The original edition was issued in 1876 (No. **89** above), and reissued in July and Oct. 1929, in Macmillan's Cardinal Series.

Hunting of the Snark (1941)

The Hunting of the Snark: An Agony in Eight Fits. By Lewis Carroll. Illustrated by Mervyn Peake.

Chatto and Windus, 'Zodiac Books', (London) 1941. Cr. 8°, pp. 48. Published November 1941, price 1s.

The Snark, in French (1929)   [606

La Chasse au Snark . . . Traduit . . . par [Louis] Aragon.

Hours Press (Miss Nancy Cunard), Chapelle Réanville, Eure: 1929: Pp. [8]+29+[3]: 4°.

The only French translation of the *Hunting of the Snark*. Mrs. Ffooks, of Dorchester, Dorset, possesses a copy, and also the Harvard College Library in America, and Mr. M. L. Parrish.

It was reprinted in 1949 by P. Seghers, Paris.

The Snark, in Latin (1934)

1934. (London: Macmillan). Rendered into Latin Verse by P. R. Brinton. [Also in Toronto.]

1936. (Oxford.) Translated into Latin Elegiacs, by H. D. Watson. Foreword by Gilbert Murray.

Jabberwocky, &c., in Latin (1937)

1937. (Oxford.) More English Rhymes with Latin renderings, by H. D. Watson.

American Editions of 'Sylvie and Bruno'

Date	Publisher	Pagination	Illustrator	Notes	
S.B. 1890	N.Y., Macmillan				[619
S.B. concl. 1894	N.Y., Macmillan	423+			[620
S.B. 1898		400+	H. Furniss	8°.	[621
S.B. n. d.	N.Y.			12°.	[622
S.B. concl. n. d.	N.Y.			12°.	[623
American Editions of the Story of Sylvie and Bruno					
1904	N.Y., Macmillan	400	H. Furniss		[624
1905	N.Y., Macmillan		H. Furniss	12°.	[625

Rhyme? and Reason? (1884)   [580

Rhyme? and Reason?

New York (Macmillan): 1884: pp. 214+, illustrated by H. Holiday. A copy is in the Amory Collection at Harvard.

The Lewis Carroll Book (1931)

The Lewis Carroll Book, edited by Richard Herrick (New York, 1931: 8°: pp. xx+439+[3]). This contains Dodgson's chief works: *Alice*, *Looking-Glass*, *Tangled Tale*, *Phantasmagoria*, &c.
[Madan: *Supplement* (1935), p. 13.]

Bruno's Revenge (1924)   [595

Bruno's Revenge by Lewis Carroll. Edited by John Drinkwater . . .

London and Glasgow, Collins's Clear-type Press: [1924]: (twelve) 8°: pp. 48: in limp red cloth binding: at head of title is 'The John Drinkwater Series for Schools', and on the front cover, the title and 'Standard B': advertisements on the inner covers, of Collins's Press books.

The editor writes an introduction (pp. 3–5) for schoolboys, dated 1923. The text occupies pp. 7–38, and pp. 39–48 are seven poems from *Alice's Adventures*.

British Museum, &c.

Alice's Adventures in Wonderland, with *Bruno's Revenge* (1925)

With illustrations by Harry Rountree.

Thomas Nelson & Sons, Ltd. London and Edinburgh [n.d.]. Pp. viii+160.

Pp. 121–32, 'On Thinking it Over' (no author named) gives originals of some of the parodies.

Alice's Adventures in Wonderland, with *Bruno's Revenge* (1933?)

With illustrations by Helen Munro.

Thomas Nelson & Sons Ltd. London, Edinburgh, New York, Toronto, and Paris. [n.d. Bodleian copy received 31 Jan. 1933.] Pp. iv+220 (+Advertisements).

The Vision of the Three T's, in French (1945)

La Vision des Trois T.: thrénode.
Translated by Pascaline and Alain Gheerbrant.

Paris (Fontaine), 1945.

Father William (1928)   [602

Father William; and other numbers. Taylorville, Illinois [U.S.A.], Parker Publishing Co. [1928?].

'Eight-page classics' series; presumably the song in *Alice's Adventures.*

United States Catalogue of Books (1928).

Stories for Children by Lewis Carroll (1948)

Illustrated by Leslie Butler, A.R.C.A. Colour plates by Phyllis Fenton.

London: Golden Galley Press Ltd. 1948. Pp. viii+172. Preface signed 'C. D. D.'

Two extracts from *Address to Children* (1897). Cf. *Lewis Carroll Picture Book.*

Three extracts from *Alice's Adventures.*

Two extracts from *Looking-Glass.*

Seven extracts from *Sylvie and Bruno* and *Sylvie and Bruno Concluded.*

PART III

Memoirs, Reminiscences, Memorials, Bibliographies, Etc.

A

BOOKS AND PAMPHLETS: 1898 TO 1960

1898

1. *Collingwood's Life and Letters of Lewis Carroll* (1898)
[644 a

THE | LIFE AND LETTERS | OF | LEWIS CARROLL | (REV. C. L. DODGSON) | BY | STUART DODGSON COLLINGWOOD | B.A. CHRIST CHURCH, OXFORD | *ILLUSTRATED* |

London: T. Fisher Unwin, Paternoster Buildings: MDCCCXCVIII: 8°: pp. xx+448+[12], signn. 1^{10}, $2-29^8$, +Advtt. CONTENTS: p. i, half-title: ii, Fisher Unwin's mark: iv, frontispiece, a portrait of Dodgson: v, title: vi, at foot '[All rights reserved]': vii, dedication to Child Friends, &c.: ix–xii, Preface, dated Guildford, September, 1898: xiii–xv, contents: xvii–xx, list of illustrations: 2–429, the text, in 11 chapters: 431–43, Bibliography: 445–8, index: 448, 'Unwin brothers, the Gresham Press, Woking and London': pp. a–d, g–o, Advertisements of books published by Fisher Unwin.

Mr. Dodgson's ten surviving brothers and sisters did well when they invited their nephew, Mr. S. D. Collingwood, to take up the biography of 'Lewis Carroll'. The present volume is a very readable and satisfactory Life, by one who had both an intimate acquaintance with the subject and access to his Diary and Correspondence. Every facet of Dodgson's life is dealt with, and the two last chapters are about his numerous 'Child-Friends'. His character, habits, uneventful life, and successive works are here flowingly described, and seventy illustrations (five of which are portraits of him) depict his surroundings, relations, and friends, with facsimiles and specimens of letters. The book was issued in Dec. 1898, priced 7s. 6d.: and reissued when it was in its eleventh thousand in Dec. 1899, at 3s. 6d., to accompany the *Lewis Carroll Picture Book* (No. **583**). There is also a $1s.$ edition (Messrs. Nelson & Son) in sm. 8^0 of May 1912 (pp. xiv+'15' to '372'+Advtt.), a reprint with only a few illustrations, and a similar one issued at $7d.$ in May 1913, by Messrs. W. Collins, London. [**644**[b], **644**[c].]

II. *Dodgson Sale Catalogue* (1898)   [**646**

Oxford. Catalogue of the Furniture, Personal Effects, and the interesting and valuable Library of Books the property of the late Rev. C. L. Dodgson, M.A., Ch. Ch., Oxford, more widely known as 'Lewis Carroll', the Author of 'Alice in Wonderland' and other popular publications; Also . . . Coins and Medals . . ., Books and Oil Paintings . . . [owned by] the late Rev. L. Thomas . . . which will be Sold by Auction by Mr. E. J. Brooks at the Holywell Music Room, Oxford, on Tuesday, May 10th [1898], and following days, commencing at Eleven o'clock each day. . . .

Oxford, Hall & Son, Printers: (1898): 8^0: pp. 63+[5].

The sale was well attended and successful: it occupied two days (lots 1–300, 301–963), the books being sold on the second, but the drawings and engravings were in the latter part of the first portion. Two copies of the 1865 *Alice* are lots 680 and 681, the former (with a twelve-line manuscript poem to M.A.B.) falling to Mrs. Bickmore for £50, the second fetching £24. The groups relating to Dodgson are lots 237–59 a, 680–726. Among the personal effects are a chronometer, telescope, chessmen, a human skull, a nyctograph, and many of his photographs, as well as a camera and fancy costumes for photographic purposes. The sale is mentioned in the *Oxford Magazine* of 18 May 1898 (p. 35) and *Jackson's Oxford Journal*, 14 May, p. 8. A copy of this Sale Catalogue is in the Bodleian and in Mr. Parrish's Collection, but it is rare and not in the British Museum.

[Later Madan acquired a copy 'with additions, priced throughout'. A copy, also priced, is in the possession of the Dodgson family.

Dodgson's friend Frederick York Powell, also a Student of Christ Church, was present at the Sale and wrote the following lines which seem first to have been published in Oliver Elton's *Frederick York Powell* (1906), vol. ii, p. 393:

> 'Poor playthings of the man that's gone,
> Surely we would not have them thrown,
> Like wreckage on a barren strand,
> The prey of every greedy hand.

Fast ride the Dead! Perhaps 'tis well!
He shall not know, what none would tell,
That gambling salesmen bargain'd o'er
The books he read, the clothes he wore,

The desk he stood at day by day
In patient toil or earnest play,
The pictures that he loved to see,
Faint echoes of his Fantasy.

He shall not know. And yet, and yet,
One would not quite so soon forget
The dead man's whims, or let Gain riot
Among the toys he loved in quiet:

Better by far the Northman's pyre,
That burnt in one sky-soaring fire
The man with all he held most dear.
"He that hath ears, now let him hear."

Oxford. *Nov.* 1898.']

1899

III. *Isa Bowman's Story of Lewis Carroll* (1899) [657ᵃ

THE STORY OF | LEWIS CARROLL | TOLD FOR YOUNG PEOPLE BY |
THE REAL ALICE IN WONDERLAND | MISS ISA BOWMAN | WITH A DIARY
AND NUMEROUS | FACSIMILE LETTERS ... | ... | ... ALSO MANY
... | ... | ... ILLUSTRATIONS [*ornament*] | [*Dent's device*].

London: J. M. Dent & Co. . . .: 1899: 8°: pp. [12]+132: 132, 'Printed by
Ballantyne, Hanson & Co., Edinburgh & London', 'At the Ballantyne Press'.

An intimate account of Dodgson, as he appeared to a child-
friend who became an actress and acted Alice on the stage in 1888.
Many details are given of his daily habits, when making tea, starting
for a journey, drawing caricatures and the like. The whole of an
account in prose by him of 'Isa's Visit to Oxford, 1888' is given in
facsimile on pp. 40-55, and also a verse account of Isa's sister
'Maggie's Visit to Oxford, June 9-15, 1899' [*sic*] (actually 1889) on
pp. 104-9, not in facsimile. Maggie played Mignon in J. S. Winter's
Bootle's Baby on this occasion, at Oxford. A strangely written letter
is in facsimile on p. 94, entirely written backwards, beginning 'Nov.
1. 1891. C L D, Uncle loving your' and ending 'was it, Nelly dear
my', written to Miss Nellie Bowman. The nineteen illustrations are
interesting, including one of Dodgson, one of his Christ Church
study, his house at Eastbourne, &c. 'Maggie's Visit' above mentioned

C 90   R

is reprinted in *Further Nonsense*, p. 61 (1926) [and in *Nonesuch*, &c.]. There is also an American edition of 1900, owned by Mr. M. L. Parrish. [657ᵇ] F. M.

Dodgson's 'House' at Eastbourne was in fact the lodgings at which he stayed for a couple of months each summer: this was 'Glenmore Villa', 7 Lushington Road, kept by Mr. and Mrs. Dyer. He lodged here first in 1877: 'I have a nice little first-floor sitting room with a balcony, and bed-room adjoining', he noted (*Diaries*) on 31 July 1877 when moving into them after a trial three-weeks at 44, Grande Parade. 'No. 7, Lushington Road seems like a second home now', he wrote on 15 July 1893 when arriving there for his summer holiday. But on 30 July 1896 he noted 'My new quarters (still, of course with Mrs. Dyer) are at 2, Bedford Well Road'; and he was there again in 1897.

Isa, Nellie, and Empsie Bowman, all of whom had parts in *Alice in Wonderland* in 1888, were still appearing on the London stage at least as late as 1950. Isa contributed in writing to Langford Reed's *Lewis Carroll* (1932)—see below; and all three of them in the course of personal conversations to my *The Story of Lewis Carroll* (1949).

1910

IV. *Belle Moses's Lewis Carroll* (1910) [659

Lewis Carroll in Wonderland and at Home. The Story of his Life by Belle Moses, author of 'Louisa May Alcott'.

D. Appleton & Company, New York and London: 1910: 8°: pp. viii+[2] +296+[6, chiefly advertisements].

Miss Moses has compiled a considerable account of Dodgson's Life, from various sources, and contributed her own view of his character and work. Unfortunately she never came into personal touch with him or with Oxford. Given these limitations, the book is pleasantly written and supplies a good picture of its subject. Oxford men may gasp at some of the expressions, 'the spires of the Cathedral of St. Mary' (p. 43), 'the University can trace its origin to the time of Alfred the Great' (p. 43); and may even doubt whether, in early days at Croft, Dodgson saw chipmunks in the trees or turtles sunning themselves on the banks of the river. There are many quotations from *Alice*, *Through the Looking-Glass*, and the rest, and a portrait of Dodgson, but no index. F. M.

1924

v. *S. H. Williams's Bibliography* (1924)   [660

A BIBLIOGRAPHY | OF THE WRITINGS | *of* LEWIS CAR-ROLL | (CHARLES LUTWIDGE DODGSON, M.A.) |||| *By* | SIDNEY HERBERT WILLIAMS, F.S.A. | Barrister-at-Law, of the Inner Temple. ||||

London: at the Office of 'The Bookman's Journal', 173–5 Fleet Street, E.C. 4: 1924: la. 8°: pp. xiv+142+[4], CONTENTS: p. i, 'A': ii, note of 700 numbered copies, 650 for sale, and the number of the copy: iii, half-title: iv, dedn. to Mr. Cyril Davenport, and '[Printed in Great Britain]': v, title: vi, details of Dodgson's life: vii–x, preface: xi, contents: xiii, list of facsimile title-pages: 1, 3–92; 93, 95–114; 115, 117–22; 123, 125–30; the four parts: 131, 133–5, Addenda; 137–42, Index; [1–4], advertisements. (Price 21s.)

The first 'full-dress' bibliography of Dodgson's works, preceded only by Mr. Collingwood's short-title list in the *Life and Letters*. The division adopted was (1) Books bearing Lewis Carroll's name or in the Carrollian vein, (2) Dodgson's mathematical and other serious works, (3) Contributions to periodicals, &c., (4) Books about Lewis Carroll, and Miscellanea. Some overlapping was unavoidable. The Addenda took note of the outburst of illustrated editions of 1907. The book received what is called a 'good press', has many merits, and is not entirely superseded by the present volume. It is good pioneer work.   F. M.

1925

vi. *The Poetry of Nonsense* (1925)

The | Poetry of Nonsense | By | *EMILE CAMMAERTS* | [decoration] | LONDON | George Routledge & Sons Ltd | Broadway House | 68–74 Carter Lane, E.C. 4

8°. Pp. [viii]+86+[2 blank]. 8 illustrations on shiny paper tipped in. Date on p. [ii] *First Edition, November 1925.* Bound in decorated paper over boards, with green cloth spine lettered in gold.

A general study of 'Nonsense', but with Dodgson as central figure.

1928

When the original manuscript of *Alice's Adventures* came up for sale at Sotheby's Auction Rooms in London on 3 Apr. 1928, the London papers had long notices of the book and the author, as for instance Mr. Langford Reed's article with portrait in the *Daily Mail* of that date.   F. M.

Mrs. Lennon (*Victoria Through the Looking-Glass*, 1945, pp. 370–1, lists an American pamphlet:

VII. *Alice in Wonderland*; the Manuscript and Its Story. By Robert William Glenroie Vail. With eight pages of facsimiles. New York, New York Public Library, 1928.

VIII. *Mr. M. L. Parrish's Catalogue* (1928)   [663

A LIST OF THE WRITINGS OF | LEWIS CARROLL | [CHARLES L. DODGSON] | In the Library at Dormy House | *Pine Valley, New Jersey* | [*small ornament*] | Collected by M. L. Parrish [*ornament*] ||||

'Privately Printed: 1928': la. 8°: pp. [xiv]+148+[6]+4 leaves inserted after p. 62, and 2 blank leaves after p. 96 and after p. 114 and after p. 142. CONTENTS: p. [iv], portrait of Dodgson in photogravure: [v], title as above: [vi], 'copyright 1928 by M. L. Parrish': [vii], 'a list of the writings of Lewis Carroll', [viii], 'the collection' under a photogravure of an open cupboard filled with books: [ix ('iii')], preface, signed and with address, 'May 1. 1928': [xi ('v')], contents: [xiii–xiv ('vii–viii')] list of illustrations, 32 in number: 1–62, [1–4]; 63, 65–96; 97, 99–113; 115, 117–42, the four parts: 143, 145–8, Index: [1] 'Sixty-six copies printed by William Edwin Rudge of which this is number   '.

A fine catalogue of the best and largest collection of Dodgsoniana and Carrolliana in private hands, collected by Mr. M. L. Parrish of Philadelphia, U.S.A. The four parts contain, respectively, pieces under the name of Lewis Carroll; those under the name of Charles L. Dodgson; those issued without signature; and Miscellaneous Items. The numerous illustrations are all of bibliographical interest, especially in the complicated matter of the Postage-Stamp-Case (pp. 43–48) and its Envelope: several are facsimiles of writing. There are a fair number of unique printed pieces, but the manuscript letters which Mr. Parrish possesses do not come within the scope of this Catalogue. Some might wish that Mr. Parrish had seen his way to add notes of the literary interest of each piece, but within his self-imposed limits he has issued a full and accurate account of the pieces in his own possession. Every item is noted in the present volume as *Parrish Catalogue*, and the note implies that Mr. Parrish owns a copy. This rare and valuable book is bound in full red morocco with gold lettering, and none of the sixty-six copies were offered for sale. The prefatory sheet is strictly pp. i–viii+3 inserted leaves, two bearing plates.

The standard of accuracy is so high that possessors of the book will be glad to have note of a few slips, as follows:

P. 7, l. 14. Friedrich, *not* Friederich.

P. 9, l. 9. The error on 'page 104' seems to be an accidental failure of ink in one copy only.

P. 30, l. 6 from foot. [x], blank; [xi], contents; [xii], blank.

Pp. 63–6 are not in the Index, being additions.

P. 67, l. 3 from foot. By the | Rev.

P. 87, l. 3 from foot. PROCTORIAL.

P. 88, l. 5 from foot. AS TO ELECTION.

P. 119, l. 4 from foot. him and Canon Liddon.

P. 128, l. 4. MDCCCX.   F. M.

Mr. M. L. Parrish issued in 1933 'A Supplementary List of the Writings of Lewis Carroll . . . collected by M. L. Parrish'. (Privately printed, 66 copies only: Philadelphia, U.S.A.: pp. xii+116+9 illustrations.) This contains about 200 additions to his first Catalogue, and amply proves the pre-eminence of his Carrolliana.

F. M. (*Supplement, 1935*).

IX. *Mr. De la Mare's Lewis Carroll* (1930)   [667

Lewis Carroll. By Walter de la Mare.

The tenth and last essay in *The Eighteen-Eighties. Essays by Fellows of the Royal Society of Literature. Edited by Walter de la Mare* (London, 1930, 8°: pp. 218–55). This is an essay on Nonsense Literature, chiefly as exemplified by Lewis Carroll, and chiefly that form of it which is found in England from about 1800. Of *Alice* he quotes 'It is the only child's book of nonsense that is never childish', and adds 'And not only that; it admits us into a state of being which, until it was written, was not only unexplored but undiscovered' (p. 242). He notes too that this is one of the very few books for children in which there is only one child. There is much delicate criticism of various kinds of nonsense, of Dodgson's easy crystalline writing, of the ingenious design underlying apparently effortless outpouring, of the author's 'rational poise in a topsy-turvy world' (p. 249), while Alice's repartees, apt and pungent repartees as they are, yet do not disturb the airy tissue of the dream. The penultimate page affords the finest appreciation of the atmosphere of the *Alices* which has as yet been written. But the mathematical and scientific side of the writer are not forgotten, nor the *Hunting of the Snark*.

An abridged form of this article appeared in the *Fortnightly Review* of September 1930, before the publication in fuller form.   F. M.

Published in book-form in 1932:

LEWIS CARROLL | BY | WALTER DE LA MARE ||||

London | Faber & Faber Limited | 24 Russell Square.
[On verso of title-page] First published in MCMXXXII | by Faber and Faber Limited | 24 Russell Square London W.C. 1 | Printed in Great Britain by | R. MacLehose and Company Limited | The University Press Glasgow | All Rights Reserved.
8°. $8\frac{4}{5} \times 5\frac{3}{4}$ in. Pp. 67 (+one page blank).

It should be noted that on p. 49 the reference to 'Dr. Paget' is a mistake for 'Dr. Thomas Fowler'. See Derek Hudson's *Lewis Carroll* (No. XXV below), pp. 74-76 for explanation of the mistake, and of the supposed 'incubation' of *Alice* at Whitby in 1854, which caused subsequent biographers so much trouble.

x. *Handbook of the Literature of the Rev. C. L. Dodgson* (1931)

A HANDBOOK OF THE | LITERATURE OF | THE REV. | C. L. DODGSON | (*LEWIS CARROLL*) | BY | SIDNEY HER-BERT WILLIAMS, F.S.A. | *Barrister-at-Law of the Inner Temple* | *Member of the Bibliographical Society* | AND | FALCONER MADAN, M.A. | *Hon. Fellow of Brasenose College, Oxford* || WITH SUPPLEMENTS AND | ILLUSTRATIONS || *Ridentem dicere verum* | *Quid vetat?* HORACE ||

Oxford University Press | London: Humphrey Milford | 1931.
8°: pp. xxiv+336+16 plates. Bound in blue cloth boards, lettered in gold on spine.
Certificate of issue on p. [ii]: This Edition is limited to seven hundred and fifty-four copies, four of which are on mould-made paper. ['No. . . .' added in ink.]
Contents: Preface, &c., Part I, Pieces issued by Dodgson in his lifetime. Part II, pieces issued after his death in 1898. Part III, Selected short pieces, chiefly unpublished [see No. *302* above for detailed list of these]. Supplements (Essay on *Alice* and *Looking-Glass*; Memoirs; Portraits; Dramatizations and Music; Abridgements, &c.; Parodies, &c.; Collections of Carrolliana).

SUPPLEMENT of 24 pages issued February 1935 by F. Madan; Oxford University Press as above.

HANDBOOK OF THE | LITERATURE OF | THE REV. C. L. DODGSON | (*LEWIS CARROLL*) | *By* S. H. |WILLIAMS *and* F. MADAN | 1931 | [short rule] | SUPPLEMENT | [short rule] | CORRI-GENDA AND ADDENDA | THE LATTER COVERING 1932-1934 | AND

INCLUDING THE | CENTENARY YEAR (1932) | *By* | F. MADAN || FEBRUARY 1935

N.B. This is the book of which the present LEWIS CARROLL HANDBOOK is a revised and augmented version.

XI. *Langford Reed's Life of Lewis Carroll* (1932)

THE LIFE OF | LEWIS CARROLL || BY | LANGFORD REED

W. & G. Foyle, Ltd. | 'At the Sign of the Trefoile' | London.

8°. $8\frac{1}{2} \times 5\frac{1}{2}$ in. Bound in salmon-pink paper over boards, with canvas spine, lettered on front and spine in gold. Pp. 142 (plus one leaf blank) + 12 illustrations.

Herbert Langford Reed (1889–1954), best known for his researches into the history of 'Limericks' and his collections of them, had also edited a Lewis Carroll anthology (*Further Nonsense*, see No. *298* above) in 1926. The present *Life* adds little, beyond some letters from Dodgson to Ellen Terry, and further interesting anecdotes by Isa Bowman. Reed was, to a certain extent, a 'debunker'—and he is mainly responsible for the idea of Dodgson as a 'split personality', which he describes as 'The Strange Case of Professor Dodgson and Mr. Carroll', and drives to absurd lengths in Chapter XIII. He is censured for this even in his obituary notice in *The Times*.

XII. *The Lewis Carroll Centenary in London* (1932)

For full description of this see No. *305* above.

XIII. *Columbia Centenary Exhibition Catalogue* (1932)

CATALOGUE OF AN EXHIBITION AT | COLUMBIA UNIVERSITY TO COMMEMORATE | THE ONE HUNDREDTH ANNIVERSARY | OF THE BIRTH OF | LEWIS CARROLL | (CHARLES LUTWIDGE DODGSON) 1832–1898 |||| [colophon] | NEW YORK [foot of colophon] | M.CM.XXXII | COLUMBIA UNIVERSITY PRESS

8°. Bound in red paper wrappers. Pp. [x] + 153 + [5 blank except for imprint on p. [155]].

There are some interesting short quotations from otherwise unpublished letters, notably those to Robinson Duckworth (pp. 131-3); also descriptions of unpublished MSS., notably *The Christ Church Commoner* (1851), *The Ligniad* (1853), *Number Guessing* (1896); and further quotations from miscellaneous letters. The most interesting letter (described but not quoted) is to Tom Taylor giving synopsis of a proposed play; this is dated 25 Jan. 1866; it was from Owen D. Young's collection.

XIV. *The Harcourt Amory Collection* (1932)

THE HARCOURT AMORY COLLECTION | OF | LEWIS CARROLL | IN THE | HARVARD COLLEGE LIBRARY | [small decoration] | *Compiled by* | FLORA V. LIVINGSTON || [decoration] |||| CAMBRIDGE, MASSACHUSETTS | *Privately Printed* | 1932

8°. Limited to 65 copies. Pp. xiv+190. Bound in marbled paper over boards, with cloth spine (fawn) lettered in gold.

This volume contains several items not otherwise published, the most important being:

P. 61. Acrostic poem (8 ll.) 'Florence' [Beaton] dated 2 Sept. 1876, beginning 'From the air do they come?'
Between pp. 128–9 facsimile (pp. 4) of 'Railway Rules' and ' "Live's" Railway Guide' [c. 1847].
Also short quotations from numerous letters; facsimiles of MS. and early title-pages of *Looking-Glass*, &c.

XV. *Ayres's Carroll's Alice* (1936)

CARROLL'S ALICE | BY | HARRY MORGAN AYRES | PROFESSOR OF ENGLISH | COLUMBIA UNIVERSITY || [cut of Alice] ||

New York: Morningside Heights | Columbia University Press | 1936.
8°. 5×7½ in. Bound in red cloth over boards, square spine. Lettered in gold on spine. Gold panel and medallion of Alice on front. Green end-papers.
Pp. [4]+x+98 [4 blank]; 8 illustrations and facsimiles, some included in pagination.
Printed at the George Grady Press, New York.

The Preface states that the basis of this book was a lecture delivered in the University Gymnasium, Columbia University, on 4 May 1932 'in connection with the exhibition commemorating the hundredth anniversary of the birth of Lewis Carroll and in honor of Mrs. Alice P. Liddell Hargreaves (the original "Alice"), who came from England for the occasion'.

The most interesting part of this excellent little book is 'Appendix IV: Carroll's withdrawal of the 1865 *Alice*' (which appeared originally in *The Huntington Library Bulletin*) which gives minute comparisons of the first edition with the American issues of it and the second edition, and also facsimiles of title-pages.

This is to a certain extent superseded by W. H. Bond's article in *The Harvard Library Bulletin*, x. 306–24 (1956) on 'The Publication of *Alice's Adventures in Wonderland*' which makes use of Dodgson's corrected proofs, *The Diaries*, and letters from Dodgson and Tenniel—not available to Ayres.

XVI. *Weaver's Correspondence Numbers* (1940)

Lewis Carroll Correspondence Numbers. A Table of Correspondence Numbers and Dates: From which one can determine the approximate Date of any undated Item of Carrolliana which bears a Correspondence Number.

Feb. 1940. At 160 Brite Avenue, Scarsdale, New York.

A printed pamphlet of 16 pages.

XVII. *Mrs. Lennon's Victoria through the Looking-Glass* (1945)

Victoria | through the | Looking- | Glass | [all the above printed in 'run-on' script and framed in up-right oval of yellow to resemble the frame of a mirror] | THE LIFE OF LEWIS CARROLL | *By Florence Becker Lennon* |||

1945 | Simon and Schuster, New York.

Large Crown 8°: $8 \times 5\frac{3}{16}$ in. Bound in grey cloth over boards. Lettered on spine in purple, with decorations in gold. End-papers in green on white of the De Morgan tiles in Dodgson's fire-place at Christ Church.

Pp. [2]+xvi+390. There are 7 illustrations in the text, and 9 on 4 tipped-in pages.

The book was published in England by Cassell & Co. in 1947 as *Lewis Carroll: A Biography.*

By far the most meticulous, painstaking, and fully documented biography to date, but vitiated by lack of discrimination in the use of sources and an apparent inability to understand the Victorian age or how Dodgson fitted into it. Nevertheless it is an indispensable book for all Dodgson students. A revised edition is now (1962) in preparation.

XVIII. *R. L. Green's Story of Lewis Carroll* (1949)

The Story of | LEWIS CARROLL | *by* | ROGER LANCELYN GREEN | Author of | *Tellers of Tales, Andrew Lang.* ||||

Methuen & Co. Ltd., London | 36 Essex Street, Strand, W.C. 2.

8°. Bound in blue cloth, lettered on spine in yellow. Published in 1949 (date on verso of title-page), being one of Methuen's 'Story Biographies' for young readers issued under the general editorship of Eleanor Graham.

Pp. [x]+182. Numerous illustrations in the text.

An American edition was published in 1950 by Henry Schuman of New York, consisting of sheets of the English edition with a new title-page and verso. Bound in blue; lettered in darker blue down the spine.

It was reprinted in U.S.A. in 1951, apparently by photographic methods, on thinner paper which prints the illustrations far better. Two alterations were made (without the author's knowledge) consisting of the reprinting in smaller type of the first five lines of paragraph 2 on p. 175 which, by omission of a few words, now make four lines; and by the complete omission of the last eight lines on p. 177 and the first five on p. 178—all contained criticisms of American writings on Dodgson.

XIX. *Gernsheim's Lewis Carroll: Photographer* (1949)

[Title-page in three-line panel] LEWIS CARROLL [in shaded letters] | PHOTOGRAPHER | by | HELMUT GERNSHEIM | *Fellow of the Royal Photographic Society* | *With 64 Plates in Photogravure* ||||

London | Max Parrish & Co. Limited | 1949.
Square 8°: $8\frac{3}{4} \times 6\frac{1}{2}$ in. Bound in light brown cloth boards with decoration on front and lettering on spine in gold.
Pp. xii+121+[5 blank]+64 illustrations (62 pages not numbered—between pp. 94 and 95 of text).
Published February 1950.

Besides the photographs, all of which are by Dodgson except No. 1 which is the photograph of him by O. G. Rejlander, this book contains nearly all the references to photography in the *Diaries* which were extracted specially for this book by Miss Menella Dodgson. In one or two cases entries are included which were omitted from the published edition of the *Diaries* (1953).

Pp. 106 to 121 reprint some of Dodgson's writings on photography:
1. Photography Extraordinary. *Comic Times*, 3 Nov. 1855. (Here reprinted from the published edition of *Mischmasch*, 1932).
2. Hiawatha's Photographing. *The Train*, Dec. 1857. (Reprinted from the cut and revised version in *Rhyme? and Reason?* 1883).
3. The Ladye's History. (From 'The Legend of Scotland' first published in *The Lewis Carroll Picture Book*, 1899.)
4. A Photographer's Day Out. *South Shields Amateur Magazine*, 1860.
5. Photographs. A description (not a reprint) of the pamphlet of 1860 described above (No. *23*).

All the above (except No. 5) were included in *Nonesuch*. Unfortunately Mr. Gernsheim was unaware that the earlier versions of 'Hiawatha's Photographing' contain many amusing lines about the old 'collodion process' which Dodgson omitted in 1883 when dryplate photography had come in. He also overlooked the Review of the Photographic Exhibition contributed by Dodgson to the *Illustrated Times*, 28 Jan. 1860, which was included in *Mischmasch*.

Besides the *Diary* extracts, the following items are published here for the first time:

1. 'Alice, daughter of C. Murdoch, Esq.' Poem of 22 lines, in facsimile, beginning: 'O child! O new-born denizen', on p. 38. The photograph

of Alice Murdoch was taken on 19 June 1856 (plate 5), and presumably the poem, which Dodgson copied into his album opposite it, was written on the same day.

2. Letter to Louisa Dodgson. Written apparently on 2 August 1864, this letter to his sister, from the Dodgson Collection, appears on pp. 57–58.

There are also several quotations from previously published poems and letters.

The verses on Agnes Grace Weld as 'Little Red Riding-Hood' referred to in the *Diary* entry for 6 Jan. 1858 (p. 43) do not seem to have survived. Mr. Gernsheim tells me that they were not printed in the Photographic Exhibition Catalogue, nor are they in any of the albums in his own collection.

There was a second edition with corrections and addenda in 1951.

This admirable study by the leading authority on the history of photography claims that Dodgson was the greatest photographer of children in the Victorian period, and outstanding among the portrait photographers as well. To the list of celebrities photographed by Dodgson which Mr. Gernsheim gives on pp. 101–2 may be added Gathorne-Hardy (10 May 1867) and Mrs. Craik (23 Apr. 1874).

XX. *Peter Alexander's Logic and the Humour of Lewis Carroll* (1951)

LOGIC AND THE HUMOUR OF | LEWIS CARROLL | BY | PETER ALEXANDER

Leeds | Chorley & Pickersgill Ltd. | *May 1951.*

Reprinted from the Proceedings of the Leeds Philosophical Society, Literary and Historical Section. Vol. VI. Part VIII. Pages 551–66.

An 'offprint' of these pages bound as a pamphlet $8\frac{1}{2} \times 5\frac{1}{2}$ in. in grey paper wrappers with front cover as title-page.

This study by the Assistant Lecturer in Philosophy at the University of Leeds is the most important contribution to Dodgson studies on the 'mechanics' of the Lewis Carroll 'Nonsense'.

XXI. *Elizabeth Sewell's Field of Nonsense* (1952)

The Field of Nonsense | [decorated rule] | ELIZABETH SEWELL ||||

1952 | Chatto and Windus | London.

8°. Bound in plum-coloured cloth over boards, lettered in gold on spine. Pp. [x]+198.

An interesting study of Nonsense Literature as produced by Lewis Carroll and Edward Lear—of no great depth, but most provocative.

Marred by the lack of any scholarly knowledge of the texts which occasionally makes nonsense (ordinary variety) of her assumptions: cf. *Times Literary Supplement*, 7 Nov. 1952.

XXII. *Henri Parisot's Lewis Carroll* (1952)

Lewis Carroll, un Étude: œuvres choisies, bibliographie, etc. Par Henri Parisot.

'*Poètes Aujourd'hui.*' P. Seghers, Paris, 1952.
Pp. 219.

XXIII. *A. L. Taylor's The White Knight* (1952)

[Title-page in decorated frame in double panel] THE | WHITE | KNIGHT [the above 3 words in decorated capitals] | *A Study* | *of* | *C. L. Dodgson* | (*Lewis Carroll*) | *by* | ALEXANDER L. TAYLOR, M.A. ||||

Oliver & Boyd | Edinburgh: Tweeddale Court | London: 98 Great Russell Street, W.C. |
On verso of title-page: *First published 1952.*
8°. 8½ × 5½ in. Bound in red cloth over boards, lettered in gold on spine. Pp. viii+209+[3 pages blank]. No illustrations.

The review of this controversial 'interpretation' of *Alice* in the *Times Literary Supplement* on 27 Jan. 1953 was followed by a number of letters from Mr. Taylor and the Reviewer.

XXIV. *The Diaries of Lewis Carroll* (1953)

See full description under No. *315* above.

XXV. *Derek Hudson's Lewis Carroll* (1954)

Lewis Carroll | [rule] | DEREK HUDSON ||||

Constable. London [Date on verso] *First published 1954.*
Crown 8°. 8½ × 5½ in. Bound in dark blue cloth over boards, with lettering in silver on spine.
Pp. xiv+354. Frontispiece photograph [Madan's No. ix] tipped in, and ten others on shiny paper, besides cuts in the text.

This excellent study, the first since Collingwood to make use of the *Diaries*, is the nearest approach to a 'definitive' biography that has appeared this century.

Besides many letters published for the first time, and many re-printed extracts, Mr. Hudson includes Dodgson's Preface to *The Guildford Gazette Extraordinary* (see No. *74* above) as Appendix B (pp. 327–30); Appendix A consists of 'Last Memories of Lewis Carroll' written specially for the book by Viscount Simon, Mrs. A. T. Waterhouse (Ruth Gamlen), Miss H. L. Rowell, and Mrs. Arthur Davies (Margaret Mayhew). On pp. 234–5 are printed for the first time 16 lines of verse by Dodgson headed 'Sequel to "The Shepherd of Salisbury Plain",' found by Professor Duncan Black among the Dodgson papers at Christ Church: this was written on the back of a *Punch* cartoon in answer to verses called 'The Shepherd of Salisbury Plain' which appeared in the same issue—that of 1 Feb. 1862. On pp. 252–3 is reprinted Dodgson's letter to the Ch. Ch. Senior Common Room (No. *236* above) of which no copy had been traced until Professor Black found one in his 1952 discovery.

Published in U.S.A. by the Macmillan Company.

XXVI. *Dr. Phyllis Greenacre's Swift and Carroll* (1955)

SWIFT AND CARROLL | [rule] || *A Psychoanalytic Study of Two Lives* || BY PHYLLIS GREENACRE, M.D. ||||

International Universities Press. New York. [On verso] Copyright 1955 . . . | Manufactured in the United States of America.

8°. 8½ × 5½ in. Bound in dark blue cloth over boards, lettered in gold on spine. Pp. 306. There are six illustrations tipped in and two in the text, all but two (portraits of Swift and Stella) concerned with Dodgson.

Part I, pp. 17–115: Jonathan Swift.
Part II, pp. 119–246: Lewis Carroll.
Part III, pp. 249–61: Certain Comparisons between Swift and Carroll.
Part IV, pp. 265–77: Notes on Nonsense.

An interesting study with many fully documented quotations and good bibliographical list. Not published in England.

XXVII. *Derek Hudson's British Council Pamphlet* (1958)

LEWIS | CARROLL | *by* | DEREK HUDSON

Published for | The British Council | and the National Book League | By Longmans, Green & Co., London, New York, Toronto.

Writers and Their Work: No. 96. Bibliographical Series of Supplements to 'British Book News' on Writers and Their Work. General Editor: Bonamy Dobrée.

8°. 8½ × 5½ in. Pp. 38 with Frontispiece on shiny paper (of the Herkomer portrait) tipped in. Bound in decorated off-white wrappers printed in brown and black, uniform with the series.

While supplementing and correcting his full-length study, this epitomizes the whole in short compass most admirably and sums up Mr. Hudson's conclusions on Lewis Carroll in one of the most satisfying essays that has been written on the subject.

XXVIII. *Duncan Black's Theory of Committees and Elections* (1958)

THE THEORY OF | COMMITTEES AND | ELECTIONS || BY | DUNCAN BLACK, M.A., PH.D. | *Professor of Economics in the* | *University College of North Wales* ||||

Cambridge | at the University Press | 1958.
8°. $8\frac{1}{2} \times 5\frac{1}{3}$ in. Bound in red cloth over boards, lettered in gold lengthwise on spine. Pp. [blank sheet] +xiv+242.

The Dodgson portion of this very abstruse and learned study occupies pp. 189–238, consisting of Chapter XX: 'The Circumstances in which Rev. C. L. Dodgson (Lewis Carroll) wrote his Three Pamphlets', and 'Appendix. Text of Dodgson's Three Pamphlets and of "The Cyclostyled Sheet".' After the pamphlets comes: 'Notes on Dodgson's Third Pamphlet "A Method . . ." (1876).'

The Dodgson Pamphlets are:

1. A Discussion of the Various Methods of Procedure in Conducting Elections (1873). [No. *96* above.]
2. Suggestions as to the Best Method of Taking Votes, Where More than Two Issues are to be Voted on (1874). [No. *100*.]
3. A Method of Taking Votes on More than Two Issues (1876). [No. *113*.]
4. 'The Cyclostyled Sheet' (7 Dec. 1877). [No. *114*.]

XXIX. *R. L. Green's Monograph on Lewis Carroll* (1960)

Lewis Carroll | [decorated rule] | A BODLEY HEAD MONO-GRAPH | *by* | Roger Lancelyn Green

The Bodley Head | London. [On verso of title-page, with other material]
First published 1960.
F'cap 8°. $7 \times 4\frac{1}{10}$ in. Bound in red paper over boards with square spine. Title, author, colophon, and price on front, series and title along spine, list of The Bodley Head Monographs on back—all in black.
Pp. 84+tipped-in portrait frontispiece.
The first of The Bodley Head Monographs: General Editor, Kathleen Lines. 'A series of studies of the lives and work of eminent writers for children. Each book contains a bibliography and a frontispiece portrait.'

A summing-up in 12,000 words of the conclusions derived from twenty years of Lewis Carroll studies.

B

ARTICLES IN PERIODICALS AND CHAPTERS OR IMPORTANT PASSAGES IN BOOKS:
1865–1960

[*Note*. Reviews of books are not included, except for *Alice*, and a few of particular interest on account of authorship.]

1865

Reviews of *Alice's Adventures in Wonderland* appeared in the following periodicals, amongst others:
- 18 Nov. *The Reader*
- 16 Dec. *The Athenaeum*
   The Illustrated Times
   The Illustrated London News
- 23 Dec. *The Spectator*
   The Pall Mall Gazette
- 26 Dec. *The Times*
                    (They were all unsigned.)

1866

Anonymous review of *Alice* in *The Literary Churchman*, 5 May.
GATTY, Margaret Scott (Mrs. Alfred)
   Review of *Alice's Adventures*
   Aunt Judy's Magazine, vol. i, no. 2, p. 123, June 1866.

1872

GATTY, Margaret Scott (Mrs. Alfred)
   Review of *Through the Looking-Glass*
   Aunt Judy's Magazine, vol. x, no. lxx, p. 249, Feb. 1872.

1876

LANG, Andrew
   Review of *The Hunting of the Snark*
   The Academy, ix, 326–7, 8 Apr. 1876.

1878

ANONYMOUS [? by George Saintsbury or Andrew Lang]
Lewis Carroll
London, 4 May 1878.

1887

SALMON, Edward
Literature for the Little Ones
The Nineteenth Century, Oct. 1887.

1888

ANONYMOUS
Leader on Lewis Carroll
The Standard, 25 Oct. 1888.

1898

ANONYMOUS
Lewis Carroll as a Mathematician
Nature, vol. lvii, p. 279, 20 Jan. 1898.
ANONYMOUS
Obituary: Lewis Carroll
The Saturday Review, 22 Jan. 1898.
LEATHES, E. S.
Lewis Carroll
The Academy, 22 Jan. 1898.
[See also the same for 17 Dec. 1898 and 7 Jan. 1899.]
COLEMAN, A. I. du Pont
Lewis Carroll
The Critic (New York), 22 Jan. 1898.
THOMPSON, Rev. Henry Lewis
Lewis Carroll: Obituary
The Oxford Magazine, 26 Jan. 1898.
COWLEY-BROWN, G. S.
[Recollections]
The Scottish Guardian, 28 Jan. 1898.
[See also Anonymous notices in *The Spectator*, *The Times*, *Daily
Mail*, *Daily News*, *Daily Chronicle*, and *Daily Telegraph*, quoted
by Derek Hudson, *Lewis Carroll* (1954), Chap. I.]   [**654**

HOLIDAY, Henry
   The Snark's Significance
   The Academy, 29 Jan. 1898.

[DODGSON, Henrietta]
   Lewis Carroll
   The Surrey Advertiser, 29 Jan. 1898.
   [Quoted by S. Godman in *Notes and Queries*, Jan. 1958.]

THOMSON, E. Gertrude   [650
   Letter: Lewis Carroll
   The Gentlewoman, 29 Jan. 1898.
   [Quoted by Collingwood, *Life* (1898), pp. 194–6.]

[SEAMAN, Owen]   [652
   Poem: Lewis Carroll
   Punch, 29 Jan. 1898.
   [Reprinted in Collingwood, p. 357; Madan and Williams,
      pp. 246–7.]

HEADLAM, Cecil
   Letter: Re The White Knight and Hudibras
   Literature, 19 Feb. 1898.

JOHNSON, R. Brimley
   Letter: Reply to the above, quoting letter from Dodgson on
      original of the White Knight
   Literature, 5 Mar. 1898.

STRONG, Thomas Banks (later Bishop of Oxford)
   Lewis Carroll
   The Cornhill Magazine, Mar. 1898.

LANG, Andrew
   The Death of Lewis Carroll
   In *At the Sign of the Ship*
   Longman's Magazine, vol. 31, Mar. 1898.

HATCH, Beatrice   [647
   Lewis Carroll
   The Strand Magazine, Apr. 1898.

COLLINGWOOD, Stuart Dodgson   [648
   Before *Alice*: The Boyhood of Lewis Carroll
   The Strand Magazine, Dec. 1898.

COLLINGWOOD, Stuart Dodgson   [649
   Some of Lewis Carroll's Child Friends
   The Century Magazine, N.S., vol. 57, Dec. 1898.
   [Cf. *Life*, Chapter X.]

COLLINGWOOD, Stuart Dodgson [654
    Interview with, about Lewis Carroll
    The Westminster Budget, 9 Dec. 1898.
TOLLEMACHE, Lionel A. [645
    Reminiscences of Lewis Carroll
    Literature, 5 Feb. 1898.
    [Reprinted in *Among My Books* (1898) by Various Authors,
    pp. 109–18.]

1899

AIKMAN, C. M.
    Lewis Carroll
    The New Century Review, Jan. 1899.
MAITLAND, Edith Alice (*née* LITTON)
    Childish Memories of Lewis Carroll
    The Quiver, 1899, pp. 405–15.

1900

BEERBOHM, Max
    Alice Again Awakened
    [On revival of Savile Clarke's play.]
    The Saturday Review, 22 Dec. 1900.
    [Reprinted in *Around Theatres* (1953), pp. 109–12.]

1901

LUCAS, Edward Verrall
    Charles Lutwidge Dodgson
    The Dictionary of National Biography, Supplement (1901), ii,
    142–4.
FURNISS, Harry
    Reminiscences in *Confessions of a Caricaturist*, i. 101–12.
NEWELL, Peter
    Alice's Adventures in Wonderland from an Artist's Standpoint
    Harper's Magazine, Oct. 1901.

1903

MILNER, Florence
    The Poems in *Alice in Wonderland*
    The Bookman (New York), Sept. 1903.

1906

POWELL, Frederick York
    C. L. Dodgson
    Oliver Elton's *Frederick York Powell: A Life and Selection from his Letters and Occasional Writings*, ii. 361–7.

1907

CRANE, Walter
    Reminiscences in *An Artist's Reminiscences*, pp. 184–6.

1908

FURNISS, Harry
    Recollections of Lewis Carroll
    The Strand Magazine, Jan. 1908.
ALLEN, Philip Loring
    The Sketchbooks of Wonderland
    The Bookman (New York), Feb. 1908.
PRATT, Helen Marshall
    Lewis Carroll [two articles]
    St. Nicholas Magazine (New York), Sept., Oct. 1908.
TERRY, Ellen
    Reminiscences in *The Story of My Life*, pp. 384–8.

1913

EDGAR, Randolph
    The Author of *Alice*
    The Bellman (Minneapolis), 22 Mar. 1913.

1914

HOLIDAY, Henry
    Reminiscences of My Life, pp. 165, 244–6, &c.
MACMECHAN, Archibald McKellar
    Everybody's *Alice*
    In *The Life of a Little College, and Other Papers*, (Boston), 1914.

1918

GARNETT, William
    Alice through the (Convex) Looking-Glass
    Mathematical Gazette, May 1918–Jan. 1919.

1919

EDGAR, Randolph   [839
    Lewis Carroll Memoranda
    The Bellman (Minneapolis), 1 Feb. 1919.

1924

PARRY, Edward Abbott (Judge)   [661
    The Early Writings of Lewis Carroll
    The Cornhill Magazine, Apr. 1924.
FURNISS, Harry
    Lewis Carroll
    In his *Some Victorian Men*, pp. 74–80 [based on his article in
    the *Strand Magazine*, Jan. 1908].
MACDONALD, Greville
    Various recollections in his *George MacDonald and His Wife*,
    e.g. pp. 342–3, &c.

1925

ANONYMOUS   [597
    Letter from Dodgson to Mrs. Gatty, with comments
    The Bodleian Quarterly Review, iv. 179.

1926

DURRELL, C. V.
    Alice Through the Looking-Glass
    Chapter II of his *Readable Relativity*.

1927

VARIOUS
    Lewis Carroll Letters
    The Times Literary Supplement, 19 May 1927.
HUBBELL, George Shelton
    The Sanity of Wonderland
    Sewanee Review, Oct. 1927.
MILNER, Florence   [662
    Mathematics and Fun
    St. Nicholas Magazine (New York), Nov. 1927.

1928

ANONYMOUS (?)   [654
    Alice in Eastbourne
    The Eastbourne Gazette, 19 Sept. 1928.
GALPIN, Stanton I.   [664
    Alice in Dorsetland
    The Dorset Year Book (1928), pp. 45–49.
LINCOLN, Eleanor
    Lewis Carroll, Dreamer
    In *Writing Informal Essays* (New York), edited by M. E. Chase
    and M. E. MacGregor.
REED, Langford
    Lewis Carroll's *Alice*
    The Daily Mail, 3 Apr. 1928.

1929

ARNOLD, Ethel M.   [665
    Reminiscences of Lewis Carroll
    The Atlantic Monthly (Boston, U.S.A.), June 1929
    The Windsor Magazine, Dec. 1929.
WINTERICH, John Tracy
    Lewis Carroll and His *Alice's Adventures in Wonderland*
    Books and Men (New York), pp. 266–90.

1930

MACKENZIE, Beatrice and Guy
    Harry Furniss Letters
    New York Times, 24 Aug. 1930.
DE LA MARE, Walter
    Lewis Carroll
    The Fortnightly Review, Sept. 1930.
    [Shortened form of his Lecture in *The Eighteen Eighties*, of the
    same year, reprinted as a book in 1932, see No. IX.]
FURNISS, Dorothy
    New Lewis Carroll Letters to Harry Furniss
    Pearson's Magazine, Dec. 1930.
HUTTON, Maurice
    Alice
    Chapter I (pp. 19–58) of his *The Sisters Jest and Earnest*.

1931

VARIOUS
Letters: The Mad Hatter
The Times, 13, 19, 20 Mar. 1931.

MACY, John
Her Majesty's Jesters
The Bookman (New York), Apr. 1931.

VAN DOREN, Dorothy
Mr. Dodgson and Lewis Carroll
The Nation, 2 Dec. 1931.

1932

RUSSELL, A. S.
Lewis Carroll, Tutor and Logician
The Listener, 13 Jan. 1932.

WILSON FOX, Alice (née RAIKES)
Letter: Lewis Carroll (re writing of Through the Looking-Glass
The Times, 22 Jan. 1932.
[Cf. Introduction to Letters to Child Friends (No. 311), pp. 8–9.]

PRICE, Clair
The Alice of Alice in Wonderland
The New York Times, 24 Jan. 1932.

CHESTERTON, G. K.
Lewis Carroll
The New York Times, 1932.
[Reprinted in his A Handful of Authors, 1953, pp. 112–19.]

STRONG, Thomas Banks (Bishop of Oxford)
Lewis Carroll
The Times, 27 Jan. 1932.

ANONYMOUS
Lewis Carroll
The Times Literary Supplement, 28 Jan. 1932.

ROBERTS, W. C.
Letter: On Lewis Carroll and Reverence
The Times, 29 Jan. 1932.

LEA, C. H.
A Lewis Carroll Rarity: The Wonderland Postage Stamp Case
The Bookman (London), Jan. 1932.

DE SAUSMAREZ, Frederick B.
Theatricals at Oxford: with Prologues by Lewis Carroll
The Nineteenth Century, cxi, Feb. 1932.

WATSON, E. H. L.
Lewis Carroll and His Centenary
The English Review, Mar. 1932.
MADAN, Falconer
Lewis Carroll
The Bodleian Quarterly Review, 1st Qr., 1932.
MAYNARD, T.
Lewis Carroll: Mathematician and Magician
The Catholic World, May 1932.
MILNER, Florence
Lewis Carroll: Playfellow
St. Nicholas Magazine, May 1932.
WILSON, Edmund
The Poet-Logician
The New Republic, 18 May 1932.
HARGREAVES, Alice and Caryl
Alice's Recollections of Carrollian Days, Told to her Son
Caryl Hargreaves
The Cornhill Magazine, July 1932.
BRAITHWAITE, R. B.
Lewis Carroll as Logician
The Mathematical Gazette, July 1932.
CECIL, Lord David
Lewis Carroll and Alice
The Spectator, 16 July 1932.
KNICKERBOCKER, F. W.
Those Nonsensical Victorians
The Bookman (New York), Sept., Oct., 1932.
SHUTE, Mrs. E. L.
Lewis Carroll as Artist, and other Oxford Memories
The Cornhill Magazine, Nov. 1932.
MACDONALD, Greville
Various references in his
Reminiscences of a Specialist.

1933

RUHL, Arthur
The Finding of the Snark
The Saturday Review of Literature (New York), 18 Mar. 1933.
EPERSON, D. B.
Lewis Carroll, Mathematician
The Mathematical Gazette, May 1933.

GOLDSCHMIDT, A. M. E.
Alice in Wonderland Psycho-analysed
The New Oxford Outlook, May 1933.
LESLIE, Shane
Lewis Carroll and the Oxford Movement
The London Mercury, xxviii, July 1933.

1934

KENT, Muriel
The Art of Nonsense
The Cornhill Magazine, Apr. 1934.
PHELPS, W. L.
Lewis Carroll and the Queen
Scribner's Magazine, xcv. 139, 1934.
LOVEMAN, Amy
The Philosophy of Lewis Carroll
The Saturday Review of Literature (New York), 3 Dec. 1934.

1935

SLOANE, William
Slithy Toves
Notes and Queries, 13 Apr. 1935.
WINTERICH, John T.
An 1868 New York Alice
The Saturday Review of Literature (New York), 22 June 1935.
FONTENOY, Henri
Présentation de Lewis Carroll
La Nouvelle revue française, 1 Aug. 1935.
EMPSON, William
Alice in Wonderland: The Child as Swain
Chapter in his Some Versions of Pastoral, 1935.

1936

HERON, Flodden
The 1866 Appleton Alice
The Colophon, ii. 422–7.

1937

KRUTCH, Joseph Wood
Psychoanalysing Alice
The Nation, 30 Jan. 1937.

BOAS, Guy
Alice
Blackwood's Magazine, No. 1466, Dec. 1937.
TROXELL, Janet Camp
Letters, &c., in her book
The Three Rossettis (pp. 152 et seq.).

1938

ROGERS, Bertram M. H.
Lewis Carroll: Two Unpublished Letters
The Times, 1 Jan. 1938.
WEAVER, Warren
Lewis Carroll and a Geometrical Paradox
The American Mathematical Monthly, Apr. 1938.
SCHILDER, Paul
Psychoanalytical Remarks on *Alice in Wonderland* and Lewis
Carroll
The Journal of Nervous and Mental Diseases, lxxxvii. 159–68,
1938.
OLIVIER, Edith
Recollections in her book
Without Knowing Mr. Walkley (pp. 176–9, &c.).

1939

DARWIN, Bernard
The White Knight's Stamp-Case
The Spectator, 10 Mar. 1939.
WAUGH, Evelyn
Carroll and Dodgson
The Spectator, 13 Oct. 1939.
PAGET, Elma K.
Various references in her book
Henry Luke Paget, 1852–1937 (cf. pp. 9, 58, 62).

1940

HUBBELL, George Shelton
Triple Alice
Sewanee Review, Apr. 1940.
MCPIKE, E. F., &c.
Dobson, Dodson, and Dodgson Families
Notes and Queries, 22, 27 July 1940.

ARCHIBALD, R. C.
   Bibliography of Lewis Carroll: Additions
   Notes and Queries, 24 Aug. 1940.
EHRENTREICH, Alfred
   Klassiker des englischen Kinderbuches im politischen Gewande
   Neuphilologische Monatsschrift, xi. 175–83.

1941

BURPEE, Lawrence J.
   Alice Joins the Immortals
   Dalhousie Review, xxi. 194–204.
AYRES, Harry Morgan
   Lewis Carroll and *The Garland of Rachel*
   Huntington Library Bulletin, Oct. 1941.

1942

RUSSELL, Bertrand, &c.
   Lewis Carroll: A Radio Panel Discussion
   The New Invitation to Learning (New York?), 1942.

1943

ROWELL, Ethel M.
   'To Me He Was Mr. Dodgson'
   Harper's Magazine (No. 1113, pp. 319–23), Feb. 1943.
W., L. M.
   C. L. Dodgson, Pamphleteer
   Notes and Queries, 27 Mar. 1943.
W., F.
   'What I say Three Times'
   Notes and Queries, 6 Nov. 1943.
MORGAN, Charles
   Various references and quotations from letters in his *The House
   of Macmillan*, 1943.

1944

STRACHAN, W. J.
   Lewis Carroll Revisited
   The Weekly Review, 13 Apr. 1944.
BAKER, Margaret J.
   To Meet the Rev. C. L. Dodgson
   Junior Bookshelf, viii, 2 July 1944.

GREGORY, Horace
Lewis Carroll's Alice and her White Knight and Wordsworth's
'Ode on Immortality'
In *The Shield of Achilles: Essays on Beliefs in Poetry* (New York),
1944, pp. 90-105.

1945

BROMAGE, Bernard
Creator of Alice
Everybody's Weekly, 27 June 1945.
GREEN, Roger Lancelyn
Lewis Carroll and the *St. James's Gazette*
Notes and Queries, 7 Apr. 1945.
GRAHAM, Eleanor
Nonsense in Children's Literature
Junior Bookshelf, ix. 2, July 1945.
ORWELL, George
Nonsense Poetry
In his *Shooting an Elephant*, 1945.

1946

GREEN, Roger Lancelyn
Lewis Carroll
Chapter III of his *Teller of Tales*, 1946.

1947

GREEN, Roger Lancelyn
The Voyage to Wonderland
Everybody's Weekly, 16 Apr. 1947.
WOOLLEN, C. J.
Lewis Carroll: Philosopher
The Hibbert Journal, Oct. 1947.
GREEN, Roger Lancelyn
A Lewis Carroll Parody
Notes and Queries, 15 Nov. 1947.
SKINNER, John
Lewis Carroll's Adventures in Wonderland
American Imago, iv. 3-31.
GROTJAHN, Martin
About the Symbolization of *Alice in Wonderland*.
American Imago, iv. 31-42.

1948

ATKINSON, Mrs. Gertrude (*née* CHATAWAY)
Memories of Lewis Carroll
The Hampshire Chronicle, 13 Mar. 1948.
[Issued as a pamphlet (offprint) of 8 pp.; copy in Bodleian.]

WOOLF, Virginia
Lewis Carroll
In her *The Moment, and Other Essays* (pp. 81–83).

1949

SADLEIR, Michael
Various recollections of Lewis Carroll
In *Michael Ernest Sadler 1861–1943*, e.g. pp. 90–96, &c.

1950

GREEN, Roger Lancelyn
Letter: Lewis Carroll's Photographing
The Sunday Times, 26 Feb. 1950.

TILLOTSON, Kathleen
Lewis Carroll and the Kitten on the Hearth
English, viii. 136–8. Autumn 1950.

1951

CAMMAERTS, Émile
The Poetry of Nonsense
Junior Bookshelf, Jan.–Dec. 1951.

DODGSON, Violet
Lewis Carroll
London Calling, 28 June 1951.

WRIGHT, N., etc.
Correspondence: The Walrus and the Carpenter
The Times Literary Supplement, 14 Sept.–19 Oct. 1951.

WEAVER, Warren
Alice's Adventures in Wonderland: Its Origin and its Author
Princeton University Library Chronicle, xiii. 1–17.

BERNADETTE, Doris
Alice Among the Professors
Western Humanities Review, v. 239–47.

MUNRO, D. H.
In his *Argument of Laughter* (Melbourne), 1951.

1952

MOLONY, J. T.
The Centenary of a Girl called Alice
The Sunday Times, 4 May 1952.
[A correspondence ensued, which is of interest.]

GREEN, Roger Lancelyn
Letter: The Field of Nonsense
The Times Literary Supplement, 7 Nov. 1952.

ATHERTON, J. S.
Lewis Carroll and *Finnegan's Wake*
English Studies (Amsterdam), xxxiii. 1.

WILSON, Edmund
Lewis Carroll, an Estimate
In his *The Shores of Light*, 1952.

1953

BLACK, Duncan
Discovery of Lewis Carroll Documents
Notes and Queries, Feb. 1953.

HUDSON, Derek
Review of Taylor's *The White Knight*
The Spectator, 13 Feb. 1953.

STEWART, J. I. M.
Review of Taylor's *The White Knight*
The New Statesman, 14 Mar. 1953.

GREEN, Roger Lancelyn
Lewis Carroll's Fugitive Pieces
The Times Literary Supplement, 31 July 1953.

HINZ, John
Alice meets the Don [on *Alice* and *Don Quixote*]
South Atlantic Quarterly, lii. 253–6.

1954

GREEN, Roger Lancelyn
Lewis Carroll and his Illustrators
Junior Bookshelf, xviii. 1, Jan. 1954.

GREEN, Roger Lancelyn
The Real Lewis Carroll
The Quarterly Review, Jan. 1954.

SHAWYER, Mrs. Enid (*née* STEVENS)
Lewis Carroll
The Observer, 14 Feb. 1954.

AUDEN, W. H.
The Man who wrote Alice [on *The Diaries*]
New York Times Book Review, 28 Feb. 1954.

GREEN, Roger Lancelyn
Lewis Carroll's Periodical Publications
Notes and Queries, Mar. 1954.

LAING, Allan M., and
JACOBS, Arthur
Letters: The Mad Hatter
The New Statesman, 6, 13 Mar. 1954.

KRUTCH, Joseph Wood
Review of *The Diaries*
The Nation (New York), 27 Mar. 1954.

HANSFORD, F. E.
A Heart of Sympathy: Some Lewis Carroll Letters
The Methodist Recorder, 22 Apr. 1954.

GREEN, Roger Lancelyn
Lewis Carroll and Stage Children
The Stage, 21 Oct. 1954.

VARIOUS
Letters re Hudson's *Lewis Carroll*
The Times Literary Supplement, 26 Nov., 3, 10 Dec. 1954.

WEAVER, Warren
The Mathematical Manuscripts of Lewis Carroll
Princeton University Library Chronicle, xvi. 1–9, Autumn 1954.

SCHÖNE, Anne Marie
Humor und Komik in Lewis Carrolls Nonsense-Traumärchen
Deutsches Vierteljahrsschrift, xxviii. 102–14.

1955

HUDSON, Derek
In Search of Lewis Carroll
Everybody's Weekly, 19 Feb. 1955

HEATH-STUBBS, John
Review of Hudson's *Lewis Carroll*
Blackfriars, xxxvi. 605.

GREEN, Roger Lancelyn
Centenaries of Nonsense
The Times Literary Supplement, 4 Nov. 1955.

1956

WEAVER, Warren
Lewis Carroll: Mathematician
The Scientific American, Apr. 1956.

BLOCH, Robert
'All on a Golden Afternoon'
Fantasy and Science Fiction, June 1956.

WEAVER, Warren
The Parrish Collection of Carrolliana
Princeton University Library Chronicle, xvii. 85–91.

BOND, W. H.
The Publication of *Alice's Adventures in Wonderland*
Harvard Library Bulletin, x. 306–24.

LENNON, Florence Becker
Review of Greenacre's *Swift and Carroll*
The Humanist, N.S. xvi. 145–6.

1957

GREEN, Roger Lancelyn
The Griffin and the Jabberwock
The Times Literary Supplement, 1 Mar. 1957.

GODMAN, Stanley
Letter: On Dodgson and the Rev. W. D. Parish
The Listener, 9 May 1957.

GREEN, Roger Lancelyn
Letter: Alice and Migraine
The Sunday Times, 7 July 1957.

GODMAN, Stanley
Lewis Carroll at the Seaside
The Times, 27 July 1957.

PRIESTLEY, J. B.
The Walrus and the Carpenter
The New Statesman, 10 Aug. 1957.

GREEN, Roger Lancelyn
Lewis Carroll's First Publication
The Times Literary Supplement, 13 Sept. 1957.

1958

GODMAN, Stanley
Lewis Carroll's Sister: Henrietta Dodgson
Notes and Queries, Jan. 1958.

HATCH, Ethel
Recollections of Lewis Carroll
The Listener, 30 Jan. 1958.
SKIMMING, Mrs. E. H. B.,
STRETTON, Mrs. H. T., and
SHAWYER, Mrs. E. G.
More Recollections of Lewis Carroll
The Listener, 6 Feb. 1958.
THODY, Philip
Lewis Carroll and the Surrealists
The Twentieth Century, clxiii, May 1958.
GODMAN, Stanley
Lewis Carroll's Final Corrections to *Alice*
The Times Literary Supplement, 2 May 1958.

1959

HOLMES, Roger W.
The Philosopher's *Alice in Wonderland*
The Antioch Review, Summer 1959.
BEROL, Alfred C.
Lanrick by Lewis Carroll
Papers of the Bibliographical Society of America, liii. 74.

1960

GARDNER, Martin
Mathematical Games: The Games and Puzzles of Lewis Carroll
The Scientific American, Mar. 1960.
LEE, Kenneth (the Rev.)
'The Most Curious Thing I Ever Saw in All my Life'
[Dodgson and the origin of 'To Grin like a Cheshire Cat']
Cheshire Life, xxvi. 6, June 1960.
BROCKINGTON, Leonard M.
The Old Biscuit Tin
[Wonderland Biscuit Tin given to Princess Alice]
The Globe Magazine (U.S.A.), 12 Nov. 1960.
MILLER, Margaret J.
Lewis Carroll
Chapter II of her *Seven Men of Wit*, 1960.
CARTLIDGE, J. E. Gordon (the Rev.)
Cheshire Cats
The Cheshire Historian, No. 10, 1960.

C

MISCELLANEA

1858

Catalogue of the Fifth Exhibition of the Photographic Society
This lists four photographs by Dodgson exhibited at the South
Kensington Museum. No. 174, 'Little Red Riding-hood', is reproduced by Gernsheim in *Lewis Carroll—Photographer* as Plate 10; see
pp. 41 and 91.

1874

Cakeless (1874)

'Cakeless' and 'The Adventures of Apollo and Diana. A Satire' are
two forms of a squib in verse relating to an incident at Christ Church.
The latter was printed by Shrimpton in 1874 at Oxford, but was
never issued; the former (*Cakeless*) was printed by Messrs. Mowbray at Oxford, but suppressed immediately after publication.

The Times of 16 Apr. 1928 unfortunately admitted a letter from
H. C. Ingle which stated that 'the most famous of all [Lewis Carroll's
pamphlets] was Cakeless, which was withdrawn; it was a little too
personal' and this letter was referred to when a copy of *Cakeless* was
catalogued for sale at Sotheby's on 29 July 1929.

Dodgson was in no way connected with the piece; it was written
by the Rev. John Howe Jenkins, then an undergraduate of the
House.   F. M.

Cakeless contains, in fact, a rather bitter attack on Dodgson, as
well as the Liddell family. See Chapters X and XI of Derek Hudson's
Lewis Carroll (1954) where it is described and quoted extensively.

1891

Aristophanes at Oxford (1891)   [821

Aristophanes at Oxford. O.W. By Y. T. O. [All rights reserved]. Oxford:
J. Vincent . . . London: Simpkin, Marshall . . . & Co.: [1894]: 8°: pp. viii+
85+[1]. Issued in stiff paper covers, lettered in green. Printed by Vincent at
Oxford.

The *dramatis personae* of this little medley are Socrates, Thucydides,
Aristotle, Oscar Wilde (O. W.), and Aristophanes, a Proctor, a

C 90   T

Chorus of Ladies and Undergraduates, Lewis Carroll, and so on. The three joint authors were L. S. AmerY, F. W. HirsT, and H. A. A. CrusO (Y. T. O). They all discourse on the Cherwell in canoes. Lewis Carroll utters thirteen lines of no distinction, on p. 57. The metres are blank verse, songs, and rhymes. The whole piece is a skit on the Aesthetic Movement of the period at Oxford. L. C. M. S. Amery was at that time an Exhibitioner of Balliol, F. W. Hirst a Scholar of Wadham, and H. A. A. Cruso a Scholar of Balliol: they wrote it as a contribution to the 'light literature of Eights' Week', and profess to have no personal acquaintance with Oscar Wilde.

A facsimile of the title-page, bearing the signatures of the authors, is given by Mr. Parrish as Plate XXIII in his Catalogue.

1898

In Memoriam (1898)   [653

In Memoriam, a card bearing a quotation from 'An Easter Greeting', 2 pp., with a picture of Lewis Carroll, and beneath 'Charles Lutwidge Dodgson (Lewis Carroll), Fell asleep Jan. 14, 1898'.

Parrish Catalogue, p. 130.

Dodgson Memorial Cot (1898)   [655

In Feb. 1898, only a month after Dodgson's death, a printed proposal was issued, entitled 'The "Lewis Carroll" Memorial. "Alice in Wonderland" Cot. The Hospital for sick children, Great Ormond Street, London.' On the front of this quarto leaf, under the above heading, are the names of 29 members of a General Committee (17 are ladies) and honorary Secretaries (Mrs. Herbert Fuller and Miss Beatrice Hatch), Treasurer, Auditor, and Bankers. One thousand pounds are asked for, to found the Cot. The Duchess of Fife and the Duchess of Albany are patrons. On the verso are promised subscriptions to the amount of about £115, the last name being Bernard Walch. The Cot was duly founded. I have seen a picture post-card of it, with a portrait of Lewis Carroll: a photograph of the Cot is at p. 196 of Collingwood's *Lewis Carroll Picture Book*. It will be remembered that Dodgson took much interest in Hospitals for children, and supplied them with free copies of his books.

Williams, iv. 6 (p. 127): *Parrish Catalogue*, p. 131: note in *Strand Magazine*, Apr. 1898, p. 423.

See Chapter I of Derek Hudson's *Lewis Carroll* (1954) for full account of the 'Lewis Carroll Cot' Appeal.

Dodgson's Grave [656

Dodgson's grave in the hill-side cemetery at Guildford is marked with an upright white cross surmounting three steps, a photograph is in Collingwood's *Life* at p. 334. There have been some complaints of a want of care in its upkeep, but arrangements have now been made for its preservation from neglect or decay.

The *Surrey Advertiser* of 22 Jan. 1898, after a full account of the funeral, adds a long list of those present and of those who sent wreaths or other tokens of regret.

[642

The Rev. C. L. Dodgson's Will, dated Nov. 4, 1871

Extracted from the Principal Registry of the Probate Divorce and Admiralty Division of the High Court of Justice

THIS IS THE LAST WILL AND TESTAMENT of me CHARLES LUTWIDGE DODGSON Student of Christ Church Oxford I give devise and bequeath all the real and personal estate of which I shall be possessed or entitled to at the time of my decease to be divided into equal shares one share to go to each of my brothers and sisters who shall be then living and if any one of them be then deceased but have married one share to be divided equally among the children if any be then living of such brother or sister And I appoint my brothers Wilfred Longley Dodgson and Edwin Heron Dodgson EXECUTORS of this my will IN WITNESS whereof I hereunto set my hand this fourth day of November in the year of our Lord One thousand eight hundred and seventy one—CHARLES LUT-WIDGE DODGSON—Signed by the said Charles Lutwidge Dodgson the testator in our presence who in his presence and in the presence of each other at the same time subscribe our names as witnesses—

T. VERE BAYNE Clerk in Holy Orders Student of Ch. Ch. Oxford—

A. VERNON HARCOURT Senior Student of Ch. Ch. Oxford.

Proved May 13th 1898.

Fos. 3.

A.Mc.M.

543.

[Value of Estate: £4,596 7s. 7d.
Date of will: 4 Nov. 1871.
Date of death: 14 Jan. 1898.]

1932

Sir John Squire's Speech at the Centenary Exhibition (1932)

SPEECH | AT | THE LEWIS CARROLL | CENTENARY | EXHIBITION | BY | J. C. SQUIRE

Pamphlet (F'cap 8º) of 8 pages bound in red paper and published by John & Edward Bumpus Ltd. of speech (in verse) delivered 28 June 1932. Reproduction of Mad Hatter and Dormouse on title-page from Tenniel, and of Invitation to the Exhibition by Rex Whistler on p. [8].

1934

Daresbury Church (1934)

In 1934 a window to the memory of Lewis Carroll was dedicated in Daresbury church: it is reproduced in the *Guide to Daresbury Church* on sale to visitors. There is a good photograph of the window in *The People's National Theatre Magazine*, vol. vi, No. 4, Winter 1939, tipped in to face p. 17 on which it is described in 'The Glory of Laughter' by the Editor (Nancy Price). There is a bad reproduction in R. L. Green's *The Story of Lewis Carroll* (1949); a 'close up' of a portion is excellently reproduced in Kenneth Lee's article on the Cheshire Cat in *Cheshire Life*, June 1960.

The description of the *Guide* is as follows:

Lewis Carroll | and his Birth-Place | Daresbury |||

by The Rev. Victor Dams, M.A. and The Rev. Dyott W. Darwall, M.A.
Vicar of Daresbury, Cheshire   Vicar of Walton

This is a 20-page pamphlet fully illustrated with photographs (including two of the window) bound in paper wrappers. It was first published in 1937 and reprinted 1944, '48, '52, '54, '57. It was 'Privately Printed for Daresbury Parish' by 'Truslove & Hanson, 14a Clifford St. New Bond Street.W. 1' and is on sale in the church, price two shillings. A new edition is in preparation (1961).

Gogarth Abbey Hotel, Llandudno

A pamphlet of 16 pages (undated) is issued by the Hotel which occupies the house 'Penmorfa', built on the site of Gogarth Abbey for Dean Liddell, and first occupied by him and his family during the summer of 1862. There are reproductions of nine of the Tenniel drawings, and of the painting of the Walrus and the Carpenter by Robert Fowler, R.I., of which the original hangs in the dining-room at the hotel.

The pamphlet states that it was 'here that a shy whimsical young man, Charles L. Dodgson, often came to visit' the Liddell family. 'Considerable portions of these world-famous stories were written during Mr. Dodgson's visits to Gogarth, including the poem which relates how "The Walrus and the Carpenter" dealt with the innocent and unsuspecting oysters on the sands of the Conway shore. . . . The late Sir William Richmond used to tell how, in the evenings at Gogarth, Mr. Dodgson would read to the Liddell family those chapters of the book which he had written during the day.'

Unfortunately the *Diaries* prove conclusively that Dodgson never visited the Liddells at Gogarth; and it is almost certain that he never even came to Llandudno. If he did it must have been in 1858, 1859, or 1860 (see *Diaries*, pp. 169–72): but Alice assured her son Caryl Hargreaves that Dodgson never visited *them* at Llandudno, at Gogarth or elsewhere: this contradicts a statement in the *Daily Dispatch* in 1933 purporting to be from a telephone conversation with Alice—it is probable that the visit in question was that paid by Dodgson to the Liddells at Charlton Kings in Apr. 1863 which is fully described in the *Diaries*.

Lewis Carroll Exhibitions

There have been many of these on varying scales, the most important being that in London in 1932 (see Madan's *The Lewis Carroll Centenary*), and many of them may have had catalogues.

The latest took place at The Florida State University Library in December 1960, and an excellent Catalogue was prepared with the following title: THE PARODIES | of | LEWIS CARROLL | and | THEIR ORIGINALS | Catalogue of an Exhibition | with notes by | JOHN MACKAY SHAW.

For each parody a different edition of *Alice* (or *Looking-Glass*) was exhibited open at the correct page, and beside it a first or early edition of the poem parodied. A few lines from each are printed in the Catalogue.

The parodies represented are only those in the Alice books: there is no 'original' given for Jabberwocky or Humpty-Dumpty's Poem. See Appendix.

APPENDIX

'Jabberwocky', and other Parodies

'*Jabberwocky*. Among the many fanciful creatures which live their part through this book [*Looking-Glass*], perhaps the most remarkable is the Jabberwock, whose fate is described in a poem on pp. 21-24. In this poem Lewis Carroll uses a number of what have become generally known as "portmanteau words", that is two words telescoped into one, such as *slithy*, meaning lithe and slimy. On the publication of *Through the Looking-Glass* this poem was the subject of a certain amount of discussion in the Press, and for some unknown reason was supposed by some to have been taken from the German; indeed a correspondent to the *Queen* declared that it was a translation of a German poem. Perhaps the absurdity of this assertion prompted the writing of a letter which appeared in *Macmillan's Magazine* for Feb. 1872 over the name of Thomas Chatterton. In this very clever and amusing epistle, the writer describes a seance which he had attended. He tells how a spirit with the unfortunate name of Schwindler tapped out the information "that the celebrated Jabberwocky was taken from a German ballad by the well-known author of 'The Lyar'." The spirit then proceeded "with great fluency, to tap out" six verses of what appears to be a German poem, using words in many cases suggestive of those used by Lewis Carroll. The letter is reprinted in the *Lewis Carroll Picture Book*, pp. 365-9. I do not think, however, that this letter affected the known authorship of the *Jabberwocky* to any extent, but there is no doubt that some question was raised as to the source of the poem, and indeed in a leading Sunday paper in September of the year 1924 a correspondent definitely states that Jabberwocky as it appears in *Through the Looking-Glass* is a free and easy translation of a German poem called "Das Jammerwock". The writer of the letter goes on to quote the first line of the German poem said to have been tapped out by von Schwindler in 1872. The matter, however, has been definitely settled by Mr. Walter Scott of Eastbourne, who in a letter to the same Sunday paper a week or two later said that the German poem in question "was written by my father in answer to a challenge made to him at the Deanery, Rochester, in the spring of 1872, to translate the first verse. To this he replied by producing the version in question of the whole poem the next morning." So much for the poem. Now as to the letter. Mr. Scott goes on to say "My father also wrote the mock-serious account of its origin which accompanied the poem to Macmillan." S. H. W.'

It might have surprised S. H. Williams, whose note on 'Jabberwocky' is quoted above from the original edition of this *Handbook*, to know that the writer in the *Queen* (whose letter seems to be as elusive as a Bandersnatch) was not quite as absurd as he thought in giving the poem a German original. Not, of course, in the sense which Williams so rightly condemns: 'Jabberwocky' is original with the supreme originality of great works of literature that need never be ashamed to admit a debt of inspiration.

'Jabberwocky' consists, in fact, of two parts written, so far as is known, at different times. The first stanza, which is repeated at the end, was included (in MS.) in *Mischmasch*, the last of the Rectory Magazines (see No. 6 in this *Handbook*) where it is dated 'Croft: 1855'. It is there called 'Stanza of Anglo-Saxon Poetry', and is followed by learned notes on the meanings of the words—not all agreeing with those given by Humpty-Dumpty. This version has been reprinted many times, and need not detain us here.

The main poem, however, cannot be dated with any such ease, nor is it even certain whether Dodgson wrote the rest to fit the original stanza, or combined two different poems. All that Collingwood tells us, in a footnote to page 143 of the *Life*, is that 'Lewis Carroll composed this poem while staying with his cousins, the Misses Wilcox, at Whitburn, near Sunderland. To while away an evening the whole party sat down to a game of versemaking, and "Jabberwocky" was his contribution.'

The poem is not mentioned in the *Diaries*—but nor are any other poems in either *Alice* book that were written as parts of those books. Assuming, therefore, that Dodgson took the 'Stanza of Anglo-Saxon Poetry' to re-use in *Through the Looking-Glass* (as he did with the White Knight's song and as he had done with the Evidence read at the Trial of the Knave of Hearts in *Wonderland*) the occasion at Whitburn must have been Dec. 1867, since a letter to Macmillan in Jan. 1869 suggests that it was written by then—and he did not visit Whitburn in 1868. (The events of the last four months of 1867 were 'written up' on 24 Nov.—but there are only three further entries: 12 and 14 Dec., but with a final 'write up' on 31 Dec. which gives 'On the 27th I went over to Whitburn, returning to Croft today.'

At Whitburn Dodgson frequently met a mutual cousin of his and the Wilcoxes, the poetess Menella Bute Smedley, who had advised him on his early writings and recommended them to another cousin Frank Smedley who was editor of *Sharpe's London Magazine* from 1845 to 1847, and on the staff of both the *Comic Times* and the *Train*. Dodgson certainly read all that Menella published, and records giving copies of *Poems Written for a Child*, 1868 [written by Menella and her sister Elizabeth Anna Hart, author of *The Runaway*] to child-friends; while its sequel *Child-World* (1869) contains probably the first reference to *Alice in Wonderland* in Nursery Literature.

Menella Smedley had been a constant writer for *Sharpe's Magazine*, and one of the most important of her contributions was a version in two numbers (7 and 21 Mar. 1846) of 'The Shepherd of the Giant Mountains' from the German of Fouqué; and this, as I suggested in the *Times Literary Supplement* of 1 Mar. 1957, was the 'original' of the main portion of 'Jabberwocky'.

'Jabberwocky' is neither a parody nor an imitation of 'The Shepherd of the Giant Mountains' in any strict sense. The original is in many hundreds of lines of rambling blank verse, and Dodgson was writing a different kind of poem, particularly if from the start he had determined to use the 'Stanza of Anglo-Saxon Poetry' as his first verse. The similarity cannot be pinned down precisely: much is in the feeling and the atmosphere; the parody is of general style and outlook. The 'plot', however, so far as it goes, is identical in its outlines. Gottschalk, the young shepherd, sets out to slay the terrible Griffin which has been ravaging the flocks:

> Now with his herdsman's staff, iron-tipped and sharpened,
> Like a good battle-axe upon his shoulder,

in spite of the warnings of the old shepherd Hans to beware of 'the ravening beast'. He traces it to the gigantic tree where it feeds its young, and destroys them in the nest by setting it on fire. The scorched Griffin attacks him:

> The reeling monster falls upon the grass.
> Now, shepherd, now! Where is thy ready staff? . . .
> Stroke upon stroke he hurls against the foe:
> He stabs it in the fiery eye—the beast
> Rears in wild rage, then, quick as thought, the staff
> Pierces its undefended breast, and sinks,
> Sure, deep and deadly, in the ruthless heart.

The battle over, Gottschalk brings the trophy before the Duke who has offered a rich reward 'to the valiant man'

> Who shall subdue and slay the hideous monster.

And when all the tale is told,

> The Prince cried, stooping from his balcony,
> In gratulating tones,
> 'Come to my heart, my true and gallant son!'

which has the nearest direct echo in 'Jabberwocky'

> Come to my arms, my beamish boy!

This also answers Mrs. Becker Lennon's psychological interpretation of 'Jabberwocky' (*Victoria Through the Looking-Glass*, p. 176) which turns on the fact that the beamish boy 'is welcomed by his parent instead of by a beautiful maiden'.

Dodgson is actually telescoping his original: Gottschalk is warned against the Griffin by the garrulous old shepherd Hans, who calls him 'my son'; and he is embraced by the grateful Duke—who calls him 'my son' because the victor's prize is to be

> The hand of Adiltrude, his only daughter—

and as much of the kingdom as he can drive his flock round in one day. Dodgson, of course, names no speaker: the slayer is 'my son' before the exploit and 'my beamish boy' after it; we conclude that the speaker is the same, but we need not do so, and probably Dodgson did not, if he had 'The Shepherd of the Giant Mountains' in mind.

This is almost the only controversial 'original' that has been proposed for any of the poems in the *Alice* books. With one exception (no. 11), the rest can be accepted without reservation.

1. 'How doth the little crocodile' is a direct parody of 'Against Idleness and Mischief' by Isaac Watts, first published in *Divine Songs attempted in Easy Language, for the Use of Children*, 1715. The first stanza of the original runs:

> How doth the little busy Bee
> Improve each shining Hour,
> And gather Honey all the Day
> From ev'ry op'ning Flow'r!

2. 'You are old, Father William' is a direct parody of 'The Old Man's Comforts' by Robert Southey, first published in *The Annual Anthology*, 1899. The first stanza runs:

> You are old, Father William, the young man cried,
> The few locks which are left you are grey;
> You are hale, Father William, a hearty old man,
> Now tell me the reason, I pray.

Dodgson's parody departs progressively further and further from the original and contains 8 stanzas to Southey's 6.

3. 'Speak roughly to your little boy' is only a rough parody of one stanza from a popular poem called 'Speak Gently'. This poem has always hitherto been ascribed to G. W. Langford in all books about Lewis Carroll that mention it (my own included). It first appeared, anonymously, in *Sharpe's Magazine*, Feb. 1848, and its authorship was apparently a matter of controversy not long afterwards when the poem became immensely popular. It was, however, included in *The Eolian* by David Bates in 1849 (pp. 15–16), his book of poems published in Philadelphia. John Mackay Shaw, in his catalogue of the exhibition of *The Parodies of Lewis Carroll* at the Florida State University Library in December 1960, assigns it correctly to Bates, with reference to *The Eolian* (he was not aware of its appearance in *Sharpe's Magazine*) and I had independently made the same discovery earlier in 1960 when collecting and editing *The Book of Verse for Children* (1962) for Dent's Children's Illustrated Classics. The relevant stanza (the third out of nine) runs:

> Speak gently to the little child!
> Its love be sure to gain;
> Teach it in accents soft and mild—
> It may not long remain.

4. 'Twinkle, twinkle, little bat' is a direct parody of the first stanza of 'The Star' by Jane Taylor, first published in *Rhymes for the Nursery* (1806), which runs:

> Twinkle, twinkle, little star!
> How I wonder what you are.
> Up above the world so high,
> Like a diamond in the sky.

Dodgson is supposed to have substituted a bat out of compliment to his friend and tutor Bartholomew Price who was nicknamed 'Bat'—so I was informed by Professor Price's daughter.

5. ' "Will you walk a little faster," said a whiting to a snail', loosely parodies Mary Howitt's well-known song 'The Spider and the Fly', apparently first published in her *Sketches of Natural History* in 1834. The original begins:

> 'Will you walk into my parlour,' said the spider to the fly,
> 'Tis the prettiest little parlour that ever you did spy.'

6. ' 'Tis the voice of the Lobster, I heard him declare' begins as a close parody of 'The Sluggard' by Isaac Watts (*Divine Songs*, &c., 1715), but wanders away, particularly in the additional lines added in 1886. The first stanza by Watts runs:

> 'Tis the Voice of the *Sluggard*; I hear him complain,
> 'You have wak'd me too soon, I must slumber again'.
> As a Door on its Hinges, so he on his Bed,
> Turns his Sides and his Shoulders, and his heavy Head.

J. M. Shaw suggests that Dodgson's final eight lines are modelled on William Roscoe's *The Butterfly's Ball* (1806)—but there is little similarity except in the metre, which was followed by countless anonymous writers for children who imitated Roscoe's classic poem. Odd lines in some of these seem nearer than anything in Roscoe: but the echo, if such exists, is very faint, the nearest I can find occurring in *The Peacock at Home* (1807) [by Catherine Anne Dorset, *née* Turner]:

> The Razor-Bill carv'd for the famishing group
> And the Spoon-Bill obligingly ladled the soup.

7. 'Beautiful Soup, so rich and green' parodies the popular song 'Beautiful Star' by James M. Sayles which Dodgson records in his *Diary* for 1 Aug. 1862 that he went to hear sung by Alice and Edith Liddell. I have been unable to discover the date of its first publication (Mr. Shaw gives 1885 for its first appearance in America), but it must have been well known by 1860 when H. J. Byron parodied it in his burlesque *Cinderella*. The first stanza (all that is parodied) runs:

> Beautiful star in heav'n so bright
> Softly falls thy silv'ry light,
> As thou movest from earth so far,
> Star of the evening, beautiful star,
>   Beau — ti-ful star,
>   Beau — ti-ful star,
> Star — r of the eve — ning
> Beautiful, beautiful star.

8. 'They told me you had been to her.' The earlier version of this is Dodgson's first nonsense poem ever to appear in print: as published in the *Comic Times*, 8 Sept. 1855, with two extra stanzas and several different

readings, it begins at least as a parody of William Mee's popular song 'Alice Gray' first published as a broadside ballad shortly after 1815. I quote it later under 'Disillusioned' (No. 29) which parodies it more closely.

9. ' 'Twas brillig and the slithy toves.' See the beginning of this article for a probable 'original' of 'Jabberwocky'. Mr. Shaw compares it with the Scottish ballad 'Edward, Edward' but says that while there is no evidence that Dodgson 'had any special poem in mind . . . it seems clear that he had in mind, perhaps subconsciously, the tone and the form of the ancient ballads'.

10. 'The sun was shining on the sea.' There is no direct original for 'The Walrus and the Carpenter', but it follows closely the metre and burlesques much of the spirit of Thomas Hood's melodramatic poem 'The Dream of Eugene Aram', first published in *The Gem* in 1829, which begins:

> 'Twas in the prime of summertime,
>   An evening calm and cool,
> And four and twenty happy boys
>   Came bounding out of school:
> There were some that ran and some that leapt
>   Like troutlets in a pool.

Dodgson may have got the idea for his sad tale of the Oysters' fate from a cartoon by Tenniel in *Punch* (25 Jan. 1862) 'Law and Lunacy: Or, A Glorious Oyster Season for the Lawyers'. The Walrus was suggested by the fine stuffed specimen in the Sunderland Museum; the Carpenter had no special significance as Dodgson offered Tenniel a Baronet or a Butterfly if he preferred either from the point of view of the illustrations.

11. 'In winter when the fields are white.' This may be based on a popular song, but no acceptable 'original' has so far been discovered. Mr. Shaw suggests Longfellow's 'Excelsior'—but the only similarity is the metre of the individual lines, which is not an unusual one.

12. 'I'll tell thee everything I can.' The White Knight's Song is a composite parody. The metre and form are those of Thomas Moore's 'My heart and Lute', collected with his 'Ballads, Songs, Miscellaneous Poems, etc.' in volume v (p. 195) of his 1841 edition of his Collected Works. The first four lines of the 16-line song run:

> I give thee all—I can no more—
>   Tho' poor the off'ring be;
> My heart and lute are all the store
>   That I can bring to thee.

Dodgson parodied these lines in an uncollected fragment published in the *St. James's Gazette*, 19 May 1884, in one of his letters on Proportional Representation as follows:

> I give thee all—I can no more—
>   Though small thy share may be:
> Two halves, three thirds and quarters four
>   Is all I bring to thee.

The actual poem of the Aged, Aged Man is a distant parody of Wordsworth's 'Resolution and Independence, or the Leech-gatherer', first published in his *Poems*, 1807. The earlier version, 'Upon the Lonely Moor', first published in the *Train*, Oct. 1856, is a cruder but more forceful burlesque of Wordsworth's manner. Very few lines are actually parodied; the nearest Dodgson comes is to Wordsworth's:

> My question eagerly did I renew:
> 'How is it that you live and what is it you do?'
> He with a smile did then these words repeat—

and the final line:

> I'll think of the Leech-gatherer on the lonely moor.

13. 'Hush-a-by lady, in Alice's lap' is a direct parody of the most familiar of all cradle-songs, 'Hush-a-by baby on the tree top'.

14. 'To the Looking-Glass world it was Alice that said' is a direct parody of Sir Walter Scott's 'Bonnie Dundee' first published in *The Doom of Devorgoil*, 1830, Act ii, Scene ii, beginning:

> To the Lords of Convention 'twas Claver'se who spoke,
> 'Ere the King's crown shall fall there are crowns to be broke;
> So let each Cavalier who loves honour and me,
> Come follow the bonnet of Bonny Dundee.
> 'Come fill up my cup, come fill up my can' . . ., &c.

15. 'First, the fish must be caught.' This riddle, with the obvious answer of 'An Oyster', is not likely to be a parody of any specific poem—any more than the Mouse's 'Tail' in *Wonderland*—though neither are completely ruled out.

16. 'Beneath the waters of the sea.' This song, which was sung by the Mock Turtle in the original *Alice's Adventures Underground* but for which 'Will you walk a little faster' was substituted in *Wonderland*, is a parody of another song sung by the Liddell children. On 3 July 1862, the day before the famous picnic, Dodgson records in his *Diary* that he lunched at the Deanery and thereafter, as it rained so that the river was out of the question, 'the three sang "Sally come up" with great spirit'. This was a Negro 'minstrel song' with words by T. Ramsey and music by E. W. Mackney, with the chorus:

> Sally come up! Sally go down!
> Sally come twist your heel around!
> De old man he's gone down to town—
> Oh Sally come down de middle!

This concludes the parodies in the *Alice* books. The other verses included are all popular Nursery Rhymes from the Halliwell-Phillips collection—'The Queen of Hearts', 'Tweedledum and Tweedledee', 'Humpty-Dumpty', 'I love my love with an H', and 'The Lion and the Unicorn'.

Dodgson's other parodies must be listed more shortly. Taking the order of arrangement from *Collected Verse* (1932)—all of which is included in the *Nonesuch* volume, the most obvious of these are:

17. 'Fair stands the ancient Rectory' (from *The Rectory Umbrella*) is a free parody of 'Horatius' from Lord Macaulay's *Lays of Ancient Rome*.

18. 'There were two brothers at Twyford school' (from *Mischmasch*) is a burlesque of the traditional Ballad style and metre.

19. 'The Youth at Eve had drunk his fill' (*Whitby Gazette*, 31 Aug. 1854), Dodgson's first published parody, begins in imitation of Scott's *The Lady of the Lake*:

> The stag at eve had drunk his fill,
> Where danced the moon on Monan's rill,
> And deep his midnight lair had made
> In lone Glenartney's hazel shade . . .

The 'Coronach' beginning 'She's gone by the Hilda' which is part of Dodgson's poem parodies the 'Coronach' beginning 'He is gone on the mountain' which forms Section xvi of Canto iii of *The Lady of the Lake*.

20. 'I dreamt I dwelt in marble halls' (the *Oxford Critic*, 29 May 1857) does little more than steal the first line from Arline's song 'The Gipsy Girl's Dream' from *The Bohemian Girl* (words by Alfred Bunn) first acted 1843.

21. 'Lady Clara Vere de Vere' ('Echoes', first published in *Rhyme? and Reason?*) echoes Wordsworth's 'We are Seven' and Tennyson's 'Lady Clara Vere de Vere' and 'Locksley Hall'.

22. 'From his shoulder Hiawatha' (from the *Train*, Dec. 1857, several times revised in later collections) follows the metre and style of Longfellow's *Hiawatha*.

23. 'He trilled a carol fresh and free' (from the *Train*, Nov. 1856, &c.) 'The Three Voices' is a parody of Tennyson's 'The Two Voices'—a subtle and rather destructive burlesque rather than a direct parody.

24. 'I never loved a dear Gazelle' (from the *Comic Times*, 18 Aug. 1855, &c.) is not properly a parody, each stanza beginning with a consecutive line from Thomas Moore's *Lalla Rookh*, 'The Fire-Worshippers'. Dodgson misquotes, it should read:

> I never nurs'd a dear gazelle,
> To glad me with its soft black eye,
> But when it came to know me well,
> And love me, it was sure to die!

25. 'Ay, 'twas here on this spot' (from *Punch*, 27 July 1867, &c.). 'Atalanta in Camden-Town' parodies the cadence and metre, though hardly anything else, from the final choric ode between Meleager and the Chorus in Swinburne's *Atalanta in Calydon* (1865).

26. 'The ladye she stood at her lattice high' (from *College Rhymes*, Nov. 1862, &c.). 'The Lang Coortin'' is a burlesque of the old Balled style which was being revived at the time by writers like Aytoun and Allingham.

27. 'The air is bright with hues of light' (Riddle III, first published in

Rhyme? and Reason? 1883). This imitates rather than parodies the song from Section iv of Tennyson's *The Princess* beginning:

> The spendour falls on castle walls
> And snowy summits old in story.

28. 'My mother bids me bind my hair' (from *College Rhymes*, Nov. 1861). 'Those Horrid Hurdy-Gurdies' is similar to the 'Dear Gazelle': each of the first lines of the four stanzas are quotations—the first three from popular songs, viz. 'My mother bids me bind my hair' by Mrs. John Hunter (1742–1821), set to music by Haydn; 'My lodging is on the cold, cold ground' from a song in Davenant's *The Rivals* (1668); 'Ever of thee!' by George Linley (1798–1865). The last line 'Please remember the organ, sir' seems merely to be the begging appeal of the organ-grinder himself.

29. 'I painted her a gushing thing' (from *College Rhymes*, June 1862). 'Disillusionized' (usually reprinted as 'My Fancy', with an eight-line stanza omitted) is a rough parody of William Mee's notorious ballad 'Alice Gray' published about 1815 which begins:

> She's all my fancy painted her—
> Ye gods! She is divine;
> But her heart it is another's—
> It never can be mine . . .

30. 'Museum! loveliest building of the plain' (published as pamphlet, 1867). *The Deserted Parks* is an imitation rather than a parody of Goldsmith's *The Deserted Village*:

> Sweet Auburn! loveliest village of the plain,
> Where health and plenty cheer'd the labouring swain.
> How often have I loiter'd o'er thy green,
> Where humble happiness endear'd each scene;
> How often have I paus'd on every charm,
> The shelter'd cot, the cultivated farm . . .

31. 'If thou would'st view the Belfry aright' (from *The New Belfry*, 1872, &c.). This parodies Canto ii, Section i of Sir Walter Scott's *The Lay of the Last Minstrel*, beginning:

> If thou would'st view fair Melrose aright,
> Go visit it by the pale moonlight;
> For the gay beams of lightsome day
> Gild, but to flout, the ruins grey . . .

32. 'Is it the glow of conscious pride' (from *The New Belfry*, 1872, &c.). If this is a direct parody, I have failed to find the original; but there is a certain resemblance in metre and thought to *The Lay of the Last Minstrel*, Canto vi, Section ii.

33. 'Five fathom square the Belfry frowns' (from *The New Belfry*, 1872, &c.). This is a parody of Ariel's song in *The Tempest*, Act i, Scene ii.

34. 'Look on the Quadrangle . . .' (from *The New Belfry*, 1872, &c.). This parody of Tupper's *Proverbial Philosophy*, 1838, &c., is of his general style rather than of any specific example.

35. 'Our Willie had been sae lang awa'' (from *The Vision of the Three T's*, 1873, &c.). Another parody of the Ballad form. *The Three T's* is itself an imitation of Walton's *The Compleat Angler* (1653).

36. 'Here's to the Freshman of bashful eighteen' (from *The Vision of the Three T's*, 1873, &c.). A direct parody of the song: 'Here's to the maiden of bashful fifteen' from Sheridan's *The School for Scandal* (1777). It is called 'A Bachanalian Ode' in pursuance of Dodgson's general scheme of dragging in 'Bach' whenever possible, as the scene in Tom Quad is set on 20 Mar. 1873 when Bach's *Passion Music* was being played in the Cathedral 'to about 1200 people. I did not go. I think it a pity churches should be so used.'

37. ' "Are you deaf, Father William?" the young man said.' This acrostic to Adelaide Payne (1876) may be described as a parody of Dodgson's own parody in *Wonderland*.

38. 'It is the lawyer's daughter' (Letter to Agnes Hull, 25 Mar. 1881). This is a parody of Tennyson's song in 'The Miller's Daughter'.

39. 'King Fisher courted Lady Bird' (from *Sylvie and Bruno Concluded*, 1893). This parodies the type of Medieval Court Ballad revived by Morris in 'Three Red Roses Across the Moon'—and by many lesser writers. Calverley had already parodied the kind even more cleverly in *Fly-Leaves* (1872)—'The auld wife sat at her ivied door | (*Butter and eggs and a pound of cheese*).'

40. 'In stature the Manlet was dwarfish' (from *Sylvie and Bruno Concluded*, 1893). Parodies the metre and style of Swinburne's 'Dolores' (*Poems and Ballads*, 1866).

To these may be added the only poem in *Mischmasch* not reprinted in *Collected Verse* or *Nonesuch*, 'Tommy's Dead', written on 31 Dec. 1857, which is an amusing parody—or perversion—of Sydney Dobell's poem of the same name. Dodgson's parody, and a few lines from Dobell's poem, are reprinted on pp. 133-5 of my edition of *The Diaries of Lewis Carroll*.

Finally, after presuming to 'hold my farthing candle to the sun' for so many pages, I cannot better conclude than with some lines by Dodgson (not a parody!) written before 1850 for the *Rectory Magazine*, and now first published, which may serve as a warning to all commentators:

> See the planets as they rise,
>   Each upon his starless way,
> Look on us with angry eyes,
>   Do they not appear to say,
>
> 'Stupid fellow! hold your tongue!
>   Seek not thus to goad us on!
> You in fact are much too young
>   To offer *your* opinion!'

ADDENDA

SCHILLER, Professor. 'A Commentary on *The Hunting of The Snark*'. *Mind*. (Comic Christmas issue or parody) 1901.

WILSON, O. *A Survey of the Important Issues of 'Alice's Adventures in Wonderland'*. Published by Rare Libri in Seattle, U.S.A. 1937.

[No copies available for description.]

ALICE'S ADVENTURES IN WONDERLAND. 1957.
Riverside SDP 22. Modern Voices.
Alice's Adventures in Wonderland, read and sung by Cyril Ritchard. The Lewis Carroll classic complete on 4 LP Records.

Original Music Score by Alec Wilder, played by the New York Woodwind Quintet.

'*Recorded in New York City, Spring and Summer 1957.*'

'Including a Facsimile Volume of the Rare 1865 First Edition of the Book.'

This edition produced for, and distributed exclusively by, CROWN PUBLISHERS, INC., 419 Park Avenue South, New York 16, N.Y.

Note: The Facsimile is *not* of the 1865 First Edition (*No. 42*), but of the ordinary Second (English) Edition originally dated 1866 (*No. 46*). The Facsimile omits place (London), publisher (Macmillan) and date (1866), but reproduces Clay's trademark on verso of title-page, and imprint at foot of page 192. It is bound in pink cloth over boards, imitating the original editions, but omitting Macmillan from foot of spine. No publisher or date is given.

INDEX